Essays in the History of Religions

Toronto Studies in Religion

Donald Wiebe, General Editor
Trinity College
University of Toronto

Vol. 11

Published in association with
the Centre of Religious Studies
at the University of Toronto

PETER LANG
New York · San Francisco · Bern
Frankfurt am Main · Paris · London

Robert D. Baird

Essays in the History of Religions

PETER LANG
New York · San Francisco · Bern
Frankfurt am Main · Paris · London

Library of Congress Cataloging-in-Publication Data

Baird, Robert D.
Essays in the history of religions / Robert D. Baird.
p. cm — (Toronto studies in religion ; vol. 11)
1. Religion—Study and teaching—Methodology.
2. Law—India—Religious aspects. 3. Religion and state—India—History—20th century. 4. India—Religion. 5. Cults—United States—History—20th century. 6. United States—Religion—1960.
I. Title. II. Series.
BL41.B26 1991 291—dc20 90-24985
ISBN 0-8204-1509-X CIP
ISSN 8756-1385

Printed in the United States of America.

Table of Contents

Acknowledgments

If the writing of any book necessitates that one acknowledge intellectual debts, how much more is that true in a volume like this. These essays were written over a twenty year period. During that time numerous opportunities were provided by colleagues within the United States and abroad for these essays to appear in print. These colleagues also provided much appreciated collegiality and intellectual stimulation. While one seeks to document credit for ideas gleaned from others, often such insights merge easily into one's own thought processes. Nor can the challenges of presenting these ideas to my students be ignored. Both within and beyond the classroom they have never failed to present welcome interaction. To both professional colleagues and students I am deeply indebted.

The preparation of this manuscript for publication could not have proceeded without the encouragement of Donald Wiebe, editor of the series "Toronto Studies in Religion." Leanne Seedorff, undergraduate major in religion at the University of Iowa prepared the camera ready copy. Her patience and competence and attention to detail cannot be exaggerated. Elizabeth Hin, graduate research assistant in religion prepared the index and assisted in proofreading. Valerie Carmichael, undergraduate student assistant at the University of Iowa also proofread the final copy. They have my profound gratitude.

Permission to reprint the essays in this volume has been granted by a wide range of journals and publishers as follows.

"Interpretative Categories and the History of Religions," reprinted by permission of Wesleyan University from *History and Theory, Beiheft* 8 (1969), 17-30.

"Normative Elements in Eliade's Phenomenology of Symbolism," *Union Seminary Quarterly Review*, Vol. 25, No. 4 (1970), 505-516.

"Factual Statements and the Possibility of Objectivity in History," *The Journal of Religious Thought*, Vol. XXVI, No. 1 (1969), 5-22.

"Syncretism and the History of Religions," *The Journal of Religious Thought*, Vol. XXIV, No. 2, (1967-68), 42-53.

"Hindu–Christian Dialogue and the Academic Study of Religion," *Hindu–Christian Dialogue*, ed. Harold G. Coward, Orbis Books, Maryknoll, NY (1989), 217-229.

"Religion and the Secular: Categories for Religious Conflict and Religious Change in Independent India," *Journal of Asian and African Studies* (Canada), Vol. XI, Nos. 1-2 (1974), 47-63.

"'Secular State' and the Indian Constitution," and "Uniform Civil Code and the Secularization of Law," *Religion in Modern India*, ed. Robert D. Baird, Manohar Publications, New Delhi (India) (1981), 389-445.

"Religion and the Legitimation of Nehru's Concept of the Secular State," *Religion and the Legitimation of Power in South Asia*, ed. Bardwell L. Smith, E. J. Brill, Leiden (The Netherlands) (1978), 73-87.

"Mr. Justice Gajendragadkar and the Religion of the Indian Secular State," *Journal of Constitutional and Parliamentary Studies*, New Delhi (India) (1972), 47-64.

"Cow Slaughter and the New 'Great Tradition'," *International Journal of Studies in Religion* (Canada), Vol. I, No. 1 (1991).

"Human Rights Priorities and Indian Religious Thought," *Journal of Church and State*, 11 (Spring 11969), 221-238.

"Swami Bhaktivedanta: Karma, Rebirth and the Personal God," *Karma and Rebrith: Post–Classical Developments*, ed. Ronald W. Neufeldt, State University of New York Press (1986), 200-221.

"Swami Bhaktivedanta and the Bhagavadgita 'As it Is'," *Modern Interpreters of the Bhagavad Gita*, ed. Robert N. Minor, State University of New York Press (1986).

"The Response of Swami Bhaktivedanta to Religious Pluralism," *Modern Indian Responses to Religious Pluralism*,ed. Harold G. Coward, State University of New York Press (1987), 105-127.

"ISKCON and the Struggle for Legitimation," *Bulletin of the John Rylands University Library of Manchester* (England), Vol. 70, No. 3 (1988), 157-169.

"Religious or Non–Religious: TM in American Courts," *Journal of Dharma*, Vol. VII, No. 4, Bangalore (India) (1982), 391-407.

for

P. J. B.

Introduction

Any collection of essays written over a twenty year period will manifest diversity. While continuity is a reasonable expectation, uniformity might well be taken as evidence of a lack of academic growth. Furthermore, each essay represents the understanding of the author at the point of time at which it was produced. That I present this particular collection for publication at this time indicates that I still stand by their dominant findings and perspectives. But, they must still be understood as part of an academic journey in the history of religions.

The diversity of this collection is evident in the divisions of the book itself. Part one deals with methodological issues, part two is a series of articles on religion and the state in modern India, and part three analyzes select Indian traditions in the U. S., particularly Swami Bhaktivedanta and the International Society for Krishna Consciousness.

Continuity is provided by the application of a specific method to a number of themes in the study of modern Indian religions. This positions the work of the author midway between two poles. On the one hand are the "methodologists," or those whose research and writing centers on methodological issues. Although many of them have areas of linguistic competence, this is seldom evident in their published work. For some, at least, the history of the study of religion and methods for the study of religion are legitimate fields of research which need no further justification than their intrinsic value. It is this emphasis, I believe, from which Wilfred Cantwell Smith sought to disassociate himself in his paper, "Methodology and the Study of Religion: Some Misgivings." (*Methodological Issues in Religious Studies*, edited by Robert D. Baird, Chico: New Horizons Press, 1975.) While I do not hold so radical a view as that of Smith, a glance at the essays in this volume should indicate that I am not committed to methodology apart from its application to data.

On the other pole are numerous scholars with extensive linguistic training who deal with texts and even do fieldwork, but who seldom raise methodological issues for careful examination. While this need not be done independently of an examination of data, it can be, and frequently it is only when such issues are isolated and analyzed in their own right that the full power of logic and epistemology is brought to bear. Methodology is the logical analysis of method. Moreover, it is sometimes necessary to engage in the logical analysis of method as such. While one might not be prepared to spend one's academic life sharpening tools to the exclusion of using them, one might nevertheless argue for the necessity of sharpening tools. And, a knife cannot be sharpened while it is being used.

The method that is used in these essays is systematically argued in *Category Formation and the History of Religions* (Mouton, 1971. Reissued in paperback in 1991). If I were writing that book today I might change a sentence here or there, but I remain convinced that the method presented there provides a fruitful direction for research.

A vigorous defense of a given method should not be taken to mean nor to imply that it is the only legitimate method or even that it is the best — only that it is one among others that might enable one to ask some interesting questions and uncover some interesting relationships.

A number of issues are emphasized in the methodological essays included in this volume. This author has never considered religion to be an essence that is metaphysically "out there," and which is in danger of being reduced to something other than what it really is. Rather, religion (the word, not the thing) is defined as "ultimate concern" and therefore points to a dimension of human existence. I agree with W. C. Smith, then, when he argued that religion is basically the study of persons.

The importance of the definitional issue and how it is resolved is dealt with at some length in *Category Formation and the History of Religions*, but also more briefly in "Interpretative Categories and the History of Religions." There the necessity of proceeding with a definition is argued and a certain definition of religion as "ultimate concern" is presented. As a stipulative definition this is neither true nor false, but is merely a way of marking the boundaries of a study and determining the kind of question one is asking when one asks the "religious question." It is not argued that this is the only possible definition or that everyone should follow it. Rather it is offered as an heuristically useful definition for indicating what this author seeks to do.

Certain secondary categories used by historians of religions pose a barrier to understanding religion, particularly when it is defined in such a way as to be centered in the believer. Some of these are also discussed in "Interpretative Categories" and one is discussed more fully in "Syncretism and the History of Religions."

Since all methods have self–imposed limits by reason of their definitions, assumptions, the kinds of questions they are prepared to ask, and the methods of verification used, methodology includes the analysis of these limits both where a given method recognizes them and also where it does not. In "Normative Elements in Eliade's Phenomenology of Symbolism," the search for trans–historical religious structures is unpacked and its limits are clarified. This concern is also found in "Hindu–Christian Dialogue and the Academic Study of Religion." The academic study of religion is seen as a study of religion that is based on arguments and evidence that are available to any academically trained individual. Academic study cannot rely on religious experience or intuition for verification. Within the context of the university, religion is studied as any other subject might be studied. The history of religions, as defined in *Category Formation*, is one discipline that qualifies as academic. But, within the definitions set up in the article, Hindu–Christian dialogue is more religious than academic and it is for that reason that its participants are identified religiously as "Hindu" or "Christian."

Finally, the approach taken in these essays seeks historical truth, that is, it seeks to determine, as far as possible, what actually happened in the human past, and it also seeks to point out interrelationships which can be determined on the basis of historical research. But, in no instance is the author to be seen as presenting an ideology, a theory, or a metaphysical truth. Nevertheless, the study of historical truth provides room for theses and arguments about the human past. It allows for arguing historical theses even though it does not seek the ultimate truth of things in general. Since the very possibility of this kind of knowledge has been questioned by arguing that all discourse is ideological and all historical writing is relative, the possibility of this kind of knowledge is argued for in "Factual Statements and the Possibility of Objectivity in History."

Part two applies this method, in varying degrees, to the study of religion, law and the state in modern India. An analysis of Supreme Court cases on freedom of religion ("Religion and the Secular: Categories for Religious Conflict and Religious Change in Independent India") reveals not the relationship of religion and social change, but the conflict of two *religious* systems. This is a religious conflict because it is a conflict between two systems of ultimate values and meaning. One of the systems of meaning, embodied in *The Constitution of India*, sees life as divided into the realms of "religion" and "the secular" while traditional thinking saw all life as homogeneous and permeated with religion. These categories are developed in the analyses of the thought of Jawaharlal Nehru and Justice Gajendragadkar. They are also assumed in the Indian Constitutional directive toward a uniform civil code which necessitates the secularization of law ("Uniform Civil Code and the Secularization of Law"). I have called this way of beholding the world the "New Great Tradition." While in general the "New Great Tradition" moves relentlessly in legislation and the courts, the issue of cow slaughter is at least one place where the division between the realms of religion and the secular is indistinct ("Cow Slaughter and the 'New Great Tradition' "). " ' Secular State' and the Indian Constitution" acknowledges India's apparently universal contention that she is a "secular state" and shows the elasticity of this multivalent symbol and its role in nation building.

Finally, since the history of religions is an attempt to understand the other, when the author was asked to participate in a faculty seminar on universal human rights, he felt it his duty to point out that at different times and in different contexts some equally sincere people held different views from the majority around the seminar table. This was neither a repudiation of "universal human rights," nor was it the affirmation of inequality and caste. It was an exercise in understanding the other in a context where it seemed to be useful.

This endeavor to understand the other is applied to the thought of Swami Bhaktivedanta in Part three. I was not concerned with the use of a social–scientific method to "explain" either psychologically or sociologically "why" persons joined this movement. While that can be illuminating, it might, if carried theoretically beyond its limit, suggest that the message itself had no intrinsic appeal to adherents. The application of religio–historical method to the wide range of Bhaktivedanta's writings was an attempt to determine some of the systematic dimensions of his thought which had seldom been presented systematically. Rather than attempting to provide an *explanation* of Bhaktivedanta, I was seeking a religious *understanding*. To this end, I sought to determine how he understood karma and rebirth within his theistic system ("Swami Bhaktivedanta: Karma, Rebirth and the Personal God"); how his understanding of his role might explain his mode of commentary work ("Swami Bhaktivedanta and the *Bhagavadgita* 'As it Is'"); and how he understood the relationship between his message and the message of other religions. In no case should the analyses be seen as either promoting nor demoting his message. Again, it is an attempt at understanding an other. "ISKCON and the Struggle for Legitimation" traces the struggles of the movement to be considered religious within the American scene and how they sought to legitimate their movement.

Finally, while ISKCON struggled to be considered "religious" and thereby governed by the first amendment of the U. S. Constitution, the Transcendental Meditation Movement consistently presented itself as not a religion. The reasons for this and how a specific instance was handled in the American courts is the subject of "Religious or Non–Religious: TM in American Courts."

In none of these instances is the author voicing a personal opinion on the rightness or wrongness of a doctrinal position or a legal decision. Rather it is an attempt to understand the religious positions and how these are handled within the legal processes. Often the reader imposes his or her own prejudices upon an article that does not intend to support them. If someone judges Bhaktivedanta's somewhat negative approach to other religions as judgmental it may well be because he or she evaluates a negative approach negatively. And, if someone does not agree with certain Indian Supreme Court decisions, it might appear to that reader that the author is implying the same, even though he is merely seeking to understand the process. These essays, then, are an exercise in religious, historical, objective analysis — nothing more and nothing less. But that, I believe, offers some interesting and important insights into the religio–historical process, and provides us with perspective for a better understanding of the other.

PART ONE

METHODOLOGICAL ESSAYS

1

Interpretative Categories and the History of Religions

Although considerable variations of opinion exist concerning the method and scope of the history of religions (*Religionswissenschaft*), it is generally agreed that this field of study is divided into two main areas of scholarly concern. One area is systematic, is sometimes called phenomenology of religion, and is represented by such scholars as Van der Leeuw, W. Brede Kristensen, Mircea Eliade, and C. J. Bleeker. The second area is more distinctively historical in orientation and is exemplified by the work of G.F. Moore, Raffaele Pettazzoni, or Joseph Kitagawa (*Religion in Japanese History*). America remains considerably behind Europe in the training of practicing phenomenologists, and continues to emphasize the historical aspect of the history of religions.

There exists no necessary conflict between the two endeavors, which can and should exist side by side.

> At present, historians of religions are divided between two divergent but complementary methodological orientations. One group concentrate primarily on the characteristic *structures* of religious phenomena, the other choose to investigate their *historical context*. The former seek to understand the *essence of religion*, the latter to discover and communicate its history.[1]

Since 1887 and the publication of P. D. Chantepie de la Saussaye's *Lehrbuch der Religionsgeschichte*, the phenomenology of religion has developed sufficiently to qualify as at least a branch of *Religionswissenschaft*. But in spite of this significant development,[2] the phenomenological dimension of the history of religions has developed no universally accepted interpretative categories. While such terminological categories as sacrifice, myth, or cult are commonly used, phenomenologies of religion seldom resemble one another in terms of the larger interpretative categories by which the mass of religious data is classified. Van der Leeuw organizes his material according to the categories of the object of religion, the subject of religion, object and subject in their reciprocal operation, the world, and forms;[3] Eliade organizes his material in terms of sky gods, sun and sun worship, water symbolism, sacred stones, fertility, vegetation, etc.;[4] and W. B. Kristensen interprets the religious data with the use of the categories of cosmology, anthropology, and the cultus.[5] It is true that in various phenomenologies certain themes recur, such as sacred time, sacred space, or tabu. But it has not come to be assumed that there is only one way of organizing the religious data when dealing with it systematically or phenomenologically.

An examination of historically oriented works, on the other hand (and this is particularly true of introductory handbooks), reveals the fact that there exist categories which are almost universally accepted and seldom if ever questioned. One would be astonished to find a history of religions which did not assume that the only available categories for interpreting the data are "Hinduism," "Buddhism," "Judaism," "Christianity," and "Islam." Even when such categories are seen to be oversimplifications of religious diversity, they are still used in lieu of better alternatives. The problem which I intend to consider, then, has to do with the historical rather than the systematic branch of the history of religions. I propose to show that the study of religion must begin with a definition of "religion" and that, given the task of the historian of religions, to use as interpretative categories of religion such rubrics as "Hinduism," "Buddhism," and the like, is not only misleading, but creates a situation in which the historian of religions is actually precluded from understanding the religions he or she is studying. I shall then show how such an approach throws new light on some of the questions historians of religions have been prone to ask.

The Category of Religion

It is the contention of Wilfred Cantwell Smith that the term "religion" ought to be dropped, since the term is of no concern to the person of faith, and since there is nothing which corresponds to "religion"in the objective world.[6] His view is based on the notion that what we have generally intended by the term "religion" points to an intensely personal human dimension and can never be separated from the people to whom it refers. Having made the point that "comparative religions" is the study of persons, and having argued at length that the meaning of "religion" has gradually become reified and separated from persons, Smith takes the step of rejecting the use of the term: "religion is a misleading, confusing, and distorting concept." Having quoted eminent thinkers from various traditions regarding their dissatisfaction with the term "religion," Smith concludes:

> I have become strongly convinced that the vitality of personal faith, on the one hand, and, on the other hand (quite separately), progress in understanding — even at the academic level — of the traditions of other people throughout history and throughout the world, are both seriously blocked by our attempt to conceptualize what is involved in each case in terms of (a) religion.[7]

In more theistic terms he says, "the concern of the religious man is with God; the concern of the observer is with religion."[8]

In place of "religion," Smith offers the categories of "cumulative tradition" and "faith." His definition of the former is:

> By 'cumulative tradition' I mean the entire mass of overt objective data that constitute the historical deposit, as it were, of the past religious life of the community in question: temples, scriptures, theological systems, dance patterns, legal and other social institutions, conventions, moral codes, myths, and so on: anything that can be and is transmitted from one person, one generation, to another, and that an historian can observe.[9]

By faith is meant "an inner religious experience or involvement of a particular person; the impingement on him of the transcendent, putative or real."[10] My present concern is with the validity of these categories which are offered in place of "religion."[11]

There are two reasons why I prefer not to follow Smith in rejecting the use of the term "religion." The first reason is related to Smith's alternative term "faith." While Smith's definition of "faith" certainly sustains his concern for the personal dimension of the study of religions, it must be conceded that the term "faith" has had as many variations in meaning as has "religion," and has also undergone its own reification. "There are few words in the language of religion which cry for as much semantic purging as the word 'faith'."[12] For some, faith connotes a personal dimension and refers to a personal relationship of trust. But for others it has been thoroughly intellectualized. And, while

Smith may well say "there is nothing in heaven or on earth that can legitimately be called *the* Christian faith,"[13] it must be conceded that there are those believers for whom a distinction between "*my* faith" and "*the* Christian faith" does not exist. "Faith," no less than "religion," has been reified so as to refer to a system of thought. Tillich and other religious thinkers have attempted to restore a personal dimension to both terms. Let it at least be conceded that a variety of meanings, one of which involves reification, is not sufficient ground for dispensing with "religion" without also dropping "faith." And, if one can salvage the term "faith" by defining it, one could save the term "religion" by definition as well.

The second objection is that the historian of religions (even as a professor of "comparative faith") cannot allow himself to take the side of the opponents of reification. Smith holds that the people who are *truly* religious do not concern themselves with "religion."

> I am not saying that the concept of religion is inadequate; rather, so far, that it is inadequate for the man of faith.
>
> The more direct, immediate, and profound his faith, the more he is concerned with something, or Someone, that far transcends anything that can be denominated as religion. The concept is fundamentally a distraction to his religiousness.[14]

Again, "No man has seen the point of his own religious tradition for whom the concept religion is an adequate indication of what it is all about."[15]

Such a judgment is subjective and selective. In fact, such selectivity seems to go against Smith's alleged interest in persons. Even if it is the "faith" of other persons that we want to understand, it must be apparent that there are those for whom "religion" is a meaningful way of expressing their faith. Do we dismiss Radhakrishnan as one whose faith is less than sensitive because he writes books about "religion" and is a defender of "Hinduism"?[16] The choice of statements by believers from various traditions to the effect that their traditions are not religions leads Smith to the conclusion that for persons of "sensitive faith" such a judgment must hold. But numerous others in fact use such terms. Are they not also to be understood? It may be that the authors in Kenneth Morgan's books, *Islam the Straight Path*, *The Path of the Buddha*, and *The Religion of the Hindus* are aware of the Western audience for whom they write, but they use reified concepts with little discomfort.

The important point, if we are to understand other people, is not who originated a term or whether it was first applied by an outsider.[17] If a label is utilized by a believer to refer to his or her faith, even if that label be "religion," then it need not and indeed cannot be avoided simply because it originated in the mind of an outsider. The fact that some persons find reification unacceptable is not determinative in this regard. Indeed, according to Smith's study of reification, the majority of persons from the eighteenth century onward would not qualify as "persons of faith." At this point the seriousness with which Smith takes persons is placed in question — unless we are to conclude that he means only his kind of persons.

The historian of religions is a scholar who studies as many religions as possible with the goal of understanding. The term "religion" has indeed been a nebulous term, which, if the scholar is to proceed with credibility, must be given a functional definition prior to the investigation rather than at the end of the study. The definition of religion given by Paul Tillich, namely that religion is ultimate concern, can be functional for the historian of religions. Such a definition is serviceable since it defines for the historian of religions the goal of understanding the beliefs, rites, temples, and entire life patterns of individuals or communities in the light of their ultimate concerns. Such patterns of ultimate concern can be understood on the level of an ideal system or on the level of sociological actualities.[18]

Not only can Tillich's definition be utilized by the historian of religions for identifying the object of study; it also enables him or her to deal with the personal dimension of religious faith even in cases in which that faith expresses itself in terms like "religion" or "Hinduism." If one uses the term "religion," then, and defines it as what concerns people ultimately (either as individuals or in community), it becomes necessary to reject as subordinate interpretative categories the broad and sweeping designations "Hinduism," "Buddhism," "Judaism," "Christianity," and "Islam."[19] Having affirmed the category of religion, we now turn to these other categories which have achieved almost universal acceptance.

The Category of "The Religions"

Smith discards not only "religion" but also "the religions." His argument is twofold. To begin with, he objects to "the religions" for the same reason that he wishes to drop "religion." Such categories involve reification and are not relevant to the insider, the person of faith.

> The first score on which I see the concept of a religion as tending to deceive the observer of a community's religious life is, basically, that the concept is necessarily inadequate for the man who believes and therefore cannot but be misleading for the outsider who does not.[20]

Smith here oversimplifies what is acceptable to the believer, as he did in his discussion of religion. It is simply untrue that "the religions" are unacceptable to *all* believers. "Christians" are idealized to the extent that only a fraction of those who consider themselves "Christian" can be considered when it is said, "Christian life is a new life, lived in a supernatural context. To understand Christianity, or to think that one does, is not yet to understand Christians."[21] Here Smith enters the normative realm by defining out of consideration all but the "Christians" he intends to understand. There are those who consider themselves "Christians" for whom the term "supernatural" is theoretically unfortunate, and others whose lives are lived as though only the "natural" exists. One may disagree with such a conception of "Christianity" normatively, but to begin the descriptive task with such a selective principle creates an insuperable barrier for understanding those whose faith is less "sensitive." What is said here for "Christianity" can also be extended to include those who defend *their* Judaism (e.g., Mordecai Kaplan in *Judaism as a Civilization*), commend *their* Buddhism as a solution to the problems of world peace (Sixth Buddhist Council), or offer *their* Hinduism as the national religion of India (Hindu Mahasabha). The use of these terms, reification notwithstanding, must be retained in those cases where to exclude them would mean to modify or ignore the articulation of someone's ultimate concern — even if that person happens to live on this side of the eighteenth century. When religion is defined as ultimate concern, every person (even a reificationist) is a potential believer suitable for study by the historian of religions.

Smith's second argument for the rejection of "the religions" is an historical one. These categories were applied to impossibly large segments of historical data before the full force of historical flux had been realized.

> If it [a "religion"] exists in one country (or village), it exists in somewhat different form in the next. The concepts were formed before the ruthlessness of historical change was recognized, in all its disintegrating sweep. They have in practice been

> abandoned as awareness has since grown. It is time now definitely to reject them theoretically, as inherently inept.[22]

A recognition of the complexity and rapidity of historical change makes Smith's second argument compelling.

How does such a recognition, however, fit into the approach which proposes to study religion as ultimate concern? If it is the task of the historian of religions to study the ultimate concerns of persons, whatever these concerns happen to be in differing historical contexts, then it is even more compelling that one discard "the religions" as interpretative categories. Such categories make the study neither historical nor religious.[23] A study utilizing "the religions" as interpretative categories is not historical since "the religions" are categories which, rather than growing out of an examination of historical data, are imposed upon a mass of material prior to its examination. And the use of "the religions" as interpretative categories makes the study not genuinely religious, when the goal is understanding the ultimate concerns of persons in their givenness, since it imposes one religion or pattern of ultimate concern upon another. Hence to proceed under such interpretative categories precludes the possibility that the results will be either authentically historical or genuinely religious.

Implications of a Definitional Approach

The Essence of Religion

If this definitional approach is to be taken seriously, then certain questions that historians of religions have been inclined to ask will be seen in a somewhat different perspective. The first has to do with the search for the essence of religion. According to Eliade, phenomenology of religion (the search for structures) seeks to understand the essence of religion. C. J. Bleeker sees this search as the final goal of the historian of religions as well. He concedes that the historian of religions proceeds with a certain notion of what religion is, but that one's final goal is to determine the essence of religion.

> The student of the history of religions and of the phenomenology of religion starts his study with an intuitive, hardly formulated, axiomatic notion of what religion is. His ultimate aim is an inclusive formulation of the essence of religion. Such a definition is the crowning of the whole work.[24]

Bleeker considers various attempts to express the essence of religion in the form of a short definition and finds them wanting. An example is his rejection of the key word "power" as getting to the heart of religion.

> . . . "power" in itself is not sufficiently qualified and does not furnish a valid guarantee that it represents the object of genuine religion: besides divine power there is also demoniacal and satanical power.[25]

In announcing the failure of a host of considered definitions, however, Bleeker does not sufficiently appreciate the circular method that is employed in attempts to determine the essence of religion by examination of historical data. To criticize a definition of religion, one requires a certain knowledge of what religion really is — that is, one is laboring under another definition. And to contend that one cannot define what one is examining prior to its examination, even though one continues under a vague notion of what it is, not only raises the question whether such a vague notion will suffice in enabling one to identify that for which one is looking, but also makes it difficult for other scholars to ascertain whether what is being examined is indeed religion, and whether the "resulting" definition is actually its essence. There is no way for one who proposes to study religion to avoid the methodological necessity of beginning with an explicit functional definition of what is intended by the term, that is, a definition that will enable one to identify the object of inquiry.[26] Since the essence finally arrived at is already contained in the original definition (even if implicit or vague), there is no real point in asking the question of essence. The difficulty with most definitions is not that they already imply the essence (here we are dealing with analytic truth which makes the subsequent search only a broadening and deepening of what is already contained in the definition), but that the definition includes a normative decision for one world–view over another. By defining religion as the ultimate concerns of persons or communities, however, we are operating under a non–judgmental functional definition which will enable us to move toward an understanding of *whatever* has concerned persons ultimately. The concern of Bleeker to distinguish pure from impure religion[27] is no longer relevant, since our definition, while allowing us to identify religion, offers no norm for distinguishing "pure" religion from that which is "impure." Our concern is rather to describe and understand the religions of men and women.[28]

Dropping the question of essence does not involve a loss, for such a question involves insuperable logical problems. The essence of religion could only mean what all religious persons have in common. But all religious persons have in common whatever it is that one decides to use to identify them as "religious." That is, we are dealing with analytic and not synthetic truth. To suggest that what is common to all ultimate concerns involves more than that they concern people ultimately is to raise what is basically a non–religious question. In searching for this level of commonness, one is forced to deal with characteristics that, while included in all patterns of ultimate concern, are not equally important to all. This seems to point to the fact that the ultimate concerns are not actually the same. To consider something essential to all ultimate concerns which goes beyond the definitional tautology would demand that one insist either that all persons are in agreement on the content of their ultimate concerns (an obviously indefensible position), *or* it would necessitate emphasizing universal elements which are central to one religion but peripheral to another. But if religion is seen as ultimate concern, to compare what is in one case ultimate and in another case peripheral is not to compare similarities at all. Hence in the former alternative one is giving a religious answer which the historical data do not confirm, whereas in the latter the answer is supported by historical data only because it is no longer religious.

The search for the essence of religion is subtly normative rather than historical–descriptive. It implies that the historical accidents can be forfeited without loss. But the "essence" that is "found" as the result of this historical inquiry turns out to be simply another *Anschauung*, historically speaking. The logical fallacy of such a procedure is nowhere more clearly seen than in the attempt of Arnold Toynbee to disengage the essence from the non–essentials in "the religions."[29] According to Toynbee, one of the human family's perennial problems is self–centeredness, and the historian's method is well suited to correct this. Once one, through studying another culture, has interested oneself in other people for their own sake, one will come to see that these other people in their time and place had as much right to consider themselves at the center of the universe as we do. One will also see how little right one has to do so. I will not presently go into detail regarding the extent to which the claim to have found the essence of religion amounts to claiming to occupy a new center of the universe.

When Toynbee talks about the essence and the non–essentials, he has reference to what he calls the "higher religions," of which there are seven: Hinduism, Theravada Buddhism, Mahayana Buddhism, Christianity, Judaism, Islam, and Zoroastrianism. But the material included in such categories is not nearly as unified as the labels imply. Hence, when Toynbee points out that all seven religions agree that Ultimate Reality has both an impersonal and a personal aspect, his point is readily supported. There are some in each "religion" who have espoused an impersonal ultimate and others who have opted for a decidedly theistic view. By dividing the religious world into these seven categories, one would be more surprised if points of agreement could not be found. But this does not touch the question of ascertaining the essence of all religions. Apart from the fact that these categories leave out a large segment of religious people in non–literate cultures, it would be easier to find a commonness among "the religions" than it would be to find it within them. It is easier to point out that some "Hindus" and some "Christians" affirm a personal dimension to Ultimate Reality than it is to find what is agreed upon by all "Hindus" — or all "Christians" for that matter. Mordecai Kaplan has pointed out that there is no distinctively Jewish concept of God. He argues that in this matter the continental divide is Kant, and that post–Kantian "Jews" and post–Kantian "Christians" have more in common in their views of God than either of them have with pre–Kantian "Jews" or "Christians." The point is that the varieties of religious expression and ultimate concerns are in such classifications as great within each category as among the categories.

Having erred regarding "the religions," Toynbee continues by making a second methodological fallacy. In the "higher religions," he claims, there are two ingredients: (1) essential counsels and truths, and (2) non–essential practices and propositions. The essential counsels are valid for all time. On the other hand; the great religions have influenced their environments and have been influenced by them in return. These influences have left their marks on the religions in the form of accretions which can be verified by the historian who can trace them back to their origin and show that they were independent of the essential truths and counsels. "He can show that they have attached themselves to the religion, in the course of its history, as a result of historical accidents."[30] Toynbee recognizes that the "accidental accretions" are the price that the essential counsels must pay in order to be communicated to people in a given situation. In Christian language, the price of redemption is incarnation. The message is eternal, permanent, and universal, but must be put into terms which are local and temporary. Toynbee would do well to remember this. The fact is that the so–called essence is always found in local garb, and Toynbee's list of essential counsels is itself no exception.[31] What he is doing is merely translating what he considers essential from one local garb to another which he feels he can affirm and which he hopes will strike an accord with others as well. But to claim that he has in fact stated the pure essence, apart from historical accidents, is absurd.

The historical method which enables Toynbee to identify the accretions actually turns everything into an accretion. The reason for this is that historical method seeks for antecedents and sources, but not for origins in the strict sense. Apart from what the theologian might say about the beginnings of Christianity, the historian is aware that even the sources of "essential Christianity" are legitimate objects for historical investigation. When the historian, as historian, speaks of the origin of an idea, he or she means the source from which it came with reference to the object under consideration, and not an absolute beginning. For the historian the "beginning" does not exist in principle, but only arises when one's historical data run out and one is unable to pursue the matter any further.[32] Historical method is quite capable, given the appropriate evidence, of showing that Toynbee's "essence" is, within another frame of reference, an accretion.

The Essence of "The Religions"

It is also historically inappropriate to search for the essence of "the religions." I am assuming that although definitions may not exhaust reality, terms must nevertheless be defined to indicate to the reader what is intended by their use. This I have done with "religion," and am now arguing that anyone who insists on utilizing "the religions" as interpretative categories must, in the interest of clarity, indicate what is meant by such terms and how they assist the historian of religions in understanding religion. I have previously argued that to utilize such categories makes a study neither authentically historical nor genuinely religious.

Since the question of essence is actually analytical–circular in nature, as we have seen in discussing the essence of religion, to give a definition of "the religions" implies having made a decision regarding *their* essence. If, for example, one defines "Hinduism" in the manner of a neo–Advaitin such as Radhakrishnan or Vivekananda, one will hold that Brahman is ultimately indescribable and transcends personality. Following Śankara, bhakti movements will be valued but relegated to a lower level of reality. Personal deities such as Kṛṣṇa will be seen at best as Saguṇa Brahman or Iśwara. They will ultimately be a concession to ignorance (*avidyā*). Mokṣa will be seen as transcending all dual conceptions inherent in theistic world views. This is one pattern of ultimate concern. But if one accepts such a view of "Hinduism," one is in a position of foisting one particular religion upon other particular religions. How can one adequately deal with the "Hinduism" of Ram Mohan Roy and Debendranath Tagore, who were thoroughly theistic and who rejected a metaphysic based on the ultimate identification of Self and God? How do we honestly come to grips with the devotion to a personal deity found in the hymns of the Āḻvārs or Nāyaṉmārs, or how can we understand the views of Tamil Śaivites, for whom the emancipated in becoming "Śivamaya" does not become Śiva himself nor lose separateness, when we have already accepted the interpretation of another believer? Is it of no consequence to the study of religion that, for Śankara, bhakti is at best preliminary to jñāna while for the *Nārada Bhakti Sūtras* not only is it not preliminary but it is its own reward. It may be the case that from the Brahmanical point of view Kṛṣṇa is an avatār of Viṣṇu who is a manifestation of Brahman. But in passages of the *Bhagavadgītā*, Kṛṣṇa absorbs the transpersonal Brahman (XIII, 12-17: XIV, 27). In the latter reference Kṛṣṇa is the foundation of Brahman.

> For I am the foundation of Brahman,
> The immortal and imperishable,
> And of the eternal right,
> And of eternal bliss.[33]

Surely we will not understand the Vṛndāvin Gosvāmins who based their theology on the *Bhāgavata Purāṇa* (not the *Chāndogya Upaniṣad* or the *Vedānta Sūtras*), and who were eager to prove that Kṛṣṇa was not merely an avatār of Viṣṇu but full god himself, if we see them through the categories of Śankara. Vivekananda is the final authority for *his* "Hinduism," but that is the end of it. Each person or community that arises must be seen in the light of that person's or community's formulations. This is truly to take the believer seriously.

When Smith says that it is the task of comparative religion "to construct statements about religion that are intelligible within at least two traditions simultaneously,"[34] he is contending that the believer is the final authority on his or her own faith. But it must be emphasized that it is sometimes necessary to bypass one believer in order to understand another. This is the limitation of the witness of the believer — he or she can never speak authoritatively for the vast bodies of religious data that have in the past been categorized within "the religions." A believer or a community of believers can at best speak authoritatively regarding that believer's or community's "Hinduism." Hence an historical interpretation of Upaniṣadic faith need not have the *imprimatur* of

Radhakrishnan in order to be authentic. With living religions we have a check against subjectivity — the living believer. But in the study of the religions of persons or communities of previous generations we are thrust upon the hard realities of the text. This is not to devalue the ultimate role of the believer, but to take that believer seriously. When the believer is taken seriously, it is realized that another believer cannot speak for him or her in any final sense.

Since, then, any definition of "Hinduism" implies an essence and therefore necessitates interpreting one believer through the ultimate concern of another, and since this is equally true of the other "religions" on the descriptive level, "the religions" should be dropped as interpretative categories. Retaining the terms as part of the description wherever they appear (more frequently in the modern period), and not imposing them where they do not would be a step toward the understanding of religion. But having defined religion as ultimate concern it becomes impossible to understand the religions of *all* persons and groups by utilizing the interpretative categories of "the religions."

Historians of religions would be much ahead in the study of religion (as defined in this paper) if they would formulate their study according to areas in place of "the religions." They could then deal with religion in India, religion in China, Africa, Japan, or the Middle East, finding appropriate labels for their subject matter as do other historians.[35] The labels should not be categories imposed a priori, but should grow out of the material studied.[36] The final step would involve, not the classification of dissimilar ultimate concerns within the categories of "the religions," (as we have done in the past) but the development of *types* of ultimate concern regardless of their appearance in time and space, within or across the categories of "the religions." This final step would be the task of phenomenology, the systematic branch of the history of religions.

Notes

1. Mircea Eliade, *The Sacred and the Profane* (New York: Harper and Brothers, 1961), 232.

2. C. J. Bleeker, "The Phenomenological Method," *The Sacred Bridge* (Leiden: E. J. Brill, 1963), 1-15.

3. *Religion in Essence and Manifestation* (New York: Harper and Row, 1963).

4. Mircea Eliade, *Patterns in Comparative Religion* (Cleveland: The World Publishing Company, 1963).

5. W. Brede Kristensen, *The Meaning of Religion*, transl. John B. Carmen (The Hague: Martinus Nijoff, 1960).

6. His argument is more fully developed in his book, *The Meaning and End of Religion* (New York: The Macmillan Company, 1962).

7. *Ibid.*, 50.

8. *Ibid.*, 19.

9. *Ibid.*, 156-157.

10. *Ibid.*, 156. How these two categories operate in the study of religion can be found in the last two chapters of Smith's book.

11. It is relevant to state at this point that a decision in favor of the category of "religion" or the categories of "Hinduism," "Buddhism," "Judaism," "Christianity," or "Islam" is not decided on the basis of widespread usage. The issue is not settled by calling attention to the fact that numerous people (including scholars) use the term, or that numerous people are confused as to its meaning, but by determining whether and to what extent certain categories enable us to understand the "faiths" (or "religions") of other people.

12. Paul Tillich, *Systematic Theology* (Chicago: University of Chicago Press, 1963), III, 130.

13. Smith, *loc. cit.*, 191.

14. *Ibid.*, 128.

15. *Ibid.*, 129.

16. Cf. *Eastern Religions and Western Thought; Religion and Society; East and West in Religion.* In this same context one might ask what meaning might any longer be given to J. Sinha, *The Foundation of Hinduism* or T. M. P. Mahadevan, *Outlines of Hinduism.* Both of the authors are "Hindus."

17. Smith himself rejects the "nature and origin" theory, whereby one limits a religion to its original form and sees subsequent developments as aberrations. The faithful application of his principle makes the question of who originated the term quite irrelevant to the religious question. Cf. *The Meaning and End of Religion*, 148.

18. There is a tendency on the part of believers to see their own religion in terms of an ideal construct without imperfections and to see the religion of others in its historical and inevitably imperfect giveness. The study of religion is incomplete if it cannot deal with both levels: the ideal constructed in thought which points to a religious aspiration and the sociological and psychological realities which are usually imperfect in comparison with the ideal.

19. In this paper, these categories will subsequently be referred to as "the religions."

20. *Loc. cit.*, 134.

21. *Ibid.*, 135.

22. *Ibid.*, 142.

23. We will return to this point later when discussing the search for the essence of "the religions."

24. "The Key Word of Religion," *The Sacred Bridge*, 36.

25. *Ibid.*, 42.

26. This explains why it is necessary to *begin* with a definition of religion. But if one decides that the object of one's study is to understand the

ultimate concerns of people, then choosing interpretatively any definition of "Hinduism" or "Buddhism" over another presents a barrier to understanding the other definitions of these terms that have been offered by believers. Hence a definition of religion such as I am using does not opt for any world view but merely indicates at the beginning that for which I am looking and the limitations of my study. But, to labor under any definition of "the religions" for use in interpreting the ultimate concerns of people is only partially effective in that it enables one to understand only those who also accept such a definition.

27. "The 'Entelecheia' of Religious Phenomena," *The Sacred Bridge*, 21.

28. Tillich, as a theologian, also makes a normative distinction between valid and invalid ultimate concerns. While this is certainly a legitimate question, it is not necessary on the descriptive level. Ultimate concern, used as a functional definition, contains no form for distinguishing valid from invalid ultimate concerns. What it offers is a criterion for *identifying* religion, not for *evaluating* it. It provides the possibility of beginning our historical work by indicating *what* we are studying when we say we are studying religion, but it does not have built into it a decision as to what is the *true* religion if there is one. Our argument that defining religion in terms of ultimate concern is non–judgmental is based on the way the definition is being used, namely as a means of identifying religious data, not as a means of determining truth content.

29. *An Historian's Approach to Religion* (New York: Oxford University Press, 1956), chapter 19.

30. *Ibid.*, 266.

31. For the list of "essential counsels and truths" see *ibid.*, 274-275.

32. Cf. Robert D. Baird, "Syncretism and the History of Religions," *The Journal of Religious Thought* 24 (1967-68), 44 ff. Also a chapter of this volume.

33. *The Bhagavad Gītā*, transl. Franklin Edgerton (New York: Harper and Row, 1964), 72, 154. First published in Harvard Oriental Series.

34. "Comparative Religion: Whither — and Why?" in *The History of Religions: Essays in Methodology*, ed. Eliade and Kitagawa (Chicago: University of Chicago Press, 1959), 52.

35. It should be observed that we do not suggest "Indian Religions," "Chinese Religions," "Japanese Religions," etc., which would be as inadequate as "the religions." The areas are simply designated as convenient ways of dividing the effort of religious study. They are not to be taken as new interpretative categories. To attempt to ascertain an "Indian Mind" or an "Indian Mentality" would be just as misdirected as the search for the essence of "Hinduism."

36. To ask what one should use as categories if we dispense with "the religions" is a non–historical request. Historical categories must come from an examination of the data in a specific period and definite geographical location. To criticize one set of categories because they threaten the authentically historical nature of the study and then to concede the need for another set of equally broad a priori categories is hardly a significant solution. Alternative labels cannot be given in advance of an historical study.

2

Normative Elements in Eliade's Phenomenology of Symbolism

It is commonly held that the history of religions is not purely descriptive as history or sociology are imagined to be, nor predominantly normative as theology or philosophy of religion are assumed to be.[1] There is a sense in which a purely historical or descriptive statement is normative in that it is intended to be a true description of the object or event under consideration. But, when certain disciplines are described as normative, it is usually meant that they not merely attempt to describe certain views about reality, but propose to describe reality itself. That is, normative disciplines are so called because of their ontological stance. Theology is called a normative discipline because it offers statements which speak about the way it *is* with human nature, the world, Ultimate Reality, and not merely what some people think about these matters.

The question which we should ask is: How normative is the history of religions, of which phenomenology or the search for religious structures is a part? Our examination of Mircea Eliade's phenomenology of symbolism will lead us to the conclusion that, at least in his case, the history of religions is as normative as theology because it is based on an assumed ontology which is neither historically derived nor descriptively verifiable. We will develop this thesis by revealing four normative elements in Eliade's phenomenology of symbolism.

The Sacred and Ontology: The Point of Departure

There are two principal ways to proceed with the study of religion. The one is definitional and the other is intuitive. The definitional approach begins with an explicit definition of religion as a prior necessity for identifying the religious rite, ritual, object, and ideology. It sees no reason to assume that we know *what* religion *is*; indeed, it is overwhelmed with the vast divergence of meanings which have been given to the term.[2] The definitional starting point finds it difficult to understand how one can distinguish religion from other legitimate levels of human activity without indicating the meaning which one chooses to give to the term.[3]

The intuitive approach avoids a preliminary definition. It implies that we all know what we mean by religion and that our only difficulty is in offering a definition that will fit all its instances. The term religion corresponds to something that has ontological status, and it is intuitively identifiable by historians of religions.[4] Hence one does not proceed with a definition of religion, which is thought to prejudice the case from the start; but, after an examination of as many religions as possible, one attempts to construct the definition at the end of one's study — perhaps even at the end of one's career.[5] Usually the procedure used to determine the adequacy of a given definition is to indicate that it is either too broad or too narrow.[6] Such argumentation either implicitly posits a second definition of the term which is then used to judge the first, or it is based on the assumption that there is a reality to which the term corresponds whose manifestations are readily identifiable and are, therefore, usable as norms for determining the adequacy of a given definition.[7]

Both the definitional and the intuitive points of departure agree in resisting reductionism by holding that reality is so structured as to include the religious level — whether that level is determined definitionally or intuitively.

Eliade proceeds intuitively rather than definitionally. In the foreword of his book, *Patterns in Comparative Religion*, he affirms his desire to study the religious phenomenon as something religious.[8] He makes a correlation between religion and "the element of the sacred." While explicitly stating that one of the problems his volume is attempting to answer is "What is religion?"[9] he nevertheless doubts the value of beginning with a definition of the religious phenomenon.

> As I doubt the value of beginning with a definition of the religious phenomenon, I am simply going to examine various "hierophanies" — taking that term in its widest sense as anything that manifests the sacred.[10]

Rather than defining "the sacred," Eliade reiterates, by quoting Roger Callois, that it is difficult to define. The assumption is, of course, that it is nevertheless readily identifiable. However complex the labyrinth of facts might be, they are identifiable even though they cannot be reduced to a handy definition.

> At bottom, the only helpful thing one can say of the sacred in general is contained in the very definition of the term: that it is the opposite of the profane. As soon as one attempts to give a clear statement of the nature, the *modality*, of that opposition, one strikes difficulty. No formula, however elementary, will cover the labyrinthine complexity of the facts.[11]

That Eliade is proceeding intuitively and operating implicitly under the assumptions of the intuitive approach is beyond dispute when we read: "We are dispensed from any *a priori* definition of the religious phenomenon; the reader can make his own reflections of the nature of the sacred as he goes."[12]

Eliade continues by describing the modalities of the sacred as revealed in hierophanies of the sky and water, biological hierophanies, local hierophanies, myths and symbols.

> We must get used to the idea of recognizing hierophanies absolutely everywhere, in every area of psychological, economic, spiritual and social life. Indeed, we cannot be sure that there is anything — object, movement, psychological function, being, or even game — that has not at some time in human history been somewhat transformed into a hierophany.[13]

While never clearly articulating the difference between a hierophany and a kratophany, he also seems confident that in any given case he would be able to distinguish between the two.[14]

Historians of religions have occasionally distinguished themselves from theologians and philosophers of religion in that they do not begin with an *a priori*, but with the historically given religions.

> Wach maintained that the point of departure of *Religionswissenschaft* is the historically given religions. While the philosophy of religion proceeds from an *a priori* deductive method, *Religionswissenschaft* has no speculative purpose.[15]

In a concern to be historical, *a posteriori*, and not held by the philosophical and theological givens which bind other disciplines, historians of religions have attempted to avoid the definitional starting point, and have promised to present any definition that they might offer at the end of their investigations. They have begun with the historically given religions, assuming that they exist and that they are readily identifiable.[16] But in so doing an ontological stance is taken; and, unlike theologians or philosophers of religion, historians of religions have not felt the need to give argued defense for their implied ontologies.

C. J. Bleeker gives us some insight into the practical working out of this intuitive approach to religious phenomena. Referring to historians of religions and phenomenologists of religion, he says:

> They choose religious data. Thus they operate (*sic*) a certain notion of religion. Actually this criterium of religion is present both at the beginning and at the end of their investigations. The student of the history of religions and of the phenomenology of religion starts his study with an intuitive, hardly formulated, axiomatic notion of what religion is. His ultimate aim is an inclusive formulation of the essence of religion. Such a definition is the crowning of the whole work.[17]

By declining to go the definitional route, Eliade has opted for the intuitive point of departure. Religion, or the sacred, or the human response to the sacred, is something that can be identified without the need for a definition. How one is able to verify an authentic response to the sacred when it is intuitively identified, and how such a response can be distinguished from the demonic, remains a problem.

Eliade, then, begins intuitively. But the avoidance of a definitional starting point succeeds not in eliminating an ontological stance, but only in making that ontology less clear. It is still assumed that there is something out there that corresponds to the term "religion" or "the sacred," and also that the historian of religions can identify it intuitively. One can proceed to examine religion, reflecting on the nature of "it" as one goes along. This ontological status afforded "the sacred" is the first normative element in Eliade's phenomenological method.

Symbolism and Ontology

The meaning and methodological handling of symbolism also participates in this ontology. By this we mean more than that symbolism implies an ontology for "archaic man" who uses the symbols.[18] An ontological stance is presupposed in the methodology itself.

The technical meaning of symbolism is more extensive than the mere assertion that a particular stone or a specific tree is a hierophany. Symbolism is the coherence of many symbols into a system which is implied in any one of them. For example, the symbolism of the moon implies a system of hierophanies which cluster about the moon. The varied symbolism of snakes, women, etc., all have a lunar character, the moon acting as a symbol around which this symbolism seems to organize itself.

In the case of water symbolism there is no such central symbol, but rather various hierophanies. Nevertheless, they fit together into a coherent system. Water is the seed of things, the universal mother. There are water cosmogonies, the water of life, and the symbolism of immersion. Water symbolism involves the common element of water, but lacks a central hierophany such as unites lunar symbolism.[19]

> We have only to recall the consistency of the symbolism of immersion in water (Baptism, the Flood, submersion of Atlantis), of purification by water (Baptism, funeral libations), of the time before the creation (the waters, the "lotus," or the "island," and so on), to recognize that there is a well-ordered system. This system is obviously implied in every water hierophany on however small a scale, but is more explicitly revealed through a symbol (as for instance "the Flood" or "Baptism"), and is only fully revealed in water symbolism as displayed in *all* hierophanies.[20]

In the case of water symbolism, then, some hierophanies such as Baptism and the Flood are more clear in their intention. But there is, for Eliade, an overarching system which implies a meaning which is more comprehensive than any hierophany standing alone, and this system is *implied* in each particular hierophany. These systems manifest more clearly, more fully, and with greater coherence what each of the individual hierophanies intends. To interpret the hierophanies individualistically would be to lose their deepest meaning. "This is, moreover, the law for all symbolisms: it is the *entire* symbolism which gives value to (and corrects!) the various meanings of the hierophanies."[21]

Eliade states that he is not arbitrarily deducing a symbolism that is not there. Nor is he rationalizing the materials so that they fit into such a preconceived system.[22] By examining many symbols, myths, rites, and by many cross references, he is able to find some clear hierophanies, some that are semi–veiled, and some that are obscure.[23] A study of all hierophanies issues in a gradual understanding of what the symbol means. One can almost say that the clear hierophanies illuminate the obscure "hierophanies." The system is not something that is merely in the mind of the investigator, for each water hierophany actually implies the others.[24] Eliade does not seem to mean that men always *consciously* see in the symbol the implications of the whole logical system. The fact that some do not consciously understand all that is involved in a particular symbolism does not invalidate that symbolism.

> For a symbolism does not depend upon being understood; it remains consistent in spite of every corruption and preserves its structures even when it has been long forgotten, as witness those prehistoric symbols whose meaning was lost for thousands of years to be 'rediscovered' later.[25]

This leads naturally into certain statements which Eliade has made regarding the subconscious or transconscious activity of human beings. The use of symbols comes before language and discursive reason and reveals the deepest aspects of reality. Hence the study of symbols assists us in a better understanding of man. This is a knowledge of man as such before he is particularized in history. Every historical individual carries a great deal of this prehistoric humanity, but the archetype of "primordial man" is never fully realized in history. Eliade seems to suggest that it is that subconscious of the race which explains the coherence that he finds in symbolism.

Eliade maintains that depth psychology has freed the historian of religions from any hesitations that he or she might have had about interpreting symbols according to universally valid systems. Depth psychology has shown the survival of myths in the psyche of modern man irrespective of race or historical surroundings.

> This internal logic of symbols raises a problem with far–reaching consequences: are certain zones of the individual or collective consciousness dominated by the *logos*, or are we concerned here with manifestation of a 'transconscious'? That problem cannot be resolved by depth psychology alone, for the symbolisms which decipher the latter are for the most part made up of scattered fragments and of the manifestations of a

> psyche in crisis, if not in a state of pathological regression. To grasp the authentic structures and functions of symbols, one must turn to the inexhaustible indices of the history of religions.[26]

Such statements as these which imply an ontology are merely attempts to account for the logical system of symbolisms which have been found by an examination of the phenomena. But that is not the end of the matter. Ethnologists are sometimes confused by Eliade's "history of religions" since it is unlike any "history" with which they are familiar. The confusion is due to the fact that for Eliade phenomenology of religion is a subdivision of the history of religions. It is an ahistorical approach which organizes material into structures irrespective of time and place. This method is best served if the phenomena are sufficiently removed from each other so that similarities in structure cannot be explained in terms of historical connections.

As suggested previously, Eliade holds that it is not profitable to question the legitimacy of interpreting obscure symbols in the light of clear ones. Myths decay and symbols become secularized, but they never disappear. Even in the most profane society they exist in some form.[27] But such assertions, again, are based on an implied ontology which is nowhere philosophically defended. This ontological stance is most apparent when clear hierophanies are used to clarify the "intention" of obscure "hierophanies." Such an hermeneutic is possible only if one assumes not only that the sacred has ontological status, but also that its structures (and hence the systems of symbolism) also have ontological status. Only on this basis could a *symbolism* reveal the meaning or intention of a *symbol*.

But a method for verifying the ontological nature of such structures is neither used nor suggested. It is difficult to improve on the observation of Willard Oxtoby.

> Analogous in a sense to Gestalt psychology, the eidetic vision constitutes a confident, self–validating sense that the pattern which one has distilled represents the real essentials of the data. . . . There is nothing outside of one's intuitive grasp of a pattern which validates that pattern. The phenomenologist is obliged simply to set forth his understanding as a whole, trusting that his reader will enter into it. But there is no procedure stated by which he can compel a second

> phenomenologist to agree with the adequacy and inconvertibility of his analysis, unless the second phenomenologist's eidetic vision happens to be the same as the first's. For this reason phenomenological expositions of religion are in fact very personal appreciations of it, akin more to certain forms of literary and aesthetic criticism than to the natural or even the social sciencs.28

The ontological status of symbolic structures is a second normative element in Eliade's phenomenological method.

Authentic Existence and Ontology

There is another area in which Eliade's ontological approach makes possible a shift that would be otherwise unconvincing, He sees in "archaic man" a model for authentic existence. Eliade begins by convincing us that we should be prepared to admit that *homo religiosus* has had a tendency to extend hierophanies indefinitely. Almost everything had been a hierophany to someone at some time. This is particularly true for "archaic man." It is suggested that moderns are poorer because, for example, the human body or the process of eating is no longer a sacrament, in fact the entire cosmos has become desacralized. A shift has been effected — a shift that is made possible only because an ontological basis has already been posited. If not before, at least here it is clear that he is not dealing merely with what human beings have held to be sacred, but indeed with the structures of the sacred. His focal point, that is, is not only subjective, but also objective and hence ontological. Not only are the hierophanies which he describes hierophanies for those involved, but they are *in fact* hierophanies. One would normally expect further argumentation when a shift is made from the apparently descriptive to the normative. Here, however, an ontology has been posited from the start.

Once one sees the sacred or religion as an ontological reality, and one operates as though its structures are also ontologically real, having identified these structures, one has discovered reality. It then follows that those whose lives are lived in the sacred as completely as possible are the most authentic since they exist closest to reality.

It might be worth pointing out that not all phenomenologists of religion have taken such a step with Eliade in seeing "archaic man" as the most authentic. Bleeker, for one, states:

> Modern man has a clearer view of what is genuinely religious, is more able to distinguish the religious from the secular and makes higher demands as to the quality of religion.[29]

It is not the lack of an ontological basis that pushes him in a different direction at this point, but it is because his intuitive identification of religions differs from Eliade's. This might lead one to question the notion that we all know what religion is and can readily identify it, even though we have definitional difficulties.

Eliade's use of "archaic man" as a model of authentic existence, nevertheless, points to a third normative element in his phenomenological method.

The Urge to Philosophize

Eliade maintains that it falls within the realm of the historian of religions to articulate a systematic and theoretical interpretation of the religious facts that he finds as a phenomenologist.

> The second prejudice of certain historians of religions, that you must turn to another 'specialist' for a worldwide and systematic interpretation of religious facts, is probably to be explained by the philosophical timidity of a great number of scholars.[30]

In a footnote Eliade laments the fact that "general theories" which have dominated the history of religions from its beginnings have been the work of linguists, anthropologists, sociologists, and philosophers.[31] These are bold statements when one remembers the concern of other historians of religions to dissociate themselves from the work of theologians and philosophers of religion.[32] Eliade's prescription for the historian of religions to philosophize adds little to the method. An ontology has been implied from the start. What is more surprising is that this prior ontology is seldom if ever recognized as such. The result is that it is assumed that the philosophizing will come at the end of an examination of the given religions, when it would have been logically more appropriate in this method to find it at the beginning. For, if the ontological dimension of Eliade's phenomenological approach to the sacred and to symbolism is not validly supported, the conclusions remain equally unsupported. But Eliade thinks the philosophizing must conclude the study. If one fails to philosophize at this point,

> . . . [it] amounts to saying that the historian of religions hesitates to complete his *preparatory work* as a philologist and as a historian through an effort of *understanding*, which, to be sure, presupposes an act of thinking.[33]

Eliade laments the fact that the discipline of the history of religions has had a rather modest role in influencing modern culture.[34] This is largely because historians of religions have been too cautious. Having remained specialists, they fail to recognize the unlimited possibilities that are open to the history of religions. In attempting to remain scientific, thereby avoiding broad generalizations, historians of religions have paid the price of creativity. Eliade urges the historian of religions to go beyond the mere comprehending of religious facts to the level of philosophizing.[35] By this kind of thought the history of religions can help to create cultural values.[36] The reason why this does not happen often enough is that the majority of historians of religions defend themselves against the messages contained in the documents they study. Eliade is suggesting more than a spontaneous enlivening of the subconscious of moderns, for if his theoretical structures of symbols are true, this would simply happen apart from the philosophizing efforts of historians of religions.

The contention that historians of religions should philosophize and theorize is a fourth normative element in Eliade's method.

It is true that artificial disciplinary barriers have been erected so that if one wants to wear his or her label with cultic dignity, whether as "historian of religions," "anthropologist," or "theologian," there are some things that one is well advised not to do. But there is no valid reason why the historian of religions should be excluded from the possibility of philosophizing, or theologizing for that matter. There are various stages in Eliade's method which are philosophical — at the point of departure as well as at the point of destiny. And at all points at which ontology is assumed such philosophizing becomes essential. A failure to recognize the ontological point of departure and the assumption that he is beginning with the given religions which we can all readily identify without the need of a definition leads Eliade to miss the fact that, wherever an ontological stance is introduced, philosophical argumentation is needed. It must be said that if historians of religions are going to engage in a phenomenological approach to symbolism comparable to Eliade's, and if they are going to be called upon to develop the theoretical and philosophical implications of their findings, then simply being "most familiar with the religious facts" is insufficient preparation.[37] One who engages in such work also needs ability in philosophical method.

Whatever theories or conclusions flow from the work of those who call themselves historians of religions will be acceptable and valid only to the extent to which one's descriptions are accurate *and* to the extent to which his normative stages are adequately supported. In other words, a label (i.e. "historian of religions") does not forbid a scholar from making either normative or descriptive type statements, but when either type is made it must be adequately supported. Theoretical conclusions will then flow naturally from one's scholarly work and need not be urged to preserve an existing "discipline."

Notes

1. "In short, the history of religions is neither a normative discipline nor solely a descriptive discipline, even though it is related to both.

   "Our thesis is that the discipline of *Religionswissenschaft* lies between the normative disciplines on the one hand and the descriptive disciplines on the other." Joseph M. Kitagawa, "The History of Religions in America," *The History of Religions: . Essays in Methodology*, edited by Mircea Eliade and Joseph M. Kitagawa (Chicago: University of Chicago Press, 1959), 19.

2. Cf. Wilfred Cantwell Smith, *The Meaning and End of Religion* (New York: Macmillan, 1962); C. J. Bleeker, "The Key Word of Religion," *The Sacred Bridge* (Leiden: E. J. Brill, 1963), 36-51.

3. Cf. Robert D. Baird, "Interpretative Categories and the History of Religions," *On Method in the History of Religions*, edited by James S. Helfer, Beiheft 8 of *History and Theory*, 1968. Also Chapter 1 in this volume.

4. That historians of religions commonly take the intuitive point of departure is seen in their general reluctance to begin their work with a definition of religion.

5. Erwin Ramsdell Goodenough, "A Historian of Religion Tries to Define Religion," *Zygon: A Journal of Religion and Science*, Vol. 2, No. 1 (1967), 7-22.
6. Cf. Bleeker.

7. Cf. "Interpretative Categories and the History of Religions" (Chapter 1), for a discussion of the circularity of the search for the essence of religion and the "religions."

8. Eliade, *Patterns in Comparative Religion*, trans. by Rosemary Sheed (Cleveland: The World Publishing Company, 1963), p. xiii.

9. *Ibid.*, p. xiv.

10. *Ibid.*

11. *Ibid.*

12. *Ibid.*, p. xvi.

13. *Ibid.*, 11.

14. On page fourteen of *Patterns* he says: "I will come later to the question, how far such things can be considered hierophanies. They are in any case kratophanies, that is manifestations of power, and are therefore feared and venerated." Three pages later, without further clarification he is using the terms interchangeably. "You will find the fear of such an upheaval — ever present because of this indifference in the order of being between what is profane and what is hierophany or kratophany. . . ." 17.

15. Joseph M. Kitagawa, "Theology and the Science of Religions," *Anglican Theological Review*, Vol. 39, No. 1, (January, 1947), 47.

16. It seems to me that Charles H. Long is right when he writes: "To say

that you are studying or teaching Islam, Buddhism, Hinduism, or primitive religions does not necessarily mean that you are concerned with the specifically religious element in these complex systems of human experience." in "The Meaning of Religion in the Contemporary Study of the History of Religions," *Criterion*, Vol. 2 (Spring, 1063), 23.

17. Bleeker, 36.

18. Eliade, *Mephistopheles and the Androgyne* (New York: Sheed and Ward, 1965), 202-203.

19. *Patterns in Comparative Religion*, 499. "Of course this water symbolism is nowhere concretely expressed, it has no central core, for it is made up of a pattern of interdependent symbols which fit together into a system: but it is nonetheless real for that."

20. *Ibid.*

21. Eliade, *Images and Symbols* (New York: Sheed and Ward, 1961), 153.

22. *Patterns in Comparative Religion*, 450.

23. *Images and Symbols*, 24ff.

24. *Patterns in Comparative Religion*, 450. "The primitive mind did genuinely have the experience of seeing each hierophany in the framework of the symbolism it implied, and did always really see that symbolic system in every fragment which went to make it up."

25. *Ibid.*

26. *Images and Symbols*, 37.

27. *Ibid.*, 25. "Symbols and myths come from such depths: they are part and parcel of the human being, and it is impossible that they should not be found again in any and every existential situation of man in the Cosmos."

28. Willard Gurdon Oxtoby, "Religionswissenschaft Revisited," *Religions in Antiquity*, edited by Jacob Neusner (Leiden: E. J. Brill, 1968), 597.

29. C. J. Bleeker, 23.

30. *Mephistopheles and the Androgyne*, 195.

31. *Ibid.*

32. Cf. C. J. Bleeker, "The Phenomenological Method," *The Sacred Bridge*, 7. "In my opinion the phenomenology of religion is an empirical science without philosophical aspirations."

33. *The History of Religions: Essays in Methodology*, 92.

34. "Crisis and Renewal in the History of Religions," *History of Religions*, Vol. 5 (1965), 1-17.

35. *Ibid.*, 7. "But in the case of the History of Religions, hermeneutics shows itself to be a more complex operation for it is not only a question of comprehending and interpreting the 'religious facts.' Because of their nature these religious facts constitute a material on which one can think — or even ought to think — and think in a creative manner, just as did Montesquieu, Voltaire, Herder, Hegel when they applied themselves to the task of thinking about human institutions and their history."

36. *Ibid.*, 8.

37. Eliade urges that if general theories are not produced by historians of religions who are most familiar with the religious facts, then "we shall continue to submit to the audacious and irrelevant interpretations of religious realities made by psychologists, sociologists, or devotees of various reductionist ideologies." If historians of religions do not complete their theoretical work the "autonomous discipline" may die. "In this case we must expect a slow but irrevocable process of decomposition, which will end in the disappearance of the History of Religions as an autonomous discipline." See "Crisis and Renewal in the History of Religions," 16.

3

Hindu–Christian Dialogue and the Academic Study of Religion

The issue I intend to address is the extent to which the academic study of religion is able, within the limits imposed by its method, to handle the religious phenomenon of Hindu–Christian dialogue. But the precise nature of this issue will not be clear until I have indicated precisely what I mean by the "academic study of religion" and "Hindu–Christian dialogue." As is the case with many, if not most, terms in the study or religion, these are ambiguous. Verbal ambiguity means that, lexically speaking, such terms have referred to more than one thing. The way to eliminate verbal ambiguity is through stipulation.[1] To stipulate a specific meaning for the designations "Hindu–Christian dialogue" and the "academic study of religion" is to indicate how these designations will be used in the present discussion, even though it must be recognized that the terms have been and will probably continue to be used in other ways in other discussions. Stipulation is a formal activity that has to do with the use of words rather than with the meaning of things.

While stipulation has to do with the meaning of words rather than the significance of things, it is also clear that one uses such words to point to things. Stipulation is not a word game, but a means of clarifying precisely what thing it is to which a given word "points." In offering stipulative definitions of "Hindu–Christian dialogue" and the "academic study of religion," I am not, then, creating a set of relationships that are purely logical. That to which I am pointing with each stipulative definition does exist in the real world, even though the real world contains a great deal more than that.[2] Furthermore, a great deal more than that, or something quite different, might be intended when these same words are used in other discussions. The definitions that I am using, then, do not limit the range of reality, but only the present range of meaning for certain terms.

Stipulation is also a neutral activity. The meaning of the "academic study of religion" used in this discussion should not be seen as suggesting what can legitimately be pursued within the confines of the university or how departments of religion should be organized. Nor should it be taken to suggest that one such identified activity is somehow superior to others. Stipulation is no more than a means of clarifying the meaning of certain words in a given discussion.[3]

Clarification of Terms of Discourse

By "the academic study of Religion," I mean a study that not only proceeds with all the scholarly tools required of the subject matter, that is, languages, knowledge of history and culture, and so on, but also with a spirit of detachment or epoché, logical precision and verbal clarity.

The academic study of religion, then, is only one form of the study of religion. Religion may be studied for the purpose of *spiritual enrichment* by attending to Upaniṣadic texts in Sanskrit or biblical texts in Greek or Hebrew. And one may study Greek or Latin texts with the purpose of arriving at a true view of the nature of Christ. A doctrinal system that one is prepared to believe in and act upon may even be one's purpose for the *scholarly* study of religion. But the *academic* study of religion, as I am using the term, has no such spiritual or theological purpose. It seeks to understand religious persons and phenomena on its level of inquiry, recognizing that its tools do not permit it to exhaust the religious phenomena. One might be quick to point out that there is no single level on which religious phenomena are exhausted.

The academic study of religion is willing, even eager, to study myth but not mythologically, poetry but not poetically, ambiguity but not ambiguously. It places a high premium on clarity of analysis and is uncomfortable with contradictions. While it recognizes that believers frequently express themselves in ways that violate the law of contradiction, an exposition of those expressions by the academic study of religion would not embody such contradictions (even though the believer may consider them as paradoxes). The epoché that it embodies is not merely a preliminary attitude which enables a person to hear another before appropriation takes place. In *dialogue*, epoché is sometimes seen as "a *temporary* suspension of the consideration of our own tenets, convictions and opinions (emphasis added)."[4] In this view it is a stage in the process, for "when the aim is reached, everything which had been put aside in the process of dialogue will be recovered."[5] In the academic study of religion, when one puts epoché aside, one is no longer engaged in the academic study of religion.

The term "dialogue" is also ambiguous. Richard W. Taylor distinguishes "Socratic dialogue," "Buberian dialogue," "Discursive dialogue" and "Pedagogic dialogue."[6] All forms of "Hindu–Christian dialogue," however, regardless of how discursive or scholarly they may be are also religious. Interreligious dialogue in general and "Hindu–Christian dialogue" in particular, at least as I am using the term here, presupposes at least two people who meet as equals to advance their experience of God, to come to a more satisfying theological system, or to solve a human problem together. They must be open to the other, and willing to change and appropriate something from the other's experience or ideas.

Certain forms of "religious dialogue," whose practitioners claim exclusive right to the term, feel that the result of their endeavor is beyond language and is not to be subjected to such superficial analysis. Some hold that in dialogue theological contradictions are often resolved. This resolution is not a logical resolution, but a satisfying and apparently self–authenticating experience that is beyond logic and dissolves the logical problem by dissolving logic itself. "Niels Bohr once pointed out that, besides the 'simple truths' whose opposite could not be defended, there are also 'deep truths' of which the opposite also contains deep truth!"[7] This "real dialogue" is also seen as synonymous with "dialogue in depth."

> By dialogue I do not mean any talk about religion, which can be mere gossip — and often is. Nor do I mean the exchange of views between theologians of different religions. Interesting and necessary as it is, it is not "dialogue" but "comparative religion." The real dialogue is an ultimate personal depth — it need not even be a personal talking about religious or theological topics.[8]

When this is coupled with the assertion that dialogue is not a means, but an end in itself, it becomes clear that this level of dialogue is not merely a method that produces religious results, but that the very act of dialogue is a religious act and that dialogue itself is a religious experience. "Strictly speaking, dialogue has no goal: like love, dialogue is an end in itself, it is the full expression of our human experience."[9] That dialogue in general and Hindu–Christian dialogue in particular has no goal outside of itself is also affirmed by Klostermaier:

> Dialogue has no ulterior or extrinsic purpose. We cannot use it for private ends or manipulate it without destroying the spirit of dialogue. But we appreciate the fact that there is a built in purpose in all dialogue, insofar as we share in and through it what God is and what He gives to both the participants. It is in this sense an experience of our deepest oneness in God and of our being men for other men even in our differences.[10]

The history of religions encounters believers in almost any cumulative tradition who denigrate the intellectual or discursive level of religion and who seek to place their position or experience beyond the jurisdiction of logic. It is also familiar with believers who seek to say that one should not subject to analysis religious experiences one has not experienced, an assertion that is also common in the context of Hindu–Christian dialogue. One even finds articles written which, if they do not disparage the mere academic approach, do seem to suggest that they are more beneficial since they grow out of experience.[11] While some scholars might return the favor and denounce such blatant anti–intellectualism, the academic study of religion should not. It accepts this witness to a self–authenticating experience as an object of study, and it does not censure it any more than it approves it or participates in it. Nor, on the other hand, does it apologize for the differing rules that govern its own discourse. The fact that it simply *asserts* logical clarity as part of the rules of its game is seen in the fact that any argument for or against logic must use logical categories or it will not be taken seriously. Within the academic study of religion, even the argument that really cannot be exhausted by logical categories would have to proceed logically to be taken seriously. Logic is not argued for, but assumed, and any attempt to refute it must proceed logically, which makes the argument circularly destructive.

Understanding, then, that "Hindu–Christian dialogue" and the "academic study of religion" operate on two different levels (neither higher nor lower) and that there has been suspicion on both sides, we now turn to two scholars who have attempted to narrow the gap.

Attempts at Convergence

Just as Hindu–Christian dialogue has been initiated predominantly from one side, that is, the "Christian" side,[12] so attempts to narrow the gap have come more from the side of participants in dialogue than from the academic study of religion. In each of the two instances cited below the individuals are serious scholars of religion, but scholars engaged in dialogue, who seem to have a religious stake in the matter but who do not want to be considered unscholarly in their endeavor.

John Carman seeks to minimize the conflict between dialogue and the academic study of religion by proposing that the academic study of religion is a preparation for a more existential dialogue, that it can provide an environment (as at the Center for the Study of World Religions at Harvard University) in which dialogue can take place, and that it actually creates a new form of dialogue.[13] In support of his last point, Carman describes one facet of the academic program at the Center which requires that the student not only have a minimal theological grounding in one's own tradition, but also in a major "second tradition." "The relation of the student's 'first tradition' and 'second tradition' is the heart of our conception of comparative religion."[14]

However, the extent to which this issues in dialogue, Carman admits, is dictated not so much by the disciplines involved as by the interest (or lack of it) of the students themselves. Some may seek to interpret the "second tradition" in the light of the "first tradition"; others may treat the second in a more existential manner; while still others might simply do comparative religion. And comparative religion is not necessarily dialogue.[15]

To seek to bring the two approaches together by placing them in a common environment may succeed if there are students of the academic study of religion who are also interested in engaging in dialogue. But there is nothing in either approach to religion that requires that the one lead to the other. As we have defined the two terms, it might be quite possible for a single scholar to engage in the academic study of religion as well as to participate in Hindu–Christian dialogue. But when he or she does so, he or she will be doing two distinct things that cannot be done *simultaneously*. One simply cannot be detached and engaged simultaneously. Carman's lament and Wilfred Cantwell Smith's admission that little dialogue in fact takes place at the Center would seem to support this observation.[16]

Klaus Klostermaier pleads that dialogue be considered a legitimate method for the study of religion. He, too, recognizes the potential animosity on both sides, but urges the reader to agree that engaging in dialogue is a necessary human activity, which cannot be avoided, and which is essential to the study of both science and religion.[17] He is aware that "dialogue" has been used to describe a variety of activities, but here and elsewhere in his writing he pleads that "real" dialogue or "serious" dialogue takes place in depth when individuals open themselves existentially to each other, when they come together as equal partners and expect to learn from each other. A "sensitive" study of religion should proceed on the same principle. He holds, for example, that one cannot explain the beginning of Buddhism by examination of the cultural setting in which the Buddha lived, but only by attention to his message, the four noble truths and dependent origination. He goes on to propose that without the proper spiritual experience one cannot hope to understand a religious position:

> Similarly, Vedānta is not "explained" by describing the socioeconomic conditions of India in 1000 B.C.E., but it requires an *extensive meditational practice* and familiarity with the texts of the upaniṣads and their commentaries throughout the ages to understand what a contemporary Advaitin wishes to say when entering into a dialogue [emphasis added].[18]

An appeal is made to modern physics to support his position on dialogue in depth. "The impossibility of cutting out the subject from a description of reality has been recognized by modern physics: deep subjectivity is a necessary component of all in–depth dialogue."[19] The study of religion cannot any longer proceed with integrity if it concentrates only on one tradition. It is obvious to Klostermaier that the historical, sociological, psychological and other types of study of religion do not exhaust the possibilities of the study of religion, for "the issues of enlightenment and justification, of self–realization and salvation are not entered into by any of the other methodologies."[20]

Klostermaier is correct in noting the limits of academic method. It is true that it does not exhaust the study of religion and that dialogue can surely be considered another method for the study of religion. But the goal(s) of dialogue are still distinct from the academic study of religion. As Carman's language points out, while Klostermaier's does not, the academic study of religion is more restricted than the study of religion. While that does *not* make it superior, it *does* make it different. The academic study of religion is not only more restricted than the study of religion, but as I am using the terms, it is also more restricted than the *scholarly* study of religion. One may be competent in the relevant languages, well–versed in the history and culture of an area, produce learned commentaries on sacred texts and not be engaging in the *academic* study of religion. For the academic study of religion operates on agreed–upon principles regarding what kinds of questions one asks and what counts as evidence or constitutes an argument. In the academic study of religion, private (or personal) experience, no matter at what depth, or revelation as held within a particular tradition, simply does not count.

> No veridical proposition can be generated on the basis of mystical experience. As a consequence it appears certain that mystical experience is not and logically cannot be grounds for any final assertions about the nature or truth of any religious or philosophical position nor, more particularly, for any specific dogmatic or theological belief. Whatever validity mystical experience has, it does not translate itself into 'reasons' which can be taken as evidence for a given religious proposition."[21]

Hence, for the academic study of religion, one can determine the belief of Śankara by quoting from his *bhāṣyas*, but such a quote will not settle a dispute regarding the actual status of the world. The academic study of religion does not always engage the whole person. It is not required that a person believe or not believe, have certain experiences or not. The only requirement is that one have the necessary academic training, the critical faculties and the desire to apply them to the study of religion. Hence the practice of meditation is not a prerequisite for the understanding of Advaita on this level any more than one must pray or respond to an altar call to understand Billy Graham.

Since "dialogue in depth" takes place on an interior and spiritual level, it is not methodologically compatible with the academic study of religion. The latter will be interested in such dialogue as a religious phenomenon, but participation in interreligious dialogue will not be part of the academic discipline. Whether some academics engage in dialogue as Christians or Hindus is another matter. If they do so they will do so as Hindus or Christians and not as academics, regardless of how much their academically derived information contributes to the dialogue. The participants are identified in a religious, not an academic way, and that is the way they participate.

What about dialogue on the discursive level? Again, I would submit that it is not the academic study of religion. The reason for this is that in "discursive dialogue" as well, the two partners come together as equals, open to each other and willing to change. When an academic engages in discussion with a believer, it is not as equals. We have already pointed out that this is not an assertion of superiority of inferiority, but of difference. They have different goals. The Hindu or the Christian, even on the level of discursive dialogue, will be open to an emendation or perhaps even radical change of his or her doctrinal systems. But the academic is interested in understanding the believer's doctrinal system, not in searching for a viable one for himself or herself. The academic as academic always stops short of appropriation. If, as John Carman suggests is possible, the academic may later appropriate some of the material for his or her own doctrinal system, that is nevertheless beyond the academic study of religion. To include interreligious dialogue, then, in the forms of "deep dialogue" or "discursive dialogue" in the academic study of religion, is to run the latter into a form of religion, and thereby dissolve it as a distinct level of inquiry. So, while it may be true that under certain circumstances and with particular goals in mind, "engaging in structured interreligious dialogue on these issues is certainly an eminently sensible and fruitful way of studying religion,"[22] it is *not* appropriate for the *academic* study of religion. I must conclude that the desires of Carman and Klostermaier notwithstanding, Hindu–Christian dialogue and the academic study of religion operate on two distinct levels.

Academic Study and the Phenomena of Dialogue

To what extent, then, is the academic study of religion interested in Hindu–Christian dialogue, and to what extent can it handle the phenomena of dialogue within the limitations of its method?

Even with discursive dialogue, which operates on a propositional level, the goals, the questions that are asked and the types of data that count as evidence, all differ from the academic study of religion. The academic and the partner in discursive dialogue are simply not on the same quest. But, the academic study of religion will find the dynamics and results of such dialogue exceedingly fruitful for its investigations. In discursive dialogue the academic study of religion is dealing with a phenomenon within its frame of reference in the sense that it operates on the propositional level. And, to the extent to which candid discussion transpires, the academic will come to a more precise, more complete and more profound understanding of the Hindu or Christian systems being articulated. Of course, no Hindu or Christian can do more than articulate or clarify his or her Hinduism or Christianity.[23]

But to what extent can the academic study of religion achieve an understanding of a phenomenon that claims to go beyond, or even in some instances cancel out, conflicting propositions? In interreligious dialogue the form designated "dialogue in depth" or "interior dialogue" would appear to be most removed and hence of least interest to the academic study of religion.

But if the academic study of religion is interested in studying all religious forms and expressions, then it is interested in this form as well. Nevertheless, the participants in this form of dialogue frequently claim that their experience transcends logical contradictions and is an interior spiritual experience. How would the academic study of religion handle such claims?

First we must document this position more fully. "Interior dialogue" or "dialogue in depth" centers in a mystical or contemplative experience. "A basic (though not always acknowledged) assumption is that all intellectualization, doctrinal or otherwise, is of limited relevance, useful only as a means of approach to the divine mystery."[24] Swami Abhishiktananda states that "the most essential qualification for a fruitful interreligious dialogue is not so much an acute mind, as a contemplative disposition of the soul."[25] The Bombay Consultation on the Theology of Hindu–Christian Dialogue (1969) urges that one pay more attention to negative theology in dialogue since,

> it is more a spiritual discipline than an intellectual exercise. It negates the primacy of logic and conceptual knowledge and relies on experiences, intuition and contemplation. It agrees with the unique character of advaitic experience.[26]

Dialogue in this spiritual and mystical sense lies beneath theological formulations and indeed may lie beneath several propositionally conflicting theological formulations.

> Dialogue thus proves to be not only an encounter of one intellect with another intellect, but a meeting of faith with faith. A theological discussion between Hindus and Christians conducted in terms of propositions and logical arguments will soon come to a dead end, and there is no end to the list of examples. Dialogue does however continue when it is based on a meditative approach to the word rather than an analytical one, finding a common basis in a certain awareness of an inner dynamism of reality communicating itself to the seeker.[27]

It is for this reason that Klostermaier finds promising the practice of meditation on parallel upaniṣads to find Christ in them as he was found in the Old Testament. This is not to misread these texts, but to find "their true inner meaning."[28] The point of this is to probe beneath the discursive to the "level of spirituality," which is the only level on which actual encounter can take place.[29] Dialogue, then, is not merely the only authentic encounter between human beings, but is where God encounters human beings as well.

> Dialogue is an end in itself — it is not preliminary to the traditional methods of proselytizing. In dialogue the essential encounter of God and man takes place — far more than in the mass–attacks from pulpits and raised platforms.30

In response to C. Murray Rogers, Sivendra Prakash quotes approvingly from the "Report on Dialogue with Other Religions" issued at the All–India Seminar on the Church in India Today (Bangalore, 1969): "Dialogue at its highest level is spiritual and religious communion, the experiencing in common of the religious reality."[31]

Not only, then, does this take place at a level other than theology, but it is an experience of truth in distinction from the truth of propositions. And since it is an experience of truth in distinction from the truth of propositions, it is an experience that breaks the "barrier of words," for it speaks of "the possibility of a communion and exchange of experience that go beyond and behind words."[32] Included as a characteristic of this level of dialogue is "ineffability."[33]

This experience of God in "dialogue in depth" is not only beyond words, inexpressible in words, and deeper than words, but includes silence as well as utterances. "It may be either spoken or silent — and seems usually partly both."[34] Klostermaier reiterates in a variety of places that those who learn dialogue only from books tend to distort it,[35] and C. Murray Rogers calls the experience an experience of "supernatural complementarity."

> At this point the difference and contrast between Christian and pre–Christian have to be stressed and seen in their clear light. Rationally these contrasts will be seen to be insoluble while at a deeper level we will begin to perceive a "supernatural complementarity," a coming together in Christ of all that is genuine in non–Christian spirituality and experience.36

The question before us is whether, since the academic study of religion is so far removed from this experience, it is simply incapable of handling it and should therefore refrain. It is to be conceded that the academic study of religion does not have access to the "ineffable" or to "supernatural complementarity" or any other experience of a mystical nature that is personal, private or reserved for a religious few. But the academic study of religion is interested in pursuing its understanding of religion as far as its methods will permit. It should also beware lest it become reductionistic by implying that when its methods are no longer applicable, what is said to be left simply does not exist.

Fortunately for the academic study of religion, those who engage in this activity of "deep dialogue" do not remain silent, do indeed speak, and seem to write an ample supply of books and articles on the topic. If the reading of their books and articles inevitably distorts the reality to which they seek to point, it is hardly the academic's fault. But, the academic study of religion is interested in these writings, even when they claim that that about which they are writing or speaking goes beyond the words that are being written or uttered. And this *can* be understood academically.

Furthermore, it is not new in the history of religions. It is a claim that mystics have repeatedly made. And if the academic study of religions does not participate in the mystical experience, it has increasingly been interested in analyzing the statements made about that experience by those who claim to have had it. That an art historian does not work with oils does not make him or her any less an art historian. When the statements of the believer contradict each other, the academic cannot appeal to "supernatural complementarity," but he or she can note that such an appeal is made.

If the only response to the experience of "dialogue in depth" is silence, there is little the academic study of religion can do with that. *Silence is ambiguous.* It may point to a lack of understanding of the question, to inability to offer an appropriate answer, or to enlightenment, to suggest a few possibilities. The Buddha's "Flower Sermon" is interpreted by Zen as a non–verbal transmission of the satori experience. But without some verbal explanation, the smile of Mahakasyapa at the silent holding of a flower communicates nothing definite. The silence of the Buddha in the face of certain questions of a metaphysical nature has been the subject of considerable discussion. The *avyākṛta* and their interpretations are discussed by T. R. V. Murti at some length.[37] Although silence is of itself uninterpretable, it takes on meaning within Madhyamika when it is interpreted in the context of the transcendent nature of the real and that the real transcends all thought. In that context the erroneous nature of all metaphysical views of the real is communicated through silence. Fortunately, as Taylor points out, the response is usually a mixture of silence *and* words. To that extent the academic study of religion can understand, but it reaches its limit in the face of pure silence.

Partners in "deep dialogue" sometimes want to affirm in spiritual experience something which, when put in propositional form, is in conflict with other propositions to which they also give assent. A preliminary attempt has been made by James D. Redington to give an account of how one can affirm in "deep dialogue" the truth of an experience while different and sometimes conflicting statements may be made about the experience. He appeals to Bernard Lonergan's distinction between faith and beliefs, and similar distinctions made by Raimundo Panikkar and John A. T. Robinson. For Lonergan, as interpreted by Redington, a faith is a dimension of the human being by which a person relates to his or her destiny. Beliefs are the formulations a person makes for oneself and others of that faith.[38]

> Once again, then, a distinction between faith and beliefs is seen as essential for a world in dialogue. The immediate intention of Lonergan's distinction may be to render intelligible how two very different sets of beliefs stem from a faith and love whose Source is the same. But the belief seems applicable to our present problem too: the question of whether another religion's belief, now seen as stemming from that profound faith and love that grounds beliefs, can be affirmed as in some way true for *all* who see it.[39]

Another well-known attempt to distinguish the interior experience from the external manifestation is that of Wilfred Cantwell Smith. Smith uses the term *faith* to refer to "an inner religious experience or involvement of a particular person."[40] "Cumulative tradition" refers to

> the overt mass of objective data that constitute the historical deposit, as it were, of the past religious life of the community in question: temples, scriptures, theological systems, dance patterns, legal and other social institutions, conventions, moral codes, myths

> and so on; anything that can be and is transmitted from one person, one generation, to another, and that an historian can observe.[41]

The difficulty with both of these formulations for the academic study of religion is that "faith" is inaccessible. The academic study of religion can only work with Smith's "cumulative tradition." "Theology is part of the traditions, is part of this world. Faith lies beyond theology, *in the hearts of men.* Truth lies beyond faith, in the heart of God."[42] One can grant that for the believer these external phenomena merely point beyond themselves and one can draw inferences and surmise what that to which they point might be. But the inferences are seldom necessary (as distinct from possible), and the fact is that surmise is not sufficient evidence for conclusions within the academic study of religion. And so, one who engages in academic study must limit himself or herself to the "cumulative traditions," the beliefs and other data that can be used by the historian. That is not to deny the "reality" to which they point — nor is it to affirm it. There is a sense in which the academic study of religion is going too far when it states either that the conflicting words that purport to point to an experience beyond themselves actually point to a uniform or similar experience *or* that they point to differing ones. They certainly say things differently. But if we have no access to the thing itself, how do we verify if the experience itself is the same (though *variously* described) *or* different (*as* described)? Perhaps the believer will want to say more, and the participant in Hindu–Christian dialogue will want to say more, and that more will be duly noted. But noting it does not constitute either assent or dissent.

The academic study of religion, then, operates within limits. It is difficult to see how one engaged in dialogue can object to that so long as it does not claim that its level of investigation exhausts reality. And it is equally difficult to see how the academic study of religion can justify ignoring Hindu–Christian dialogue, which is a prominent religious phenomenon in the modern world.

Notes

1. For an analyses of the nature of stipulative definition see Richard Robinson, *Definition* (Oxford: Oxford University Press, 1954), and for an application of these distinctions to the study of religion see Robert D. Baird, *Category Formation and the History of Religions* (The Hague: Mouton & Co., 1971).

2. This means that there are *in fact* those who see the "academic study of religion" and "Hindu–Christian dialogue" as I am using these terms, even though they do not comprise all who study religion or all those who engage in dialogue.

3. If the reader still has doubts about this, a careful reading of Richard Robinson on the distinction between stipulative, lexical and real definitions will be invaluable.

4. Swami Abhishiktananda, "The Way of Dialogue," in *Inter–Religious Dialogue*, ed. Herbert Jai Singh (Bangalore: Christian Institute for the Study of Religion and Society, 1967), 86.

5. *Ibid.*, 87.

6. Richard W. Taylor, "The Meaning of Dialogue," in *Inter–Religious Dialogue*, 55-64. For other helpful analyses see Eric J. Sharpe, "The Goals of Inter–Religious Dialogue," in *Truth and Dialogue in World Religions: Conflicting Truth Claims*, ed. John Hick (Philadelphia: Westminster Press, 1974), 77-95; Arvind Sharma, "The Meaning and Goals of Interreligious Dialogue," *Journal of Dharma* vol. 8, no. 3 (July-September 1983), 225-47; and Anand Nayak, "Hindu–Christian Dialogue in India," *Pro Mundi Vita Bulletin* 88 (January 1982), 1-30.

7. See Klaus Klostermaier, "Interreligious Dialogue As a Method for the Study of Religion, *Journal of Ecumenical Studies* 21:4 (Fall 1984), 757.

8. Klaus Klostermaier, "Dialogue — The Work of God," in *Inter–Religious Dialogue*, 119. Cf. also Klostermaier, *In the Paradise of Krishna: Hindu and Christian Seekers* (Philadelphia: Westminster Press, 1969), 102.

9. Nayak, 27.

10. Klaus Klostermaier, "Hindu–Christian Dialogue," in *Dialogue Between Men of Living Faiths*, ed. S. J. Samartha (Geneva: WCC, 1971), 20.

11. Cf. Monika Konrad Hellwig, "Bases and Boundaries for Interfaith Dialogue: A Christian Viewpoint," in *Interreligious Dialogue: Facing the Next Frontier*, ed. Richard W. Rousseau, S. J. (Scranton, PA: Ridge Row Press, 1981), 68, where the author commences by saying: "This paper is written directly from experience."

12. Nayak, 2.

13. John Carman, "Inter–Faith Dialogue and Academic Study of Religion," in *Dialogue Between Men of Living Faiths*, 81-86.

14. *Ibid.*, 85.

15. There is a tendency on the part of those engaged in Hindu–Christian dialogue, in an attempt to gain the support of history, to see dialogue in almost any exchange between "Hindus" and "Christians," or any historical influence of the one upon the other. This an extremely elastic use of the term and does not qualify as "dialogue" as I have defined the term above.

16. Carman, 86.

17. Klostermaier, "Interreligious Dialogue As a Method for the Study of Religion," 757.

18. *Ibid.* (emphasis mine).

19. *Ibid.*

20. *Ibid.*, 759.

21. Steven T. Katz, "Language, Epistemology and Mysticism," in *Mysticism and Philosophical Analysis*, ed. Steven T. Katz (New York: Oxford University Press, 1978), 22.

22. Klostermaier, "Interreligious Dialogue As a Method for the Study of Religion,, 759.

23. Cf. Wilfred Cantwell Smith, *The Meaning and End of Religion* (New York: Macmillan, 1962), chap. 5; and Baird, 134-152.

24. Sharpe, "The Goals of Inter–Religious Dialogue," 87.

25. Abhishiktananda, 85.

26. Quoted by Sharpe, 88.

27. Klaus Klostermaier, "Hindu–Christian Dialogue: Its Religious and Cultural Implications," *Sciences Religieuses/Studies in Religion* (1971), 89.

28. Klaus Klostermaier, "Hindu–Christian Dialogue," 12.

29. *Ibid.*

30. Klostermaier, "Dialogue — The Work of God," 125.

31. *Dialogue Between Men of Living Faiths*, n. 13, 26.

32. Matthew John, "The Biblical Basis of Dialogue," *Inter–Religious Dialogue*, 72.

33. Richard W. Taylor, "The Meaning of Dialogue," *Inter–Religious Dialogue*, 56.

34. *Ibid.*, 58.

35. "Dialogue — The Work of God," 121.

36. C. Murray Rogers, "Hindu and Christian — A Moment Breaks," in *Inter–Religious Dialogue*, 113.

37. T. R. V. Murti, *The Central Philosophy of Buddhism* (London: George Allen & Unwin, 1955), 36-54.

38. James D. Redington, S. J., "The Hindu–Christian Dialogue and the Interior Dialogue," *Theological Studies* 44 (1983), 601-1.

39. *Ibid.*, 602.

40. Smith, 156.

41. *Ibid.*, 156-57.

42. *Ibid.*, 185.

4

Syncretism and the History of Religions

One of the purposes of the study of World Religions today is to enable us to understand the faiths of other people. It is with this purpose in view that Wilfred Cantwell Smith proposes that "it is the business of comparative religion to construct statements about religion that are intelligible within at least two traditions simultaneously."[1] This means that a description of Hinduism or Buddhism or Islam[2] that is to be considered valid must be both intelligible to outsiders and acceptable to that religion's believers. "Anything that I say about Islam as a living faith is valid only in so far as Muslims can say 'amen' to it."[3] Our present concern is to inquire to what extent, if any, the concept of syncretism contributes to such understanding.

The concept of syncretism has been used frequently to describe certain manifestations in the history of religions. Although seldom defined, the term is usually assumed to be abundantly clear, even though examination of its usage reveals that it is used in various and conflicting ways. The term does not always communicate anything definite, and the meaning that is intended could often be more clearly expressed if another term were used.

Among those who have studied the history of religions few have used the term as frequently as Hendrik Kraemer. He has written on this theme at some length as both a theological problem and as a missionary problem.[4] Even in Kraemer's writings, however, the term is used with several meanings, and there are times when he employs the term in a manner which he has elsewhere stated is a confusing and misleading use of the word. There are, for example, those instances where he states explicitly that syncretism is inevitable, necessary, and universal.

> One could go on enumerating, but these examples may suffice to demonstrate the simple fact that syncretism, cultural and religious, is for many reasons a persistent and universal phenomenon in human history. It cannot but happen, unless peoples live in entire isolation.[5]

In this sense it would be possible, one would think, to agree with Radhakrishnan when he says that Christianity is a syncretistic faith and with Hermann Gunkel whose history of religions approach to the Bible led to the same conclusion.

In another context, however, Kraemer denies that Christianity and Islam are syncretistic religions and that to so label them is misleading. It is, in his view, the Eastern religions which are by nature syncretistic, and that clearly includes Radhakrishnan himself.[6] Kraemer would contend that while one can, in a certain sense, hold that the Christian Scriptures and also the Qur'an are syncretistic, that this is not the best use of that term. Nevertheless, the confusion in usage remains when he also maintains that syncretism is inevitable and universal.

This much should be abundantly clear. Although the term has been used by not a few historians of religions, and although the term is assumed to communicate its own meaning, that meaning varies not only from one writer to another, but also within the writings of a single author. Some have apparently sensed this ambiguity when they distinguish between conscious and unconscious syncretism.

> In a certain sense every religion, 'primitive' as well as religions related to a big cultural area or claiming to be world–religions, may be and often are called syncretistic to some degree as a result of their growth through history. In these cases, however, the word has various connotations. It then means that rites or conceptions of different origin, or of a different degree of affinity, have become incorporated in a given religion and have been adapted to its dominant spirit and concern in such a way that they have become a genuine and accepted part of this religion. This, however, has nothing to do with syncretism as a *conscious*, organizing religious principle, such as we have described in the form of genuine, full–fledged syncretism in the Roman Empire.[7]

This distinction is similar to the one that differentiates syncretism as naive or indiscriminative and intentional or reflective.[8] Such distinctions do not solve the problem of varied usage, however, for in either case the meaning of syncretism is determined by what practices or ideas are synthesized and into what kind of apparent unity they are brought, rather than whether it was a conscious synthesis on the part of the participants.

It is our contention that the concept of syncretism has been used in both a historical and a theological sense. An analysis of these two general uses will show that in the former case the term serves no useful purpose at all. The only legitimate use of syncretism theologically is not applicable to the faith of those it is sometimes used to describe, but is in reality a barrier to understanding those faiths.

Syncretism as a Historical Phenomenon

Historical analysis limits itself to an explanation of events, persons, movements or ideas which is on the plane of history. While it may or may not be theologically true that the source of the Qur'an is Allāh, it is not legitimate to make that judgment within the limits of historical knowledge. It has been this concern for historical explanation that has led to the historian's preoccupation with the "roots" of certain movements, or the "sources" of a person's thought. The historian is led to relate the contents of the Qur'an to its Arabian setting, and to attempt to show how the Meccan suras and the Medinan suras exemplify a different emphasis, no matter how theologically disconcerting it may be to some Muslims. Historicism goes so far as to imply that an entity cannot be understood unless its history has been traced, and that the significance of the twentieth century approach to life is not that it is scientific, but that understanding itself has become historical. This type of approach goes some distance in explaining the quest for origins whether it be a search for the Jesus of history, the authentic preaching of the early Christian church, or the authentic teaching of the Buddha.

But such a concern for origins runs counter to the very method that is employed. Within the historical method there is no real room for a beginning, a first cause. The historian must jump into the stream of history somewhere if he or she is to study anything. The study of Buddhism might possibly begin with Sakyamuni, but that is not to deny the historical legitimacy of another study showing the Brahmanical context that made Sakyamuni's position relevant, or still another study showing the features of the Vedic Age which preceded both. The only limitation placed on the historian's quest is in the limits of the information available as one moves into the remote past. However, this is not a logical limitation imposed by method but a limitation imposed by the availability of data. If and when more material becomes available, the historical method will push the historian back still further in a search for historical antecedents.

If the appeal is made to divine revelation such as in the Qur'an or the New Testament, the same search is relevant. Even if the Qur'an is held to come from Allāh, it was communicated by human beings and written in Arabic — an

Arabic used and understood by the people of Muhammad's day. It has been this search that has involved historians of religions when they apply their method to the study of the Bible. The result has been an insight into the historical relationship between the ideas and practices of the Old Testament and those of the ancient Near East, and the relationship between the New Testament and the Greco–Roman world. Such endeavors are legitimate historical quests even though they may not have the theological implications that have sometimes been attached to them.

One use of the term "syncretism" is to describe the interrelationship between ideas and movements historically. In this sense syncretism is universal and inevitable. Here it is merely a term which is used to describe a dictum of historical knowledge — any subject fitting for historical research has historical antecedents.

> Commercial intercourse, political events, the extension of power from a certain centre, often shows such spiritual, religious or cultural encounters and struggles as a mostly unintended consequence. We see, therefore, in the history of mankind many samples and varieties of syncretism. Everywhere, where genuine 'culture–contact' take place, it appears as an inevitable effect.[9]

It is this method of history which led Hermann Gunkel to say that Christianity is a syncretistic religion. For Gunkel, extraneous elements did not wait until the fifth century to enter the church, but were detectable in the Apostolic Age itself. Following a historical method, he located elements in early Christianity that were found in other contexts in the Greco–Roman world and concluded that indeed Christianity is "a syncretistic religion." It is this same observation that lends some point to Radhakrishnan's judgment that "Christianity is a syncretistic faith, a blend of various earlier creeds. . . ."[10]

Now, if it is true that such borrowing and blending and influencing on the plane of history is part of the whole historical process and is both inevitable and universal, then no real purpose is served by applying the term syncretism to such a phenomenon. Historically speaking, to say that "Christianity" or the "mystery religions" or "Hinduism" is syncretistic is not to say anything that distinguishes it from anything else and is merely equivalent to admitting that each has a history and can be studied historically. Although Kraemer himself calls this historical phenomenon syncretism, on other occasions he seems to sense that this usage is inadequate, as when he says:

> The smell of the earth, the brightness of the sky, the natural and spiritual atmosphere, which in the course of ages wrought the soul of a people, have to manifest themselves in the kind of Christianity that grows there. This is far from being syncretism in the technical sense in which it is currently used, but it is a certain kind of coalescence, of symbiosis without losing identity.[11]

We propose, however, that the term syncretism be dropped as a designation of a historical phenomenon. Since in this sense it applies equally well to all expressions of religion, to use it to describe a particular expression tells us nothing specific.

Syncretism as a Theological Phenomenon

When we turn from the meaning of syncretism as a historical phenomenon to what syncretism might mean theologically, we find a certain confusion in the way the term is used. To distinguish between a syncretism that is reflective and conscious and one that is spontaneous may be interesting but it is not a significant distinction logically. Here we are interested in what takes place theologically when one uses the term syncretism, whether that which takes place does so consciously, unconsciously or both.

We shall begin by pointing out that merely to define syncretism as the uniting of religious elements of different origin, or merely as the "fusion of various beliefs and practices,"[12] is too general to avoid the application of the concept to any religious expression. The origin of the elements to be united is not of prime import, and that various beliefs and practices are fused says nothing that would distinguish one movement from another.

Usually, when the concept of syncretism is applied, it connotes an element of conflict or inconsistency. Care must still be taken, however, lest the term be used in a manner which is meaningless. To say that syncretism is what takes place when one brings two conflicting ideas or practices and unites them into a harmonious whole is to say nothing coherent. If the two original ideas or practices are in conflict, then they cannot, without modification, produce a harmonious unity. If a harmony is produced, then it follows that either the two original elements were only apparently in conflict, or that changes have been effected so that it is not actually the two conflicting elements which produce the harmony but a modification of those elements which produces elements no longer in conflict. To say that two genuinely conflicting concepts were harmonized is a contradiction.

When elements which have come from differing sources are united into a harmonious unit then the term synthesis might be used to describe the phenomenon. This term indicates the unity achieved without implying the logically impossible statement that the harmony is produced by the union of two contradictory practices or ideas.

What, then, can be intended by the concept syncretism? This term should be reserved for cases where two conflicting ideas or practices are brought together and and are retained without the benefit of consistency. Syncretism occurs only when the result is not a harmonious unity. Kraemer expresses this view in the following manner:

> It is in these circles taken in the sense of a systematic attempt to combine, blend and reconcile inharmonious, even often conflicting, religious elements into a new, so called synthesis.[13]

This is the same idea found in Hocking when he mentions the view whereby one brings together elements from various sources into a whole "devoid of any principle of coherence."[14] The same essential lack of unification in syncretism is implicit in H. R. Mackintosh's definition. "To be strict, syncretism is only present when elements derived from various religions are admitted on equal terms. . . ."[15] Here various elements stand side by side without an attempt to reconcile or give priority to either one.

If, on the other hand, a unity is produced by modifying one's religious complex so that the previously extraneous element is comfortable in that context, then one is referring to what Hocking called "reconception".

> Either that good thing you have found belongs uniquely to the religious organism from which it came — in which case you must adopt *that* unity — or it belongs to *yours* — in which case you must *reconceive* the essence of your own faith, to include that new element. You cannot live religiously within a divided house, or a house whose roof covers only part of its floor area![16]

From a theological point of view, reconceptionism may be as unhappy a situation as syncretism but the two are not the same. In reconceptionism, the result is a unity which has been effected through a modification of the very essence of a religion. This concept, of course, can only be used when one defines the essence of one's religion theologically. The attempt to arrive at the essence of a religion by examining its numerous historical manifestations has been unsuccessful. Syncretism, however, merely retains the conflicting elements without having successfully reconciled them.

We conclude, then, that this is the only meaningful use of the concept of syncretism, and that although the term has been used to designate other types of religious expressions as well, it is, in such contexts, misleading and confusing. The pejorative connotation attached to the term now becomes partially understandable. What could be objectionable in synthesizing religious elements which are not in conflict? It is the willingness to maintain contradictory elements side by side that has been objectionable.

Syncretism, a Barrier to Understanding

The term syncretism is usually not used by a believer to describe his or her own religion. One of the most common uses of the term in the history of religions is to describe certain Eastern religious expressions. Ryobu–Shinto is described as "syncretism",[17] as is the Hindu philosophy of Śankara, or the Chinese attitude which enables one to be simultaneously a Buddhist, Confucianist, and Taoist.

> In the grand Mahayanist and Hindu philosophies of religion, for instance, elaborated in Japan in Ryobu–Shinto or in India by Shankara, every stage and expression of religion, from the 'highest' to the 'basest' gets, on this basis, full recognition and justification as to its necessary and relative value. On this syncretistic approach, the claim of absolute tolerance, the pride of all genuinely eastern spirituality, depends. Radhakrishnan is, as we have seen, a modernized but essentially unchanged defender of this syncretistic philosophy.[18]

It seems to be implied that in each case the Eastern religious expressions have brought elements together that are conflicting and illegitimate. This is never the religious attitude of those involved, however, who sense no such logical problem. This failure to find a recognition of inconsistency where it might be expected has been problematic for Western scholars.

In the thought of Śankara, for example, there are both levels of Being and stages of experience. What is true of one level is not necessarily true of another level. All distinctions, including logical ones, are part of the phenomenal world of appearance. The world of appearance, however, is *māyā*, that is, illusory from the vantage point of the indescribable and undifferentiated Nirguṇa Brahman. The phenomenal world is valid on its own level, but it can be transcended.

> So long as the right knowledge of the Brahman as the only reality does not dawn, the world appearance runs on in an orderly manner uncontradicted by the accumulated experience of all men, and as such it must be held to be true. It is only because there comes such a stage in which the world appearance ceases to manifest itself that we have to say that from the ultimate and absolute point of view the world appearance is false and unreal.[19]

From the standpoint of Brahman, then, all distinctions of the phenomenal world are obliterated, including ideas and practices that are contradictory on the lower level of being. There is no uncomfortable sense of living with conflict in Śankara's total system. The conflict exists for those who reject the notion of levels of Being and who deny the ultimate reality of Nirguṇa Brahman.

> Another supposed illustration of syncretism is a Chinese expression. One of the best-known features of Chinese universalism is that the three religions — Confucianism, Buddhism and Taoism — are virtually treated as one. The religious allegiance of the average man is not related to one of the three religions. He does not belong to a confession or creed. He participates unconcerned as to any apparent lack of consistency, alternatively in Buddhist, Taoist or Confucian rites. He is, by nature, a religious pragmatist.[20]

The important point here is noticed by Kraemer himself. To the Chinese believer there was no inconsistency in such a religious practice for they were treated virtually as one. The reason for this is that there was a broader and over–arching religious attitude which made it possible to incorporate all such practices and beliefs as seemed useful. Kraemer says that the Chinese was in this case a pragmatist by nature. If that be true, then that was his religious attitude, and it was hardly inconsistent to act in the described manner. It is the outsider who does not share such an attitude, and fails to recognize its significance. It is also the outsider who uses the term to describe the phenomenon.

Ryobu–Shinto is often given as a good example of syncretism. Here the Shinto kami and the Buddhist bodhisattvas are identified and the two religious expressions are merged.

> A really gigantic and systematic attempt towards religious syncretism is Ryobu–Shinto (bi–lateral Shinto). In it Buddhism and Shinto have thoroughly amalgamated on the basis of naturalistic kinship. The great leader in this enterprise of religious amalgamation has been Kobo Daishi, the founder of Shingon.[21]

Here again, however, Kraemer recognizes a basic kinship. The system of Ryobu–Shinto conceives of Ultimate Reality, or the unobservable source of all existent things, as the cosmic Buddha Maha–Vairochana or Dai Nichi. The universe is the body of Dai Nichi.

> In this manifestation of the Great Life of the Universe on the side of the observable events of experience, the *kami* of the Shinto pantheon appear as the avatars of the divine beings of Buddhism, and thus these two faiths are in essence one and the same.[22]

In this system, every Shinto god or goddess becomes a manifestation of the special Buddhist divinity. Hence, Amaterasu–Omikami becomes a particular manifestation of Maha–Vairochana or Dai Nichi.

That some were opposed to Ryobu–Shinto and that others made attempts to eliminate those aspects which were foreign, is no refutation of the unity here expressed but merely underlines the well–known fact that the terms "Hinduism," "Buddhism," "Christianity," or "Shinto" do not correspond to a clear and always consistent system of practices and ideas. "Every faith appears in a variety of forms."[23]

Buddhism had long shown the ability to adjust to Chinese religion. Shinto had a similar history of adjustment. As Anesaki puts it, "Now this Double Aspect Shinto was an expression of the compromising attitude so characteristic of the Japanese mind."[24] Of the utmost importance here is that those involved did not look on their amalgamation as involving opposing or conflicting positions. Rather it was a unification that appeared to those involved to be quite legitimate and natural.

Syncretism, then, is irrelevant to those who are inside the so–called syncretistic faiths. "For those naturalistic religions, which are by nature syncretistic, syncretism is no problem at all. They cannot see it."[25] If, then, one is attempting to understand such faiths or is attempting to communicate the meaning of such faiths, the term is misleading since it does not correspond to the believer's understanding of his faith.

Syncretism and the Encounter of Religions

Kraemer labels most Eastern religions as expressions of religious syncretism. Mahayana Buddhism, Advaita Vedanta, Chinese religions in general, Ryobu–Shinto, and the so–called primitive faith encountered in Java, are all syncretistic because they are basically naturalistic (naturalistic–cosmic or naturalistic–monistic).[26] It has already been observed that the insiders in the above cases sense no conflict in their approach. "In view of the fundamental nature and structure of these religions it is nothing capricious or unprincipled; it is consistency itself. It would be abnormal if this were not so."[27] The term serves no real purpose *within* the value system of these religions, but reflects instead the value system of the one who uses it. Such an observation is basic to understanding what is involved when the concept of syncretism is used.

We have argued that the only fruitful use of the term "syncretism" is to describe a situation in which conflicting ideas or practices are brought together into a new complex which is devoid of coherence. But the religious complexes represented by the above illustrations of syncretism are not devoid of coherence to the believers. The term syncretism most clearly denotes not only a lack of coherence in the new complex of ideas and practices, but also the distinction between the insider or person of faith and the outsider or observing scholar.

It is no secret that the term syncretism commonly carries a pejorative connotation.

> The scholars intended their statements to be taken objectively and scientifically, but they allowed subjective overtones to creep in. This is well seen in the concept of 'syncretism' which has a deprecatory connotation. If a religion is said to be 'syncretistic', it is held to be *ipso facto* inferior.[28]

This pejorative connotation is readily understandable when it is realized that the concept not only implies a contradiction, but that it is applied from outside the circle of a given faith. The concept of syncretism not only describes the encounter of religions, but is itself a part of that encounter. Syncretism is a concept applied to a religion by those who stand outside its circle of faith and hence fail to see or to experience its inner unity. Hence, Kraemer can say that Śankara's philosophy is syncretistic and Radhakrishnan can hurl the same label at Christianity.

Basically, syncretism is a concept that not merely points to the encounter of one religious complex with another but it is itself a part of that encounter. Hence, its use must be guarded. If one of the purposes of the History of religions is to come to an understanding of the faith of other people, then it is imperative that the term be avoided since it implies a conflict which is not experienced by the insider.

> It is rather interesting to note that the term syncretism is, properly speaking, inadequate if we judge this phenomenon from the stand point of the fundamental nature and structure of the religions in which it occurs, which scientifically considered, is the only legitimate method to be followed.[29]

If, however, one's purpose carries one to theological evaluation of other religious practices and ideas (and this is a legitimate purpose as well), then the word is legitimate but of limited service. To label a religious complex syncretistic is to say it is inconsistent — in which case more specific arguments are required.

Those works, of which the purpose is descriptive rather than normative, should avoid the label "syncretism" since, rather than assisting communication, the concept proves to be a barrier.

Notes

1. W. C. Smith, "Comparative Religion" Whither — and Why?" in Eliade and Kitagawa, *History of Religions: Essays in Methodology* (Chicago: University of Chicago Press, 1959), 53.

2. Since his article in the above volume, Smith has rejected these designations in favor of "the faith of Hindus" or "the faith of Buddhists," designations more in keeping with his personalist approach. cf. *The Faith of Other Men* (New York: New American Library, 1963) and *The Meaning and End of Religion* (New York: The Macmillan Company, 1962).

3. Smith, "Comparative Religion. . .," 43. We are not implying that there is no place for theological studies or critical evaluations which involve the truth question, but merely that understanding is a prior task for the History of Religions.

4. *The Christian Message in a Non–Christian World* (Grand Rapids: Kregel Publications, 1963, first published 1938), 200-211; *Religion and the Christian Faith* (Philadelphia: The Westminster Press, 1956), 387-417. Asked to contribute an article to *The Theology of the Christian Mission*, Kraemer responded with a letter indicating that he could say little more on the subject than he had already said.

5. *Religion and the Christian Faith*, 389.

6. *Ibid.*, 406.

7. *Ibid.*, 297 (italicization mine).

8. *Ibid.*, 200 and 401.

9. *Ibid.*, 389.

10. S. Radhakrishnan, *East and West in Religion* (London: George Allen and Unwin , Ltd., 1933), 62.

11. Kraemer, *loc. cit.*, 390-391.

12. "Syncretism" in *The Oxford Dictionary of the Christian Church*, (London: Oxford University Press, 1957), 1314.

13. Kraemer, *loc. cit.*, 392.

14. William Ernest Hocking, *The Coming World Civilization* (New York: Harper & Brothers, 1956), 146.

15. H. R. Mackintosh, *Types of Modern Theology* (London: Nisbet and Co. Ltd., 1956), 185.

16. Hocking, *loc. cit.*, 147.

17. cf. John B. Noss, *Man's Religions* (New York: The Macmillan Company, 1963) third edition, 436. Also D. C. Holtom, *The National Faith of Japan* (London: Kegan Paul, Trench, Trubner & Company Ltd., 1938), 38.

18. Kraemer, *loc. cit.*, 401.

19. S. DasGupta, *A History of Indian Philosophy*, Vol. I (Cambridge: Cambridge University Press, 1922), 446.

20. Kraemer, *loc. cit.*, 201.

21. *Ibid.*, 201. Cf. also Noss and Holtom.

22. Holtom, *loc. cit.*, 38.

23. Smith, *The Meaning and End of Religion*, 2.

24. M. Anesaki, *History of Japanese Religion* (London: Kegan Paul, Trench, Trubner& Co., Ltd., 1930), 137.

25. Kraemer, *loc. cit.*, 402.

26. *Ibid.*, 403.

27. *The Christian Message in a Non–Christian World*, 203.

28. William Montgomery Watt, *Truth in the Religions* (Edinburgh: Edinburgh University Press, 1963), 61.

29. *The Christian Message in a Non–Christian World*, 203.

5

Factual Statements and the Possibility of Objectivity in History

When the question of the possibility of historical knowledge is the issue, one is in the realm of logic or perhaps epistemology. Considerable confusion has been bred by a poor choice of terms, and through using the same term for several levels of meaning. One view is that historical work should be based on the "facts," while another throws into question the availability of such "facts." Some declare that we must distinguish between fact and interpretation, while others hold that there is no such thing as a fact apart from interpretation. What do we mean when we speak of "the facts," and what does the answer to this question contribute to our understanding of the limits or possibilities of a knowledge of the past?

One of the more influential discussions of the nature of historical facts is an article by Carl Becker, "What are Historical Facts?"[1] This discussion on the nature of historical facts has become a viable way of viewing the possibility of historical knowledge for a considerable number of historians. The intention of the article is to use Becker's analysis as a touchstone whereby an alternative can be entertained.

Carl Becker and Historical Facts

> Historians feel safe when dealing with the facts. We talk much about the "hard facts" and the "cold facts," about "not being able to get around the facts," and about the necessity of basing our narrative on a "solid foundation of facts." By virtue of talking in this way, the facts of history come in the end to seem something solid, something substantial like physical matter . . . something possessing definite shape, and clear persistent outline — like bricks or scantlings; so that we can easily picture the historian as he stumbles about in the past, stubbing his toe on the hard facts if he doesn't watch out.[2]

Becker sets himself squarely against any such view that there are "hard facts," "cold facts," or "simple facts." That the facts are anything but simple is his point when he asks his first question: "What are historical facts?" Take the apparently simple fact "In the year 49 B.C. Caesar crossed the Rubicon." This "fact" is actually a symbol in the sense that it is a generalization of many smaller incidents which are included in it. If the crossing of the Rubicon took any time at all it must have included numerous acts and thoughts. The statement itself, then, is a symbol whereby one is able to generalize about several acts and implications such as the relationship between Caesar and millions of people in the Roman world.

> It is so far as we can know it, only a *symbol*, a simple statement which is a generalization of a thousand and one simpler facts which we do not for the moment care to use, and this generalization itself we cannot use apart from the wider facts and generalizations which it symbolizes.[3]

Becker's argument continues by maintaining that the significance of a given fact is known by virtue of its relationship with other facts and its place in a certain interpretive structure. About the fact "Indulgences were sold in Germany in 1517," Becker states:

> This fact can be proven down to the ground. No one doubts it. But taken by itself the fact is nothing, means nothing. It also is a generalization of a thousand and one facts, a thousand and one actions of innumerable sellers and buyers of indulgences all over Germany at many different times; and this also acquires significance and meaning only as it is related to other facts and wider generalizations.[4]

Becker adds that the historian does not have access to the historical event itself. Directly, we can only deal with statements about the event which is precisely what a fact is. A fact is a statement about an event. We shall shortly utilize this observation to develop an alternative approach to an understanding of "facts."

If one accepts Becker's analysis of the nature of a historical fact, his answers to two further questions are sound. "Where is the historical fact?" If the historical fact is anywhere it is in the mind of the historian or someone else. The event *was*, the historical fact *is*. The two may be closely related but they are never identical. The event is gone, and can never again be experienced by any living person. The facts can be directly experienced. "Where are the historical facts? They are, as I said before, in his mind, or in somebody's mind, or they are nowhere."[5]

"When is the historical fact?" If one has agreed with Becker's argument thus far, then the answer here is obvious. The historical fact is in the present. When Becker first presented this theory in 1926 as an address, he included in it an aside which indicated that he was aware that few of his audience would agree with his analysis. Today, one might fairly say the the situation is reversed. The pitch for relativism in history has been heard for so long that it has become part of the atmosphere that we breath. Now, one must marshall cogent arguments indeed if one is to be heard, and then one's voice may be barely audible.

An Alternative Approach

Thought on this topic would be considerably cleared if, instead of speaking of "facts," we spoke of factual statements. Becker is correct when he observes that the event is past. The events are gone, data remains, and the factual statements based on the data in each case (artifacts, diaries, theological treatises, etc.) are made by the historian. "In the year 49 B.C. Caesar crossed the Rubicon" is a factual statement, and this is what is meant when it is called a fact. But to say that a statement is factual is not to say that it is a true statement about the past. It is the intention of all historical statements that they intend to describe or interpret. To say that a statement is factual merely points to the type of statement that it intends to be. If we say, for example, "Kobo Daishi founded the Shingon sect of Japanese Buddhism in the fourteenth century," we are making a factual statement. But, since the evidence available to us indicates that Kobo Daishi lived in the 9th century, the above factual statement probably is not a true statement about the past.[6]

Factual statements are sometimes distinguished from interpretive statements; however, it is not uncommon to be told that all historical statements involve some interpretation. Part of the confusion lies in the usage of the term "interpretation" as a synonym for "judgment." It is true that no historical statement is made apart from the judgment of the historian, but to use the term "interpretation" so broadly is confusing. If the term "interpretation" is used to include all statements that historians make, then we are left with the need for another term to distinguish between levels of "interpretation."

In historical writing, one is making an interpretive statement when that statement involves a level of meaning which must come from a source other than the historical data available.[7] An interpretation of historical events based upon the assumption that economics is determinative for human life is such a statement. In his study of Henry VIII, J. C. Flügel has made so many interpretive statements that the work itself might be called interpretive.

> Nevertheless, we cannot but suppose that the difficulties and dangers which surrounded his father's throne must have exercised a powerful influence over the younger Henry's mind. The envy with which, even in ordinary families, a son is apt to look upon the superior power and privileges of a father is liable to be intensified when the father enjoys the exceptional influence and honor appertaining to a king. Under these circumstances any threat to the father's authority almost inevitably arouses in the son the idea of superceding the father.[8]

That difficulties attended the throne of Henry's father is something that can be verified or rejected according to historical method. The extent to which these difficulties could have influenced Henry's mind, the relationship of sons to fathers, and the psychological conditions under which a son might think of superceding his father, lead to statements which depend upon one's psychological point of view; and that discipline has its own methods of verification. What we have, then, is a set of statements of a psychological nature which are used to interpret another set of historical import. In such a case the verification of the statement in question is not a simple one of examining the historical data, because, even when that evidence is in, something remains for an adequate verification of the statement.

> Furthermore, this failure in the fertility of his marriage aroused superstitious fears connected with Henry's Oedipus complex. The idea of sterility as a punishment for incest is one that is deeply rooted in the human mind, and in the case of a union such as that of Henry and Catherine, there was scriptural authority for the infliction of a penalty of this description.[9]

Here we are introduced to the psychological judgment passed on a dead man who cannot even lie down on our couch, that he had an Oedipus complex, and that incest is deeply rooted the human mind as being punished by sterility. The footnote used to support that statement is not taken from any data that might substantiate the fact that Henry expressed such fears, but rather from a reference to Frazer's *Totemism and Exogamy*. The author in effect says, since this is the way men are and this has been the case elsewhere with certain frequency, it must be characteristic of men and therefore also of Henry. The next statement is even more bold.

> It is true that Henry is reported to have himself denied the truth of this; but even if (as is very possibly the case) the rumor itself is exaggerated, it may well have been founded on some genuine attraction which Henry may have felt for the Lady Elizabeth. If this is so, in the light of psychoanalytic knowledge, it would appear not overbold to suggest that the mother and daughter, Elizabeth and Mary Blount, were, to Henry's unconscious mind, substitutes for Elizabeth and Mary Tudor — his mother and sister respectively.[10]

Here the author is bold enough to venture an interpretation (which is contrary to a report of Henry's own statement), probably based on the assumption that one's unconscious motivation is not always what one's language states. One further illustration will suffice.

> Now there can be little doubt that Henry was a person whose Oedipus complex found expression in such a way. On this hypothesis it becomes possible to explain two very constant features of his love life; his fickleness (which tended to make him unable to love a woman, once his possession of her was assured) and the desire for some obstacle between him and the object of his choice. We shall come across sufficient examples of these.as we study the further course of his checkered conjugal career.[11]

This theory is based on Freud's analysis of love life which the author has used to interpret the available historical data.

However, simply because a statement is interpretive does not make it valid or invalid. Interpretive statements cannot, by their very nature, be verified solely with historical evidence. Such statements can be verified, but the verification must be both historical and theoretical. Interpretive statements always rest on two poles. The biblical statement "Christ died for our sins" is truly interpretive since it involves a theology. Perhaps, also, theological interpretation is legitimate, but then the statements depend not only on the probability of the historical aspect, but also on the validity of the theology involved.[12]

What is the difference, then, between an interpretive statement and a factual one? A factual statement is one which involves levels of meaning that are implied in the data itself. There are many statements which historians make that are more significant than "In the year 49 B.C. Caesar crossed the Rubicon" which are still of a factual nature. This does not mean that all factual statements are of equal probability, but it does mean that they do not have imposed on them a level of meaning which comes from a source other than the data itself. Factual statements, then, are dependent for their probability on the historical data available for their support.[13]

This distinction between a factual statement and an interpretive one is related to the difference between objectivity and relativity in history. Historical relativism is the view that "no historical work grasps the nature of the past (or present) immediately, that whatever 'truth' a historical work contains is relative to the conditioning processes under which it arose and can only be understood with reference to those processes."[14] Mandelbaum continues:

> Now the fact that every historical work, like any intellectual endeavor, is limited by psychological and sociological conditions (to mention only two) is indisputable. The radical novelty in historical relativism lies in the fact that it claims that the truth of the work, its meaning and validity, can only be grasped by referring its content to these conditions. In short, the relativist believes that to understand a history we must not only understand what is said in it but also why this is said.[15]

Mandelbaum adds that this is what philosophers have called the genetic fallacy. The validity of the arguments for relativism remains to be considered, but here it may be of value to point out that if such a position were followed consistently, no valid knowledge of the past would be possible. This position holds that a knowledge of the past is always dependent not only upon what is said by the historian, but why and out of what context he or she said it. An infinite regress then becomes necessary: a third party is needed to analyze not only the analysis of the second, but also the context out of which it was made; and then the analysis which he makes is in turn made in some cultural context, and hence necessitates a fourth; and on *ad infinitum*.

This is the view of historical relativism, and it is related to the way this position conceives of historical facts.

> In the first place the facts of history never come to us "pure," since they do not and cannot exist in a pure form: they are always refracted through the mind of the recorder. It follows that when we take up a work of history, our first concern should be not with the facts which it contains but with the historian who wrote it.[16]

This quote indicates clearly an important characteristic of relativism. Carr is not speaking of some history or some facts. He says, "the facts of history *never* come to us 'pure,'"; "they do not and *cannot* exist in a 'pure' form"; "they are *always* refracted" (italics mine). The invalidity of the relativist position is not that it fails to describe something that historians do or that it fails to describe that something accurately. The failure is that it universalizes the particular and states unequivocally that this is what *all* historians *must* do. When the case is stated in terms as boldly and universally as this, knowledge of the past is no longer possible.

What, then, do we mean by historical objectivity? "Where we are fully entitled to speak of the 'objectivity' of a piece of knowledge, the knowing subject knows an object before him, independent of himself; the personality of the knower has no significance for the content of the piece of knowledge...It thus claims to be valid in precisely the same manner for every subject."[17] The ability to gain valid knowledge about the psychological processes of the historian is not denied, but that is another matter. Nor are we saying that such knowledge is never relevant to an understanding of what some historians write. It is, nevertheless, possible to know something about the past since a consideration of who claims to know this is *not always a necessary* consideration. I do not imply that all history is objective in this manner, but that some can be. Objective knowledge about the past remains a possibility if objections to this position can be met.

Critique of Becker

Having presented Becker's analysis of the historical fact, and having developed an alternative to it, we are now prepared to consider the validity of Becker's arguments. Facts are not like bricks or stones upon which the historian stumbles (although there is data and one may stumble on that). If we can think of facts as factual statements about the past (as Becker has), some of his other problems become unreal.

Becker holds that a historical fact is a symbol in the sense that it is a generalization of many smaller facts. It is confusing, however, to call the statement "In the year 49 B.C. Caesar crossed the Rubicon" a generalization. Generalizations are statements which are based on other statements of fact and summarize their implications. At least a generalization is "a proposition that describes some attribute common to two or more objects."[18] The Caesar statement is simply a factual statement about an event. That one could possibly make numerous other factual statements of greater or lesser import about the same event is simply to say that some events are sufficiently complex to allow numerous factual statements to be made about them. That one does not make all the factual statements about an event that might possibly be made does not make those statements that are made generalizations. From the realization that the historian cannot say everything about a given event even if he chooses to, that is, from the fact that the historian's knowledge is finite and not God's knowledge, it is often reasoned that what he or she says is less than accurate. This I deny. That written history is less than complete should be obvious. But that one must say everything that could be said in order that anything that one might say about the past could be accurate, or that one must know everything in order to know anything must be rejected unless one is also willing to forfeit the possibility of any knowledge at all.[19] Many factual statements about the past are highly probable and are therefore valid as long as one does not imply that they are more than they really are — a part. There is a profound difference between holding that one can make accurate statements about something and holding that because one can only make statements about something even those statements cannot be accurate. All factual statements, then, are not generalizations.

What, then, are generalizations, and to what extent are they either factual or interpretive statements? There are numerous types of generalizations which permit verification to varying degrees. Some are so boldly conceived that it is difficult even to imagine what kind of historical confirmation could possibly verify the statement. Some generalizations are universal in scope and admit of no possible variants. Consider the generalization by Seymour Lipset: "It is obvious that the distribution of wealth is the most important source of interest–conflict in complex societies."[20] This generalization is so universally conceived that it is difficult for the historian to verify it. Universality is not the only problem such a statement presents. Because it is based on a certain theory of economics, this statement rests on more than the data of history. The statement is therefore an interpretive one since its verification depends on historical data (if relevant data for such a statement does exist) plus a necessary theoretical justification of the economic theory involved.

Consider another generalization by Crane Brinton: "The man of the nineteenth century has a sense of *belonging* (deeper than mere optimism) that we lack."[21] It is not only difficult to document a *sense* of belonging, but to imply that the nineteenth century is so simple that one is able to talk about the "nineteenth century man," may well be an example of a historian asking a question that is too simplistic for the complexity of the material. By this type of reasoning Jonathan Edwards is for Vernon Parrington an anacronism,[22] and in nineteenth century America one is stuck not only with Bushnell and Emerson, but also with Charles Hodge. If Hodge is not a nineteenth century man there are things about Bushnell that are not nineteenth century either if one can speak in this way at all. It might be urged that such generalizations are not meant to be infallible, but only approximations. That is apparent — but they are erroneous since, in such simplistic form, they do not correspond to anything real. This generalization, however, is a statement of factual intent that may have a very low degree of probability according to the historical method.

The next generalization is more limited in scope and is based upon other highly probable factual statements. "All the wars here discussed were preceded by a fall in prices on the London Stock Exchange and by a rise in the number of trade union members reported as unemployed."[23] The important point here is that not only can a generalization be verified in some cases with as high a degree of probability as simple statements, but generalizations may be factual statements just as readily as they may be interpretive statements. A generalization, then, is different from some types of simple historical statements, but can be either factual or interpretive, depending on the nature of the statement. The type of evidence demanded for the verification of a generalization depends upon whether it is factual or interpretive and not that it is a generalization. Factual statements can be made which do not involve the value system of the historian.[24] Generalizations can be factual statements and are then subject to the same kind of verifying evidence as statements like "In the year 49 B.C. Caesar crossed the Rubicon." Sometimes, moreover, generalizations can have a higher degree of probability than more simple statements regarding the date of an event for which the data is either slight or conflicting.[25]

Interpretive studies are legitimate, but in such cases verification depends upon historical evidence as well as a substantiation of the theory involved. When some historians hold that all written history involves the value system of the writer, they not infrequently fail to see the necessity of justifying the theoretical system, and seem to assume that since everyone imposes a value system anyway, verification is either impossible or unnecessary. Such procedure can satisfy only the most unquestioning mind.

Causal statements are similar to generalizations in this regard. One of the questions about the past which the historian attempts to answer is "why"? To deal with the problems related to causation raised by Hume would be a lengthy task. The point is that historians do make statements of a causal nature, and that their statements about past events seem to imply that the causal connection lies not only in the mind of the historian but also that it was true of the past event itself. Some have denied the clear intent of their own historical statements, however, by contending that it is the mind of the historian that imposes the structure on the past. Mandelbaum points out that since Hume and Kant it has often been assumed that the structure which the objects of our knowledge possess are the results of the activity of the human mind upon a world of flux. Mandelbaum offers an opposing position: "We hold that the order to be found in nature and history as they are known by us may really characterize the events of the world independently of the mind's activity."[26] While not going into the matter in detail, Mandelbaum points out that if one holds that the human mind has an ordering activity, then this is to say that either the mind is not a part of nature, or that at least one element of nature, the mind, somehow has order implicit to it. If one chooses to see the mind as outside the order of nature one must accept the consequences of the statement for both one's psychology and theology as well. Furthermore, if one holds that all structuring is due to the activity of the mind, "why is it that the mind attributes one form of order to certain of the elements in its experience and another form of order to certain other elements?"[27] Mandelbaum explains his choice:

> On any assumption such as the Kantian this problem must remain to the end of time what Windelband calls "a sacred mystery". Let him who will, acknowledge such mysteries as the ultimate terminus of philosophic

> discussion. To us it seems preferable to start with mysteries and conclude with some definite knowledge, rather than to start from grounds of which we feel ourselves to be sure and proceed to a point where the very search for an answer becomes meaningless.28

Historians do use causal statements and intend to say that the causal connection indicated was in the event. The point to be made for our purposes is that causal statements may be either factual or interpretive and that their verification in this regard is similar to the verification of generalizations.

> We have seen that Brahmanism had hardly been formulated before vigorous dissent appeared. The Kshatriyas were particularly aroused to dissent. They did not like either the social or the religious implications of Brahmanism.29

The intent of these statements is causal. The writer is saying that the dissent of the Kshatriyas was caused, at least in part,30 by their dislike of the social or religious implications of Brahmanism. This is also a factual statement since it can be verified by examining the available data. The probability of this factual statement, however, depends on the type of historical evidence that can be brought forth in its defense. There is, therefore, a possible and legitimate historical answer of a factual nature to the "why" of an event. When, on the other hand, Flügel says "...this failure in the fertility of his marriage aroused superstitious fears connected with Henry's Oedipus complex," he is making a causal statement of an interpretive nature. The validity of this causal statement rests on two kinds of evidence. Here the answer to the question "why" is answered not in the light of historical data, but in the light of Freudian psychology. An answer to the causal question may therefore be given at various levels, some of which are factual and others of which are interpretive.

Becker continues by stating that the simple fact "In the year 49 B.C. Caesar crossed the Rubicon" has strings attached to it. This fact has significance only because of its relationship to other facts and to the interpretive structure into which it is placed.31 If causal statements and generalizations can be either factual or interpretive, as we have argued, then the relationship between statements can be interpretive or factual. Becker's statement implies that factual statements take on meaning only as they are related to other factual statements. But if such relationships are themselves factual (not involving a level of meaning not contained in the data), then one must either distinguish between levels of interpretation or better still limit the use of the term as we have indicated.

It has been conceded that interpretive statements give meanings to factual statements that they never had when they stood alone, but it has been argued that some statements which are called "interpretive" hardly qualify for the title. Becker seems to assume that the "facts" exist in a vacuum. Actually, factual statements are based upon data from which a number of different, and sometimes related, factual statements can (not infrequently) be made. If this is so, then the connection made between some types of factual statements are themselves factual in that they are based as solidly upon the data as any single factual statement. When Becker says, "...generally speaking, the more simple an historical fact is, the more clear and definite and provable it is, the less use it is to us in and for itself,"[32] there is a certain amount of truth being stated. But, much depends upon what use one wants to make of the available data. It is possible for a historian to ask questions of the data that it could not possibly answer. It may be necessary for the discerning historian to admit that some factual statements cannot be used to answer certain questions no matter how interesting or profound they may be to the human spirit.

When Becker indicates that a fact, if it is anywhere, must be in the mind of the historian or someone else, he is stating what should be obvious to anyone. If what we are talking about is historical statements, then they must be in the present and they must be in someone's mind. To this anyone would agree. Is this not where most ideas are found? It is the implication that is not valid — that since it is in the mind of the historian it must of necessity undergo change there. This is an inference that remains to be supported. Were it true, one would be forced to conclude that no one has any valid knowledge since all ideas with which we are familiar are found in the mind of someone. This is true of mathematics or physics no less than of history.

So much for a critique of Becker's analysis. It remains for us to speak of some of the implications that he draws from his analysis. He says, "by no possibility can the historian present in its entirety any actual event, even the simplest."[33] This statement is emphasized because nineteenth century "scientific historians" emphasized that they would "present all the facts and let them speak for themselves." It is Becker's contention that one cannot present all the facts. This simply means that one cannot make all the factual statements about an event that could possibly be made. This should be evident, and those who made the above claim should at least have been more careful in their use of words. But that does not exempt Becker from a similar care.

Becker makes two statements that he believes are valid inferences from this observation of selectivity. Our concern is to see if they are necessary inferences, for one can hardly doubt that they are possible inferences. If they are not necessary, then objectivity remains a possibility. The first statement he makes is: "What is it that leads one historian to make out of all the possible true affirmations about a given event, certain affirmations and not others? Why, the purpose he has in mind will determine that."[34] This is true, but the real question is whether the purpose he has in mind is a legitimate one given the data at his disposal. The issue is not that the historian exercises judgment, for that is part of an interesting psychological question. The question is whether or not his selection does violence to the data.[35] If we are going to support the notion that all selection does violence to the data, then we must also accept in that parcel the view that no knowledge of the past is possible.

Becker goes even farther when he states that the purpose in the mind of the historian not only determines his selectivity but also imposes any meaning that the written history might have. "The event itself, the facts, do not say anything, do not impose any meaning. It is the historian who speaks, who imposes a meaning."[36] If by facts we mean factual statements, it is absurd to say that they "do not say anything" or even that they do not mean anything. They say whatever it is that they say as is true of all adequately constructed sentences. We have indicated that there are different levels of meaning. To say that a factual statement means nothing is simply to say that one does not consider that level of meaning significant. That may be correct, but it does not therefore add up to the elimination of all levels of meaning so that one can say that statements of fact have *no* meaning. The factual statement "Indulgences were sold in Germany in 1517" is a factual statement which may not explain the existence of Protestantism until it is put in a context with other factual statements, but even alone it does mean something, namely, that in 1517 in Germany indulgences actually were sold. A deeper meaning may not be available unless one includes a theological analysis of indulgences, but that is another matter. There are levels of meaning and the statement exhibits one level of meaning even when it stands alone.

Becker's second implication is that the historian cannot eliminate the personal equation. This argument takes various forms among relativists, but it essentially states that in the writing of history the writer inevitably inserts his or her own value system so that what is written never really corresponds to the past event. It should be pointed out, however, that few if any logical reasons for the position are given. Some illustrations are given of how different people have seen events differently, and then the position is simply stated as Toynbee does: "Thus the historian's transcendence of self–centeredness is never more than partial and imperfect; and even contemporaries who have been brought up in different cultural milieux find it difficult to appreciate one another's mutually alien cultural heritage...."[37] It is stated that the historian selects, but that, as well as the statement that the historian cannot eliminate the personal equation, does not make it so. No number of illustrations as to how persons have been influenced by the values of their culture or of historians who have written biased history will show that this is the very nature of *all* knowledge of the past.

There is a very basic distinction to be made between the psychology of history and the logic of history. Morton White has pointed out this distinction in his analysis of the relativism of Charles Beard. "Beard was guilty of a confusion which is typical in the philosophy of history, the confusion between the psychology of historical interpretation and its logic."[38] The question is not whether the historian has interests — who doesn't? There is still the point that what stands or falls as being adequate or inadequate is the conjunction of statements that he or she finally writes down. This must pass the rigid criteria that historians are capable of applying. The fact that the historian has certain interests is irrelevant since his or her interest at this point *may not be* relevant to the topic being researched, or it may be merely the neutral interest in knowing something about the past.[39] As Sidney Hook puts it: "The possession of bias or passion on the part of the historian does not preclude the possibility of his achieving objectivity in testing his hypothesis any more than a physician's passion to relieve men from the ravages of a disease...precludes the possibility of a discovery of a medical...truth."[40]

The whole question of self–transcendence can be seen in the same light. When it is stated that the historian can never completely transcend his or her cultural and historical context, one is making a statement of a psychological nature. The question to which we want an answer is not whether one can achieve complete psychological self–transcendence. That is a meaningless question since it involves a contradiction in terms. The sentence seems to be asking whether or not a person can cease to be oneself. The issue is whether the written history under consideration stands in such a way that the emotional concerns of the historian are of no significance for the accuracy of the work. I know of no thinker on this subject who is proposing that one can always live in a condition of personal suspension or self–transcendence. Nor is the real issue whether one can withhold one's concern on any subject at will. The question is if any one person can write on any one topic in such a way that if he or she has any values that are relevant to the subject they will not intrude into the study as written. I would contend that logical self–transcendence is possible if for no other reason than that it is possible to write on a subject in which one has no particular stakes except curiosity about the past. It is not only the historian who has values. The ability of the historian to restrain them, or not to write on subjects for which one is emotionally disqualified, may go a long way toward indicating one's ability as a historian. If one is too involved even to recognize such involvement, then we simply cannot expect an objective account from that historian. But it does not follow that since some or even many written histories fit this category, therefore all do.

Relativism or Probability

Having argued for the possibility of objectivity, we have repeatedly asserted that statements in history can only be highly probable at best. One of the problems in the discussion of this issue is the confusion of relativism with probability. The opposite of relativism is objectivity, and the opposite of absolutism is probability. We have argued against relativism since it seems to forfeit the possibility of knowing anything. This is not to argue that any work of history can be absolute (either in the sense of total knowledge or in the sense of absolute certainty).

It might be argued that in our position the validity of the statement is relative to the evidence available to support it. This is a less technical use of the term relative. Relativity proposes that the statement is relative to the viewer regardless of what kind of evidence one marshals to its support. It is our contention that the validity of the statement does not depend upon understanding how or why it was stated by the person who stated it, but whether and to what extent the data bears it up. This can be analyzed without concern for Mannheim's "sociology of knowledge." To say that the probability of a statement is relative to the evidence would be a truism to which any staunch objectivist would submit. But it is not saying anything more than that the probability of a statement depends on the amount and kind of evidence that can be used to defend it. It is quite another thing when one says that no matter what the evidence, the statement is less than adequate, not because of a lack of evidence, but because it happens to be a culture–bound person who makes the statement.

It is necessary to grant that no historical statement can be more than highly probable. But to say this is to admit the possibility of objective statements about the past. If all statements or written histories are relative, then from the standpoint of testing them, none are more probable than others, and therefore all statements are merely relative to the culture and stance of the historian. The concept of probability makes sense only as one concedes that objectivity is possible, and, I would suggest, this is implied when a historian makes a judgment that this written history is more true to the data than is another one. Given the logic of the relativist approach, one is hard pressed to object to any written history.

Notes

1. This article appeared in *The Western Political Quarterly* in September, 1955, and has since been republished in Hand Meyerhoff, *The Philosophy of History in Our Time* (Garden City: Doubleday Anchor, 1959), 120-137. It was originally presented as a paper at the 41st annual meeting of the American Historical Association at Rochester in December, 1926.

2. Carl Becker, "What are Historical Facts?" in Hans Meyerhoff (ed.), *The Philosophy of History in Our Time* (Garden City: Doubleday Anchor Books, 1959), 120-212.

3. *Ibid.*, 123.

4. *Ibid.*

5. *Ibid.*, 125.

6. Statements can be true and yet not highly probable since probability has to do with the degree of verification. Some statements could be true which we do not have the means to verify, but such statements have no

right to be included in a historical writing based on evidential data. Historical writing is based on probability and hence must exclude statements which are improbable because little historical data supports them, even though the statement might be true or even verifiable if the proper data were available.

7. It should be remembered here that we are speaking of historical knowledge. What is clearly fact or interpretation in history might be something else in another discipline.

8. "On the Character and Married Life of Henry VIII," in Bruce Mazlish (ed.), *Psychoanalysis and History* (Englewood Cliffs: Prentice–Hall Inc., 1963), 126.

9. *Ibid.*, 131.

10. *Ibid.*, 133.

11. *Ibid.*, 138.

12. There may also be interpretive statements which are true but improbable, perhaps because the appropriate evidence is not available to support their probability. The possibility remains that such statements might become probable if further data became available.

13. This use of factual statement differs from Professor Mead's use of "facts". His view (and Becker's) is that when we use the term "fact" we commonly mean those assertions that are highly probable. The point is that there are statements which are factual in intent which are improbable although verifiable in the same way as more certain statements of identical form. We are using the phrase to indicate the intention of the sentence since some statements have another intention. Such a distinction also supports an important difference in the area of fact and interpretation. "...So far as the nature of knowing is concerned there is no fence separating an area of settled 'facts' from an area of 'interpretation'" ("Church History Explained," *Church History*, 32:1, 21.) But this is too easy for "interpretive statements," as we have seen, need verification by at least two methods while factual statements stand on verification by historical method alone.

14. Maurice Mandelbaum, *The Problem of Historical Knowledge.* (New York: Liveright Publishing Corporation, 1938), 19.

15. *Ibid.*, 20.

16. E. H. Carr, *What is History?* (New York: Alfred A. Knopf, 1964), 24.

17. Fritz Medicus, "On the Objectivity of Historical Knowledge," in *Philosophy and History*, edited by Raymond Klibansky and H. J. Paton (New York: Harper & Row, 1963), reprint from Clarendon Press, 1936, 137.

18. Louis Gottschalk, "The Historian's Use of Generalization," in Leonard D. White (ed.), *The State of the Social Sciences* (Chicago, 1956), 437.

19. Ernst Nagel points out that this is a corollary to the idealistic doctrine of the internality of all relations. He continues: "It will suffice here to note that, were the doctrine sound, not only would every historical account ever written be condemned as a necessarily mutilated and distorted version of what has happened, but a similar valuation would have to be placed on all science, and indeed on all analytic discourse." in "The Logic of Historical "Analysis," Meyerhoff, 209.

20. Seymour Martin Lipset, *Political Man: The Social Basis of Politics*, (Garden City, N.Y., 1960), 40. This and some other generalizations utilized here are found in William O. Aydelotte, "Notes on Historical Generalizations," in Louis Gottschalk (ed.), *Generalization in the Writing of History* (Chicago: University of Chicago Press, 1963), 145-177.

21. Crane Brinton, *Ideas and Men: The Story of Western Thought* (New York, 1950), 442. Also in Aydelotte.

22. Vernon L. Parrington, *Main Currents in American Thought: The Colonial Mind* (New York: Harcourt, Brace & Company, 1927), 165.

23. Quoted by Sidney Hook in "Problems of Terminology in Historical Writing — Illustrations" in *SSRC Bulletin 54* (New York, 1946), 127.

24. It is true that the very method which involves the strict use of historical evidence implies that one values this method itself. The question, however, is not a valueless historian but whether the historian's values must intrude in the history as written. Such values tend to eliminate bias and values from written history and therefore cannot be appealed to as a refutation of objectivity. That such types of values exist is evidence that not all values are detrimental to objectivity. The value which proposes to write objective history is certainly a value, but can in itself do nothing but contribute to the goal.

25. An example in point would be the date of the Exodus.

26. *Loc. cit.*, 203-204.

27. *Ibid.*, 204.

28. *Ibid*, 204-205.

29. John B. Noss, *Man's Religious*, 3rd edition (New York: Macmillan, 1963), 253.

30. Because historians are unable to rerun experiments and change the variables and constants as the chemist might do, one could hardly speak of "the" cause of an event in the past. One could, however, speak of "a" cause with some degree of probability.

31. This is involved in Becker's article and also in another by Charles Beard, "Written History as an Act of Faith," in Meyerhoff, particularly 150.

32. Becker, *loc. cit.*, 123.

33. *Ibid.*, 129.

34. *Ibid.*, 131.

35. "If selection simply means paring down the original list (known to be true), the result of selection will also be true. Any part of a true conjunction remains true." Morton White, "Can History Be Objective?" in Meyerhoff, 193.

36. *Loc. cit.*, 131.

37. Arnold Toynbee, *An Historian's Approach to Religion* (New York: Oxford University Press, 1956), 9.

38. *Loc. cit.*, 199.

39. It is quite neutral curiosity that Lovejoy contends was his reason for researching the history of "The Great Chain of Being," in Arthur Lovejoy, "Present Standpoints and Past History" in Meyerhoff, 178.

40 Charles Beard and Sidney Hook, "Problems in Terminology in Historical Writing," in *Theory and Practice in Historical Study* (New York: Social Science Research Council, 1946), 126.

PART TWO

RELIGION AND LAW IN MODERN INDIA

6

Religion and the Secular: Categories for Religious Conflict and Religious Change in Independent India

Constitutional provisions for "religion" in modern India and the subsequent determination of the realm of "religion" by the courts have been the subjects of several books by political scientists.[1] Legal scholars have also analyzed this material to determine the legal extent of religious freedom.[2] It is my intent to submit these documents to religio–historical analysis. Religio–historical analysis operates with the functional definition that religion is what concerns people ultimately. Religion is what is more important to them than anything else in the universe.[3] While religio–historical analysis can be used on materials which have traditionally been considered religious, it can also be useful in analyzing the religious dimensions of materials not commonly considered religious — in this case legal documents.

In these terms, *The Constitution of India* not only makes provision for "religion" in the modern Indian State, but is itself a religious document.[4] By providing a value structure for the modern Indian State, the Constitution not only orders priorities, but also embodies religious conflict and religious change.

The Constitution: The Conflict of Religions

When the study of religion is defined as the study of what people have considered of ultimate importance and the structure of reality consequent to such determinations, religion can take the form of a non–transcendent concern. The Constitutional religious model is non–transcendent. The Constitution neither affirms nor denies life beyond the present existence — it is simply not a relevant consideration. The preamble to the Constitution suggests the religious orientation of the document.

> WE, THE PEOPLE OF INDIA, having solemnly resolved to constitute India into a
> SOVEREIGN DEMOCRATIC REPUBLIC and to secure to all its citizens:
> JUSTICE, social, economic and political;
> LIBERTY of thought, expression, belief, faith and worship;
> EQUALITY of status and opportunity; and to promote among them all
> FRATERNITY assuring the dignity of the individual and the unity of the Nation;
> IN OUR CONSTITUENT ASSEMBLY this twenty-sixth day of November, 1949, do
> HEREBY ADOPT, ENACT AND GIVE TO OURSELVES THIS CONSTITUTION.

By limiting itself to concerns relating to this life, the Constitution stands in marked contrast with traditional religious models such as the one contained in the *Manusmṛti*.[5] For example, both the Constitution and *Manusmṛti* place considerable emphasis on justice. But in *Manusmṛti* the doctrines of karma and rebirth require that justice be defined in terms of considerations which take place before and after one's present existence. The Constitution defines justice in such a way that it must be actualized in the present existence. The doctrines of karma and rebirth are not denied — they are simply ignored.

Closely related to this is the fact that for the Constitutional religious model the content of justice is based on equality. All people are to be considered equal before the law and are to be afforded equal opportunity for employment, education and access to public facilities. Article 17 abolishes untouchability. If Article 16(4) provides for the possible reservation of positions for persons in backward classes, it is not because they are deemed superior, but because reverse discrimination seemed necessary to balance previously inherited handicaps which are themselves inconsistent with the theory of human equality.

By way of contrast, *Manusmṛti* rejects the inherent equality of all persons. Not limiting itself to this life, it interprets present inequalities as the result of past deeds. *Manusmṛti* begins with a chapter on creation in which the class system is seen as a part of the created order. Brahmans, Kṣatriyas, and Vaiśyas are to offer sacrifices and study the Vedas, and perform other functions peculiar to their respective classes. Śūdras are to serve the other classes. Since they are not *dvijas*, they do not have access to the Vedas nor do they perform sacrifices. Manu is declared to be omniscient and of equal authority with the Vedas.[6]

Because people are different by birth, justice must be dispensed so as to take such inequalities into account. Some men are lower than other men, and women are lower than men. *Manusmṛti* is as convinced that this is the way things are as the Constitution is that reality is not so structured. Women are by nature passionate and not to be trusted alone. They must be subject successively to their fathers, their husbands, and their sons.[7] Marriage should not be contracted with some kinds of people,[8] and contact with impure people renders one impure.[9] In implementing justice, *Manusmṛti* emphasizes the importance of honesty in testimony and trustworthiness in witnesses. Perjury has its penalty, but as in other cases the penalty is determined by where you stand in the class hierarchy.[10] And, if a Śūdra arrogantly goes against the nature of things by trying to teach Brahmans their duty, "the king shall cause hot oil to be poured into his mouth and into his ears."[11] Now this is conceived as a scheme of justice in that it indicates how one ought to conduct oneself in the light of the way things are. But assumed in this scheme are the notions of karma and rebirth. Life is not limited to the present and the mundane. Here lies a significant contrast between the Manu religious model and the Constitutional religious model.

The non–transcendent orientation of the Constitutional religious model is further revealed in the status given to more traditional religious expressions.[12] N. A. Subramaniam has noted that "The importance of Articles 25 and 26 lies not so much in the *grant* of religious liberty but in its *restriction*."[13] Article 25 is subject to the other provisions of Part III of the Constitution regarding "Fundamental Rights." These include the elimination of untouchability, equality before the law, and provisions for members of backward classes. Furthermore, religious freedom is "subject to public order, morality and health…," and cannot stand in the way of social reform.

Now these restrictions on the otherwise free exercise of "religion" constitute an admission that a conflict exists. It suggests that the Constitutional religious system may well be in conflict with traditional religious practices. Hence religious freedom cannot be granted without restriction. In the event that a conflict surfaces, the Constitution provides that the constitutional religious model will prevail. Traditional religious systems have the freedom to exist within the provisions of the Constitution. But those provisions make it clear that the traditional religious expressions cannot exist if they are in conflict with the Constitutional religious model. In cases where there is religious conflict of this nature, religious change becomes a necessity for survival. But the survival can be only partial, as the conflicting tradition is modified so as to ease the grounds for the conflict.

One of the devices for handling religious conflict is through the categories of "religion" and the "secular." According to the Constitutional religious model, life can be divided into these two all–encompassing categories. It is the category of "religion" which is granted freedom. But over against "religion" is the "secular" for which the same degree of freedom is not provided. Sometimes the realms of "religion" and the "secular" are closely related, but it is the view of the Constitution that they ought not to be confused.

"Religion" and the "secular" are not only part of the Constitutional religious model, but they are part of the religious conflict in that they run counter to much traditional religious thinking in India which sees life as homogeneous. In *Manusmṛti*, for example, the place of women, the nature of marriage, etc., are justified by the same sanction as more traditional "religious" matters. And, it has been common for Muslims to hold that personal law and inheritance was as much a matter of Muslim faith and tradition as was prayer. Such religious models did not consider "religion" as a segment of existence. Even the Supreme Court recognizes this to have been the case.

> ...Sometimes practices, religious and secular, are inextricably mixed up. This is more particularly so in regard to Hindu religion because as is well known, under the provisions of ancient Smritis, all human actions from birth to death and most of the individual actions from day to day are regarded as religious in character.14

These categories are not only a means for handling religious conflict and religious change, but are at the same time a part of the religious system whose survival is constitutionally guaranteed. Hence it is determined that the religious conflict will be handled through categories contained in one of the conflicting religions. These categories have become axiomatic, so that neither side of a litigation is able to deny the categories themselves. The categories are given sanction as part of the Constitutional religious model. Whether one is arguing one's case on the side of the Constitutional religious model or from a more traditional point of view, the case must be made within these categories. Once the legitimacy of the two categories is no longer questioned, certain activities can be relegated to the "secular," thereby cut off from the

Constitutional provisions for "religious" freedom. But when this method proves insufficient, other alternatives must be taken.

Although the categories of "religion" and the "secular" are an integral part of the Constitutional religious model, and although they are axiomatic, they are not constitutionally defined. This has been left to the courts. We now turn to the attempt at definition by the Supreme Court.

The Supreme Court: Defining "Religion" and the "Secular"

Supreme Court judgments reveal an ambivalence with reference to the definitional problem. The Court expresses a difficulty in distinguishing between the two realms when it says: "The question, is, where is the line to be drawn between what are matters of religion and what are not?"[15] In the case of a Mahant, for example, one is dealing with the spiritual leader of an institution who by virtue of his position also exercises wide powers of property management. Moreover, such a definition is not only difficult, it is virtually impossible. "The word 'religion' has not been defined in the Constitution and it is a term which is hardly susceptible of any rigid definition."[16] If the term "religion" is difficult to define, then "secular" would be no easier since its intelligent use presupposes a meaning for "religion."

While the Supreme Court states that there are difficulties in making the separation, the Constitution enjoins it, and there are times when the Court seems to make the required distinctions with little effort. There is no doubt, for example, that the administration of properties is a "secular" matter and thereby subject to law.

> It is clear, therefore, that questions merely relating to administration of properties belonging to a religious group or institution are not matters of religion to which clause (b) of the Article applies.[17]

In seeking to determine the limits of "religion," whose freedom from legislation is guaranteed, the definition offered by the American Supreme Court in *Davis* v. *Benson* (133 U.S. 333 at 342) is quickly discarded. That definition was:

> that the term "religion" has reference to one's views of his relation to his Creator and to the obligations they impose of reverence for His Being and character and of

> obedience to His will. It is often confounded with *cultus* or form of worship of a particular sect, but is distinguishable from the latter.[18]

Whatever view of "religion" the Supreme Court of India is to take it cannot define out of existence Buddhists and Jains (who do not affirm any Supreme Being).

"Religion" goes beyond mere belief. It can include ceremonies, ethical obligations and can even extend to matters of food and dress.

> A religion may not only lay down a code of ethical rules for its followers to accept, it might prescribe rituals and observances, ceremonies and modes of worship which are regarded as integral parts of religion, and these forms and observances might extend even to matters of food and dress.[19]

By taking account of the constitutional reference to the "practice of religion" (Article 25), the Supreme Court makes observable activity as much a part of "religion" as private belief systems. But since the State can legislate on matters which are economic, financial or political, the question still remains as to how far "religious practices" will be permitted to extend themselves. Communities might claim that almost anything is "religious" in order to be exempted from governmental control. How, then, has the Supreme Court attempted to distinguish "religion" from the "secular"?

In *Commissioner, Hindu Religious Endowments, Madras* v. *Sirur Mutt*, the Attorney–General from Madras State introduced the concept of essentiality as a means for determining what is to be granted freedom under Article 26(b). But since, in fact, the determination of essentiality already presupposed the identification of the realm of "religion," it did not advance the Court's ability to distinguish between "religion" and the "secular." The Attorney–General's argument was that "all secular activities, which may be associated with religion but which do not really constitute an essential part of it, are amenable to State regulation."[20] While rejecting implications which the Attorney–General wanted to draw from his observations, the Supreme Court nevertheless expressed itself on the subject on essentiality. "...What constitutes the essential part of a religion is primarily to be ascertained with reference to the doctrines of that religion itself."[21] Here, again, the determination of essentiality presupposes the identification of "the doctrines of the religion."

The manner in which essentiality presupposes the realm of "religion" and is therefore unable to define it is more clearly revealed in *Panachand Gandhi* v. *State of Bombay*.[22] In that case the manager of a Svetamber Jain public temple and the trustees of Parsi Panchayat Funds and Properties in Bombay challenged the validity of the Bombay Public Trusts Act of 1950. This Act required that the trustee of every religious or charitable trust register that trust. A fee of Rs. 25 was levied, and further fees were required to defray expenses incurred in regulating public trusts. Counsel for the appellants argued that

> ...according to the tenets of the Jain religion the property of the temple and its income exist for one purpose only, *viz.*, the religious purpose, and a direction to spend money for purposes other than those which are considered sacred in the Jain scriptures would constitute interference with the freedom of religion.[23]

To spend religious funds for governmentally imposed fees would be contrary to Jain "religion." The judgment does not indicate how such an assertion was supported. Nevertheless, the Supreme Court rejected the contention as unsound.

> These expenses are incidental to proper management and administration of the trust estate like payment of municipal rates and taxes, etc., and cannot amount to diversion of trust property for purposes other than those which are prescribed for any religion.[24]

Whether the objection of the appellants was sound or not, or whether it is in reality contrary to the Jain "religion" to pay such fees is less important for our analysis than the fact that here a religious institution through its counsel made a statement about the nature of its "religion" and it was not accepted by the Court. It is true that in order to gain one's ends before the Court such an argument may have been conjured up irrespective of the beliefs of the community. But it is the way the objection is handled that is instructive for our purposes. Although the religious institution made an explicit statement about their "religion," since it extended into the area which the Court considered the "secular" no further discussion was necessary.

In *Commissioner, Hindu Religious Endowments, Madras* v. *Sirur Mutt* it was stipulated that

> a religious denomination or organization enjoys complete autonomy in the matter of deciding as to what rites and ceremonies are essential...25

It was also stipulated that just because such matters involved the outlay of funds they were not any less "religious." However, in *Panachand Gandhi* v. *State of Bombay* the power of the religious community to define the extent of its own "religion" does not extend beyond the sphere of "religion" as intended in the Constitution and explicated in the Courts. If it is determined that it is the "secular" role of government to register a trust to ensure it proper management, and if it is the constitutional right of the government to levy fees to defray the cost thereof, then this is part of the "secular" realm. Although the religious institution has unchallenged right to determine its own affairs in matters of "religion," the extent of the "religion" cannot reach into the constitutionally determined realm of the "secular." Hence, it can define its "religion" and what is essential to it, but only within the bounds of "religion" as distinct from the "secular." It becomes clear that the concept of essentiality is not helpful in defining "religion," since an assumed realm of "religion" is logically prior to essentiality. *Panachand Gandhi* v. *State of Bombay* does not resolve the question of how one determines what is "religion."

In *Shri Govindlalj* v. *State of Rajasthan*,[26] the applicability of the Nathdwara Temple Act of 1959 was challenged on the ground that the temple was the property of the Tilkayat and was not a public temple. The Court then attempted to determine if it was an essential part of the tenets of the Pushtimargiya Vaishnava Sampradaya that they could only worship in private temples owned and managed by the Tilkayat. They decided that it was not. But a new element arises.

The judgment of the Supreme Court reiterated that when one is deciding a religious practice it must be an essential or integral part of the "religion." And, this must be decided by whether the practice is considered integral by the community itself. But what if the community does not speak with a united voice?

> Take the case of a practice in relation to food or dress. If in a given proceeding, one section of the community claims that while performing certain rites white dress is an integral part of the religion itself, whereas another section contends that yellow dress and not the white dress is the essential part of the religion, how is the Court to decide the question.27

How will the Court decide? Gajendragadkar's judgment returns to essentiality. Unless this test is used, even secular practices might be confused with "religion."

> The question will always have to be decided by the Court and in doing so, the Court may have to inquire whether the practice in question is religious in character and if it is, whether it can be regarded as an integral and essential part of the religion, and the finding of the Court on such an issue will always depend upon the evidence adduced before it as to the conscience of the community and the tenets of its religion.[28]

A new problem is introduced: the possibility of lack of unanimity within a community. However, no new criterion is offered for determining the extent of "religion." But since in the above statement a practice's "religious" character comes prior to its essentiality, essentiality is again no help in determining "religiousness." And, no further indication is given as to the criterion that the Supreme Court will use to decide "if the practice in question is religious in character."

The difficulty which the Court has had in defining "religion" is not due to its indefinability. All communicable symbols are definable.[29] But the Court is unable to handle what has been considered "religion" within the categories of "religion" and the "secular," because to do so creates religious conflict and requires dealing with traditional religious expressions in terms provided by a new and conflicting religious model. The Supreme Court has been unsuccessful in defining the categories explicitly. But, defined or undefined, the categories continue to be used. How the Supreme Court handles the categories is a study of the progressive victory of the Constitutional religious model. That the victory is neither swift nor complete does not change the nature of the conflict nor the direction of the required religious change.

The Supreme Court: When the Categories Are Adequate

Although "religion" and the "secular" are never clearly defined by the Court, they are nevertheless used to handle religious conflict. Sometimes a practice is declared unessential, while on other occasions the Court seems to act on its own advice in *Panachand Gandhi* v. *State of Bombay* that in difficult cases the "court should take a common–sense view and be actuated by considerations of practical necessity."[30]

In *Commissioner, Hindu Religious Endowments, Madras* v. *Sirur Mutt* it was held that the determination of what rituals were necessary was a "religious" matter, but that the scale of expenses for the rituals was a "secular" matter and could legitimately exist under governmental control. Financial matters, and the acquiring and administering of property are "secular" matters. Hence, there is no interference with "religion" if a governmentally appointed Commissioner oversees the daily affairs of the temple, for that is a "secular" matter.[31] When Sikhs contested governmental action legislating the method of representation of the Board which manages their Gurdwaras, it was determined that the manner of representation was "secular" and could be determined by the State.[32]

In *Bira Kishore Deb* v. *State of Orissa*,[33] it was argued that the Shri Jagannath Temple Act of 1954 deprived the Raja of Puri of his personal property. The appellant, in representing his case within the categories provided, distinguished two functions of the Raja. He was the chief servant of the temple (*adya sevak*) and also the sole superintendent in charge of the secular affairs of the temple. The Court accepted the categories and maintained that the Act in no way limited the Raja in his "religious" functions but only intended to regulate the "secular" affairs of the temple. Section 15, cl.(1) of the Act required that an appointed committee provide for the proper performance of worship in accord with the Record of Rights. The Court pointed out that there are two aspects to Sevapuja. The one aspect has to do with the provision of the proper materials for the puja and this is a "secular" matter. After this the servants use the materials according to the dictates of "religion." Section 15(1) of the Act deals with the "secular."

It seems clear that it is the committee that decides what is demanded by the Record of Rights and not the servant of the idol. And, it is the duty of the committee to see that the servants carry out the Record of Rights properly. Since this is intended as a guarantee of "religious" integrity, held the Court, it cannot be an interference with "religion." But what the *adya sevak* is left with is the performance of duties mandatory upon him as determined by the committee in the light of the Record of Rights.[34] Hence the determination of duties which are "religious" in accord with the Record of Rights is not itself a "religious" determination. So long as the committee allows (even enforces) the *sevaks* to perform the duties, their "religious" rights have not been touched. The "secular" management of the temple includes not only the financial matters but also the determination of the "religious" rites demanded by the Record of Rights.

Several petitions representing Vaiṣṇava and Śaivite temples in Tamil Nadu contended that the Tamil Nadu Hindu Religious and Charitable Endowments (Amendment) Act (1970) infringed upon their "religious" rights in doing away with the hereditary right of succession to the office of *Archaka* (*pujari*) in their temples.[35] The petitioners held that their rights had been violated under Article 26(b) since

> The freedom of hereditary succession to the office of Archaka is abolished although succession to it is an essential and integral part of the faith of the Saivite and Vaishnavite worshippers.[36]

Examining the *Agamas*, the Court found that only a qualified Archaka could step inside the *sanctum sanctorum*. The touch of anyone else would defile the image. Moreover, a Śaivite cannot serve in a Vaiṣṇavite temple, nor can a Vaiṣṇavite serve in a Śaivite temple. It was this rule that the principle of hereditary succession was intended to protect. The Court agreed that failure to appoint a person from the appropriate denomination would "interfere with a religious practice the inevitable result of which would be to defile the image."[37]

In this regard the Court also expressed itself on the matter of essence. In effect, it rejected the contention that hereditary right was essential, but held that it was essential that the images not be polluted.

> An Archaka of a different denomination is supposed to defile the image by his touch and since it is of the essence of the religious faith of all worshippers that there should be no pollution or defilement of the image under any circumstances, the Archaka undoubtedly occupies an important place in temple worship. Any State action which permits the defilement or pollution of the image by the touch of an Archaka not authorized by the Agamas would violently interfere with the religious faith and practices of the Hindu worshipper in a vital respect, and would, therefore, be prima facie invalid under Article 25(1) of the Constitution.[38]

The Court admitted that the hereditary principle was common usage and was in practice from antiquity. "The real question, therefore, is whether such a usage should be regarded either as a secular usage or a religious usage."[39] It was the contention of the petitioners that it was indeed a "religious" practice. They held that priests who are to perform "religious" ceremonies may be chosen by the temple on whatever basis the temple decides, and sometimes it is hereditary. They objected to the classification of the Act as social reform.

> Under the pretext of social reform, he (Mr. Palkhivala on behalf of the petitioners) contended, the State cannot reform a religion out of existence and if any denomination has accepted the hereditary principle for choosing its priest that would be a religious practice vital to the religious faith and cannot be changed on the ground that it leads to social reform.[40]

The Court agreed that the priest was appointed to a "religious" function, but questioned whether the appointment itself was "religious." Even the priest appointed in the hereditary manner is subject to the disciplinary power of the trustee. Furthermore, any lay founder of a temple can appoint a priest. Appointment is therefore by a "secular" authority, and hence it is a "secular" act. Neither the fact that some temples have followed the principle of heredity, nor the "religious" nature of what the Archaka does in the temple makes the act of appointment any less "secular."[41]

The Amendment Act was an expression of the Constitutional religious model.

> The Amendment Act was enacted as a step toward social reform on the recommendation of the Committee on Untouchability, Economic and Educational Development of the Scheduled Castes.[42]

As such, it posed a conflict with the traditional hereditary practices of denominational temples. The Court resolved the conflict in favor of the Act by declaring that, although what the Archaka did within the temple in his function as pujari was "religious," the appointment of the Archaka and the manner in which it was done was a "secular" matter, and legitimately under the jurisdiction of the State.

In *Saifuddin Saheb* v. *State of Bombay*,[43] the religious conflict which we are tracing is built into opposing judgments rendered by members of the Court, but resolved by the majority in terms of the categories of "religion" and the "secular." The issue at stake was whether the Bombay Prevention of Excommunication Act (1949) was in conflict with Articles 25 and 26 of the Constitution. The petitioner in the case was the Dai–ul–Mutlaq who was the head of the Dawoodi Bhora Community of Shia Muslims. Part of the Dai's authority was the power of excommunication. An earlier case determined that under certain conditions it was within the power of the Dai to excommunicate.[44] The petitioner argued that the practice of excommunication was essential, for without it the purity and continuity of the denomination could not be safeguarded by removing persons unsuitable for membership. It was further contended that the right to worship in a mosque and burial in a graveyard dedicated to the community were "religious" rights not to be enjoyed by a person rightly excommunicated.

It was the contention of the State of Bombay that the Dai had the right to regulate religious practices but that excommunication was not an essential part of the "religion" of the Dawoodi Bohra community and hence was a "secular" matter which affected the civil rights of persons.

The religious conflict which we have been tracing becomes explicit in a contention of the Attorney–General for the State of Bombay when he argued that in abolishing excommunication the Act was "in consonance with modern notions of human dignity and individual liberty of action even in matters of religious opinion and faith and practice."[45] The preamble to the Act itself includes the following words: "And whereas in keeping with the spirit of changing times and in the public interest it is expedient to stop the practice..."

In his minority judgment, Sinha, C. J., interprets the Act as the culmination of the history of social reform which began with provisions of the Bengal Code which were later incorporated in the Caste Disabilities Removal Act of 1850. Again, the conflict with a new religious system arises:

> The impugned Act, thus, has given full effect to modern notions of individual freedom to choose one's way of life and to do away with those undue and outmoded interferences with liberty of conscience, faith & belief. It is also aimed at ensuring human dignity and removing all those restrictions which prevent a person from living his own life so long as he did not interfere with similar rights of others. The legislature had to take the logical final step of creating a new offence by laying down that nobody had the right to deprive others of their civil rights simply because the latter did not conform to a particular pattern of conduct.[46]

In coming to his decision, Sinha, C.J., introduced a slightly different category. Instead of merely speaking of "religion" and the "secular," he referred to excommunication as not being "purely religious" or "wholly religious." It has been recognized that the separation of "religion" from the "secular" was not simple. But when an act is not "purely religious" this means that there are civil consequences to the activity under consideration.[47] As a member of the Court, Sinha, C.J., held that he was not called upon to comment upon the "purely religious aspects" of excommunication, nor was he interested in distinguishing what they might be. He was responsible for making a judgment about actions touching on the civil rights of members of the community. Since excommunication treated the excommunicated much as a pariah, and since the Constitution abolished untouchability, the Act is valid. Sinha, C. J., then, decided in favor of the civil rights while recognizing implications for "religion" which did not concern him.

> Hence, although the Act may have its repercussions on the religious aspect of excommunication, in so far as it protects the civil rights of the members of the community, it has not gone beyond the provisions of Art. 25(2)(b) of the Constitution.[48]

The majority of the Court judged the Act unconstitutional. In arguing for the essentiality of excommunication, Das Gupta, J., appealed to an article in *Encyclopedia of Social Sciences* on "Excommunication" where it was argued that the practice had been a principal means of maintaining discipline and solidarity in a religious community. Furthermore, it was noted that at the time of initiation the Dawoodi Bohras take an oath of unquestioning faith and loyalty to the Dai. Das Gupta, J., indicated that this did not demand an answer to the question of whether every case of excommunication by the Dai was based on "religious" grounds. But by invalidating excommunication on any ground, the Act made it impossible to maintain the strength and continuity of the "religion."

> What appears to be clear is that where an excommunication is itself based on religious grounds such as lapse from the orthodox religious creed or doctrine (similar to what is considered heresy, apostasy or schism under the Canon Law) or breach of some practice considered as an essential part of the religion by the Dawoodi Bohras in general, excommunication cannot but be held to be for the purpose of maintaining the strength of the religion.[49]

What does Das Gupta, J., do with the attendant "civil rights" which are thereby curtailed? He does exactly what Sinha, C. J. did with the "religious" matters entailed in his "civil decision." They are secondary and are not his concern.

> The fact that civil rights of a person is affected by the exercise of this fundamental right under Art. 26(b) is therefore of no consequence.[50]

In this case the majority argument was in favor of the traditional practice. But is is interesting to note that although both sides of the Court made their decisions as though the categories were adequate to handle the conflict, both had to ignore one side of it. Both seemed to recognize that excommunication had a "religious" and a "secular" or civil side. Sinha, C. J. acted in the light of the "secular," ignoring the "religious," while the majority judgment passed on "religion" ignoring the "secular." So the conflict is resolved by the power of the Court, but not because the categories of "religion" and the "secular" adequately handled it. We will now turn to instances where the breakdown is even more apparent.

The Supreme Court: When the Categories Are Inadequate

In some instances additional methods or principles have been introduced to assist "religion" and the "secular." Three of these are reification, superstition, and the rule of harmonious construction.

Reification

Reification is the treatment of an historical process characterized by diversity and change as a single objective entity. In the study of religion it is the treatment of "Hinduism," "Buddhism," and the like, as units of thought and practice.[51] Where there exists a conflict between the religious claims of a community and the Constitutional religious model, the Court has used reification in aid of "religion" and the "secular."

This method is particularly useful in reinforcing the Constitutional model in *M. H. Quareshi* v. *State of Bihar*.[52] Contesting the constitutionality of three acts for the prevention of cow slaughter, the petitioners argued that their fundamental rights guaranteed under Article 25 of the Constitution were abridged, since it was their custom to sacrifice a cow on Bakr Id Day. The petitioners claimed that this was enjoined in the Holy Qur'ān, but the Court contended that the verses referred to merely stipulated that people should pray and offer sacrifice. Operating under a reified concept of

Islam, the Court made a search for a scriptural statement making the sacrifice of a cow obligatory. A lack of obligatoriness would suggest that the practice was not essential to Muslim faith. Although the petitioners pointed out that it was their custom to sacrifice a cow, and although this was not denied by the Court, their custom was not sufficient. By treating Islam as a reified entity and considering the petitioners as Muslims, their specific contemporary practices could be ignored. When it was found that it was optional for a Muslim (according to "Hamilton's translation of Hedaya Book XLIII at page 592") to sacrifice a cow or camel for every seven persons or a goat for each person, it was apparent that for Muslims there was an option. Since the petitioners were Muslims, it must be optional for them as well. Although financial considerations would put the option out of reach for many, that was considered an economic matter and not a "religious" one. Since the sacrifice of a cow was optional for Muslims, it was optional for these Muslims, and since it was optional it was not essential, and since it was not essential it was not protected under Article 26 of the Constitution.

> We have, however, no material on record before us which will enable us to say, in the face of the foregoing facts, that the sacrifice of a cow on that day is an obligatory overt act for a Mussalman to exhibit his religious belief and idea.[53]

Superstition

Another concept which presents possibilities for use beyond its present actualization is the principle of superstition. In *Durgah Committee* v. *Hussain Ali*,[54] the issue was the respective rights of attendants of the shrine of Nasrat Khawaja Moin–ud–din Chishti in Ajmer. The shrine was run by the Chishti order of Sufis and the issue was the result of the Durgah Khawaja Saheb Act of 1955. In the judgment, written by Justice Gajendragadkar, the previous decisions relating to Articles 25 and 26 were recounted. But he also thought it advisable to "strike a note of caution." Once it was stated that practices were as much a part of "religion" as beliefs, it became possible for all kinds of practices to be judged "religious" by a given community. It was possible that even with the criterion of essentiality there might be practices which conflicted with the Constitutional religious model. Such practices would appear to fit under the Court's interpretation of Article 26, but they still could not be accorded the freedom stipulated therein. There is a difference between essential "religion" and superstitious accretions which may attach themselves to that essence in history.[55] Hence an historical community might sincerely believe that a practice is essential to their "religion," but that is because they mistake superstition for "religion."

> Similarly even practices thought religious may have sprung from merely superstitious beliefs and may in that sense be extraneous and unessential accretions to religion itself.[56]

No definition of superstition is offered and the principle does not play a role in deciding this case.

In *Yagnapurushdasji* v. *Muldas*,[57] the issue was whether the temples of the Saminararyan Sampradaya sect come under the Bombay Hindu Places of Public Worship Act (1956), since the appellants contended that they were not Hindus but a separate religion. At the end of a lengthy consideration of the nature of Hinduism and the tenets of the Swaminarayan Sampradaya sect it was concluded that they were Hindus. Of some importance was the fact that the sect had not objected to being so classified in Census reports. This case was decided as a matter of social reform. But Gajendragadkar J., held that although the contention of the sect began in sincerity, it was founded on superstition.

> It may be conceded that the genesis of the suit is the genuine apprehension entertained by the appellants; but as often happens in these matters, the said apprehension is founded on superstition, ignorance and complete misunderstanding of the true teaching of Hindu religion and of the real significance of the tenets and philosophy taught by Swaminarayan himself.[58]

The use of this concept is seen to go hand in hand with reification. First, there was a determination of the essential tents of Hinduism. Since the appellants contended that they were not Hindus, it was also necessary to find out what the Swaminarayan sect ought to believe if it were true to its founder. The result of the Court's research was that, although the appellants were sincere in their contention, they did not properly understand their own faith. And, not to understand one's own faith is to operate with "superstition, ignorance, and complete misunderstanding..."

The Rule of Harmonious Construction

In *Sri Venkataramana Devaru* v. *State of Mysore*,[59] the Gowda

Sarawath Brahman sect contended that the Madras Temple Entry Authorization Act (1947) which opened their temple dedicated to Sri Venaktaramana to all Hindus was in violation of Article 26(b) of the Constitution. They held that who was entitled to participate in temple worship was a matter of "religion." Admitting the precedent that "religion" includes practices as well as beliefs, the Court proceeded to determine whether exclusion of a person from a temple was a matter of "religion" according to "Hindu ceremonial law."[60] The Court observed that along with the growth of temple worship, there also grew up a body of literature called *Agamas* which stipulated how the temple was to be constructed, where the principal deity was to be consecrated, and where the other deities are to be installed. One such text includes degrees of participation.

> In the Nirvachanapaddathi it is said that Sivadwijas should worship in the Garbhagriham, Brahmins from the ante chamber or Sabah Mantabham, Kshatriyas, Vyasias (sic) and Sudras from the Mahamantabham, the dancer and the musician from the Nrithamantabham east of the Mahamantabham, and the castes yet lower in scale should content themselves with the sight of the Gopurum.[61]

It is pointed out by the Court that violation of such regulations results in pollution of the shrine and requires purificatory ceremonies. In a 1908 case, *Sankarakinga Nadam* v. *Raja Rajeswara Dorai*,[62] it was agreed by the Privy Council that trustees who agreed to admit persons into the temple whom the Agamas did not permit were guilty of breach of trust. The Court agreed that temple entry was a matter of "religion."

> Thus under the ceremonial law pertaining to temples, who are entitled to enter into them for worship and where they are entitled to stand and worship and how the worship is to be conducted are all matters of religion.[63]

But another factor had to be taken into account. Article 25(2)(b) of the Constitution provides that nothing in the Article should prevent the State from making a law

> providing for social welfare and reform or the throwing open of Hindu religious institutions of a public character to all classes and sections of Hindus.

The Court admitted that "the two Articles appear to be apparently in conflict."[64] The position of the "Hindu social reformers" which culminated in Article 17 of the Constitution abolishing untouchability was then recounted. The reformers objected that "purely on grounds of birth" some Indians were denied access to public roads and institutions which were open to the general Hindu public. This was not defensible on "any sound democratic principle."

After considerable argumentation it was finally admitted that this case involved two constitutional provisions, Article 26(b) and Article 25(2)(b), which are of equal authority. Appeal was then made to the "rule of harmonious construction" whereby two conflicting provisions are interpreted in such a manner as to give effect to both. The Court then agreed to the opening of the temple to all classes of Hindus. The right of the denomination to exclude members of the public from worshipping in the temple, although protected under Article 26(b), must give way to Article 25(2)(b). But this does not mean that anyone can go into any part of the temple at any time. Hence the denomination was permitted the right to exclude the general public from certain religious services. The Court felt that it had given effect to both provisions inasmuch as even after the the exclusions from certain religious services, "what is left to the public of the right of worship is something substantial and not merely the husk of it."[65]

In this case the Court faced the existence of religious conflict. On the surface this solution seems sensible. But in terms of religio–historical analysis it must be observed that while a portion of the denominational right under Article 26(b) was preserved, another portion was taken away. For, while traditional religious practice as described in the *Agamas* did distinguish degrees of participation and involvement in temple worship, it also included the degree of exclusion. Some persons were to "content themselves with the sight of the Gopurum." The issue of temple pollution was ignored by the Court. The judgment said, in effect, that traditional practices could not be maintained in their entirety because Article 25(2)(b) denied such practices. Part of the denomination's traditional religious practices are maintained under the "rule of harmonious construction." But, under the same principle another rather significant portion of their religion must be eliminated. This case, then, admits the existence of religious conflict and again implements religious change. It may also point out the inadequacy of the categories of "religion" and the "secular" to solve the issues of religious conflict introduced by the Constitutional religious model.

A religio–historical analysis of *The Constitution of India* and later Supreme Court cases reveals the existence of religious conflict. The categories of "religion" and the "secular" both provoke and also attempt to resolve the conflict. Although these categories have not been defined, and although they frequently prove inadequate, they nevertheless continue to be used. They are one means whereby the Supreme Court has attempted to resolve the conflict in favor of the Constitutional religious model.

Notes

1. Donald Eugene Smith, *India As a Secular State* (Princeton: Princeton University Press, 1963); Ved Prakash Luthera, *The Concept of the Secular State and India* (Calcutta: Oxford University Press, 1964).

2. N. A. Subramaniam, "Freedom of Religion," *Journal of the Indian Law Institute*, July-Sept., 1961, 323-350; Harry E. Groves, "Religious Freedom," *Journal of the Indian Law Institute*, April-June, 1962, 191-204; B. Parameswara Rao, "Matters of Religion," *Journal of the Indian Law Institute*, Oct.-Dec., 1963, 509-513; J. Duncan M. Derrett, *Religion, Law and the State in India* (London: Faber and Faber, 1968); G. S. Sharma (ed.), *Secularism: Its Implications for Law and Life in India* (Bombay: N. M. Tripathi Private Ltd., 1966); V. K. Sidha (ed.), *Secularism in India* (Bombay: Lalvani Publishing House, 1968).

3. For a more extended treatment of this approach see the author's *Category Formation and the History of Religions* (The Hague: Mouton & Co., 1971).

4. For the purpose of this paper, "religion" will refer to the realm for which the Constitution provides freedom, while religion will refer to the functional definition of religion as ultimate concern.

5. G. Buhler (trans.), *The Laws of Manu*, Vol. XXV, S.B.E., (Delhi: Motilal Barnarsidass, reprint 1964). First published by Oxford University Press, 1886.

6. *Ibid.*, II, 7.

7. *Ibid.*, V, 148.

8. *Ibid.*, III, 6-7.

9. *Ibid.*, V, 85.

10. *Ibid.*, VIII, 122-123.

11. *Ibid.*, VIII, 272.

12. Articles 25 and 26 of the Constitution read as follows:

    25. (1) Subject to public order, morality and health and to the other provisions of this Part, all persons are equally entitled to freedom of conscience and the right freely to profess, practise and propagate religion.

    (2) Nothing in this article shall affect the operation of any existing law or prevent the State from making any law —

    (a) regulating or restricting any economic, financial, political or other secular activity which may be associated with religious practice;

    (b) providing for social welfare and reform or the throwing open of Hindu religious institutions of a public character to all classes and sections of Hindus.

    Explanation I. — The wearing and carrying of *kirpans* shall be deemed to be included in the profession of Sikh religion.

    Explanation II — In sub-clause (b) of clause (2), the reference to Hindus shall be construed as including a reference to persons professing the Sikh, Jaina or Buddhist religion, and the reference to Hindu religious institutions shall be construed accordingly.

    26. Subject to public order, morality and health, every religious denomination or any section thereof shall have the right —

    (a) to establish and maintain institutions for religious and charitable purposes;

    (b) to manage its own affairs in matters of religion;

    (c) to own and acquire movable and immovable property; and

    (d) to administer such property in accordance with law.

13. *Loc. cit.*, 350.

14. *Shri Govindlalji* v. *State of Rajasthan, All India Reporter.* 1963 SC 1638 at 1661.

15. *Commissioner, Hindu Religious Endowments, Madras* v. *Sirur Mutt, The Supreme Court Journal*, Vol. XXVI, 1954, 348.

16 *Ibid.*

17. *Ibid.*

18 *Ibid.*

19. *Ibid.*, 349.

20. *Ibid.*

21 *Ibid.*

22. S.C.J., Vol. XVII, 1954, 480.

23. *Ibid.*, 487.

24. *Ibid.*

25. *Loc. cit.*, 351.

26. A.I.R. 1963 SC 1638.

27. *Ibid.*, 1660.

28. *Ibid.*, 1660-1661.

29. cf. *Category Formation and the History of Religions*, Chapter I.

30. S.C.J., Vol. XVII, 1954, 487.

31. *Digyadarshan R.R. Varu* v. *State of A.P.*, A.I.R. 1970 SC 181.

32. *Sardar Sarup Singh* v. *State of Punjab*, S.C.J., Vol. XXII, 1959, 1123.

33. A.I.R. 1964 SC 1501.

34. *Ibid.*, 1510.

35. *Seshammal and Others* v. *State of Tamil Nadu, Supreme Court Cases.* Vol. II, Part I, 1972, 11 ff.

36. *Ibid.*, 18.

37. *Ibid.*, 23.

38. *Ibid.*, 20-21.

39. *Ibid.*, 24.

40. *Ibid.*

41. *Ibid.*, 25.

42 *Ibid.*, 12.

43. A.I.R. 1962 SC 853.

44. A.I.R. 1948 PC 66.

45. A.I.R. 1962 SC 859-860.

46. *Ibid.*, 860-861.

47. *Ibid.*, 865.

48. *Ibid.*

49. *Ibid.*, 869.

50. *Ibid.*

51. cf. *Category Formation and the History of Religions*, Chapter V.

52. S.C.J., Vol. XXI, 1958, 975.

53. *Ibid.*, 985.

54. A.I.R. 1961 SC 1402.

55. For a discussion of Gajendragadkar's view of the essence of "religion" see the author's "Mr. Justice Gajendragadkar and the Religion of the Indian Secular State." Also, Chapter XI.

56. A.I.R. 1961 SC 1415.

57. A.I.R. 1966 SC 1119.

58. *Ibid.*, 1135.

59. S.C.J., Vol XXI, 1958, 382.

60. *Ibid.*, 389.

61. *Ibid.*, 390.

62. I.L.R. 31 Mad.

63. S.C.J., Vol. XXI, 1958, 390.

64. *Ibid.*, 391.

65. *Ibid.*, 396.

7

Religion and the Legitimation of Nehru's Concept of the Secular State

Although in ancient India distinctions were made between the responsibilities of king and priest, the primary aim of the state was to promote *dharma*. Hence, "the Hindu kings built temples, granted them large endowments, and exercised strict supervision over their affairs."[1] Under governments claiming Muslim norms, Aurangzeb destroyed Hindu temples and schools. Akbar, as part of his religious quest, supported the Persian translations of (among others) the *Atharvaveda*, the *Mahābhārata*, and the *Rāmāyana*.[2] During the British period, in addition to attempts at religious neutrality, there were occasions when the state assumed responsibility for the administration and patronage of South Indian temples. Hence, although the modern distinction between religion and the secular (so important for the thought of Nehru) was known in principle, the two realms were distinguished but not separated. It was frequently the case that government considered itself responsible for the religious well–being of its subjects. This responsibility was implemented directly or indirectly, and with varying conceptions of the nature of religious well–being.

In this setting, Nehru's notion of the secular state carries with it the necessity for political and social change.[3] The purpose of this paper is to determine in what sense and to what extent religion can be said to be a means whereby Nehru legitimated his concept of the secular state. This determination requires some prior methodological considerations.

Religious Legitimation: Sacred and Profane

To speak of religion as a means of legitimating power or justifying the directions of political and social change is to understand religion as distinct from the power to be legitimated or the political or social change to be justified. Failure to make such a distinction would require one to show how a given use of power or political or social change is legitimate without recourse to any principle outside of itself. Power would then be justified because it was power, and a given political or social phenomenon would be legitimated because it was indeed that political or social phenomenon.

For this reason it is not uncommon to find that in such discussions religion is understood in terms of the "sacred" over against the "profane."

> The dichotomization of reality into sacred and profane spheres, however related, is intrinsic to the religious enterprise. As such it is obviously important for any analysis of the religious phenomenon.[4]

Peter Berger intends to take the "sacred" in the "sense understood by *Religionswissenschaft* since Rudolph Otto...."[5] The three characteristics of the experience of the holy for Otto are summarized by W. Richard Comstock as follows:

> First is the sense of the *tremendum* that refers to a feeling of awfulness, and *majestas* or overpowering might that includes the sense of urgency. Second, *mysterium* refers to the uncanniness and mysteriousness that also pervades the experience. Finally, there is the element of *fascinans* as the experience seems to participate in an aspiration toward some ultimate value.[6]

In terms of the legitimation of power, this means that one is attempting to discover how the dimensions of the sacred are utilized to legitimate dimensions of the profane. Under these categories, secularization, or the profanization of the world, poses a problem for religious legitimation.[7] In terms of these categories, to the extent to which secularization has occurred, to that extent religious legitimation will cease to be a logical possibility. Hence, the topic under consideration in this symposium remains a real topic only to the extent to which secularization has not been complete. For the problem to be phrased in terms of these categories, some sense of the sacred must remain.

Closely related to these categories is the approach found in Donald Eugene Smith's *Religion and Political Modernization*. Here religion is seen in terms of "the religions," i.e., the sacred traditions of "Hinduism," or "Buddhism," or "Islam." The question of religious legitimation in the modern world is then framed as follows:

> The question that engages us here is this: Despite their traditionally conservative role, can the major religious systems be reformulated to provide positive ideological support for largely secular political systems committed to rapid socioeconomic change? Can reformulated Hinduism, Buddhism, Islam, and Catholicism significantly reorient the motivation and behavior patterns of large numbers of people and help to mobilize them for the tasks of development?[8]

In this vein Miriam Sharma and Jagdish P. Sharma show how the Sarvodaya movement utilized traditional religious terminology and concepts to justify social change. Bhoodan became the moral duty of good Hindus. Indeed, all good human beings should give one–sixth of their land to the landless.

> Expressed almost exclusively in a religious idiom, Sarvodaya uses a reinterpreted Hinduism to legitimize revolutionary change toward a utopian society.[9]

To examine Nehru's concept of the secular state under the categories of "sacred" and "profane" will abort an attempt to understand Nehru's thought. It might show us what he did not believe, but would not show how it was that his concept of the secular state was legitimated. There are at least two reasons for this. *First*, Nehru was not firmly committed to any religious or sacred tradition. Hence, he could not be expected to attempt the type of reformulation to which Smith refers. Many of his statements about "the religions" indicate that rather than reformulate them Nehru would prefer to see their scope compressed. If this compression is considered a type of reformulation, it is a reformulation which made "the religions" irrelevant to the social or political systems which they might be thought by others to legitimate. Religion as sacred tradition had no hold on Nehru. It does not, therefore, come as a surprise that he does not attempt to justify his concept of the secular state by appeals to a sacred tradition. There were moments in Indian religious history which Nehru appreciated, but he did not use them for legitimation.

Second, and closely related to the first, for Nehru there is no relationship between the realm of the "secular" and "religion." One of the things which most disturbed Nehru about Gandhi was his religious interpretation of the freedom movement.

> Gandhiji was continually laying stress on the religious and spiritual side of the movement. His religion was

> not dogmatic, but it did mean a definitely religious outlook on life, and the whole movement was strongly influenced by this and took on a revivalistic character so far as the masses are concerned...10
>
> I used to be troubled sometimes at the growth of this religious element in our politics, both on the Hindu and the Moslem side. I did not like it at all. Much that Moulvies and Maulanas and Swamis and the like said in their public addresses seemed to me most unfortunate. Their history and sociology and economics appeared to me all wrong, and the religious twist that was given to everything prevented all clear thinking. Even some of Gandhiji's phrases sometimes jarred upon me — thus his frequent reference to *Rama Raj* as a golden age which was to return. But I was powerless to intervene, and I consoled myself with the thought that Gandhiji used the words because they were well known and understood by the masses. He had an amazing knack of reaching the heart of the people.11

Nehru was willing to submerge his feelings about the intrusion of the sacred tradition into what he considered a purely political quest for at least two reasons. First, he was aware that he was powerless to do anything about it. Furthermore, although he did not agree with Gandhi's interpretation, nor with his theory, his method did get results.

The commonly used categories of "sacred" and "profane," then, have limited use for an analysis of the stance of one whose thought is predominantly "profane." But one is not bound to these commonly used categories in this analysis. Peter Berger does not intend to suggest that "sacred" and "profane" are the only legitimate terms for religious analysis.

> Definitions cannot, by their very nature, be either "true" or "false," only more useful or less so. For this reason it makes relatively little sense to argue over definitions...
>
> In the long run, I suppose, definitions are matters of taste...12

Religious Legitimation: Ultimate Concern

It is possible to study religion as ultimate concern. Religion, then, is studied as that which is more important than anything else in the universe to the individual or group involved.[13] Its application to the study of Nehru's thought would be to ask what Nehru considered of ultimate importance for human beings. If it was not the performance of puja, or sacrificial rites, or the achievement of some non–dual moksha, then what was it? In view of the topic of this paper, two subordinate questions then present themselves. What place does the secular state have in relationship to that ultimate goal, and, how did Nehru attempt to legitimate his view?

It was in contrast to the approach of organized "religion" that Nehru revealed his own approach to reality, and the ultimate human goal. "Religion" is emotional and merges with mysticism. Although some insight might come from it, there is an equal likelihood of self–delusion.

> Religion merges into mysticism and metaphysics and philosophy. There have been great mystics, attractive figures, who cannot easily be disposed of as self–deluded fools. Yet mysticism (in the narrow sense of the word) irritates me; it appears to be vague and soft and flabby, not a rigorous discipline of the mind but a surrender of mental faculties and a living in a sea of emotional experience. The experience may lead occasionally to some insight into inner and less obvious processes, but it is also likely to lead to self–delusion.[14]

Gandhi's use of "religion" in his 1932 "fast unto death" angered Nehru. It was the introduction of emotion and sentimentality into politics.[15] Over against "religious" emotionalism, Nehru opted for reason and clear thinking.

> Again I watched the emotional upheaval of the country during the fast, and I wondered more and more if this was the right method in politics. It seemed to be sheer revivalism, and clear thinking had not a ghost of a chance against it.[16]

"Religion" also has a tendency to sponsor superstition, magic, dogmatic beliefs, and unthinking credulance and reliance on the supernatural. This was true even when practiced by "thinking minds."[17] During his prison stay in

1933, a friend sent him books on Catholicism and copies of some of the papal encyclicals. He realized the hold that Catholicism had on many people and the safe anchorage from doubt and mental conflict which it and other "religions" offered their adherents. But to Nehru, the "religions" had no appeal. "I am afraid it is impossible for me to seek harborage in this way. I prefer the open sea, with all its storms and tempests."[18] Over against this, Nehru chose what he considered a "more or less scientific" view of things.[19]

Moreover, "the religious outlook does not concern itself with the world."[20] It has engaged in metaphysics and vague speculation which has often had little relevance to modern problems. Nehru's approach is decidedly this–worldly.

> Essentially I am interested in this world, in this life, not in some other world or a future life. Whether there is such a thing as a soul, or whether there is a survival after death or not, I do not know; and important as these questions are, they do not trouble me in the least.[21]

Perhaps most important of all, Nehru was not concerned with God nearly as much as he was with humanity. "A kind of vague humanism appealed to me."[22] God did not take up his attention, for the very concept seemed odd.

> What the mysterious is I do not know. I do not call it God because God has come to mean much that I do not believe in. I find myself incapable of thinking of a deity or of any unknown supreme power in anthropomorphic terms, and the fact that many people think so is continually a source of surprise for me. Any idea of a personal God seems very odd to me.[23]

But if God did not take up his attention, man did. "No, one may not lose faith in Man. God we may deny, but what hope is there for us if we deny Man and thus reduce everything to futility?"[24]

At this point Nehru's religious goal becomes clear. Committed though he was to "the scientific spirit,"[25] Nehru recognized the limits of science. "Science does not tell us much, or for the matter of that, anything, about the purpose of life."[26] Hence he could not settle for a mere scientific approach, but held out for "a kind of scientific humanism."[27] His ultimate goal, his religious goal was to create

> *a fully integrated human being* — that is, with what might be called the spiritual and ethical counterpart of the purely material machinery of planing and development being brought into the making of man.[28]

It was this goal of "a fully integrated human being" that gave meaning to Nehru's struggle for freedom: political, economic and social. A planned economy and a secular state were not ends in themselves, but were the most adequate means to his religious goal.[29] Convinced that people were not equal in abilities, he nevertheless held that they should be granted every opportunity to develop to their fullest potential. This was the goal of socialism.

> I am trying to search for the correct solutions, keeping before me certain objectives, *the broad objectives being human welfare and human development, providing opportunity to every human being to develop to the fullest measure possible...*
>
> Now when you ask for a definition of Socialism, what you mean presumably is a definition of an *economic policy* which would lead to the desired goal. This is a means to an end: *the end being, basically, as I have said, human betterment, everybody having the chance to concrete betterment.*[30]

Nehru's ultimate goal, then, is humanistic and scientific, it is rational, and, unlike antiquated "religious" superstitions, it is modern. It includes a higher material standard of living while retaining an ethical and spiritual approach to reality. It is, in his terms, "a fully integrated human being."

The Religious Goal and Freedom

In order for this growth into a fully integrated person to take place, people had to be free. Not only did the Indian people need independence from British domination, but national strength and national unity were also required.

> Some fissiparous tendencies have sprung up, as they were bound to, in a country of so many diversities, but I am confident that these will be conquered so as to have all the strands harmonized into a central unity. What is needed is education and culture, a common

> education and culture which makes every citizen of this vast land *think, feel and act the Indian way*.[31]

It is wrong to think that individuals can grow by pressing for communal advantages. Communalism weakens India and a weakened India threatens individual well–being.

> The one thing that should be obvious to all of us is this, that there is no group in India, no party, no religious community, which can prosper if India does not prosper. If India goes down, we go down, all of us, whether we have a few seats more or less, whether we get a slight advantage or we do not. But if it is well with India, if India lives as a vital, free country then it is well with all of us to whatever community or religion we may belong.[32]

On his return from Europe, Nehru had enlarged his outlook so as to add social and economic freedom to political freedom. Of what use, he held, was freedom from foreign domination if Indians remained bound by poverty and antiquated social restrictions?[33] The only justification for national freedom is a real freedom for the Indian masses.

> The only real justification for Indian freedom is the promise of better government, of a higher standard for the masses, of industrial and cultural growth, and of the removal of the atmosphere of fear and suppression that foreign imperialist rule invariably brings in its train.[34]

In a broadcast from New Delhi on August 15, 1947, Nehru reiterated the theme that the freedom that was gained when Indians lost the yoke of foreign domination had to be preserved and enlarged. What that enlargement entailed was indicated when he continued by expanding his theme in terms of the basic needs of food and clothing, economic production, industrialization, and the equitable distribution of goods.[35] In a speech on the anniversary of independence, on August 15, 1948, he made freedom a matter of the heart, an internal matter.

> For freedom is not a mere matter of political decision or new constitutions, not even a matter of what is more important, that is, economic policy. It is of the mind and heart and if the mind narrows itself and is befogged

> and the heart is full of bitterness and hatred, then freedom is absent.[36]

Freedom also entails equality, for it implies that all persons should be free. But equality in turn requires a limited freedom.[37] Otherwise, the unlimited freedom of one citizen might hamper or unduly limit the freedom of another. In a 1949 speech in San Francisco, he addressed himself to this issue of freedom and equality.

> Take equality. I am not quite sure if ultimately the concept of equality can be co–ordinated with freedom, because when you bring equality it may interfere with someone's freedom. So there is a slight conflict — not a final conflict, but there is a conflict. Perhaps in understanding the problems of the world today, you might put it in this way: that while in the nineteenth century, and later, the concept of freedom was given considerable emphasis and very rightly, in this middle–twentieth century the idea of equality is gaining more force. Until you balance the two ideas of freedom and equality, both of which are important, and each of which has to be limited to some extent in order to co–ordinate with the other, you will not solve the problems of today.[38]

The limitation of religious freedom should be seen in this light. Nehru would concur with *The Constitution of India* where religious freedom is subject to public order, morality and health, and is not to be used as an obstacle to social reform.[39] Freedom must be expanded to the fullest extent possible. But this requires the conscious limitation of freedom so that the overall scope of freedom can be maximized.

Freedom and the Secular State

The secular state is the means of maximizing freedom and hence enabling each individual to fulfill himself or herself in keeping with his or her optimum potential. Individual progress depends on national progress and strength. In a country like India, only the secular state will enable this to occur.

> The Government of a country like India, with many religions that have secured great and devoted

> followings for generations, can never function satisfactorily in the modern age except on a secular basis.[40]

But, the secular state involves certain limitations and one is the limitation of "religion." This means that Nehru operates with the categories of "religion" and the secular. It also means that in the secular state "religion" has its own sphere which is to be separated from other legitimate and important spheres of life. These spheres which have traditionally been closely related to "religion" must be secularized, that is, made distinct from the sphere of "religion" and purged of "religious" elements. This is all ultimately related to Nehru's religious goal. For the secularization of these endeavors is a necessary part of the secular state. The secular state maximizes human freedom and hence provides the opportunity for persons to achieve a fully integrated existence.

The Secularization of Politics

Part of what it means to be a secular state is that each citizen, regardless of his other associations, is to have equal rights and obligations as part of that citizenship. The citizen must be free to practice "religion," but "religious" association neither grants one special rights nor deprives him of any. Nehru drafted the Congress Election Manifesto of July, 1951, which stated that "As India is a secular State, every citizen has the same duties, rights, privileges and obligations as any other. He has full freedom to profess and practice his religion."[41] Citizenship, then, is determined on an individual basis, quite apart from one's status in a "religious" community. It was this secular basis for citizenship which made Nehru so much opposed to the Pakistani solution to the Kashmir question. The idea of two nations, each based on a "religion," was against the secularity upon which the Indian state was established.

> India is a secular nation which guarantees equality of citizenship to people of all religions. We consider our Muslim population — we have some fifty millions of them — as part of our nation, the Indian nation, and not some other Muslim nation. We have Hindus, Muslims, Sikhs, Christians and other religious communities, and we obviously cannot consider them as different nationalities. Such an approach would be absolutely fatal from our point of view. If we concede this two-nation theory which Pakistan is sponsoring, what happens to our vast Muslim population? Do we have

> to consider them as a different nation just because they have a different religion? The very concept is fantastic. It might lead to further trouble, division and disruption of the nation.[42]

Since citizenship is secular, so is politics. The individual's citizenship in the secular state is not dependent on "religious" affiliation, and "religion" is irrelevant to politics in the secular state. Indeed, the introduction of "religion" into political issues angered Nehru. Gandhi's announcement of a "fast unto death" in 1932 was interpreted as the introduction of "religious" means to achieve a purely political end. In the secular state, politics must be secularized.

> I felt angry with him at his religious and sentimental approach to a political question, and his frequent references to God in connection with it. He even seemed to suggest that God had indicated the very date of the fast. What a terrible example to set![43]

Although Nehru was pleased with the way Gandhi seemed to be able to mobilize the masses, his introduction of "religion" into the realm of politics was unacceptable. Moreover, he was concerned lest this bad example encourage others to mix "religion" with politics.

The threat to the secularization of politics was ever present in India in the form of communalism — the attempt to gain political power through alliances of a "religious" nature. Nehru spoke frequently against the communalist view that "religion" could serve as a national bond.[44] Communalism was undemocratic and was seen to go against the concept of citizenship found in the secular state.

> Our State is not a communal state, but a democratic state in which every citizen has equal rights. The Government is determined to protect these rights.[45]

In a speech delivered before the Constituent Assembly on April 3, 1948, Nehru addressed himself to the dangerous alliance of "religion" with politics in the form of communalism.

> ...The combination of politics and religion in narrowest sense of word resulting in communal politics is — there can be no doubt — a most dangerous combination and must be put an end to. It is clear, as

> has been pointed out by the Honourable Mover, that this combination is harmful to the country as a whole; it is harmful to the majority, but probably it is most harmful to any minority that seeks to have some advantage from it. I think even the past history of India will show that. But in any event a minority in an independent State which seeks to isolate and separate itself does some injury to the cause of the country, and most of all it injures its own interests, because inevitably it puts a barrier between itself and others, a barrier not on the religious plane but on the political plane — sometimes even to some extent on the economic plane; and it can never really exercise the influence which it legitimately ought to aspire to exercise, if it functions in that way.[46]

Ultimately, not only does communalism go against the secular concept of the state and weaken the state's solidarity, but it weakens the group which is seeking to strengthen itself through "religious" alliances. By placing a barrier between its members and other citizens, it hinders its members from achieving self–fulfillment and the extent of personal development which the secular state makes possible.

The exclusion of "religion" from politics would exclude all forms of communalism. Ideally, it would eliminate the reservation of seats along communal lines. Seeing that some reservation of seats might be in the offing, Nehru urged moderation. In response to the discussion about joint or common electorates, he urged:

> I hope personally that the less reservation there is the better, and I think that is so mostly even more from the point of view of the group or the minority that might have that reservation than from the point of view of any other group or majority.[47]

Not only does the concept of the secular state exclude "religion" from politics, but it also makes it an irrelevant consideration for social and economic planning.

Secularization and the Social Order

Regardless of the extent to which the caste system has been justified on "religious" grounds, within the context of the secular state, social order and social change must be decided on modern and "non–religious" grounds. Nehru spoke approvingly of the position of Vivekananda in which "caste was a form of social organization which was and should be kept separate from religion."[48]

Nehru recognized that simple equality was impossible, for people's capacities and talents, the Government notwithstanding, were dissimilar.

> You cannot make everybody equal for the simple reason that people are different, intellectually and physically different. There are clever people, there are stupid people, and there are all types of people. But what you can do is to equalize opportunities for all and apply the same standards for everyone.[49]

Equality of opportunity is an inference from the secular state's notion of citizenship which is granted equally apart from religious status of affiliation. But the caste system, which served a purpose in the past, had come to be in conflict with such equality.

> In the context of society today, the caste system and much that goes with it are wholly incompatible, reactionary, restrictive, and barriers to progress. There can be no equality in status and opportunity within its framework, nor can there be political democracy, and much less, economic democracy. Between these two conceptions conflict is inherent, and only one of them can survive.[50]

It was indeed the tendency for Hinduism and Islam to order society and give their ordering "religious" sanction.

> Thus Hinduism and Islam, quite apart from their purely religious teachings, lay down social codes and rules about marriage, inheritance, civil and criminal law, political organization, and indeed almost everything else. In other words, they lay down a complete structure for society and try to perpetuate this by giving it religious sanction and authority. Hinduism has gone farthest in this respect by its rigid system of caste.[51]

But the social order cannot be "religiously" determined. The social and economic changes which are to take place must be governed by the secular goal of equality of opportunity. Fortunately, reformers arose whose work led to "increasing secularization of the State and of many institutions — that is to say they were separated from religion."[52] A secular state requires the secularization of society and a caste-dominated society cannot be secular.

> Thus, a caste-ridden society is not properly secular. I have no desire to interfere with any person's belief, but where those beliefs become petrified in class divisions, undoubtedly they affect the social structure of the State.[53]

Secularization and Law

Article 44 of *The Constitution of India*, as part of the Directive Principles of State Policy, stated that "The State shall endeavour to secure for the citizens a uniform civil code throughout the territory of India." At the moment of Independence, Muslims and Hindus were governed by different laws regarding inheritance, marriage, divorce and other matters of personal law. Nor was Hindu law unified. In 1954, Nehru stated that he thought a unified civil code was inevitable, but that the time was not ripe to push it through in India.[54] This was in support of the "Hindu Code Bill" which had floundered as a unified bill, but was being passed in sections. Supporting the separate bills, Nehru argued from his understanding of Hindu history. In the past, he stated, Hindu society evidenced a capacity for change. Furthermore, the attempt on the part of any religion to support practices in conflict with modern trends would only weaken the credibility of the "religion." This was not an attempt by Nehru to offer religious legitimation for the Hindu Code Bill. The uniform civil code of which the Hindu Code was the first step was validated on the grounds of the secular state. That being settled, if a reminder of past Hindu flexibility could be used to get Hindus to take the first pill, that would be utilized. But the movement toward a unified civil code was based on the nature of citizenship in the secular state.

Religious Legitimation of the Secular State

With the categories which we have been using, religious legitimation of the secular state asks what ultimate values are appealed to in support for the Indian secular state. By the nature of the case, ultimate values are not defended, for such argumentation would necessarily appeal to other values which are "more" ultimate. Ultimate values are those which the thinker cannot justify by an appeal to something beyond. They are themselves the ultimate appeal. It might well be that the very values which are ultimate and hence not called to the bar of justification by a given thinker are only penultimate and hence in need of further justification for another. But that is only because ultimate values are not uniform or universally shared. What we want to know in the present instance is what ultimate values does Nehru use to give force or justification to his views of the legitimacy of the secular state for modern India?

We have found Nehru's religious goal to be a fully integrated human being, and that in his conception the secular state is the most effective means for reaching that goal. Nehru also offers some characteristics of his view which are clearly valued but never defended. These valued characteristics are that his view is *rational and scientific*, *Indian*, and *modern*. When a debate over his position actually arises, it is not an appeal to a sacred tradition, but these values which are offered to clinch the validity of his approach. They are ultimate or religious values because they are inseparable, in his view, from his ultimate or religious goal.

Not infrequently in his speeches, Nehru will settle a point by indicating that he does not see how any sensible person could possibly hold to anything else. In his speech moving the Objectives Resolution at the Constituent Assembly in 1946, he stated:

> ...We adhere to certain fundamental propositions which are laid down in this Declaration. These fundamental propositions, I submit, are not controversial in any real sense of the word. Nobody challenges them in India and *nobody ought to challenge them*, but if anyone should challenge them, well, we shall accept that challenge *and hold our position*.[55]

The reason why Nehru's fundamental position ought not to be challenged is that it is the only possible modern, scientific, and Indian approach that can be taken. Nehru does not defend modernity, he does not argue for science over superstition, and he does not buttress his appeal to it as being Indian. All of these are self–evident. No one should disagree with them, and if they do, then, "we shall accept that challenge and hold our position." These three qualities or characteristics of his position are brought together in an interview.

> But on the whole I think that Congress is infused not with anything like a Nehru ideal or any other individual approach, but what is basically and fundamentally the Indian approach, the modern approach, the scientific approach, that is, the Socialistic approach — the only possible approach in the modern world.[56]

These three qualities are interrelated. Sometimes Nehru refers to his approach as rationalistic, and the rational is frequently coupled with scientific. Nehru presents his approach as one which is opposed to dogmatism, and he thereby distinguishes his from traditional "religious" approaches. The Indian approach is not an appeal to past authority, but the assumption that in modern India with its varied "religious" traditions, the only possible Indian approach is that of the secular state.

Those who want to make "religion" the basis of statehood are less than modern. Pakistan's approach is "antediluvian."

> Pakistan, of course, thinks otherwise. She calls herself a Muslim State, that is a religious and theocratic state. And the conflict over Kashmir arises from this different approach of theirs. They insist that because Kashmir has a Muslim majority it must go to Pakistan. We cannot agree to such theory. *We consider it an absurd, obnoxious and antediluvian theory to divide people into nations on a purely religious basis.*[57]

This last statement is not an argument, but an assertion of basic values.

To introduce "religion" into politics as the Swatantra party wants to do is a "throw–back to the past."

> You may call it counter–revolution. And as you see, as usual, it covers both our domestic and foreign policy. It is, if I may say so, a *complete throw–back to the past*...*Dharma* is good so long as it does not get into conflict with a rational and scientific outlook — but don't you see that is exactly what these Swatantra gentlemen want to do![58]

If, in London, Nehru denounced South African apartheid, it was also because it was an "evil development opposed to the whole concept of modern thinking."[59] Socialist objectives were considered an important and necessary consequence of the goals of freedom and equality. Hence socialism can be argued for as a means to reach the goals of the secular state. But socialism too is modern, and is commended on that ground.

> I am not embarrassed about being a Socialist or our objectives being Socialist. That should be the ideal of every sensible nation or society or individual. Modern thinking all over the world is increasingly becoming Socialist and only people who have lost touch completely with contemporary trends can think otherwise.[60]

In 1964, Mr. R. K. Karanjia asked Mr. Nehru to what he would attribute the success of the past "golden decade" of Indian freedom? His answer was that his policies of democratic socialism and non–alignment for peace have been based on a correct ideology which reflects the "genius of our own country" and is "in step with our times."[61] But what if some future regime, following Nehru, were to get out of step, what then? Nehru held that such would not be possible in the long range for it would go against the natural evolution of history and those who seek to break this will only break themselves. His position, then, is modern (in step with the times), it is rational and scientific, and it is historically guaranteed.

> Our philosophy and ideology, as I have always maintained, are not some private fad or creations of mind. They belong to the *ethos* of our nation and people. They arise from the spirit of our times. If we accept this premise, there is no getting away from them. Any person or regime that tries to divert the course of our freedom and its natural evolution, will succeed only in injuring itself. I do not think our parliamentary democracy will permit any such reversal of our basic policies.[62]

The secular state as a political solution for modern India, then, is based on the argument that it affords the optimum freedom for people to develop into fully integrated human beings. The goal of fully integrated human beings is a modern goal, a rational and scientific goal, and an Indian goal. These ultimate values should be apparent to all, and it is because of this that they are for Nehru both ultimate and the final legitimation for the secular state.

Notes

1. Donald Eugene Smith, *India As a Secular State* (Princeton: Princeton University Press, 1963), 57.

2. *Ibid.*, 64.

3. Although social reformers, using the categories of "religion" and the "secular," call the change social, there are cogent reasons for admitting considerable religious change as well. For a discussion of this see the previous chapter.

4. Peter Berger, *The Sacred Canopy*, (Garden City: Doubleday & Company, Inc., 1967), 27.

5. *Ibid.*, 178.

6. W. Richard Comstock, *The Study of Religion and Primitive Religions* (New York: Harper & Row, 1972), 22.

7. Chapter 7 of *The Sacred Canopy* shows how this has unfolded in "Western religions."

8. Donald Eugene Smith, *Religion and Political Modernization* (New Haven and London: Yale University Press, 1974), 23.

9. *Ibid.*, 223.

10. Jawaharlal Nehru, *Toward Freedom: The Autobiography of Jawaharlal Nehru* (Boston: Beacon Press, 1958. First published in 1941), 71.

11. *Ibid.*, 71-72.

12. Berger, *loc. cit.*, 178. Also see the author's *Category Formation* where the same point is made.

13. I have discussed this definition and the method employed in this paper at greater length in *Category Formation and the History of Religions.*

From this point onward in this paper, when the term religion appears it should be understood in the sense of ultimate concern. When "religion" appears it should be understood in terms of Nehru's use of the word as referring to the institutional sacred traditions of "Hinduism," "Buddhism," "Christianity," "Islam," etc., and the traditional practices and values usually associated with traditions.

14. Jawaharlal Nehru, *The Discovery of India* (New York: The John Day Company, 1946), 14-15.

15. Nehru, *Toward Freedom*, 237.

16. *Ibid.*, 240.

17. *The Discovery of India*, 14.

18. *Toward Freedom*, 242.

19. *The Discovery of India*, 13.

20. *Toward Freedom*, 242.

21. *The Discovery of India*, 15.

22. *Ibid.*, 13.

23. *Ibid.*, 16.

24. *Ibid.*, 477.

25. *Ibid.*, 571.

26. *Ibid.*, 14.

27. *Ibid.*, 571.

28. R. K. Karanjia, *The Mind of Mr. Nehru: An Interview with R. K. Karanjia* (London: George Allen & Unwin Ltd., 1960), 34. *Emphasis* in text).

29. *Ibid.*, 56.

30. *Ibid.*, 37. *Emphasis* in text.

31. R. K. Karanjia, *The Philosophy of Mr. Nehru: As Revealed in a Series of Intimate Talks with R. K. Karanjia* (London: George Allen & Unwin Ltd., 1966), 27.

32. Jawaharlal Nehru, *Independence and After: A Collection of Speeches, 1946-1949* (New York: The John Day Company, 1950), 360.

33. *Toward Freedom*, 128.

34. *Ibid.*, 300.

35. *Independence and After*, 7-8.

36. *Ibid.*, 5.

37. *Ibid.*, 362.

38. Nehru, *Visit to America* (New York: The John Day Company, 1950), 136.

39. Karanjia, *The Mind of Mr. Nehru*, 60.

40. Quoted in Donald Eugene Smith, *Nehru and Democracy: The Political Thought of An Asian Democrat* (Calcutta: Orient Longmans Private Ltd., 1958), 154.

41. *Ibid.*, 152.

42. Karanjia, *The Philosophy of Mr. Nehru*, 128-129.

43. *Toward Freedom*, 237.

44. *Ibid.*, 292.

45. *Independence and After*, 45.

46. *Ibid.*, 48.

47. *Ibid.*, 49.

48. *The Discovery of India*, 339.

49. Karanjia, *The Mind of Mr. Nehru*, 38.

50. *The Discovery of India*, 254.

51. Nehru, *Glimpses of World History* (London: Lindsay Drummond Ltd., 1934. Using 4th edition, 1949), 736.

52. *Ibid.*

53. Quoted in Smith, *Nehru and Democracy*, 151.

54. *Ibid.*, 165.

55. *Independence and After*, 351, emphasis added.

56. Karanjia, *The Mind of Mr. Nehru*, 59.

57. Karanjia, *The Philosophy of Mr. Nehru*, 129, emphasis added.

58. Karanjia, *The Mind of Mr. Nehru*, 60. Emphasis in text.

59. *Ibid.*, 91.

60. *Ibid.*, 57.

61. Karanjia, *The Philosophy of Mr. Nehru*, 38.

62. *Ibid.*

8

"Secular State" and the Indian Constitution

Two books on the concept of the secular state and India have set the stage for much of the subsequent discussion of that topic. Donald E. Smith's *India As A Secular State* is a comprehensive treatment of the relations between religion and the state.[1] Smith's treatment is basic to most later serious discussions of the subject.[2]

Ved Prakash Luthera's *The Concept of the Secular State and India* is a less extended discussion and its influence has been less impressive.[3] However, it was available to Smith in dissertation form,[4] and Smith had discussions with Luthera prior to the publication of his volume. Furthermore, Luthera takes a position counter to Smith's. The dispute between them is not over the data. Rather, it is a difference in definition and interpretation.

Smith's position is that India intends to be a secular state. "The ideal is clearly embodied in the Constitution, and it is being implemented in substantial measure."[5] While reminding us that a "*completely* secular state does not exist,"[6] India is as secular as it is democratic. And, in spite of the ever present threat of communalism, Smith's prognostication is that "the secular state has far more than an even chance of survival in India."[7]

Smith's assessment is based on the definition that "the secular state is a state which guarantees individual and corporate freedom of religion, deals with the individual as a citizen irrespective of religion, is not constitutionally connected to a particular religion, nor does it seek either to promote or interfere with religion."[8] Luthera, stressing one aspect of Smith's definition, separation of religion and the state, holds that a secular state is "One which is separated from, unconnected with and not devoted to religion. Or, to use a terminology which is generally employed to indicate such a relationship between the state and religion, it is a state where there is a separation of the state and the church."[9] Armed with this definition and the historical data available to Smith, Luthera concludes that India "is not and cannot be a secular state."[10]

Smith disagrees with Luthera's position, arguing that Luthera "proceeds from too narrow a definition of the secular state," and that Hinduism has a greater potentiality for organizational development than Luthera's more static view allows it.[11] Luthera retorts that the three prongs to Smith's definition are all dependent on the basic principle of the separation of religion and the state. His response to Smith's second criticism is that his judgment that India is not a secular state is based on the present social circumstances even though he does see the prospects for future organization among Hindus as slight.

Both Luthera and Smith note the fact that (at the time of their writing) the term "secular state" did not appear in the Constitution. Both also mention the two unsuccessful attempts by Professor K. T. Shah to have the term included. While neither Luthera nor Smith ventures an explanation for this action on the part of the Constituent Assembly, Luthera seems to imply that it is because India does not intend to be a "secular state" in the proper sense of the term.[12] Smith, on the other hand, sees the inclusion of the proposed amendment as producing an internal conflict in the Constitution. "The inclusion of such an article in the Constitution, however laudable the intention behind it, would certainly have produced a conflict with article 25 which, as we shall see, permits extensive state intervention in matters connected with religion in the interest of social reform."[13]

If the rejection of Shah's two efforts to have India constitutionally designated as a "secular state" were deliberate rejections by the Constituent Assembly because they did not consider it their goal, then the 44th Constitution Amendment Bill, approved by the Lok Sabha on November 2, 1976, and by the Rajya Sabha on November 11, 1976, must be seen as marking a major shift in constitutional goals. If the rejection was because the concept of secularity was inconsistent with article 25 (an argument not offered by members of the Constituent Assembly), then the recent introduction of the term must mean either that the inconsistency has now been belatedly introduced, or that the concept of "secular state" has changed so that it is no longer in conflict with article 25.

It is the contention of this paper that India was uniformly designated a "secular state" by members of the Constituent Assembly, by leaders as diverse as Nehru and Radhakrishnan, and that the insertion of the term "secular" in the Preamble of the Constitution by the Constitution Amendment Bill of 1976 did not modify the Constitution as far as its secular intention was concerned. It is further maintained that the designation "secular state" functioned in a way that enabled political leaders with a variety of ultimate concerns to share in nation building without sacrificing their deepest convictions. As such, the designation "secular state" will be found to have a minimal universally affirmed content while at the same time it is used to support a wide range of differing and sometimes contradictory issues.

"Secular State" and the 1949 Constitution

First, then, we must address ourselves to the fact that the Constituent Assembly twice had the opportunity to incorporate the term "secular" in the Constitution, but declined to do so.

On November 15, 1948, Professor K. T. Shah moved to insert in clause (1) of article 1 the words "Secular, Federal, Socialist" so that the amended article would read: "India shall be a Secular, Federal, Socialist Union of States."[14] His argument for the inclusion of the term "Secular" is that it will help India to avoid the communalism and sectarianism of its past, and will eliminate the interfering element of "extraneous considerations or authority," thereby decreasing the possibilities for injustice or inequality.[15] His motion was rejected by Dr. Ambedkar, chairman of the Drafting Committee, on two grounds. FIrst, the Constitution should not fix the social and economic organization which the people should determine through their duly elected representatives. It is conceivable that in the future a form of social organization superior to socialist organization will be conceived and the people should be free at that time to adopt it if they choose and not be tied in perpetuity to a particular form because it is stipulated in the Constitution. Second, the amendment was superfluous since all of the goals of socialism have found a place in article 31 of the Draft Constitution.[16]

While Ambedkar addressed himself to the reasons for rejecting the term "socialist," K. V. Kamath argued against including the term "federal." As he saw it, the tendencies toward disintegration dictated a need for emphasis on union rather than on the rights of the parts which would be true were the term "federal" to be inserted. When the amendment was brought to a vote, it was rejected.[17]

It is less than precise, however, to state that in rejecting Shah's amendment, the Assembly was rejecting the "secular" nature of the Indian state. Although the "secular" part of the amendment was never addressed, it went down with the other aspects of Shah's amendment. And, under the procedures followed, it would have been out of order to raise it again in this context even if it were raised independently.

On December 3, 1948, Shah again sought to include the term "secular" in the Constitution, this time in the form of amendment no. 566.

> 18-A. The State in India being sector [*sic*] shall have no concern with any religion, creed or profession of faith; and shall observe an attitude of absolute

> neutrality in all matters relating to the religion of any class of its citizens or others [*sic*] persons in the Union.[18]

In his explanation of the significance of his amendment, Shah comes close to the view of the secular state held by Donald E. Smith. In the area of citizenship, equality is to prevail: "All classes of citizens should have the same treatment in matters mundane from the State."[19] As for religion and the state, Shah proposes a strict doctrine of separation: "The State of India being secular shall have no concern with any religion, creed or profession of faith" (proposed amendment). Neutrality not only means equal treatment, but complete separation. Shah sees the state as quite capable of taking over "all mundane services, all worldly activities and utilities which are for the benefit of the community collectively."[20] This would leave religious people with "the actual profession of faith and belief" in which the state should have no concern.[21] This is "by its very essence, a non–worldly activity."[22] Not to make the separation complete, but to allow the state to contribute to the support of mundane services while they are still promoted by specific religious groups, is not in the interest of the state since it would suggest that one or another group is being favored, assisted, or aided. Shah is therefore not only arguing against favoring any religious group, but also against assisting or aiding them through support for mundane services which they sponsor.

Unlike Shah's first attempt, this amendment was not discussed. It was read and then rejected. The rejection of this amendment offers no more proof that the Assembly did not see India as a "secular state" than did the rejection of the first attempt. Here a very specific definition of the "secular state" is offered, and if anything is being rejected it is that specific view. This would not be the last attempt by Shah to introduce amendments relating to religion and numerous other themes. In addition to favoring the secular state above described, he was ideologically committed to secularism.[23] He confesses before the Assembly that he himself professes no religion,[24] a fact most of them already knew. Furthermore, many subscribed to the view of S. Radhakrishnan that a "secular state" is not an irreligious state. Shah's second amendment makes no room for such a distinction. By not only pushing for the inclusion of the term "secular state" in the Constitution, but also defining it so that it could mean only one thing, Shah lessened the possibility for its inclusion.

It is difficult to ignore the personal factors brought to bear on the rejection of Shah's amendments. Anyone who has read the entire twelve volumes of the proceedings of the Constituent Assembly cannot miss the heavy influence of Dr. Ambedkar. If he accepted an amendment it generally passed. His rejection of an amendment (with or without reasons offered) spelled its death. Ambedkar had spoken against Shah's first amendment. This fact must be added to the arguments made above for its rejection.

If Ambedkar's influence hung heavily over the Constituent Assembly, Shah's presence meant defeat for numerous proposed amendments. He himself was not oblivious to this, for on one occasion he indicated his expectation that since *he* was proposing the amendment it was bound to fall.[25] While these personal factors may have been influential in the Assembly, I am offering them only as further illumination for a point that has already been adequately supported. That point is that although the Draft Constitution did not describe India as a "secular state," and although two attempts to insert the term failed, this is not sufficient reason to argue that members of the Constituent Assembly did not think of India as a "secular state."

Throughout the Assembly it was common to hear India called a "secular state." Indeed, I am aware of no instance where the term was explicitly rejected. It was accepted as a designation of the Indian state by people like Shah, who wanted complete separation of religion and the state, and by those who, like K. V. Kamath, could say: "But to my mind, a secular state is neither a Godless State nor a [*sic*] irreligious nor an anti–religious State."[26] It is important to note that when India is described as a "secular state," it is never a point that is argued. Rather, it is an assertion that is made as a preface to another point for which the speaker desires support.

Immediately following the rejection of Shah's second attempt which was the amendment exclusively depicting the nature of the secular state, speakers continued to refer to India as a "secular state" in such a way as to suggest that it was common knowledge and commonly accepted. On the same day, and within one page of the rejection of Shah's amendment, Mr. Tajamula Husain, in arguing against the propagation of religion and for its privacy, said: "I submit, Sir, that this is a secular State, and a secular state should not have anything to do with religion. So I would request you to leave me alone to practise and profess my own religion privately."[27] He also used the concept of "secular state" in support of his contention that kinds of dress that identify a religious community should be eliminated. "We are one nation. Let us have one kind of dress; one kind of name; and no visible signs. In conclusion, I say we are going to be a secular State. We should not, being a secular State, be recognized by our dress. If you have a particular kind of dress you know at once that so and so is a Hindu or a Muslim. This thing should be done away with."[28] Also, the same day, while rejecting the notion that the concept of the "secular state" implies complete separation from religion it is still assumed, in very strong language, that India *is* a "secular state." "Sir, we have declared the State to be a secular State. For obvious and for good reasons we have so declared."[29] Nor did the defeat of his amendment deter Shah himself from offering arguments based on the assumption that India is a "secular state." "The State of India, if it claims to be secular, if it claims to have an open mind, should have, in my opinion, a right not merely to regulate and restrict such practices but also absolutely to prohibit them."[30] Throughout the ensuing discussion, which was taken up on December 6, the legitimate application of the designation of "secular state" to India is commonly assumed.

"Secular State" and Nationhood

Independence from British domination did not itself guarantee nationhood. The diversity of cultures and languages, the exclusiveness of caste, and fear on the part of minorities, all threatened Indian national unity. Shah had proposed that the word "federal" be inserted into the Constitution, but it was objected that the emphasis should be on union. India required a strong center if it was to survive as a nation.

Partition created a context in which members of the Constituent Assembly made significant concessions to minorities in order to instill in them the feeling that their potentially threatened position would be replaced with complete freedom and equality. The proceedings were delayed in the early days of the Assembly as Muslims who had not joined the Assembly were urged to join in the historic event of nation building. Provision for the propagation of religion was a concession to Christian and Muslim demands, and the reservation of seats was intended as a guarantee of minority representation.

At the least, the designation "secular state" promised no preferential treatment on religious grounds. On the basis of this hope, national consolidation could be achieved. Of what use would national freedom be without a nation? The creation of an Indian nation required not only self–rule, but also a "secular state." The designation "secular state," then, had a dual function (intended or unintended). On the one hand, it was a rejection of a theocratic state either along Muslim or Hindu lines. It suggested that no religion would get preferential treatment, and that equality would be the national goal. On the other hand, the designation was multivalent in that its lack of sharply defined limits allowed various points of view to take shelter under its broad branches. It was a designation by which many Indians could commit themselves to nationhood while at the same time not reject their individual religious commitments.

I have elsewhere discussed the religious conflict inherent in the joint constitutional provisions of equality and religious freedom within the Constitution, and attempts to handle such conflict by the Supreme Court.[31] The same divergency of ultimate goals existed when the Constitution was being debated. "Secular state" was a designation whose affirmation enabled religious conflict to be held in check while a constitution was in the process of being formed. It supported a common goal (nationhood), while its multivalent nature permitted ambiguity, which enabled religious people to retain their particular meaning for it. No one spoke against the designation "secular state" in the Constituent Assembly. Having affirmed the designation people were then enabled to speak for or against each others' positions or even against the Draft Constitution, and yet maintain the minimal unity required for the construction of a constitution which is basic to nationhood.

In his argument for the possibility of an oath in the name of God, Mahavir Tyagi states what is implied in much of the other discussion surrounding the "secular state." It provides for the consolidation of the nation. "I will understand the philosophy or the logic of the State being secular. For, in every land, where there are so many religions and so many communities, one cannot give any particular colour to the State. The State must in some cases be secular, *so that the consolidation of the nation may be achieved*."[32] If the secular state requires the restriction of religion to certain spheres it too is for the sake of a strong and consolidated nation, according to K. M. Munshi. "Religion must be restricted to spheres which legitimately appertain to religion, and the rest of life must be regulated, unified, and modified in such a manner that we may evolve, as early as possible, *a strong and consolidated nation*. Our first problem and the most important problem is to produce national unity in this country."[33]

It is true that "secular state" had clearly defined limits for Nehru, Shah, or Ambedkar.[34] But from the beginning of the Constituent Assembly, it contained no more than a minimal universally affirmed meaning, while continuing to be multivalent. What then are some of the divergent positions argued for on the basis of a "secular state?"

Relevance or Irrelevance of Religion

On the one hand, the symbol was used to argue for a strict separation of religion and the state in the manner of Shah. This view of the "secular state" was the basis for Chaudhari Ranbir Singh's opposition to the reservation of seats for minorities.

> Our aim today is to set up a secular State — a non–denominational State. I cannot, therefore, see any reason why seats should be reserved for minorities or sectarian groups. I do not see any sound reason for the adoption of such a course of action. Would not its adoption defeat the realization of Ideals we have in view? Our object in establishing a secular State in this country would remain merely an unrealised dream if we decide to provide safeguards on grounds of religion.[35]

This sentiment was echoed by Shrimati Renuka Ray.[36]

In the same vein, the designation "secular state" was used to argue against a type of reverse discrimination in appointments to posts.

> If this clause is accepted, it will give rise to casteism and favouritism which should have nothing to do in a secular State. I do not mean that necessary facilities and concessions should not be given to backward classes for improving their educational qualifications and raise general level of their uplift. But, Sir, appointments to posts should be only left to the discretion of the Public Service Commission, to be made on merit and qualification, and no concession whatever should be allowed to any class on the plea that the same happens to be backward.[37]

On the other hand, the designation "secular state" was used to affirm the relevance of religion. A recurring theme surrounding "secular state" is that the designation ought not to be considered the equivalent of irreligious. Hussain Imam, a Muslim from Bihar, made the distinction between non–religious and irreligious! "Secular State does not mean that it is anti–religious State. It means that it is not irreligious but non–religious and as such there is a world of difference between irreligious and non–religious."[38] H. Kamath moved that a new subclause be added to the Constitution: "The State shall not establish, endow or patronize any particular religion. Nothing shall however prevent the State from imparting spiritual training or instruction to the citizens of the Union."[39] Although the amendment was not accepted by the Assembly, it is important to note that Kamath accepts the secularity of the State while rejecting with equal force the implication that the state is anti–religious. "But to my mind a secular state is neither a Godless State nor a [*sic*] irreligious nor an anti–religious State."[40]

For Kamath, the real meaning of the term "religion" is *dharma*, which in its widest meaning is taken to be "the true values of religion or of the spirit."[41] He agrees with Radhakrishnan's assessment of the spiritual malaise of the world and of India's mission of bringing spirituality to the world. Moreover, it is imperative that India preserve for herself the imparting of spiritual instruction to its citizens since only the inculcation of such values will create an Indian unity. Kamath is arguing for the imparting of spiritual values and basic religion to Indians. He sees this as compatible with the designation "secular state." "When I say, Sir, that the State shall not establish or endow or patronise any particular religion, I mean the formal religions of the world; I do not mean religion in the widest and in the deepest sense, and that meaning of religion as the highest value of the spirit."[42]

M. Ananthasayanam Ayyangar also finds it necessary to make it clear that just because the state is "secular" does not mean that its citizens have nothing to do with religion. "We are pleased to make the State a secular one. I do not, by the word 'secular,' mean that we do not believe in any religion, and that we have nothing to do with it in our day–to–day life. It only means that the State or the Government cannot aid one religion or give preference to one religion against another. Therefore it is obliged to be absolutely secular in character, not that it has lost faith in all religion."[43] Ayyangar is confident that members of the Assembly are all believers in one religion or another, and he only regrets that it has not been possible to evolve a "universal religion" that might be taught to all Indians. "We all believe in the existence of one God, in prayer, in meditation and so on."[44] Lacking an agreed upon "universal religion," it is regrettable that the state will not be able to offer religious instruction to its children. R. K. Sidwa makes it clear that for him "a secular State does not mean that an individual cannot believe in God."[45]

K. M. Munshi, too, recognizes that the designation "secular state" does not mean that the citizens of that state will be irreligious, but also suggests that the state itself can take some account of the religion of its citizens without ceasing to be "secular." Munshi was even of the opinion that to have the name of God in the Preamble to the Constitution would not threaten the "secular" character of the state to which it referred. "A secular state is not a Godless State. It is not a state which is pledged to eradicate or ignore religion. It is not a State which refuses to take notice of religious belief in this country."[46] "We must take cognizance of the fact that India is a religious–minded country.

Even while we are talking of a secular State, our mode of thought and life is largely coloured by a religious attitude to life."[47] These statements were echoed by Rev. Jerome D'Souza.[48]

Mahavir Tyagi is as committed to a "secular state" as he is to "Ram Raj." Since it was announced that India was to be a "secular state," all sorts of misunderstandings entered the picture, and it was thought by some that the government intended to banish God completely. When All India Radio officials concluded that they should ban the recitation of the *Gītā, Rāmāyana, Qur'ān* and *Bible* from broadcast on A.I.R., this was stretching the meaning of "secular state" too far. "We worship God and our faith must be recorded. India believes in God and therefore the Indian State must remain a State of God. It must be a godly State and not a godless State. *This is our meaning of secularity.*"[49]

It must be recognized that some of the concern to disavow the irreligious significance of "secular state" might have been intended to temper the fears of those who saw the designation as actively anti–religious. On the other hand, some of the statements disavowing the non–religious nature of "secular state" appear to be sincere efforts to explain that since all Indians are religious, and since there is a basic commonality, if broadly sought, a truly "secular state," while not embodying one of the organized religions, will embody the spiritual or religious ideals of the Indian people. The argument goes so far as to suggest that only in that way will the "secular state" realize its objective of a unified nation.

To argue that such speakers lack precision as to what the implications of the "secular state" are merely reinforces the point of this paper — beyond the minimal content of a non–theocratic, non–communal state embodying equality for all, the designation did lack a universally accepted content. It was that very multivalence that enabled persons with a variety of religious goals to use it as a banner under which they could endeavor to build a nation together.

For and Against Religious Education

The ambiguity of the designation "secular state" made it possible for the designation to be used both in support of and rejection of religious instruction in institutions supported by the state.

Mohamed Ismail Sahib, a Muslim from Madras, argues that it is not necessary for a "secular state" to ban religious education in state institutions. It would be contrary to the "secular state" to compel students to study a religion to which they do not belong. "But, if the pupils or their parents want that religious instruction should be given in the institutions in their own religion, then, it is not going against the secular nature of the State and the State will not be violating the neutrality which it has avowedly taken in the matter of religion."[50]

Tajamul Husain, however, argued against religious instruction in schools wholly maintained out of state funds on the grounds that it was contrary to the designation "secular state." Without offering an extended discussion of the characteristics of "secular state," he argued: "What is the use of calling India a secular State if you allow religious instruction to be imparted to young boys and girls?"[51]

Those favoring inclusion or exclusion of religious instruction in state institutions did not fall along communal lines, and the discussion included a wide range of persons. In response to the discussion, Ambedkar indicated that there were three different points of view expressed. Ismail's view was that "there ought to be no bar for religious instruction being given. The only limitation which he advocates is that nobody should be compelled to attend them."[52] The second view, argued by Tajamul Husain and others, was that "there ought to be no religious instruction at all, not even in institutions which are educational."[53] The third view, that of K. T. Shah, is "that not only no religious instruction should be permitted in institutions which are wholly maintained out of State funds, but no religious instruction should be permitted even in educational institutions which are partly maintained out of State funds."[54] All three views are presented as a necessary, or at least a possible, inference from the designation of India as a "secular state." None of the advocates argued that India was not to be a "secular state." No one argued that India *was* to be a "secular state" either, as though it were a matter for debate. All seem to have assumed that that was the intention — there resides the unity. But by filling that designation with a meaning that was amenable to their views it was possible to engage in nation building while at the same time they were able to dispute the character of the nation they had agreed to build.

For and Against the Propagation of Religion

The multivalent nature of the designation "secular state" made it useful in support of and in opposition to the propagation of religion. Tajamul Husain agreed that people should have the right freely to profess and practice religion. But, in his view, religion is a "private affair between oneself and his Creator. It has nothing to do with others."[55] Since, then, religion is a personal matter between a person and the Creator, and since each will achieve salvation according to his or her own religion, there is no point to the propagation of religion. Each person should profess religion and practice it at home. Moreover, his aversion to the propagation of religion is connected to the fact that India is a "secular state." "I submit, Sir, that this is a secular State, and a secular State should not have anything to do with religion. So I would request you to leave me alone, to practise and profess my religion privately."[56]

Lokanath Misra does not feel that propagation of religion should be ruled out, but that putting it down as a fundamental right will encourage it — a thing that should not be done. He is concerned that propagation will enable some religions to swell their numbers at the expense of "Hinduism," and thus pave the way for the annihilation of the Hindu culture and way of life.[57] Moreover, it was the propagation of religion that led India to its present unfortunate state (i.e., partition), and if Muslims who introduced propagation had never come, India would have been a perfectly "secular state" and a Hindu one at that.

> Sir, we have declared the State to be a Secular State. For obvious and for good reasons we have so declared. Does it not mean that we have nothing to do with any religion? You know that propagation of religion brought India into this unfortunate state and India had to be divided into Pakistan and India. If Islam had not come to impose its will on this land, India would have been a perfectly secular State and a homogeneous state. There would have been no question of Partition. Therefore, we have rightly tabooed religion. And now to say that as a fundamental right everyone has a right to propagate his religion is not right. Do we want to say that we want one religion other than Hinduism and the religion has not yet taken sufficient root in the soil of India and do we taboo all religion? Why do you make it a Secular State? The reason may be that religion is not necessary, but as India has many religions, Hinduism, Christianity, Islam and Sikhism, we cannot decide which one to accept. Therefore let us

> have no religions. No. That cannot be. If you accept religion, you must accept Hinduism as it is practised by an overwhelming majority of the people of India.[58]

If Husain and Misra argue that because India intends to be a "secular state," the propagation of religion should be outlawed, there were others who argued that "secular state" permitted propagation. Pandit Lakshmi Kanta Maitra rejects the view that "secular state" and propagation of religion are in conflict. He sees the essence of the "secular state" in the principle that there is to be no discrimination or preferential treatment on the basis of religion. But there is nothing wrong with guaranteeing the freedom of propagation.

> Even in a secular State I believe there is necessity for religion. We are passing through an era of absolute irreligion. Why is there so much vice and corruption in every stratum of society. Because we have forgotten the sense of values in things which our forefathers had inculcated. We do not at all care in these days, for all these glorious traditions of ours with the result that everybody now acts in his own way, and justice, fairness, good sense and honesty have all gone to the wilderness. If we are to restore our sense of values which we have held dear, it is of the utmost importance that we should be able to propagate what we honestly feel and believe in. Propagation does not necessarily mean seeking converts by force of arms, by the sword, or by coercion. But why should obstacles stand in way if by exposition, illustration and persuasion you could convey your own religious faith to others? I do not see any harm in it.[59]

L. Krishnaswami Bharati presses the "Hindu" doctrine of tolerance into an argument for propagation.[60] One must remember that all religions, if properly understood, are one and the same. There is only one God even though he is known under different names. And furthermore, "It is not at all inconsistent with the secular nature of the State."[61]

K. M. Munshi argues that whatever political advantage the Christian community might have had under the British was only true of the old regime. Under the "secular state" propagation will never offer any advantage to one community over another, nor in a "secular state" will there be any political advantage to a religious community by increasing its numerical population.

"In the present set–up that we are now creating under this Constitution, this is a secular State. There is no particular advantage to a member of one community over another, nor is there any political advantage by increasing one's fold. In those circumstances, the word 'propagate' cannot possibly have dangerous implications, which some of the members think that it has."[62] It is not remarkable that there should be disagreement over the desirability of making propagation of religion a fundamental right.[63] However, both sides are in effect claiming that since India is a "secular state" it should outlaw or provide for the propagation of religion. Again, "secular state" is a designation on which both sides agree while they continue to argue the merits of an issue on which they differ. "Secular state" provides the minimal meaning under which they can engage in nation building even though their points of view on a variety of issues are at odds.

For and Against a Uniform Civil Code

The multivalent "secular state" also becomes a basis for arguing for or against a uniform civil code. The Constitution provided in its "Directive Principles of State Policy" for the eventual formation of a uniform civil code for all its citizens. Although this was not to be pushed through rapidly because of strong Muslim opposition and restlessness on the part of Hindus as well, Nehru and others held that a "secular state" which treated all citizens with equality should eventually issue in a uniform civil code. But if this was seen as an implication of the "secular state," the reverse argument was also used. Mahboob Ali Baig Sahib Bahadur argued that in the "secular state" communities should have the freedom to practice their own religion which would mean that Muslim personal law should not be violated.

> Now, Sir, people seem to have very strange ideas about secular State. People seem to think that under a secular State, there must be a common law observed by its citizens in all matters, including matters of their daily life, their language, their culture, their personal laws. That is not the correct way to look at this secular State. In a secular State, citizens belonging to different communities must have the freedom to practise their own religion, observe their own life and their personal laws should be applied to them.[64]

The designation "secular state" was also used as an argument against prohibition,[65] as a reason for uniformity of dress among all citizens,[66] and as a basis for arguing that all property, including temples and churches, should be taxed.[67] It was important for arguments for taking oaths in the name of God,[68] against the necessity of taking such oaths,[69] and against providing for both possibilities to accommodate persons who favored such an oath and those who did not.[70]

The range of uses for the designation is remarkable. That such a range of ideas existed or that such differences would be discussed is hardly surprising. But that the designation "secular state" had sufficient plasticity to accommodate such a wide range of contentions while never being raised as a point of contention itself, is important. It reinforces the contention of this paper that it was not a term with sharply defined limits, but a multivalent designation under which discussion leading to nation building could take place.

"Secular State" and the 44th Amendment Bill

If it is the case that members of the Constituent Assembly considered India a "secular state" even though they saw fit not to include the designation in the Constitution, what is to be made of the inclusion of this designation in 1976 as part of the 44th Amendment Bill?

At the time that this Bill was being considered, India had been under a "state of emergency" for approximately a year and four months. While under the emergency, a scheduled election had been passed, and the existing Parliament had extended its term to a fifth year. One opposition member humorously objected to being called M. P. (Member of Parliament) and suggested M. P. P. (Member of Permanent Parliament). Others argued that the 44th Amendment Bill was so extensive that it required a new Constituent Assembly. The majority replied that extension under the emergency was indeed constitutional, that Parliament had acted on other matters during the emergency without a challenge of competency, that the competence of Parliament to amend the Constitution was constitutionally guaranteed and had been exercised forty–three times before.

The opposition contended that under the emergency free discussion had not been permitted. Dr. V. K. R. Varadaraja Rao contended that

> in the prevailing atmosphere of oppression and fear due to this emergency no free and open public debate could be possible. Opposition party leaders and other

> leaders of public opinion were mostly in jail. As my friend, Shri Sezhiyan pointed out in his speech on this Bill, meetings to discuss the Bill by Opposition leaders were until ten days back completely banned and the press was effectively gagged. The complete denial of rights of the freedom of speech and association and other fundamental freedoms, the erosion of judicial processes and the blackout of opposition viewpoints in the press, have made it impossible for the people to know, discuss and understand the drastic constitutional changes proposed in the draconian Constitution Amendment Bill.[71]

To this the majority responded that now in Parliament free discussion was possible, and the opposition had boycotted that discussion instead of participating.

Other provisions in the amendment made the Supreme Court incompetent to judge the constitutionality of constitutional amendments, required questions regarding state laws to be adjudicated before High Courts, and central laws to be challenged only before the Supreme Court. A growing resentment on the part of Parliament was increased substantially by the Golaknath case, for Parliament felt that its power had been usurped by the courts.[72] Certain attempts to implement the "Directive Principles of State Policy" were held to be in conflict with the section on "Fundamental Rights." Parliament sought in the 44th Amendment Bill to secure its supremacy. To assure the constitutionality of programs intended to implement the "Directive Principles" this amendment provided that the "Directive Principles" should take precedence over the "Fundamental Rights."

In addition to these more substantive issues, the amendment also provided for the inclusion of two words in the Preamble: "secular" and "socialist."

Whatever objections were made to this part of the amendment were strictly procedural. It was argued that the Preamble could not be amended since it was dated and not technically a part of the Constitution. Although P. G. Mavalankar's rejection of the Bill was total and strong, even he did not reject the term "secular" on any other than technical grounds.

> But I want to ask you: can we change the preamble which was passed on 26 November 1949 and that was specifically mentioned in the Preamble which says: "We the people of India etc." The Preamble is a part of the Constitution, not strictly; though undoubtedly it is the key of the Constitution, as the hon. Law Minister

> rightly said. Therefore, if you put words today "socialist" and "secular," in the preamble, I am afraid a time will come when some people might say: remove the word "democracy." Already the substance has gone; the word may also go next time.73

Moreover, on various occasions when the discussion moved toward the terms "secular" and "socialist" the speakers would confine their remarks to the term "socialist." It is clear that the latter term generated much more interest than the former even though it was occasionally said that the two go together and that if the country were to move toward socialism it would also have to be "secular."

Throughout the entire discussion no one opposed the inclusion of the term "secular" or objected in any way to India being designated as a "secular state." No one argued that the inclusion of the term "secular" suggested new departure. On the contrary, it was common to hear the sentiment of C. M. Stephen. "At the time when the Constitution was framed, the words were not used, but these elements were there in the Constitution."74 Parliament merely explicated what had always been intended. Many speeches held a view similar to that expressed by K. Manoharan.

> Regarding the minority rights, regarding the religious sections, there is no discrimination whatsoever. Our concept towards that particular direction is secularism. *The people knew it very well right from the beginning, after the liberation of the country, after the Independence of the country, that we are for a secular State, not a theocratic State.* The people knew about it. The people know about it. But still the fathers of the constitutional amendments, including Shri Swaran Singh, thought it fit that a particular word must find a place in it. I am happy about it.75

The use of the designation "secular state" in nation building is as apparent here as it was in the Constituent Assembly. Considerable support was found for the "state of emergency." The threat to national unity and the potentially debilitating effect of excessive strikes on the part of labor unions had become an issue. That this was a time when the majority was a threat to national unity and hence national existence is clear from the fact that an article was included which outlawed "anti–national activity." As explained by K. Manoharan, "This Article says that anti–national activity in relation to an individual or

Association means any action taken by such individual or Association which is intended to threaten or disrupt the harmony between different religious, racial, language or regional groups or castes or communities."[76] The corollary to this is that as the concept of secularism is strengthened, so is national unity. In the words of Swaran Singh,

> It will be found that in the clause where the concept of duty is spelt out, there are elements of both these concepts of secularism and of integrity in the list of duties apart from other things. Then again in the new clause that is proposed to be added where anti–national activities are defined both these concepts have been mentioned and the intention is to see that the concept of secularism is strengthened and the country remains united.[77]

Part of the concern at this juncture in nation building was socio–economic justice. "Secularism" in conjunction with socialism will contribute to this goal. "I would like to say that the addition of the words 'secular' and 'socialism' in the Preamble of our Constitution are very significant as they clearly indicate the direction in which the nation is to move in order to achieve socio–economic justice in our society."[78] These references support the notion that the term is important in maintaining national unity and in nation building, with special reference to socio–economic justice.

The usefulness of the designation "secular state" in the Constituent Assembly was seen to be due to its possessing a minimal universally accepted meaning coupled with a multivalent nature. This continues to be true in the Parliamentary discussion of 1976. The minimally affirmed content continues to be a state that is non–theocratic, non–communal, granting equality to all. First, India is not a theocratic state, but a state which prohibits establishment and enjoins equality of treatment to all persons of all religions or of no religion. "It is very welcome also that the word 'secular' is being introduced. We want to understand what is the significance behind this. Because our State is a secular State, our State respects and recognizes, and gives equal rights to people belonging to all religions or faiths or to people of no religion, in law."[79]

Furthermore, "secular state" is a guarantee against communalism of the sort proposed by the Jan Sangh party. "Jan Sangh is going about with a sectarian point of view and a divisive philosophy. Therefore, it is necessary that the Preamble reminds the nation that the nation has been committed to secularism and there can be no going away from secularism.[80] Seeking to return to a Hindu state, Jan Sangh would threaten the nation in which persons of all religions or none would be equal before the law. This, then, is the minimal content of secularity which enables Indians to engage in building a nation. It is non–theocratic and non–communal, guaranteeing equality to all before the law.

Although there was a minimally affirmed meaning for the designation "secular state," it continued also as a multivalent symbol. The extent of meaning was more limited than it was in the Constituent Assembly Debates. To some extent this was due to the fact that the main thrust of this amendment was in other directions. Moreover, if the designation functioned as a device for use in nation building so that those engaged in the building will have a basic agreement while they continue to differ on specifics, the meaning of "secular state" for India is whatever the state happens to be a given point in her history.[81] Since some twenty–five years have elapsed since the original Constitution was framed, some content has been filled in. That will place certain restrictions on its elasticity.[82] On the other hand, certain issues seem to be more pressing at this juncture, and they find their way into the discussion and are supported by suggesting that they are a necessary implication of secularity.

We have seen that the "secular state" does not envisage the establishment of any religion as proposed by Jan Sangh. Although the majority knows this, there are still those who are committed to their "Hindu" view of life and its superiority over all other views. For them it is comforting to know that the concept of the "secular state" finds its source in the ancient "Hindu" past as well as in the "Hindu" present. Jagannath Rao says:

> Our spiritual philosophy is contained in articles 25 to 30, universal love and universal brotherhood; those articles deal with secularism. We have been a secular country; our ancient philosophy contained in Vedas and Upanishads speak of universal love and universal brotherhood. Service of man is service of God — that is our philosophy. Only subsequently, the priestly class came into prominence and the Hindu society came down from the high pedestal with the introduction of the caste system. Our original philosophy was expounded by Swami Vivekananda in 1893 in the World Parliament of Religions in Chicago.[83]

It was even argued that secularism was the exclusive possession of "Hinduism" because it alone was tolerant while other religions sought converts through force and coercion.[84]

It is to be noticed that in the above reference it was argued that caste was introduced into Hindu society late and was not part of the pristine purity of the religion. Hence it was not to be included in the argument for the "secular state." Indeed, R. K. Khadikar argued that in a "secular state" there is little room for caste. He urged the sponsors of the amendment to sharpen the limits of secularism in such a way as to make it clear whether secularism and caste are compatible. "Do you say that secularism includes caste abolition or not? I want a clear answer."[85] Although he wanted a clear answer, none was forthcoming. This part of the content of the designation would have to await the determinations of legislative history.

The "secular state" has been seen as a protection for the rights of minorities. In the original Constitution the secularity of the Indian state was a way of guaranteeing non–Hindus that the majority religious community would not force its religion and culture upon them. It has continued, in the discussion of the amendment, to be associated with the minority issue. "I take it that what we want to assure the people of all faiths and communities and religions particularly the minorities is that on our part we mean to take some further action, legislative and others, to strengthen and secularize the content of our democracy."[86]

However, in the elevation of the "Directive Principles" above the "Fundamental Rights," the Muslim community saw the potential for the elimination of Muslim personal laws. From the beginning, one of the Directive Principles was: "The State shall endeavour to secure for the citizens a uniform civil code throughout the territory of India" (article 44). It was seen that now the way was open to contend that the articles regarding religious freedom must be subordinate to the concern for a uniform civil code. But the interesting point for our purposes is that the concept of "secular state" was used, on the one hand, to argue that the rights of Muslims to maintain their system of personal laws should be guaranteed. On the other hand, it was used to maintain that there should be uniformity before the law and that religious affiliation should be irrelevant in the "secular state."

The former position was clearly articulated by Ebrahim Sulaiman Sait. He welcomed the inclusion of the designation "secular" in the Preamble, but held that from this should emerge a greater concern for the rights of minorities. He quoted Indira Gandhi as saying, "The Indian version of secularism was based on respect to all religions and not opposition to any religion."[87] But Muslims are a backward community and have not been afforded equal opportunities. Muslims have been voicing their concern over article 44 ever since it was included in the original Constitution. Since the president, prime minister and law minister had all re–assured the Muslim community that their Personal Law would not be violated, Sait wanted a radical revision of the Directive Principles. Now that they are to take precedence over the Fundamental Rights, only this would protect the religion of the Muslim minority.[88] He concluded:

> I still hold and maintain that once the precedence is given to the Directive Principles over the Fundamental Rights, the minorities rights definitely become weak and get eroded.
>
> We are now going to declare our country as secular, socialist and democratic. I feel very strongly that in case we are in a position to carry on as per our personal laws and keep our identity, neither the secular character, nor the socialist character nor the democratic character of our country gets affected in any manner.[89]

It was clearly the view of others that a "secular state" ultimately meant a uniform civil code and that hopefully Muslim sentiment would evolve in that direction. In the words of K. Narayana Rao:

> On a point of clarification. I fully appreciate the sentiments, the fears and apprehensions expressed by the hon. Member. The complete deletion of this article is not called for in the sense that even today there are some liberal Muslims in India who are for the codification of personal law. Even in some foreign Muslim countries, they have changed the personal law. In future, probably the consent of majority of Muslims may be forthcoming. In such a case the complete deletion of this article will fore–close that possibility.[90]

Sait's response is unbending: "I want to make it clear that as far as this is concerned, the Muslims unanimously do not want a change in personal law. This has been made clear during the Muslim Personal Law Board Convention. As regards the foreign countries, we are not guided by the foreign countries.

We are guided by our Holy Book Koran and Suna. Therefore, the question does not arise at all."[91]

In addition to these rather weighty considerations, there were those who saw the "secular state" as requiring the removal of "superstition and blind faith,"[92] as justifying all manner of dress,[93] and as providing for the possibility of a "secular prayer." Holding to a spiritual basis for the state, and believing that the prosperity of the state is dependent upon prayer, S. N. Misra proposed a "secular prayer" that could be used in educational institutions and all public places: "Oh, you the creator, in whom I have faith. Give me the strength to do the right and throw out the wrong and serve the country and the people."[94] That even prayer is an implication of the "secular state" indicates how far some were willing to stretch the designation in support of their concerns. But here is the one place where an exchange takes place to correct the effort to stretch the designation that far.

> SHRI S.A. SHAMIM: How does it affect non–believers?
> SHRI S.N. MISRA: I have not come across even a single individual who has not recognized the existence of God. You take it from me that everybody has recognized the existence of God before death.
> SHRI S.A. SHAMIM: I do not believe in God.
> SHRI S.N. MISRA: You are not dying yet.
> SHRI S.A. SHAMIM: After your speech I will.[95]

While there were several calls issued for the greater clarification of the concept "secular," none of them was answered. H. R. Gokhale captured what I am proposing when he said: "But I would like to say that in a country like ours where we have to go step by step further ahead, we cannot say that anything done is the last word."[96]

"Secular state" continues to be a designation with minimal meaning under which nation building can proceed. But its multivalent nature also continues. If its scope has been somewhat lessened, it may be because the strong majority in Parliament in 1976 had less need for the symbol or that other symbols such as socialism were given more weight. Nevertheless, the use of the designation found in the Constituent Assembly has not been lost. Whatever clarity comes to the concept of the Indian "secular state" will await subsequent legislative history.

Notes

1. Donald E. Smith, *India As a Secular State* (Princeton: Princeton University Press, 1963).

2. It has also been the occasion for two extensive reviews and a rejoinder by Smith. Mark Galanter, "Secularism, East and West," *Comparative Studies in Society and History* 7, no. 2 (January 1965: 133-59); John T. Flint, "India as a Secularizing State," ibid., 160-65; Donald E. Smith, "Secularism in India: A Rejoinder," Ibid., 166-72.

3. Ved Prakash Luthera, *The Concept of the Secular State and India* (Calcutta: Oxford University Press, 1965).

4. Ved Prakash Luthera, "The Concept of the Secular State and India," (Ph.D. diss., University of Delhi, 1958).

5. Smith, *India As a Secular State*, 500.

6. *Ibid.*, 499.

7. *Ibid.*, 501.

8. *Ibid.*, 4.

9. Luthera, *The Concept of the Secular State and India*, 15.

10. *Ibid.*, viii.

11. Smith, *India As a Secular State*, 110, footnote. Since "Hinduism" does not have any organizational structure which could effect reform or desirable change, it has become necessary in India for the state to step into the void.

12. In the context of discussing the rejection of Shah's proposed amendments, he points out that the term does not appear in the "Objectives Resolution" moved in the Constituent Assembly nor in the speech of the prime minister. Luthera, *The Concept of the Secular State and India*, 62-63.

13. Smith, *India As a Secular State*, 101. That such conflicts exist anyway are seen in subsequent attempts by the courts to deal with cases of religious freedom. See the author's "Religion and the Secular: Categories for Religious Conflict and Religious Change in Independent India," in *Religion and Social Conflict in South Asia*, ed. Bardwell L. Smith (Leiden: E. J. Brill, 1976).

14. *Constituent Assembly Debates*, VII, 299. (Hereafter cited as CAD).

15. *CAD*, 7: 400.

16. *CAD*, 7: 402. Article 31 reads as follows:
"The State Shall, in particular, direct its policy toward securing —
(i) that the citizens, men and women equally, have the right to an adequate means of livelihood;
(ii) that the ownership and control of the material resources of the community are so distributed as best to subserve the common good;
(iii) that the operation of the economic system does not result in the concentration of wealth and means of production to the common detriment;
(iv) that there is equal pay for equal work for both men and women.

17. *CAD*, 7: 403.

18. *Ibid.*, 815.

19. *Ibid.*, 816.

20. *Ibid.*

21. *Ibid.*

22. *Ibid.*

23. By secular*ism* is intended a world view which excludes religion and limits itself to the material world. The secular state envisaged by Nehru, for example, made religion irrelevant to social and economic policy, but did not require an ideological commitment which excluded it.

24. *CAD*, 7: 821.

25. *Ibid.*, 827, 1156.

26. *Ibid.*, 825.

27. *Ibid.*, 818.

28. *Ibid.*, 819.

29. *Ibid.*, 822.

30. *Ibid.*, 827.

31. See Robert D. Baird, "Religion and the Secular: Categories for Religious Conflict and Religious Change in Independent India." Also Chapter XI of this volume.

32. *CAD*, 7: 1050.

33. *Ibid.*, 548.

34. See Robert D. Baird, "Religion and the Legitimation of Nehru's Concept of the Secular State," *Religion and the Legitimation of Power in South Asia*, ed. Bardwell Smith (Leiden: E. J. Brill, 1978). Also Chapter XII of this volume.

35. *CAD*, 7: 289.

36. *Ibid.*, 356.

37. *Ibid.*, 679.

38. *Ibid.*, 546.

39. *Ibid.*, 824.

40. *Ibid.*, 825.

41. *Ibid.*

42. *Ibid.*, 826.

43. *Ibid.*, 881-82.

44. *Ibid.*, 882.

45. *Ibid.*, 1054.

46. *Ibid.*, 1057.

47. *Ibid.*

48. *Ibid.*, 1059.

49. *Ibid* , 1051 (emphasis mine)

50. *Ibid.*, 867.

51. *Ibid.*, 871.

52. *Ibid.*, 883.

53. *Ibid.*

54. *Ibid.*

55. *Ibid.*, 817-18.

56. *Ibid.*, 818.

57. *Ibid.*, 824.

58. *Ibid.*, 822.

59. *Ibid.*, 833.

60. The doctrine of "Hindu" toleration has also been used to argue against propagation. See Smith, *India As a Secular State*, 163 ff.

61. *CAD*, 7: 834.

62. *Ibid.*, 837.

63. This is discussed in Smith, *India As a Secular State*, chapter 6.

64. *CAD*, 7: 544.

65. *Ibid.*, 559-60.

66. *Ibid.*, 819.

67. *Ibid.*, 865.

68. *Ibid.*, 1050.

69. *Ibid.*, 1051.

70. *Ibid.*, 1052.

71. *Debates Before Lok Sabha*, Fifth Series, 65, no. 3, 36-37.

72. In *Golaknath* v. *State of Punjab* (A I. R. 67 SC 1643) it was held that "*Parliament had* no power under Art. 368 to make any law taking away or abridging any of the fundamental rights under Part III," Krishna Prasad De, *Religious Freedom Under the Constitution* (South Asia Books, 1977), 5. The 24th Amendment Act of 1971 was passed to counter this decision, but as long as the Golaknath case stood, it questioned the validity of this and similar amendments. A special bench of 13 judges (A. I. R. 1973 SC 1461) unanimously upheld the constitutionality of the 24th Amendment Act of 1971, but reiterated that Art. 368 did not allow Parliament to alter the basic structure or framework of the Constitution.

73. *Debates Before Lok Sabha*, Fifth Series, 65, no. 3, 98-99.

74. *Ibid.*, no. 2, 72.

75. *Ibid.*, no. 2, 48.

76. *Ibid.*, 50.

77. *Ibid.*, 23-24.

78. *Ibid.*, no. 3, 282.

79. *Ibid.*, no. 1, 78.

80. *Ibid.*, no. 2, 73.

81. Note also the criticism of the opposite approach by J. D. M. Derrett, "Far too readily it is assumed that India, having adopted the word 'secular' for its present condition, ought to study what 'secular' means or ought to mean and then put that into practice!" *Religion, Law and the State in India* (London: Faber and Faber, 1968), 31.

82. It is of little use, for example, regarding religious education in schools since that has largely been settled.

83. *Debates Before Lok Sabha*, Fifth Series, 65, no. 1, 161.

84. *Ibid.*, no. 3, 173.

85. *Ibid.*, 44.

86. *Ibid.*, no. 1, 78-79.

87. *Ibid.*, no. 2, 152.

88. *Ibid.*, no. 2, 157-58.

89. *Ibid.*, no. 4, 77-78.

90. *Ibid.*, no. 2, 158.

91. *Ibid.*

92. *Ibid.*, no. 8, 77.

93. *Ibid.*, 113.

94. *Ibid.*, no. 2, 171.

95. *Ibid.*

96. *Ibid.*, no. 4, 31.

9

Uniform Civil Code and the Secularization of Law

If religion is defined as what is of ultimate concern to persons or groups, this definition can be used to analyze the ultimate goals of states.[1] These ultimate goals and values to which a modern state is committed are usually set forth in a constitution. In this context, *The Constitution of India*, embodies a non–transcendent religious goal. It intends to implant on the Indian subcontinent a society that is characterized by justice, equality, liberty, and fraternity. Since justice is to be implemented within the present lifespan of citizens, without reference to *karma* and rebirth, it is a this–worldly goal.

In the area of legislation, the values of justice and equality are to be dominant. The preamble to the Constitution resolves to secure for all citizens of India "JUSTICE, social, economic and political" and "EQUALITY of status and opportunity." This linkage of justice with equality has resulted in legislation that intends to provide equal opportunities for all citizens regardless of religion, caste or sex. Before the law, the *śudra* is equal to the *brahmin*, and women are equal to men. This set of values is in opposition to traditional "family law," whether one is considering the dominant "Hindu" community or the minority "Muslim" community.[2]

Although in the Constituent Assembly debates and in parliamentary debates, "secular state" was a symbol with a wide range of meanings, it would be inappropriate to suggest that it is equally ambiguous within the text of the Constitution. The Constitution distinguishes between "religion," which all persons are free to "profess, practice and propagate" subject to "public order, morality and health," and the "secular," which includes economic and political activities which are sometimes associated with "religion" and which can be regulated by the state. Legislation providing for social welfare and reform is also within the proper jurisdiction of the state even though it impinges upon what has traditionally been considered religious. And, although denominations have the right to acquire property, that property must be administered according to the laws of the state.[3]

Articles 25 and 26, then, secularize social reform, economics, and politics, which were traditionally inseparable from religion. In effect, this reduced the sphere of "religion" so that its relevance in these other spheres was erased. Article 44 further assumes that the sphere of "religion" is to be distinguished from the sphere of law.[4] For, if in civil matters Hindus, Muslims, Parsis, Christians, and Jews were previously governed by differing religious laws, to have a common civil code would be to cancel differences previously given a religious valuation.[5]

This distinction between "religion" and the "secular" is a new "Great Tradition." It is enshrined in the Constitution, has been embodied in legislation, and is clarified and protected in the courts.[6] Since independence there has been frequent opposition to it, but to little avail. This new "Great Tradition" has moved on, broadening its scope, and it would appear that it will continue to do so as long as India continues under its present constitutional system. Where conflict emerges over the new "Great Tradition" we are witnesses to religious conflict — religious because it is a conflict over the ultimate way one perceives the world. It is a conflict between those who see the world as sacred, who see a sacredness to all life, including the economic, political, social, and legal dimensions, and those who, for whatever reasons, seek to distinguish between "religion," and the "secular" realms of the economy, society, politics, and law. That the conflict over the new "Great Tradition" is a basic one is reinforced by the fact that it cuts across denominational lines to include both "Hindus" and "Muslims." If there appears to be little on which these two groups could agree, here at the root of the religious matter we find a point of contact.

The purpose of this paper is to show that article 44 is an occasion for religious conflict and religious change, and to describe that conflict in terms of the movement of the new "Great Tradition" toward the secularization of law. Article 44 is based on the assumption that the Indian secular state requires the secularization of law — that civil law should be the same for all Indians in order that nation building can continue and that all persons can be welded together equally into a modern Indian state. This requires that traditional religious expressions become modified so that they are more and more a matter of personal faith, and that the state mold a modern civil code based on justice and equality. As such, traditional religious values have to be understood anew. L. M. Singhvi states this clearly: "In my view, the evolution and emergence of a uniform civil code is a part of the process of secularisation; it is part of our quest for a new and integrated national identity based on the composite culture of India and on enlightened rationalism. This is a vital area for our nation–building and social development."[7]

At the dawn of independence, Indian law relating to marriage and divorce, inheritance, and joint family property was diverse. Being a Christian, Muslim, or Hindu meant that one would be governed by a distinct personal law. Nor was Hindu law unified. The Dayabhaga school was dominant in Bengal and Assam, and the Mitakshara school, along with its four subdivisions, prevailed throughout the rest of India.[8] Furthermore, the various High Courts interpreted the same law differently. Custom also played an important role in the application of Hindu law, and that was irreconcilably diverse throughout India.[9]

If Hindus operated under irreconcilable diversity, so did Muslims. Tahir Mahmood has summarized the situation.

> The Muslims of India are divided into *Sunnīs* and *Shī'as*; the *Sunnīs* into *Hanafīs* and *Shāji'īs*; the *Shī'as* into *Ithnā 'Asharīs* and *Ismā'īlīs*; the *Ismā'īlīs* into *Khojas* and *Bohoras*; the *Bohoras* into *Dā'udīs* and *Sulaymānīs*; and so on. Each of the groups has its own personal law. The personal laws of the *Ithnā 'Asharīs* and the *Ismā'īlīs* are very much different from those of the *Hanafīs* and *Shāfi'īs* — especially in the field of intestate succession. In regard to testamentary succession, an ordinary Muslim can opt between the *Sharī'a* and the local custom (most *Khojas* prefer the latter); but a *Shafi'ī* Mapilla of South India is bound to adhere to the law of Islam. Members of the Mapilla community have their own *Marumakkatayam* law of quasi–coparcenary, unknown to the rest of Muslims. The dower stipulated in a marriage–contract, if found excessive with regard to the husband's means, can be reduced by the courts in the Oudh area of U. P. and in Kashmir but not in any other part of India. In matters of legacies and adoption every Indian Muslim has a discretion to chose [*sic*] between *Sharī'a* law and custom, if any.[10]

Christians, Jews, and Parsis also have their own personal laws which vary according to local customs.[11]

It is against this historical legal setting that article 44 must be seen. In the state that is envisaged in the Constitution, all citizens are to be equal before the law regardless of religion, caste, or sex. As Mahmood has pointed out, the Government was competent to enact a uniform civil code even without article 44. In addition to the provisions of articles 25 and 26, the government could exercise powers vested in it under List, III, Entry 5, of the VII Schedule of the Constitution.[12] Article 44 is a Directive Principal of State Policy which was to be followed seriously by government, but was not enforceable by any court. What article 44 did was to instruct government to work toward the eventual enactment of a uniform civil code.

Secularization of Law and the Constituent Assembly Debates

When article 44 (article 35 of the Draft Constitution) was discussed in the Constituent Assembly, five Muslims spoke, and all of them opposed the article, without amending it to preserve personal law (which would have defeated the purpose of the article).

Mohamad Ismail Sahib from Madras wanted to include the words "provided that any group, section or community of people shall not be obliged to give up its own personal law in case it has such a law."[13] While he included all people (i.e., Hindus as well) and although there was considerable Hindu opposition to the Hindu Code Bill, no Hindus spoke against article 44 in the Constituent Assembly. Mohamad Ismail Sahib held that for the people who follow personal law, "It is part of their religion" and anything done to interfere with that is to interfere with the life and religion of such people, which is not appropriate in the secular state. Here it is seen that the bifurcation of life into "religion" and the "secular" is not denied, but that law is to be part of the process of secularization is rejected.

The second Muslim to speak offered the following amendment: "Provided that the personal law of any community which has been guaranteed by the statute shall not be changed except with the previous approval of the community ascertained in such manner as the Union Legislature shall determine by law."[14] As with the former speaker, the goal is to protect the personal laws of the whole community, this time by requiring consent of the affected community prior to enactment. Again, the argument is that each community has certain civil laws which are "inseparably connected with religious belief."[15] Since this is the case, violation of the personal laws would clash with the provisions of article 25 (article 19 of the Draft Constitution) which grants freedom of "religion." This speaker also grants the religion/secular distinction, but contends that the personal laws do not fit into the secular realm. While there may be some activities which are pursued in proximity with "religion" which are not themselves religious and which are therefore open to state control, this is not one of them. "I can quite see that there may be many pernicious practices which may accompany many religious practices and they may be controlled. But there are certain religious practices, certain religious laws which do not come within the exception in clause (2), viz. financial, political or other secular activity which may be associated with religious practices."[16]

This speaker held that article 44 may come in conflict with article 25. We have seen that it would have been possible to enact a uniform civil code without article 44, which merely makes its desirability explicit. The speaker is aware that there have been laws enacted during the British period that narrowed the application of personal laws. He does not object to them because even though they clashed with personal law, they arose gradually.[17] But the state has not yet interfered with marriage and inheritance. He even grants that a time may come when civil law should be uniform, but such enactment should be gradual and should only come with the consent of the people concerned. An implication of this argument is that the state should not have the power to do to Muslims what in five hundred years they have refrained from doing themselves.

The third speaker, Mahboob Ali Baig Sahib Bahadur, offered the following amendment: "Provided that nothing in this article shall affect the personal law of the citizen."[18] His view was that the designation "Civil Code" should include laws of property, transfer of property, laws of contract, and law of evidence, but should not include law observed by a particular religious community. He argued that the framers ought not to think of personal law as included in "Civil Code" because for Muslims, laws of succession, inheritance, marriage, and divorce "are completely dependent upon their religion."[19] Conceding that according to Muslim law marriage is a contract rather than a sacrament (*saṁskāra* for "Hindus"), it is nevertheless the way Muslims have handled it. If there is a way other than contract whereby a marriage is authenticated, "we refuse to abide by it because it is not according to our religion."[20] Although it is true that for Muslims marriage is validated by a contract, that validation by contract is itself a matter of religious law for the speaker.

The fourth Muslim speaker, B. Pocker Sahib Bahadur, spoke in support of the amendment offered by the first speaker, Mohamad Ismail Sahib. Bahadur, as did those who spoke before him, saw personal law as part of "religion." If "Civil Code" is to refer only to matters of procedure, such as the Civil Procedure Code, he sees no problem, but marriage, inheritance, and divorce, matters in personal law, are part of the religion of communities. "What is the purpose served by this uniformity except to murder the conscience of the people and make them feel that they are being trampled upon as regards their religious rights and practices?"[21]

Finally, Hussain Imam, Bihar, argues that uniformity of law in a country as diverse as India is not only undesirable, but impossible. He grants the possibility of a uniform law only in the remote future when the country shares an equal educational level. "Sir, I feel that it is all right and a very desirable thing to have a uniform law, but at a very distant date. For that, we should first await the coming of that event when the whole of India has got educated [*sic*], when mass illiteracy has been removed, when people have advanced, when their economic conditions are better, when each man is able to stand on his own legs and fight his own battles. Then, you can have uniform laws."[22] Although one should not entirely discount the argument made here, the speaker then proceeds to what really seems to be on his mind when he clarifies what a secular state is, and that does not mean an irreligious state, but a non–religious one. If this is true, provisions should be made for the religious sensibilities of minorities.

Although a couple of the above Muslim speakers did grant that at some future time a uniform civil code might be conceivable and acceptable, they uniformly state personal law relating to marriage, divorce, and inheritance are matters of "religion" and that they must be regulated with the consent of the religious groups to which they apply. Hence they stood in opposition to the secularization of personal law.

The discussion was not to close, however, without a spokesman for the new "Great Tradition." K. M. Munshi from Bombay argued that article 25 already made provision for laws regulating the secular activities which are associated with religious practice and for social welfare and reform. Article 44 merely adds the proposition that the personal law of the country should be united at such a time as Parliament thinks proper. As for the protection of minority rights, he throws back at the Muslim speakers the case of the Khojas and Cutchi Memons. When the Shariat Act (1937) was passed they followed certain "Hindu" customs. But since they were Muslims, they were forced to abide by Shariat according to the will of the majority of Muslims. Such codes, now as then, have to ask what is in the interest of the whole community, and a small segment cannot reasonably stand in the way of that.

More important for our purposes is the explicit admission that what is intended in article 44 is the secularization of law and the separation of law from "religion." "We want to divorce religion from personal law, from what may be called social relations or from the rights of parties as regards inheritance or succession."[23] It is necessary to legislate in matters of personal law without actually interfering with "religion," even if that means a redefinition of "religion." "We are at a stage where we must unify and consolidate the nation by every means without interfering with religious practices. If, however, the religious practices in the past have been so constructed as to cover the whole field of life, we have reached a point where we must put our foot down and say that these matters are not religion, they are purely matters for secular legislation. This is what is emphasized by this article."[24] Hindus as well as Muslims are opposed to a uniform civil code. Many Hindus also feel that their personal law relating to inheritance, succession, etc., are a part of their religion. Were that true, women could not have been given equality, but that has already been laid down in the fundamental rights by prohibiting discrimination on the basis of sex.

The first concern of India is to evolve a strong and consolidated nation. In order to effect this, "religion" must be restricted to its legitimate sphere "and the rest of life must be regulated, unified and modified in such a manner that we may evolve, as early as possible, a strong and consolidated nation."[25] Munshi, then, provides for religious diversity, once "religion" is appropriately restricted to its proper sphere, but for uniformity in the secular sphere so as to produce national unity. Although the British did provide some uniformity in certain areas, in providing for keeping the various personal laws, they did not go far enough in the secularization of law. An independent India must outgrow this and move toward the radical secularization of law.

The new "Great Tradition" is further elucidated in the final response of B. R. Ambedkar, who reemphasized that there already exists a uniform and complete Criminal Code operating throughout the country in the Penal Code and the Criminal Procedure Code. There is also the Law of Transfer of Property and the Negotiable Instruments Acts. Thus far the secularization of law has already gone. But it must take a further step. "The only province the Civil Law has not been able to invade so far is marriage and succession. It is this little corner which we have not been able to invade so far and it is the intention of those who desire to have article 35 as part of the Constitution to bring about that change."[26] Ambedkar further challenged the contentions that Muslim law was immutable. He referred again to the 1937 decision to apply a Shariat law to Muslims throughout India — even those who were previously governed by Hindu law in matters of succession.

Finally, in order to reassure objecting Muslims, Ambedkar pointed out that the article did not necessitate the immediate enforcement of a uniform civil code, but that the future Parliament might well provide such a code and at first make it voluntary for those who choose to be governed by it. All of the proposed amendments were defeated and article 44 (35 in Draft Constitution) was passed.

Secularization of Law and the Hindu Code

On January 2, 1944, the government appointed a Hindu Law Committee under the chairmanship of B. N. Rau "for the purpose of formulating a Code of Hindu law which should be complete as far as possible."[27] The committee of four, including Dr. Dwarkanath Mitter, a former judge of the Calcutta High Court, formulated a Draft Code, and it was on the basis of this (with minor alterations) that they travelled to the major population centers of India to hear witnesses both for and against the proposed code. A report of their findings and proposals was completed on February 21, 1947, over the names of three members of the committee: B. N. Rau (chairman), J. R. Gharpure, and T.R. Venaktarama Sastri. A minority report which did not support codification and which included tabulations of responses for and against codification, as well as summaries of some of the reasons given by witnesses, was submitted by Dr. Dwarkanath Mitter. I will examine some of the reasons shortly, for both sides of this report illustrate the conflict over the secularization of law.

It is the opinion of Derrett that the Hindu Code is a step in the direction of a uniform civil code.[28] His understanding of the Hindu Code is commonly accepted by other scholars as well.[29] Not only is this the view of scholars, but it seems to have been the attitude taken by those involved in the legislative process itself. In answering a proposal that a uniform civil code be enacted, since that was what the Constitution called for and not a partial codification of Hindu Law, Nehru is reported to have responded: "The honourable member is perfectly entitled to his view on the subject. If he or anybody else brings a Civil Code Bill, it will have my extreme sympathy. But I confess I do not think that at the present moment the time is ripe in India for me to try to push it through. I want to prepare the ground for it and this kind of thing is one method of preparing the ground."[30] The draft Hindu Code Bill was introduced into the old central assembly in 1947 prior to the partition of India, but received such opposition that it was dropped temporarily.[31] The bill was again debated on the floor of the Constituent Assembly (legislative), but again, as a result of intense reaction, was dropped in September 1951. But a new Parliament in 1955 and 1956 passed the substance of the code in the form of four separate bills: Hindu Marriage Bill, Hindu Succession Bill, Hindu Minority and Guardianship Bill, and Hindu Adoptions and Maintenance Bill. The debate that took place over these separate bills did not center on the secularization of law, for the desirability of codification was not at issue. By this time those who were opposed to codification because of the secularization of law saw that codification was inevitable, so they attempted to effect what were to them desirable changes.

Although the majority report of the Hindu Law Committee attempted to minimize the extent of opposition ("There is however no doubt in our minds that, taking quality into account, the opinion which favours codification decidedly outweighs that which is opposed to it"[32]), Dr. Mitter in his minority report did not feel that he could ignore the overwhelming opposition to codification.

> From the examination of witnesses and of the opinions set forth in the written memorandum of all the Provinces in India the only conclusion that I can come to is that the majority of Hindus incline to the view that the codification of Hindu law is neither possible nor desirable.
>
> From a conspectus of the evidence and written opinions given in the whole of India through which the Committee had to tour, it will appear that the majority are against codification of Hindu law and it is only a *microscopic minority* that favours codification.[33]

In response to why he, along with the rest of the committee, formulated a draft Hindu Code in the light of such formidable opposition, Dr. Mitter explained, "The answer is that when we conceived of the possibility of an uniform Code of Hindu law we little knew that there would be such strong opposition to the reforms suggested."[34] Mitter indicated that he did not agree with the position held by some that reforms should be introduced even though public opinion was opposed to them.

An analysis of the arguments used by those who opposed codification suggests that they were sometimes a subterfuge for the retention of vested interests. For example, the majority report holds that many of those who argued that secularity required a uniform civil code and not a codification for Hindus alone would have been equally opposed to the uniform civil code. It is also true that some of the arguments are more easily refuted or shown to be self–contradictory than others. None of this is our concern. Of particular significance for our purpose are those statements that deal with the conflict over the secularization of law.

During the debate, a variety of pamphlets in opposition to the Hindu Code Bill were distributed. One, whose distribution spanned the time before and after the enactment of the bills of 1955-56, was *Why Hindu Code is Detestable*, which was distributed by Shastra Dharma Prachar Sabha. The level of its appeal is revealed by the fact that over half of its 104 pages are filled with excerpts from Western newspapers which report divorces, rapes, and murders — a situation which is intended to show the "shape of things to come after Hindu Code" is enacted.[35] Nevertheless, the pamphlet does outline the demands of the *śāstras* (by quoting from Manu) and equates them with "God's spoken words." "Yet these vicious bills are directed to (1) provide for intercaste marriage, (2) Sagotra marriage, (3) introduce divorce, (4) make bigamy punishable by law, and (5) give a married daughter share in her father's property. The bills go against fundamental principles of the Hindu Shastras, God's Spoken Words, on which the Society is based."[36] The pamphlet makes it clear that Hindu law and society should be based on the *śāstras* alone since they reflect God's will, and that there is therefore no room for the secularization of law.

On a somewhat higher level was a pamphlet, *Comments on the Hindu Code*, which was published and distributed by the author, B.D. Khaitan. This pamphlet deals with the various provisions of the bills and makes suggestions for changes which would preserve some of the traditional laws of Hindus. It deals with marriage and divorce, divorce and judicial separation, adoption, minority and guardianship, joint family property, women's property, and succession. Khaitan emphasizes again that the Hindu Code is not the will of the majority of Hindus and suggests a referendum to provide evidence of majority will. But it is important to note that for him Hindu law is equated with Hindu religion. "India is a land of religion and people here cling to their faith at all costs. Religion is their dearest object. They live for religion and die for it. Nothing is more shocking to a Hindu than an attack on his faith. If that be so, if both the Hindu male and the female do not like to be touched so far as their religion is concerned, where is the necessity of introducing this piece of legislation?"[37] Furthermore, Khaitan holds that the nature of the secular state is such as to guarantee that the "religion" of each community be left untouched. "The Constitution clearly and unambiguously gives the liberty of thought and conscience to every citizen of India and by declaring India to be a Secular State, the religion of each and every community and sect is sought to be left untouched and undisturbed."[38]

In his minority report, Dr. Mitter offers a chart covering over 100 pages, indicating all those witnesses who were for or against codification. Those against codification well outweigh those in favor of it, and those against codification frequently link Hindu law with "religion" or seek to resist the secularization of law. A written opinion received from the British India Association was received in Calcutta which read in part: "The legislative interference in the personal law of Hindus, connected as they are age–old religious practices, is unwise, if it is not called for, and the Association considers the proposed legislation as uncalled for, an unjustifiable interference."[39]

At Allahabad several pandits and professors representing the All–India Sanatan Dharma Mahasabha objected to codification "on the ground that the Dharma Shastra is not purely secular and is based on religion and should not be interfered with by Government."[40]

Mr. Laxmi Narain Sudan, representing the Sanatana Dharma Prathinidhi Mahasabha in Rawalpindi, was a witness at Lahore. He testified:

> We oppose the Code altogether. In fact we do not think that there should be a codification of the Hindu law at all. The Hindu law is not a mere mundane thing. It is a Dharma Shastra or a divine law regulating Hindu life. The expression "Dharma" does not connote mere law. It is not merely for this world: it is also for the other world.[41]

A number of representatives of the Sanatana Dharma Pratinidhi Sabha of Punjab said in Lahore:

> The draft Code was opposed by the Sabha on the following grounds: (i) Hindu law is a part of the Dharma Shastra and is not ordinarily secular law. Peculiar sanctity attaches to our Dharma Shastras.[42]

Several pandits and professors representing the Sanatana Dharma Bidyapith of Lahore testified:

> We are altogether against the Code. It is not a mere collection of existing laws, but makes several innovations. According to our belief, no man has a right to alter the Hindu law. Our law forms part of our religion and nobody has a right to change our religion.[43]

Sardar Sahib Iqbal Singh, an advocate representing Sikh opinion, stated:

> I am totally opposed to the codification of the Hindu Law. It constitutes an interference with the Hindu religion. Hindu law cannot be divorced from the Hindu religion, the two are intimately mixed. Nobody has a right to tinker with the Hindu religion. The source of the Hindu law is the Vedas and no earthly individual has a right to alter the Vedas.[44]

Mr. Kasturchand Agrawal, a Pleader, testified in Nagpur:

> The idea is repugnant and offensive to our feelings. We believe that our law is divine. It forms part of Hindu scriptures which have been revered from time immemorial.[45]

Pandit Nilakanta Das of Cuttack testified:

> I am against the codification of personal laws of the Hindus. The whole basis of the sacramental law is that its source is the Holy Text and not a statute. This basis is wholly lost by codification.[46]

A survey of the interviews conducted by the Hindu Law Committee will show that statements such as those above abound, and are distributed over the whole geographical area of India. To continue to supply quotes would be unduly repetitive.

Even the majority report of the committee is forced to admit that this linkage of law and "religion" is widely held. Although they may be correct historically in pointing out that Hindu law based on texts interprets those texts differently, that Hindu law has not in fact been immutable, that some of the provisions for divorce and women's rights have support in texts of the *śāstras*, that is, even though some of the claims made for Hindu Law may not stand up under historical scrutiny, the religious fact remains that numerous Hindus did indeed believe that their personal law was identical with or based upon or inextricably linked with Hindu "religion," and that to tamper with the one was to interfere with the other. This was itself a religious belief.

Although the majority report does not explicitly advocate the secularization of law, and in this case Hindu law, it is interesting to note the basis on which some of its decisions were made.

In addressing itself to the contention that it is only a minority that actually wants codification, the committee suggests that it is not a matter of numbers but of rightness. "And so the real question to be considered is not how many or how few demand the changes proposed, but whether the proposals themselves are on the right lines and worthy of acceptance."[47] But how should one determine if they are on the right lines and worthy of acceptance? What norms are to be used for settling matters that are in dispute? In discussing the matter of a woman's right to inherit when a father dies intestate, the committee is driven logically from one point to another until it is forced by that logic to grant daughters a portion of the inheritance. Against those who would have argued otherwise, they saw no logical stopping place.

> For example, we put to some of the witnesses the case of a Mitakshara father dying leaving a daughter and a brother; his interest in the coparcenary property goes to the brother by survivorship and if the brother subsequently dies leaving a daughter, the interest goes to the brother's daughter, the original owner's own daughter being thus ousted. No one desired such a result, but it could only be prevented by a further inroad upon the existing Mitakshara Law: *e.g.* by giving the daughter a right by birth similar to that of a son or by giving the father a right to dispose of his coparcenary interest by will or by some such device. Again if the daughter is to have an absolute estate in the property which she gets from her father, how can we consistently refuse a similar estate to the son by insisting on the Mitakshara rule that his son, grandson and great–grandson shall have a right by birth in such property. And so we are driven from point to point; we can find no logical halting–place until we abandon the right by birth as well as survivorship and completely assimilate the Mitakshara to the Dayabhaga in these respects.[48]

But reasonableness and the use of logic has to begin with certain axiomatic norms or values. One of these is equality, particularly between the sexes. This principle is clearly stipulated in the Constitution, although justice is based on inequality in Manu. Hence, in discussing their stand for monogamy against polygamy, the committee found the argument of witnesses, that monogamy merely gives to women the same position that men already have, a forceful one. Coupled with that, the permission to take a second wife was seen as archaic and to be superseded in the present time. "In fact, this corresponds to the position now occupied by Hindu women, and these witnesses therefore wanted Hindu men to be put in the same positions as Hindu women."[49] "The conditions on which a second wife was permitted to be taken in the ancient Smritis are few, and there seems to be no necessity for keeping these somewhat archaic rules alive at the present day."[50] Nor was the committee oblivious to the impression that the possibility of polygamy gave in other parts of the world. "We would like to add that a strong practical argument in favour of monogamy is the force of world opinion."[51]

Those who opposed divorce argued that marriage was a sacrament and created a bond between husband and wife not only throughout life, but even after death. Although widowers were free to remarry, widows should not be since they are to treat their husbands as gods even after death. For this they appealed to textual support. While the committee could have appealed to texts to show that divorce was indeed permitted under some conditions, they were more impressed with the social realities which created hardships for some women. "From the evidence adduced before us, we are satisfied that there are thousands of women in British India who have been deserted by their husbands. The visits which some of us made to Rescue and Destitute Women's Homes both in Calcutta and Madras and advertisements frequently appearing in newspapers, especially in the Bombay Presidency, fortify this conclusion."[52] Traditionalists argued that in such cases women might well exemplify patient suffering, but the committee objected that they were not willing to demand the same of men, for whom they desired the possibility of remarriage.[53] The committee was more governed by their own views of social utility than by textual stipulations when they provided for divorce in the draft Code. "We are satisfied that far from injuring Hindu society, the provision for divorce which we are now including will be found to be socially healthy and beneficial."[54]

There was also considerable discussion as to whether a man's keeping a concubine should be sufficient grounds for divorce. Some argued that it was not sufficient ground unless the man actually brought the concubine into the home to live. While doubting that many wives would file for divorce on this ground alone, the committee nevertheless held that it was a valid ground. If the wife were to become the concubine of another man, the sacramental bond of the marriage would presumably have been broken and divorce would become possible. If that is true for the woman, it should also be true for the man. Modern society could not be considered to tolerate such an unequal distribution of justice. "As far as possible the law should operate equally between man and woman, and public opinion will not, in our opinion, tolerate differential standards in this respect at the present day."[56]

Since the Code distinguished between sacramental and civil marriages, the question arose as to whether insanity, leprosy, and venereal disease, which were considered grounds for divorce within the civil marriage, should also be so considered for the sacramental marriage. Some had argued before the committee that they should be inapplicable in sacramental marriages, since in such cases marriage is not for pleasure alone and it is important to maintain such marriages. But on "human considerations" the committee disagreed. "We however disagree with this view and feel that there is no need to maintain any distinction between civil and sacramental marriages in regard to this matter, as the same human considerations apply to both."[56]

Although the committee recommended that both monogamy and divorce should be part of the Hindu Code, they made it clear that monogamy was so important to them that it should be enacted even if there were no provision for divorce. Some had argued that with polygamy, provision was made whereby a man could, if his wife contracted some serious communicable disease or were barren, marry a second wife while still maintaining the previous wife for her security. If monogamy were enforced, divorce would be required in such cases. The committee disagreed, based on the principle of equality. "Again, Hindu women are not bound by the rule of monogamy, although they are not entitled to divorce except where their communities allow it. It is not after all unreasonable to require that men should be subjected to the same rules and restrictions as women are at present."[57] Toward the end of their report, the majority of the committee once again reiterated modern standards over against traditional ones. They were impressed with the weight of world opinion and the government's stand on fundamental rights.[58]

It should not be thought that Dr. Mitter was sensitive to the will of the Hindu public while the majority of the committee was not. They spent considerable time hearing the objections forwarded against the Hindu Code. And they were receptive to some of them. But the norms by which they found a position "reasonable" were not traditional nor textual, but were based on human rights, equality of the sexes, social utility, and world opinion. The Svamiji of the Jai Guru Society, U. P., in the course of his evidence stated: "I am in favour of having one law for all Hindus, but Hindu culture must be maintained by the uniform Code which we make, and the Code must not offend against the spirit of Hindu culture and institutions."[59] The committee responded: "We may say that it is in the above spirit that we have laboured throughout."[60] They felt that they offered a genuine Hindu Code. But it was a Code based on a new foundation. Although the Hindu Law Committee did not complete the secularization of law, for after all, it was still a "Hindu Code," it did take significant strides in that direction.

The new "Great Tradition" embodying the move toward the secularization of law exemplified in the Hindu Law Committee is explicit in the thought of Nehru and Gajendragadkar. It should come as little surprise to find that P. B. Gajendragadkar, a former chief justice of the Supreme Court of India, is also an advocate of the new "Great Tradition." According to Gajendragadkar, the secular state aims at the implementation of article 44, the introduction of a uniform civil code throughout all of India.[61] The Hindu Code was merely a step in that direction, while the government prepared Muslim public opinion for the acceptance of the secularization of Muslim family law as well. "Whether or not polygamy should be allowed, what should be the line of succession, what should be the shares of different heirs, what should be the law of divorce, are matters which should be determined not by scriptural injunctions, but by rational considerations. These are matters secular in character and are outside the legitimate domain of religion as contemplated by Articles 25 and 26 of the Constitution."[62] Gajendragadkar affirms the division between "religion" and the "secular" as determined by the Constitution. He also grants that traditionally Hindus did not operate under any category that might correspond with that he means by the "secular."

> It would thus appear that the modern notion of law that it is the command of a sovereign was virtually unknown to the ancient Sanskrit texts on *dharma*. In the vast literature of Hindu law we do not find any trace of the notion of positive or secular law as such and there is no recognition of the idea that such law is a human institution, started and modified from time to time by rulers or legislatures.
>
> On the whole I think it would not be wrong to say that in the earliest stages Hindu law was regarded as consisting of commands issued, not by a political sovereign or by any legislature, but by the Supreme Ruler of the Universe, and ancient Hindu literature on *dharma* seems to be agreed that it was the imperative duty of the political sovereign to enjoin the divine commands and to enforce obedience to them by his subjects.[63]

The popular opposition to the Hindu Code Bill is based on the assumption that "religion" and civil law are inextricably bound up, and that to deal with aspects of civil or family law is to deal with the Hindu "religion."[64] This is in keeping with the ancient texts, but is an error that must be corrected. Once the public is led to distinguish between the realms of "religion" and the "secular," it will become clear that law is in the realm of the "secular," and all opposition to the Hindu Code Bill will disappear.[65] It is the view that "religion" and law are intimately connected that has also led many to believe erroneously that Hindu law has not changed over the years. It is clear that for Gajendragadkar the implementation of the Hindu Code and the uniform civil code are dependent on the secularization of law. "The task of secularism is to separate the secular from the essentially religious, and to allow the secular to be governed by the state, leaving the essentially religious to be dealt with by religion. Matters of personal law clearly fall under the secular category and have to be dealt with by the state in modern times."[66]

In a previous article I showed that Nehru legitimated his view of the secular state on the unquestionable ground that it was modern, rational, scientific, and Indian.[67] This is a continuation of the norms which appeared in the work of the Hindu Law Committee. These values are also found as the ground for Gajendragadkar's decisions. The day is gone when one can appeal to ancient texts to settle legal matters. "It would be totally unscientific and unreasonable to go back to these ancient texts to find out how we should regulate our daily life today."[68] Law is part of the "secular" realm, and law changes according to the social and political conditions in which it is found. Hindu law has indeed changed, and it is certainly not of divine origin.[69] Being merely preliminary to a uniform civil code, the Hindu Code Bill must be based on modern principles and not religious ones. That is the meaning of the secularization of law. Hence, it should not be surprising to hear Gajendragadkar argue that the Hindu Code should not be based on texts, but on principles which are enunciated in the Constitution. "It seems to me that it is the preemptor requirement of the present age that we must have a Hindu Code which is based on absolute equality amongst all Hindus, irrespective of their caste, creed or sex. If we are all agreed on this elementary proposition, there must be unanimity amongst us all in bringing about this reform."[70]

Gajendragadkar discusses at some length the textual bases for Mitakshara and Dayabhaga treatments of joint family property, showing that they differ significantly and that each purports to be based on ancient Sanskrit texts. But once one has accomplished the secularization of law, the law governing joint family property is based on social utility and not on textual exegesis. "Texts there are in support of either view and it is for us today to consider which view would serve the social interests best."[71]

The Hindu Code also proposed to deal with all Hindus equally apart from caste. The division of society into four *varṇas* is in modern times "totally obsolete" and highly objectionable. This is so obvious that no argument is necessary in its behalf. Law must be based on equality.[72]

Questions of monogamy, divorce, and inheritance are secular matters to be determined by the legislature in keeping with the principles of rationality, science, and social utility. And that is as true for Muslims as it is for Hindus.

> While educating Muslim public opinion in regard to the necessity and significance of secularizing the personal law, it would be idle to ignore the fact that in the traditional minds of the common Muslim men and women we notice resistance to any social change and this resistance proceeds from the honest, though mistaken, belief that a change in personal law necessarily invades the realm of Muslim religion. Traditional Muslims oppose any effort to secularise the Muslim law just as the traditional Hindus did, and we must satisfy the generality of Muslim men and women that no invasion of Muslim religion properly so called is intended when the adoption of a common civil code is advocated by the secular intellectuals of this country.[73]

Again, the movement of the new "Great Tradition" and its corollary, the secularization of law, was not victorious without dissension and religious conflict. But with the enactment of the bills comprising the Hindu Code in 1955-56, the "Great Tradition" picked up new momentum in its movement toward the secularization of Law. In the final analysis it was the views of Ambedkar, Nehru, and Gajendragadkar that carried, and the resistance that lost.

Secularization of Law and Uniform Civil Code: The Muslim Case

With the move in the direction of secularization in Hindu law, attention has increasingly turned to Muslim law. As the Constituent Assembly revealed, Muslims have been as inclined to the view that religion and law are inextricable bound together as have the Hindus. Most of the Indian '*ulamās*,' who are the influential teachers of the masses, stand opposed to the secularization of law. Moreover, there is the added reluctance on the part of the government to legislate in the area of the religion of a minority. Although it was an elite minority which pushed through the codification and reform of

Hindu law, it did so in a Parliament that was primarily Hindu. For those Hindus to "update" Muslim law becomes a more touchy matter.

If Muslims are not pleased with the suggestion that they modernize Muslim law, neither are they in support of a common civil code. "The Muslim public opinion, if that term could apply to the views of an overwhelming majority, is deadly opposed to the replacement of their personal law by a common civil code."[74] Regarding the All India Muslim Law Convention in 1972, Mahmood reports, "At the recent All India Muslim Personal Law Convention held at Bombay, the Muslims belonging to various schools of law, religious groups and political parties, united themselves to resolve that — far from the merger of their personal law into a uniform civil code — they will not 'tolerate' even the slightest reform of any of its principles by the Indian legislature."[75]

It was their view that if any evils had entered Muslim social life, the '*ulamā*' themselves would take care of them. The convention declared that their personal law was "an inseparable part of religion."[76] In 1963 the central government planned to set up a committee to study the ways in which Muslim personal law had been reformed in other Muslim countries, but due to the strong Muslim opposition it was given up.[77] In December 1972, in Bombay, there was a "Conference for the Protection of *Sharī'a*," in which a variety of Muslim religious, social, and political groups who were otherwise opposed to each other's ideologies, united to vote for an absolute immutability of their existing personal law. Their reason for opposing legislative efforts to reform Muslim personal law was their fear that the next step would be its replacement with a uniform civil code. As Mahmood explains: "The result is that even those few who actually are conscious of the existence of certain drawbacks in their social life do not want them to be remedied by legislation, since they are convinced that if they agree for the reform of their personal law today, tomorrow they will have to digest its replacement by a common civil code."[78]

Shortly after the bills which were labelled the Hindu Code were passed, a booklet entitled *Uniform Civil Code: A Challengeable Proposition* appeared.[79] Its publication was prompted by a reading of Donald Smith's *India As a Secular State*. Tyabi agrees with Smith that replacement of *sharī'a* with a uniform civil code will modify Islam by stripping it of the "socio–legal institutions" which will have made it a way of life. However, he takes exception to Smith's view that "the secularization of law is absolutely essential to the evolution of a modern sovereign state."[80]

Tyabi affirms the secular state, but holds that if the state reduces Hinduism and Islam to a religious core of private faith against the will of 90 percent of the Muslims of India, the state will have negated the secular concept.[81] As he sees it, Ambedkar never intended India to be truly secular and that is why he refused to insert the word "secular" in the original Constitution. Had he intended a secular state, he would also have exempted Muslim personal law from article 44. We have already noted that this view of the secular state was voiced in the Constituent Assembly. But this understanding does not fit with the new "Great Tradition" we have been describing, which sees the secularization of law, and consequently a uniform civil code, as a necessary embodiment of the secular state.

Of special concern to Tyabi is the Islamic law of succession and the move to prohibit polygamy. Tyabi sees the imposition of monogamy as coming from the West. "The ideal of Christianity is celibacy, the second best is monogamy. The ideal of Islam is monogamy and the second best is necessitous polygamy."[82] Monogamy encourages divorce and prostitution, while polygamy encourages a man, when he takes a second wife out of necessity, to continue to care for the first wife and not turn her out. Although economic conditions have led to the decline of polygamy, who is to say when war will again deplete the male population and make polygamy a viable option.

As for inheritance, wills should not be encouraged. According to Tyagi's understanding of Islamic law, both man and his property are under the rule of Allah, and when the man dies, his property becomes Allah's property. During his lifetime, a man may earn and spend and give to charity. But what one leaves in death is Allah's and that is divided among fixed shares with no heir being disinherited. With one–third of the property a man is permitted to make a will. Exceptions must be agreed upon by the person's heirs. The wayward son, whom one might like to disinherit, might later mend his ways. Modern man, believing himself the creator of his wealth, desires to satisfy his ego by being the sole dispenser of that wealth. However, "some day — too late he finds himself, with his property, in the pocket of Allah."[83]

But Tyabi also objects to the secularization of law and clearly links the *sharī'a* with religion. "The challenge is, that if a uniform Civil Code were imposed on the minorities with their respective religions in India or in any other country such a Code would definitely destroy the religious laws such as the Shariah of Islam; furthermore the imposition of such a uniform Civil Code would definitely destroy the disciplinary powers of guidance and management by the Community through the religious head of its own affairs in matters of religion."[84]

In September 1968, a Seminar on Muslim Personal Law was held at Aligarh Muslim University to provide an academic forum for a discussion of the "true nature of Muslim personal law in India."[85] Eight of the twenty formal participants were among the Maulana. While there was recognition of the need for change and that there was a valid distinction to be made between Islamic law and Muslim personal law, most participants held that it was up to the Islamic community itself to initiate such religious change. Moreover, it was repeatedly stated that religion and law were inextricably bound together. As the organizer of the seminar reflected, "For Other Communities law giving is an entirely secular activity. But not so with the Muslims. To them law giving is part and parcel of religion. In so far as Quran and Sunnah clearly state the course of action to be followed, there is no choice for a Muslim."[86]

There are also Muslim thinkers who stand firmly in the new "Great Tradition" and who thereby do not stand with Tyabi's rejection of the secularization of law. One of these is A. A. A. Fyzee. Fyzee sees that in other Muslim countries secular law is reducing the extent of influence of the *sharī'a*. Even in India the Islamic law of evidence is no longer operative and in the commercial and criminal spheres it is not followed.

> With the growth of industrialization and the change in economic conditions, there has been a great increase in legislation designed to suit the new economic and social life of the people. A glance at the legislative activity of the Indian Parliament in 1951 and 1952 will show the rapid steps that the country took to improve and ameliorate the condition of the so–called working classes. In 1952 we find the Coal Mines Ordinance, the Requisition and Acquisition of Immovable Property Ordinance, the Delhi University Amendment Act, the Mines Act, the Cinematograph Act, the Commission of Enquiry Act, and the Reserve and Auxiliary Forces Act, to mention but a few of the acts that have been passed into law.[87]

For Muslims living in modern states, a whole variety of laws have been passed which govern their lives. Some of these are in areas that the *sharī'a* never anticipated, whole others take away areas of authority formerly held by Islamic law. For Fyzee, *sharī'a* is both law and "religion" as traditionally conceived. But this produces a contradiction in that law is by nature subject to change while "religion" is unchangeable. "If two such divergent forces are made to live together, there will be a clash."[88] Fyzee's solution is to distinguish "religion" from law, and in effect engage in the secularization of law. The first step in this process is to separate religious or moral law from civil law. Moral law is further classified in terms of universal moral laws, such as truthfulness, marital purity, honesty, etc., and particular moral laws, such as the prohibition of ham and wine, which are not forbidden by all religions. But moral laws apply to the conscience, are subjective, and deal with the inner life, while legal rules are objective and can be enforced by the state.[89] Fyzee is aware that such a conception would modify the Constitution of an Islamic country because of the commonly held view that God is the owner of everything and the final sovereign in a state. But "such a theory would be impractical in the modern world, and the only workable principle is as laid down by numerous modern democratic constitutions, namely, that the people of a country are sovereign within their own domain."[90]

If civil law is freed from "religion" and law is allowed to develop freely, Muslim society will progress rapidly. "Religion" should content itself with emphasizing "devotion to God, cleanliness of spirit, orderliness of life," but should give up jurisdiction over the minutiae of do's and don'ts. Fyzee offers a series of questions to be asked for determining the exact meaning of the rules of Islam. They are to be subjected to rigorous historical analysis. It is enough, however, to note that the constitutional provisions which move toward the secularization of law would be inoffensive to Fyzee.

Speaking in the symposium held at New Delhi in 1964, entitled "Changes in Muslim Personal Law," M. C. Chagla, a former judge of the Bombay High Court, affirmed the constitutional distinction between religion and the secular. "If you accept my point of view, then a distinction must be drawn between the religious and the secular aspect. The religious aspect cannot be touched. It is something personal to every Muslim in this country. But the secular aspect is entirely different from the religious aspect."[91] According to Chagla, the state has no right to interfere with religion, faith, tenets — that which is intensely personal. But when it comes to the area of social good and social justice, the state is fully justified in interfering if it believes it is for the good of all citizens. In a secular state, it is inappropriate to produce legislation for the social good and social justice of only a segment of society. It is granted that legislation will infringe upon the personal rights of individuals. But that principle has already been accepted. "If we have accepted that position in the field of economics, in the field of politics, why is it that we should not accept that position in the field of social welfare, social justice and social reform?"[92]

Legislation should certainly include provisions for monogamy. If laws requiring monogamy are seen as socially beneficial to society as a whole, the state has every right to pass such legislation. Law, as politics and economics, must be secularized. And, if the social sphere (including personal law) is secularized, that means that the content of social good and social justice will be decided by the state and not by religious leaders. Since Muslims have a part in electing Parliament in the modern secular state, and since Parliament is the arm of legislation, "The duty of every citizen in this country is ultimately to submit to the decision of Parliament in regard to what is the social good that legislation is going to produce.... Parliament is the ultimate arbiter in regard to what is social good, what is social justice and what is the interest of the people as a whole."[93]

This new "Great Tradition," then, proposes a clear distinction between "religion" and the "secular" and the subsequent secularization of law in a uniform civil code for all citizens of India.

Notes

1. For a presentation of this definitional approach see Robert D. Baird, *Category Formation and the History of Religions* (The Hague: Mouton, 1971).

2. The terms "Hindu" and "Muslim" are used in this paper in a legal sense. That there are clearly defined communities who are legally considered "Hindu" or "Muslim" should not lead to the judgment that these are adequate religious categories indicating common ultimate concerns.

3. Articles 25 and 26 read as follows:

   25. (1) Subject to public order, morality and health and to the other provisions of this Part, all persons are equally entitled to freedom of conscience and the right freely to profess, practise and propagate religion.

   (2) Nothing in this article shall affect the operation of any existing law or prevent the State from making any law —

   (a) regulating or restricting any economic, financial, political or other secular activity which may be associated with religious practice;

(b) providing for social welfare and reform or the throwing open of Hindu religious institutions of a public character to all classes and sections of Hindus.

Explanation I — The wearing and carrying of *kirpans* shall be deemed to be included in the profession of the Sikh religion.

Explanation II — In sub–clause (b) or clause (2), the reference to Hindus shall be construed as including a reference to persons professing the Sikh, Jaina or Buddhist religion, and the reference to Hindu religious institutions shall be construed accordingly.

26. Subject to public order, morality and health, every religious denomination or any section thereof shall have the right —

(a) to establish and maintain institutions for religious and charitable purposes;

(b) to manage its own affairs in matters of religion;

(c) to own and acquire movable and immovable property; and

(d) to administer such property in accordance with law.

4. Article 44 reads: "The State shall endeavour to secure for the citizens a uniform civil code throughout the territory of India."

5. Cf. P. B. Mukharji, "Uniform Civil Code," in *Readings in Uniform Civil Code*, ed. N. Khodie (Bombay: Thacker, 1975), 7.

6. For Supreme Court decisions relating to freedom or religion, see Robert D. Baird, "Religion and the Secular: Categories for Religious Conflict and Religious Change in Independent India," in *Religion and Social Conflict in South Asia*, ed. Bardwell L. Smith (Leiden: E. J. Brill, 1976), 47-63. Also, Chapter XI of this volume.

7. Introduction to Tahir Mahmood, *An Indian Civil Code and Islamic Law* (Bombay: Tripathi Private Ltd., 1976), xi. Cf. also Moin Shakir, *Muslims in Free India* (New Delhi: Kalamkar Prakahan, 1972), 125.

8. Donald E. Smith, *India As a Secular State* (Princeton: Princeton University Press, 1963), 279.

9. J. D. M. Derrett, *Religion, Law and the State in India* (London: Faber and Faber, 1968), 330.

10. Mahmood, *An Indian Civil Code and Islamic Law*, 10-11.

11. *Ibid.*, 11. Also, Phiroze K. Irani, "The Personal Law of the Parsis of India," in *Family Law in Asia and Africa*, ed. J. N. D. Anderson (New York: Frederick A Praeger, 1968), 273-300.

12. Entry 5 reads as follows: "Marriage and divorce; infants and minors' adoption; wills, intestacy and succession; joint family and partition; all matters in respect of which parties in judicial proceedings were immediately before the commencement of this Constitution subject to their personal Law."

13. *Constituent Assembly Debates*, 7: 540; hereafter *CAD*.

14. *Ibid.*, 541.

15. *Ibid.*

16. *Ibid.*, 542.

17. *Ibid.*

18. *Ibid.*, 543.

19. *Ibid.*

20. *Ibid.*

21. *Ibid.*, 545.

22. *Ibid.*, 546.

23. *Ibid.*, 574.

24. *Ibid.*

25. *Ibid.*

26. *Ibid.*, 550-51.

27. *Report of the Hindu Law Committee* (Government of India Press, 1955), 1.

28. J. D. M. Derrett, *Hindu Law Past and Present* (Calcutta: A. Mukherjee, 1957), v.

29. Smith, *India as Secular State*, 277ff.

30. Quoted in P. B. Gajendragadkar, *Secularism and the Constitution of India* (Bombay: Bombay University Press, 1971), 124.

31. Smith, *India As a Secular State*, 280.

32. *Report of the Hindu Law Committee*, 5.

33. *Ibid.*, 116.

34. *Ibid.*, 120.

35. *Why Hindu Code is Detestable* (Calcutta and Allahabad: Shastra Dharma Prachar Sabha, n. d.), 41.

36. *Ibid.*, 31.

37. B. C. Khaitan, *Comments on the Hindu Code* (published by the author, 1951), 2.

38. *Ibid.*, 4.

39. *Report of the Hindu Law Committee*, 90.

40. *Ibid.*, 97.

41. *Ibid.*, 99.

42. *Ibid.*, 100.

43. *Ibid.*

44. *Ibid.*

45. *Ibid.*, 103.

46. *Ibid.*, 104.

47. *Ibid.*, 47.

48. *Ibid*, 15.

49. *Ibid.*, 22.

50. *Ibid.*, 23.

51. *Ibid.*

52. *Ibid.*, 24.

53. *Ibid.*, 25.

54. *Ibid.*

55. *Ibid.*, 26.

56. *Ibid.*

57. *Ibid.*, 30.

58. *Ibid.*, 38.

59. *Ibid.*, 39.

60. *Ibid.*

61. P. B. Gajendragadkar, *The Constitution of India: Its Philosophy and Basic Postulates* (Nairobi: Oxford University Press, 1969), 17.

62. Gajendragadkar, *Secularism and Constitution of India*, 125-26.

63. P. B. Gajendragadkar, *The Hindu Code Bill* (Karnataka University, 1951), 4.

64. *Ibid.*, 8.

65. *Ibid.*, 10-11.

66. Gajendragadkar, *Secularism and the Constitution of India*, 120.

67. Robert D. Baird, "Religion and the Legitimation of Nehru's Concept of the Secular State," in *Religion and Legitimation of Power in South Asia*, ed. Bardwell L. Smith (Leiden: E. J. Brill, 1978). Also Chapter VII of this volume.

68. Gajendragadkar, *The Hindu Code Bill*, 47.

69. *Ibid.*, 46.

70. *Ibid.*

71. *Ibid.*, 39.

72. *Ibid.*, 46.

73. Gajendragadkar, *Secularism and the Constitution of India*, 151.

74. Mahmood, *An Indian Civil Code and Islamic Law*, 73.

75. *Ibid.*, 3.

76. *Ibid.*, 4.

77. Tahir Mahmood, "Family Law Reform: Perspective in Modern India,: in *Family Law and Social Change*, ed. Tahir Mahmood (Bombay: N. M. Tripathi, 1975), 102.

78. *Ibid.*, 103.

79. Salahuddin Tyabi, *Uniform Civil Code: A Challengeable Proposition* (Hyderabad: Islamic Publications Society, 1966).

80. *Ibid.*, 54.

81. *Ibid.*, 64.

82. *Ibid.*, 38.

83. *Ibid.*, 25.

84. *Ibid.*, 44.

85. F. R. Faridi and M. N. Siddiqi, eds., *Muslim Personal Law: Papers and Proceedings of a Seminar* (Aligarh: Islamic Research Circle, 1973), 187.

86. *Ibid.*, 188. Cf. also pp. 4, 7, 8, 10, 18, 80-81 for this view voiced by other participants.

87. A. A. A. Fyzee, *A Modern Approach to Islam* (Bombay: Asia Publishing House, 1963), 63.

88. *Ibid.*, 88.

89. *Ibid.*, 99-100.

90. *Ibid.*, 100.

91. *Changes In Muslim Law* (New Delhi, 1964), 94.

92. *Ibid.*, 11.

93. *Ibid.*, 12-13. Another Muslim, Mohammad Ghouse, grants that the source of Muslim law regulating marriage, divorce and inheritance is religious, i.e., the *Qur'ān* and *Hadīth*, but that the relations it regulates are social and within the province of the state. "Therefore, marriage,

divorce, inheritance and other aspects of personal status are, despite the source of the Muslim law regulating them, social or secular activities surrounding religion. The State can validly enact measures of social welfare and reform in respect of the matter governed by the Muslim Law." *Secularism, Society and Law in India* (Delhi: Vikas, 1973), 227.

10

Cow Slaughter and the New "Great Tradition"

Since its beginning as a modern state, India has enshrined in its constitution an ideology which I have called the "new great tradition."[1] More than the transformation of a "Great Tradition," this is a radical departure. An examination of the major texts of the Sanskrit tradition makes it clear that "religion" is not a category to be distinguished from other aspects of life. There is a sacredness to all of life which includes such matters as marriage, divorce, and inheritance. Indian traditions are not religious because they deal with a special portion of life, but because they provide a special valuation which permeates all aspects of life.

The ideology of the new great tradition entered India during the British period and found embodiment in *The Constitution of India*. Constitutional provisions for "religion" make it clear that all of life cannot be considered religious. Rather, religion is provided a place alongside economics, politics, social reform, and law. *The Constitution of India* guarantees citizens the freedom "to profess, practise and propagate religion" (Article 25). However, the conditions within which this guarantee is offered constitute a higher set of values which define the goals and intentions of India as a nation. India is to be a nation in which citizens are treated equally regardless of religion, caste, or social standing, in which the freedom of one person or group has to be balanced against the potential damage to the freedom of others. It is to be a nation which offers equal opportunity and justice to all its citizens. This ideology is based on the dignity of the individual and the unity of the nation.

It is quite clear that this new great tradition is in conflict with traditional religious beliefs and practices.[2] That is why Articles 25 and 26 of *The Constitution of India* make it clear that freedom of religion is subject to "public order, morality and health" and cannot be invoked to avoid social reform or opening access to Hindu temples for all classes of Hindus. This has not been eagerly embraced by Hindus nor by Muslims who have both resisted the secularization of law.[3]

Nevertheless, this new great tradition which separates religion from the realm of the secular is enshrined in the Constitution, embodied in legislation, and is clarified and protected in the Courts. This separation means that in a "secular state" when one is deciding matters of politics, economics or law, one must argue reasonably and marshall arguments on humanitarian grounds. The citation of religious texts in support of a position is no longer appropriate. This provides insight into the detailed economic arguments against the slaughter of cows. Even persons who want the elimination of cow slaughter on religious and textual grounds are aware that within the new great tradition such arguments do not count. Since the government has no place legislating on religious matters, it can best be defended on economic grounds.

This new great tradition which separates religion from the secular has moved along in the courts in a relentless manner. It was used to determine that the scale of expenses for temple rituals was a secular matter and could legitimately fall within the province of legislation.[4] Other financial matters such as acquiring and administering property were also considered secular,[5] as was representation on the Board that manages Sikh Gurdwaras.[6] It was held that the Shri Jagannath Temple Act of 1954 did not impose limitations on the religious duties of the Raja of Puri, it merely regulated the "secular" affairs of the temple. While the utilization of materials in puja might be religious, the provision of the proper materials for puja was secular.[7] Even the hereditary right of succession as archakas in south Indian temples could be set aside by government since the method of appointment was a secular matter.[8] Admittedly, the principle was not always easily applicable, but the courts did seem to manage even when the vote was split.9

The issue of cow slaughter, however, and its present legal status seems to have resisted the new great tradition. There are two dimensions to the movement against cow slaughter. There is the religious sentiment from which it springs, and there are the economic arguments which are used to support that sentiment. An examination of the Constituent Assembly Debates and the court cases which followed independence reveals the existence of both. The Court's judgment, based on the constitution, is that religious sentiment is not a relevant consideration. My thesis is that although in the new great tradition religious sentiments are an irrelevant base for governmental and legal decision, it is the only element which explains the legal base for the prohibition of cow slaughter. In examining this thesis we will consider first, the Constituent Assembly Debates, second Supreme Court cases, and finally High Court Cases.

Constituent Assembly Debates

As the Constituent Assembly began its work there was considerable pressure to include an article prohibiting cow slaughter among the Fundamental Rights. This was rejected and there was no mention of cows or cow–slaughter in the draft constitution.[10] During the debate, however, it was proposed by Thakur Dass Bhargava that such a provision be included among the Directive Principles of State Policy.

In his contention that a prohibition of cow–slaughter should be included among the Directive Principles of State Policy, Thakur Dass Bhargava made it clear that he would prefer it to be among the Fundamental Rights. Nevertheless Draft article 38A (48) included three parts: that agriculture should be improved along modern and scientific lines; that the cattle breed should be improved; and that the cow and other cattle should be protected from slaughter. Bhargava lamented that the cattle wealth of the country had declined from 1940 to 1945. He recognized that there was strong sentiment for the protection of the cow for religious reasons throughout the country. He noted that the ancient ṛṣis and Lord Krishna himself were devoted to the cow. But he indicated that he did not want to make a religious appeal. By appealing on economic grounds, he agreed to argue within the rules of the new great tradition. Even Muslim rulers did not practice cow slaughter because it was unprofitable. Other countries such a China, Afghanistan, and Burma have outlawed cow slaughter. Burma realized that a partial ban was ineffective. Under the pretext of slaughtering useless cattle, many useful cattle are slaughtered. But, there is no such thing as a useless cow, for even when it is no longer able to bear milk or to be used for breeding or draught purposes, it is a "moving manure factory."[11] Bhargava, while alluding to religious purposes for the ban on cow slaughter, stuck close to his pledge to make his appeal on economic grounds.

Seth Govind Das was less inclined to argue within the rules of the new great tradition, making his appeal on religious and economic grounds. Cow slaughter is a religious matter.

> Great importance has been attached to this question from the time of Lord Krishna. I belong to a family which worships Lord Krishna as "*Ishtadev*." I consider myself a religious–minded person, and have no respect for those persons of the present–day society whose attitude towards religion and religious–minded people is one of contempt.[12]

The cow was also an economic and cultural matter. The decline in the number of cattle in an agricultural country like India is lamentable. No matter how much is spent on the Grow More Food Campaign, it will not succeed if the cows are not preserved.

> In New Zealand milk supply *per capita* is 56 ounces, in Denmark 40, in Finland 63, in Sweden 61, in Australia 45, in Canada 35, in Switzerland 49, in Netherland 35, in Norway 43, in U. S. A. 35, in Czechoslovakia 36, in Belgium 35, in Australia 30, in Germany 35, in France 30, in Poland 22, in Great Britain 39, and in India it is only 7 ounces. Just think what will be the state of health of the people of a country where they get only 7 ounces of milk per head. There is a huge infantile mortality in this country. Children are dying like dogs and cats. How can they be saved without milk?13

The per capita milk supply is the milk available to each inhabitant of the nation. How this will be improved by the retention of cows that do not produce milk was not addressed. But, partial bans have never worked. Only a total ban on cow slaughter will stop the erosion of this national wealth.

He returns again to the religious matter. He wants all religions to live together in harmony. To this end he urges Muslims to concede that their religion does not require them to slaughter the cow. Since Hindus have this sentiment against the cow's slaughter and there is no reason why Muslims must do so, there is a religious base for Hindus, but no religious barrier for Muslims. Muslims would be giving up something that their religion does not require anyway. As for the large sums of money needed to maintain cows in goshalas, the citizens of India will be more than glad to be taxed for it.

Prof. Shibban Lal Saksena started off by reflecting the new great tradition. "Sir, there are two aspects to this question. One is the religious aspect and the other is the economic aspect."14 Rather than argue that the religious aspect has no place in the secular state, he promoted the view that simply because an issue like cow slaughter has a religious dimension is no reason to leave it out of the constitution. His view was that the majority of Hindus feel the way they do about the cow because it has economic value.

> I personally feel that cow protection, if it has become part of the religion of the Hindus, it is because of its economic and other aspects, I believe that the Hindu religion is based mostly on the principles which have

> been found useful to the people of this country in the course of centuries.15

In addition to the arguments about the economic value of dung, the need for milk and the desire to lower infant mortality, he also lamented the need to use vanaspati ghee because of the unavailability of pure ghee from cow products.

Dr. Raghu Vira expressed his view in terms of his religious sentiments and feelings. Some of his friends have told him it is an economic question. He wants to make it clear that it is more than that.

> This country evolved a civilization and in that civilization we gave prominent place to what we call *Ahimsa* or non–killing and non–injury, not merely of human beings but also of the animal kingdom. The entire universe was treated as one and the cow is the symbol of the oneness of life and are we not going to maintain it?16

If the country forbids the killing of a learned man, it should do the same for the cow. He indicates that in his family no one could drink until the cow had drunk and no one started their meal until the cow had its meal. "The cow takes precedence over the children of the family, because she is the mother of the individual, she is the mother of the nation."17

Shri R. V. Dhulekar saw Indian independence as part of a mission that India had to declare that the whole human world as well as the animal world is free and shall be protected. He defends placing cow protection among the Fundamental Rights. One should not deny its place there because it does not pertain to humans. It is not the cow's right to protection but the right of humans to protect it that is at stake. Hindu society has included the cow in its fold.

> I can declare from this platform that there are thousands of persons who will not run at a man to kill that man for their mother or wife of children, but they will run at a man if that man does not want to protect the cow or wants to kill her.18

Two Muslim speakers rounded out the debate. Mr. Z. H. Lari, recognized that there were those who desired cow slaughter for religious as well as economic grounds. His contention was that whatever the majority wants should be placed in the clearest possible terms. He would prefer that it be among the Fundamental Rights rather than in the Directive Principles which would leave it up to the states. He recounted that on *Bakrid* many Muslims were molested or even imprisoned. While Islam does not require the slaughter of cows, it does permit it. The issue was not whether this was interference with religion but whether the Muslim minority would be denied a privilege which they presently have. Most important, the law must be clear so that there will be no basis for misunderstanding. If cow slaughter is to be banned, he and his community will submit to it. But as it stands, the article argues for the promotion of modern and scientific agriculture and also for the banning of the slaughter of cattle. This inconsistent article should be postponed until a clear statement can be submitted.

Syed Muhammad Saiadulla began with the recognition that the debate over the elimination of cow slaughter had two fronts: the religious and the economic. He recognized that there were those who wanted the prohibition of cow slaughter on religious grounds, but who argued on economic grounds. If they were to admit that it was part of their religion that cows should be protected he could not use his veto against it. But when they used economic arguments, the suspicion arose that "the ingrained Hindu feeling against cow slaughter is being satisfied by the backdoor."[19] He was suggesting that the economic arguments were merely a rationalization for a religious conviction. Saiadulla continued by questioning the economic argument. He pointed out that in 1931 there were 70 lakhs of cattle in Assam and 90 lakhs of people. But the cattle were small and unproductive. Their draught power was negligible and so cattle were imported from Bihar. If cattle were to be placed on a scientific footing many of the Assam cattle should be replaced with productive cattle. He was unimpressed by the view of Bhargava that through proper care and feeding marginally useful cattle would become useful for breeding purposes.

Finally, Article 48 found its way into the Directive Principles of State Policy. It argued for the improvement of cattle along scientific lines and also for the prohibiting of slaughter of cows and calves.

> The State shall endeavor to organise agriculture and animal husbandry on modern and scientific lines and shall, in particular, take steps for preserving and improving the breeds, and prohibiting the slaughter, of cows and calves and other milch and draught cattle.

While debate in the Constituent Assembly recognized both a religious sentiment and an economic argument and to that extent embodied the new great tradition, it could not be said that it limited itself to economic arguments. While Bhargava sought to do so, most of the other speakers either held that the religious sentiment was important or that it should not hinder the will of the majority. It is difficult not to agree with Z. H. Lari that it is inconsistent to promote scientific management of cattle and at the same time promote an end to slaughter. Religious sentiment would seem to have played a significant role in the formulation of Article 48.

The Supreme Court

Since the formation of the Constitution, there have been a number of attempts in Parliament to introduce anti cow–slaughter bills that would make it against the law to slaughter cows anywhere in India. In 1955 when the India Cattle Preservation Bill was debated, Nehru put forward the position that it was a matter for the state governments to decide. Although there were outbursts from members of the Hindu Mahasabha, Nehru stood firm and stated that he would stake his prime ministership on the issue. The bill was overwhelmingly rejected.[20]

The case which became a norm for all subsequent decisions before the court was *M. H. Quareshi* v. *State of Bihar*.[21] This case involved a series of petitions against the Bihar Act (1955-56), U. P. Act (1955-56) and Madhya Pradesh Act (1951). The Muslim petitioners who engaged in the butcher's trade and auxiliary trades, held that their fundamental rights had been offended, particularly Articles 14, 19(1)(g), and 25.

Before proceeding with the substance of the case, the Court felt constrained to deal with the contention that although the Directive Principles are not judiciable, since they are fundamental in the governance of the country, it is not only necessary that the State give effect to them, but that they are on that account more basic than the Fundamental Rights. The Court rejected this point of view and held that the Directive Principles cannot override the Fundamental Rights. Rather, one should seek to implement them harmoniously with the Fundamental Rights. If this contention had been accepted the case would have been without point for the petitioners were arguing that in the attempt to implement Article 48 their fundamental rights had been abridged.

The first complaint was that in banning the slaughter of cows their rights under article 25 were abridged. The petitioners had stated (Bihar Petition No.58 of 1956):

> As a result of the total ban imposed by the impugned section the petitioners would not even be allowed to make the said sacrifice which is a practice and custom in their religion, enjoined upon them by the Holy Quran, and practised by all Muslims from time immemorial and recognised as such in India.[22]

The petitioners were referring to their practice of slaughtering a cow on Bakr Id Day. The Court argued that in the Quranic surahs to which reference was made, the text reads that "people should pray unto the Lord and make sacrifice." In Hedaya Book XLIII at page 592, it was found that Muslims had the option of offering a cow or camel for seven persons or a sheep or goat for each person. Although the Court granted that to go the latter route would be economically impossible for many, that was not a religious compulsion. Since Muslims had several options, to take away one of them (i.e. sacrifice of a cow) did not take away their religious freedom.

The second complaint was that the restrictions did not afford equal protection before that law. The Act only affected Muslim Kasais who killed cattle but not others who killed goats and sheep. They contended that the U. P. Act and the Madhya Pradesh Act discriminated between those who killed cows and those who killed buffaloes. This discrimination is contrary to Article 14. The Court responded that although Article 14 forbids class legislation, it does not forbid reasonable classification based upon intelligible differentia if that differentia has a rational relation to the object being sought by the statute in question. It also pointed out that there is always a presumption of the constitutionality of an enactment and the burden of proof lies with those who would challenge it. The Court further held that the impugned acts were made by the states involved in fulfillment of their duty to implement Article 48 of the Constitution. The objects of these Acts, then, were "the preservation, protection, and improvement of lifestocks."[23] Now the different animals can be classified as to their usefulness to society and therefore the effects on society of those who kill the differing categories of animals can also be determined. As for the relative use of the classes of animals, the Court had this to say:

> Cows, bulls, bullocks and calves are no doubt the most important cattle for the agricultural economy of this country. Female buffaloes yield a large quantity of

> milk and are, therefore, well–looked after and do not need as much protection as cows yielding a small quantity of milk require. As draught cattle male buffaloes are not half as useful as bullocks. Sheep and goats give very little milk compared to the cows and the female buffaloes and have practically no utility as draught animals.[24]

These, then, are intelligible differentia, and so whatever objections one might have to these Acts, equal protection of the laws cannot be one of them.

The final argument of the petitioners was that the Acts abridged their rights under Article 19 (1)(g). The petitioners contended that, based on the Report on the Marketing of Cattle in India, and on 1948 figures, and figuring 7 sheep or goats as equivalent to one cow, that if a butcher of cattle were to be required to substitute sheep and goats for cattle, the number of such animals would not be available to make up the equivalency, nor would a market exist for such products in that volume. The state's defense was that to prohibit the slaughter of one type of animal was not the same as prohibiting a butcher to practice his trade. And, the subsidiary trades dealing with hides and guts could continue with the use of fallen cattle. The Court held that in U. P. the prohibition was only on cows, bulls, bullocks and calves of cows, permitting slaughter of buffaloes. M. P. also permitted the slaughter of buffaloes under certain conditions. In Bihar there was a total ban including buffaloes, but the butchers were still free to slaughter sheep and goats. The restrictions, then, did not totally shut down the trade of butchers. The real issue is the reasonableness of the restrictions placed upon their means of livelihood. The Court must decide reasonableness not on the basis of some abstract concept of reasonableness, nor what is considered reasonable by those upon whom the restrictions are imposed. The issue is whether the restrictions are "reasonable in the interests of the general public."[25] The Court forwarded the view that while the issue before them could not be settled on grounds of mere sentiment no matter how passionate it might be, sentiment was one among many elements to be taken into consideration in determining the "reasonableness" of the protested acts.

The Court then proceeded with its analysis. Cattle have a threefold use in India: "(1) to produce milk for food, (2) bulls for draught and (3) manure for agriculture."[26] A detailed statistical analysis of the cattle numbers in India revealed to the Court that India's cattle wealth was in number the highest in the world. But coupled with this, milk production was "perhaps the lowest."[27] "The average yield of milk per cow in India was 413 pounds which is about the lowest of any country in the world as against 8000 pounds in the Netherlands, 7000 pounds in Australia, 6000 pounds in Sweden and 5000 pounds in the United States of America."[28] Of this buffaloes yield 54% while cows give only 42% of the milk production. The former is higher in fat content, while the later is considered more easily digestible. In a Bihar study cows were credited with 620 pounds of milk per year, while buffaloes were credited with 1526 pounds. The Court conceded that merely from the economic point of view to maintain cows that produce less than 2 pounds of milk per day might profitably be eliminated. But to do so would have eliminated 90% of milk cows in 1958 and 70,00,000 tons out of 96,00,000 tons of annual gross production and the large number of bullocks that they might bear. It was estimated that to maintain a balanced diet would require 3,23,00,000 tons of milk per annum which was less than one third of total production. Particularly was this problematic in a country where many were vegetarians. Cow bullocks are preferred 10 to 1 over buffalo bullocks for draught purposes. While it was judged that there were about the right number of bullocks for cultivation purposes, with the growth in population and the need for more cultivated land, the need would likely increase. And, the number of breeding bulls (cattle and buffaloes) were considered insufficient. It was contended that 80,00,00,000 tons of dung are available each year of which 50% was used for fuel and 50% was used as manure. Cattle urine is also important for nitrogen, phosphates and potash. "In terms of money the dung and urine will account for a large portion of the agricultural income in India. Indeed Pandit Thakurdas Bhargava appearing as *amicus curiae* has claimed Rs. 63,00,00,000 per year as the contribution of the dung of these animals to the national income."[29] The Court concludes that "the back bone of Indian agriculture is in a manner of speaking the cow and her progeny."[30]

The Court admitted that "there exists a surplus of useless or inefficient animals."[31] While the greatest handicap in improving the efficiency of cattle was the lack of fodder, the inefficient cattle took fodder that could have been used to make the other cattle more efficient. Old and useless cattle roam in search of food creating a nuisance, and have a detrimental effect on the quality of cattle since they tend to multiply. The promotion of gosadans for old and useless cattle was considered an expensive proposition. It was estimated that the cost of 91 gosadans would be Rs. 45,50,000 non–recurring and Rs. 22,75,000 recurring each year. The government subsidy would be Rs. 19 per head while the per capita for education was Rs. 4.9 during 1955-56. That was the theory. But the plan was tried and, in the mind of the Court, with little success. After a detailed discussion of the cattle situation in the country, the Court summarized as follows:

> The country is in short supply of milk cattle, breeding bulls and working bullocks. If the nation is to maintain itself in health and nourishment and get adequate food, our cattle must be improved. In order to achieve this objective our cattle population fit for breeding and work must be properly fed and whatever cattle food is now at our disposal and whatever more we can produce must be made available to the useful cattle which are *in presenti* or will *in futuro* be capable of yielding milk or doing work. The maintenance of useless cattle involves a wasteful drain on the nation's cattle feed. To maintain them is to deprive the useful cattle of the much needed nourishment. The presence of so many useless animals tends to deteriorate the bred. Total ban on the slaughter of cattle, useful or otherwise, is calculated to bring about a serious dislocation, though not a complete stoppage of the business of a considerable section of the people who are by occupation butchers (Kasais) hides merchants and so on. Such a ban will also deprive a large section of the people of what may be their staple food."[32]

The Court also recognized the greater inclination to have a cow slaughtered over a buffalo. Since the cow produces so little milk it is uneconomical to maintain her during her dry period. The buffalo yields more milk and brings a lesser price than the cow for slaughter. Yet bullocks are more desirable for draught purposes than buffaloes. Hence the cow needs more protection. Regulation of the slaughter of cows has not worked. Veterinary inspectors can be pressured, cows can be maimed or slaughter may take place outside the municipal limits. After all of this discussion the Court's decision was the following:

> (i) that a total ban on the slaughter of cows of all ages and calves of cows and calves of she–buffaloes, male and female, is quite reasonable and valid and is in consonance with the directive principles laid down in Article 48 (ii) that a total ban on the slaughter of she–buffaloes or breeding bulls or working bullocks (cattle as well as buffaloes) as long as they are useful as milch or draught cattle is also reasonable and valid and (iii) that total ban on the slaughter of she–buffaloes, bulls and bullocks (cattle or buffalo) after they cease to be capable of yielding milk or of breeding or working

> as draught animals cannot be supported as reasonable in the interest of the general public."33

The Bihar Act then was considered invalid to the extent that it prohibited the slaughter of she–buffaloes, breeding bulls and working bullocks even though they might no longer be useful. As for when they become useless, that is a matter for legislative decision. However, to the extent that the Bihar Act "prohibits the slaughter of cows of all ages and calves of cows and calves of buffaloes, male and female, is constitutionally valid..."34

Likewise the U. P. Act was considered constitutionally valid in prohibiting the slaughter of all cows and calves, but unconstitutional insofar as it purported to "totally prohibit the slaughter of breeding bulls and working bullocks without prescribing any test or requirement as to their age or usefulness." The same judgment is made for the Madhya Pradesh Act.

In the light of the decision of the Supreme Court in *M. H. Quareshi* v. *State of Bihar* (1958), certain modifications were made in the acts involved and the revised acts were appealed in *Abdul Hakim* v. *State of Bihar*.35 Those revised Acts are: (1) Bihar Preservation of Animals (Amendment) Act, 1958; (2) Uttar Pradesh Prevention of Cow Slaughter (Amendment) Act, 1958; and (3) Madhya Pradesh Agricultural Cattle Preservation Act, 1959 (Act 18 of 1959). The petitioners contended that the legislation infringed on their fundamental rights in that it in effect placed a total ban on the slaughter of she–buffaloes, bulls or bullocks even when they have ceased to be useful. The age up to which the animals cannot be slaughtered (20 and 25 years) is unreasonably high and makes it impossible to slaughter any animals. They contended that even in countries where animal husbandry is highly scientific, cattle seldom live beyond 15 or 16 years and breeding bulls are discarded at 12 to 14 years. It was argued that in India bulls, bullocks and she–buffaloes seldom live 15 years and draught bullocks begin to age after 8 years. The responding states argued that with better animal husbandry in the State of Bihar, she–buffaloes, bulls and bullocks remain useful up to 25 years of age. U. P. responded that the age of 20 is reasonable for the useful age depends on the quality of grass on which they are grazed, and at no time do they become completely useless. M. P. argued that bulls, bullocks and buffaloes remain useful in that state well past 20 years.

Considering a large body of "expert opinion," the Court held that experts agree almost unanimously that after age 15 bulls, bullocks and buffaloes are no longer useful for breeding, draught or other purposes and that what little use they have is offset by the considerable economic disadvantage of feeding and maintaining unserviceable animals. To raise the age from 15 years to 25 is unreasonable. Also the detail of bureaucratic work required for a certificate of slaughter and to appeal if it is denied was considered unreasonable and disproportionate restrictions on their rights.

The Court then turned to the U. P. Act which raised the age from 15 to 20 for slaughterable cattle and added the condition of unserviceability. This meant that unserviceable animals under 20 years could not be slaughtered. Moreover, even if one had a certificate saying the animal was "fit for slaughter" it could not be killed for 20 days in order to give any "aggrieved" person the right to appeal. The court judged that all of the above were unreasonable restrictions.

The restrictions of the M. P. Act were also judged unreasonable because such cattle (other than cows and calves) had to be both unserviceable and over 20 years. The right to appeal within ten days was also considered unreasonable. In all of these instances the total ban on cows and calves was only mentioned and since it had already been declared valid in 1958 remained so thereafter.

As the result of a notification issued by the Jabalpur Municipality on January 12 1967 cancelling certain bye–laws which in effect withdrew the legal right to slaughter bulls and bullocks at Madar Tekdi Slaughter–House, the petitioner Mohd. Faruk held that his rights guaranteed in Article 19(1)(g) were infringed upon since restrictions were placed upon his hereditary vocation. The Court indicated that from time to time there had been attempts to circumvent the results of the Quareshi decision and that apparently this was another such attempt. The notification that cancelled the slaughter of bulls and bullocks in the aforesaid slaughter house in effect prohibited such slaughter within the Municipality of Jabalpur. The Court granted that the Municipality had the authority to cancel or withdraw bye–laws, and that the State had also the power to control or prohibit a practice, but when a fundamental right is affected through prohibition it places a heavy responsibility upon the State to show that it is done in the interest of the general public. The test of reasonableness must also show that the same interest of the general public could not be effected through some less radical restriction. The Court ruled in favor of Mohd. Faruk. But the Court went on to address itself to Hindu sentiments and the place of those sentiments in deciding the merits of the case.

> The sentiments of a section of the people may be hurt by permitting slaughter of bulls and bullocks in premises maintained by a local authority. But the prohibition imposed on a exercise of a fundamental right to carry on an occupation, trade or business will

> not be regarded as reasonable, if it is imposed not in the interest of the general public, but merely to respect the susceptibilities and sentiments of a section of the people whose way of life, belief or thought is not the same as that of the claimant.[36]

In 1958 the Court held that such sentiments were part of the test for reasonableness. But when they become dominant it is apparent that the interest of the general public is no longer the norm.

This conflict over cow slaughter continued in *Municipal Corporation, Ahmedabad* v. *Jan Mohammed*.[37] This case involved a grievance on the part of butchers of cattle that the designation of five days during the year as holidays on which the municipal slaughter house would be closed violated their rights under Article 19(1)(g) of the Constitution by placing unreasonable restrictions on their right to carry on their trade and also that it violated Article 14 by imposing restrictions which singled them out. The High Court had ruled that the standing orders were *ultra vires* and in violation of Article 19(1)(g). The Supreme Court held that the designated holidays did not place a prohibition but only a reasonable restriction on the fundamental right of the petitioner. It pointed out that the holidays were connected with Ghandi and Mahavir who were both promoters of non–violence. Others were connected with Rāma who is considered the embodiment of all virtues and Kṛṣṇa, expounder of the philosophy of the Gītā. These are generally days not only of festivity but often also of abstinence from meat. The contention that it was against Article 14 was rejected by both the High Court and the Supreme Court on grounds that were articulated in 1958.

In an attempt to implement Article 48, the State of Bombay enacted The Bombay Animal Preservation Act, 1954. This was amended in 1961 by the Gujarat Act 16 of 1961 to the effect that no certificate of slaughter would be granted in respect of a cow or any other animal that might be or later become useful for draught or breeding purposes unless it is above the age of 15 years and is not a cow. In 1978 the Governor of Gujarat issued Gujarat Ordinance No. 10 as a further amendment of the original Act when this was finally included in Gujarat Act No. 23 of 1979, the age limit was changed to apply to bulls and bullocks above 15 years which meant they had to be at least 16 years of age. In *Haji Usmanbhai* v. *State of Gujarat*,[38] the appellants challenged this as adversely affecting their trades. They appealed to *Abdul Hakim* v. *State of Bihar* where it was held that banning the slaughter of bulls, bullocks and she–buffaloes below the ages of 20 and 25 years was an unreasonable restriction since such animals did not remain useful after 15 years. The State countered that with the improved and more scientific animal husbandry in the State of Gujarat it was not an unreasonable age. The High Court rejected the appellants' contentions and when they went to the Supreme Court only two points of protest were made. The unreasonable restriction on age was the first and on it the Court sided with the State. Their second contention was that it violated their rights under Article 14 since it discriminated between dealers in cows and buffaloes, there being no uniform law regarding all cattle. The Court rejected this, as one might expect, on the grounds that dealers in different types of meat are of different classes which had already been established in the 1958 Quareshi case. The appeal failed.

In the above cases before the Supreme Court, the issue of religious sentiment was raised only twice. In *M. H. Quareshi* v. *State of Bihar* it was made clear that it was part of a consideration of reasonableness but could never be the determining factor regardless of how passionate the sentiment might be. In *Mohd. Faruk* v. *State of Madhya Pradesh* it was held that the prohibition of a fundamental right would be held unreasonable if it was imposed not in the interest of the general public but out of consideration of the sentiments of a section of the people whose way of life is different from the claimant. Restrictions on fundamental rights, therefore, are not reasonable if based on religious sentiment for the prohibition of cow slaughter, but such sentiment may play a more limited role in the determination of reasonableness.

The High Courts

Certain incidents issued in cases which reached only the High Courts. One such case was *Buddhu* v. *Allahabad Municipality (FB)*.[39] Although the slaughter of animals had been regulated by Municipal law since 1916, on 31-3-51 an amendment was made in the bye–laws which read: "No bull, bullock, cow, calf (both male and female) shall be slaughtered in any slaughterhouse or in any other place." The applicant contended that the new bye–law infringed upon his fundamental rights as found in Article 19(1)(g) on right of livelihood, and Article 14 since it made a distinction between those who slaughter sheep and goats and those who slaughter cattle. Since the petitioner could still slaughter buffaloes and sheep and goats he could not contend that his right to livelihood had been taken away. The Court concluded that the bye–law was not unreasonable since the "interest of a small class must yield place to the larger interest of the society as a whole."[40]

In February of 1950 an orthodox Brahmin was appointed chairman of Budge Budge Municipality. Using all the common economic reasons, the Commissioners of the Municipality passed a resolution closing "the Municipal Slaughter House for slaughtering cow, bull, bullock or buffaloes" and declared that no license would be issued for slaughter and sale of the flesh of such animals within the municipality. Exempted was meat for religious festivals and ceremonies. The owners of two beef shops appealed, and when the case reached the Calcutta High Court, the Court found that the appellants had not violated any provision of the Bengal Municipal Act (15 of 1932). While Article 48 of the Constitution encourages the state to pass laws for the protection of cattle, the resolution was not a law in the sense that the Bengal Municipal Act was. Hence the decision went in favor of the appellants and the municipal resolution was cancelled.[41]

Dulla v. *The State*[42] reveals that people suspected of slaughtering cows were turned in to the authorities and that the courts commonly imposed penalties which the High Court considered unreasonable. It concluded that they were led by their emotional reaction to the slaughter of cows. In May, 1956 the police investigated a report that a cow was being slaughtered at the house of one Phulu of the village of Saidpur. Arriving at 12 noon they found three men including Phulu in the inner courtyard cutting the carcass of a cow into large pieces while the other three men were cutting the large pieces into smaller ones. Phulu was arrested and the others fled. It was established that the slaughter had taken place between 4:30 and 6:30 a.m. and that the cow was not diseased. All six were found guilty by the Magistrate and given 18 month sentences. The six appealed to the Sessions Judge of Budaund and the conviction was upheld. The appeal was not based on any argument that the U. P. Prevention of Cow Slaughter Act (U. P. Act No. 1 of 1956) was unconstitutional, but rather that (i) the order of the Magistrate was bad in law and opposed to commonsense; (ii) that the order was against the weight of evidence; and (iii) that the sentence was excessive. The High Court to which this case eventually came emphasized that on both previous levels no reasons were given for what was considered an extreme sentence. Nor was this an isolated instance. "This Court is getting concerned at the punishment which subordinate Courts have been thoughtlessly inflicting on persons found guilty of a breach of the Cow Slaughter Act, and has been reducing the imprisonment to the period already undergone."[43] The Court then discussed at length the principles involved in sentencing. The prevalence of the crime in a particular area and whether the accused was a first offender should weigh heavily. But, "one's political, sentimental or religious pre–conceptions should be strictly disregarded."[44] No sentence should appear vindictive and fines are preferred to imprisonment unless the gravity of the crime demands it. The Court concluded that the lower courts looked at cow slaughter "as very heinous."[45] The Court recognized the religious dimension of cow slaughter but declared it irrelevant. "This Court is aware that large sections of the community deify the cow or surround it with a halo of religious veneration. But it is clear from a reading of the Act that it sedulously ignores as is inevitable in a secular State — the religious or sentimental aspect of the subject; it views it exclusively as an economic proposition, a weighty consideration in an agricultural economy as ours."[46] The Court voiced the view that the fact that a cow had been killed "perturbed the judicial mind." The Court would have held that a fine of Rs.50 for each offender would have been sufficient. But, even that was not necessary given the circumstantial nature of the evidence. The Court argued that there was no reason to presume that if someone is found cutting an animal at noon, that he must also have killed it six hours before. No witness saw them do the killing. When circumstantial evidence is used all evidence should exclude any other hypothesis but the one to be proved. But the evidence did not exclude the possibility that hearing that a cow had been slaughtered and that its meat was available, the defendants came to avail themselves of it. It is also possible that after killing the cow, Phulu decided to make a gift of the spare beef to his friends. The conviction was reversed.

In *Parasram Ji* v. *Imtiaz*[47] being informed that some persons had brought a number of cows (51) to a field in the vicinity of the police station for the purpose of slaughtering them, the Head Constable and two assistants arrived to find a cow tied up on the ground with two men holding it down, a third standing with a knife in his hand and three others observing. The Magistrate who tried the case convicted all six and assigned a sentence of six months in prison and Rs. 200 fine for each. On appeal before the Additional Sessions Judge it was determined that three were merely observers and the other three were making preparation for slaughter. Since that fell short of attempting to slaughter their conviction was overturned. When appealed before the High Court, the decision of the Sessions Judge was upheld. While in attacks on human beings preparation may itself be an offence, preparation for the slaughter of animals is no offence. In another case the accused were convicted because they were caught at the stage of reciting "bismillah," a rite meant to be practically simultaneous with actual slaughter. But there was no evidence that the accused in this case were reciting "bismillah" and so their convictions were overturned.

Gadadhar v. *State of West Bengal*[48] involved the attempt of government to condemn approximately 106 acres in the Hooghly district of Calcutta for the construction of a slaughter house along with a drug factory. The appeal was granted on technical grounds. The argument, however, included discussion of the cow slaughter issue. The appellants argued that the construction of the slaughter house was an attempt to appease Muslims at the expense of the sentiments of Hindus. Further, that while many states were passing laws implementing Article 48, West Bengal seemed to be going in the opposite direction. On that issue the court ruled that it was the duty of government to be concerned with the health of all Indians, and that all were not vegetarians.

Bafati v. *State*[49] was also decided on technical grounds. On report that the appellant was "coming to Khaga to sell beef as usual" he was approached by the police upon which he left his bicycle and fled on foot. He was later apprehended and convicted of violating Section 5 of the U. P. Prevention of Cow Slaughter Act. However, the prosecution failed to prove that the meat that he was transporting was "beef," that is cow rather than bullock, and that it was not suffering from contagious disease nor used for medical experimentation and public health research. Since the evidence was not presented the conviction was overturned.

In *Abdul Ameed* v. *Chitradurga Municipality*[50] apparently as the result of agitation on the part of the Hindu community regarding the sale of beef in the community, accompanied by complaints from citizens that the various beef vendors had created a public nuisance the municipality ordered the revocation of the licenses of beef vendors without indicating precisely at what point they had violated the terms of the license and without the opportunity to show cause against the charges levelled against them. The Court recognized the existence of strong Hindu sentiment against the slaughter of beef, but held that was not sufficient cause for the revocation of licenses.

In *Kitab Ali* v. *Santi Ranjan*[51] the accused were convicted of deliberately wounding the religious feelings of the complainant and other local Hindus by slaughtering a bullock within sight of their houses even though the act was done under protest. The accused held that they slaughtered the bullock in celebration of Bakr–Id–Day and had no intention of wounding the sentiments of the local Hindus. The case hinges more on Article 25 than on Article 48. The accused argued that Hindu texts show that there is sanction of cow slaughter and so the sentiments of these Hindus amounts to superstition.[52] The Court responded that although cow slaughter was sanctioned in some texts, it was abhorrent to Hindus generally. "There are various castes and sects among Hindus but no one who calls himself a Hindu can look upon cow–slaughter with equanimity and without his religious feeling being wounded."[53] Furthermore, "the idea of slaughter of cow which is repugnant to the Hindus universally cannot be held to be a mere superstition."[54] The Court rejected the appellants view that they did not intend to wound the feelings of Hindus. The slaughter was done in an open field and "in spite of the protest of the complainant whose house was close–by."[55] The application for revision was rejected.

In *Babu* v. *Municipal Board, Kheri*[56] the petitioner complained that the municipal slaughter house had been closed down and was in a dilapidated condition. He therefore slaughtered cattle at his house and was convicted of selling flesh in an unexposed manner. The Area Committee, Mahammadi, had ordered in 1955 that no cattle including buffaloes could be slaughtered in the town. The petitioner contended that this denied him the right to carry on his profession as guaranteed in Article 19(1)(g) of the Constitution. The Court pointed out that a total ban on the slaughter of cows is constitutional, but on the basis of *M. H. Quareshi* v. *State of Bihar*, that a general ban on cattle other than cows is unconstitutional. Therefore, it does offend the petitioners rights under Article 19(1)(g) and hence the respondents were ordered not to enforce their order.

In these cased there are several admissions of the existence of religious sentiment against cow slaughter. According to the Courts it is this sentiment which explains the willingness of citizens to report violations and which has also impaired the judgment of lower courts in affixing penalties for the offence. In *Dulla* v. *The State*, it was observed that the Act that was violated was not based on religious sentiment but on economic grounds. In the same manner the Courts should ignore such sentiments in sentencing. Moreover, while such sentiments may lead citizens to complain that beef vendors are a public nuisance, those sentiments are not sufficient for the revocation of licenses (*Abdul Ameed* v. *Chitradurga Municipality*).

Religious sentiment against cow slaughter seems on the whole to have been disregarded by the Courts. But it was not disregarded in the Constituent Assembly. Article 48 may be sufficient to explain most of the judgments of the Courts. But when the Court determined that to ignore the test of usefulness in the case of the slaughter of buffaloes is unconstitutional while the test of usefulness is irrelevant in the case of cows, that sentiment was surely taken into account. The Court did argue that given the need for bullocks for draught, uneconomical cows needed protection. But what economic argument could be given for protecting from slaughter a cow that gives no milk, is past breeding age, and is of no value for draught? The fact that they continue to produce dung would not have been sufficient to save the buffalo. Only religious sentiment can account for this ruling. We have in the case of the prohibition of cow slaughter, then, one of the few matters which goes against the ideology of the new great tradition.

Notes

1. cf. Robert D. Baird, "Religion and the Secular: Categories for Religious Conflict and Religious Change in Independent India," *Religion and Social Conflict in South Asia,* ed. Bardwell L. Smith (Leiden: E. J. Brill, 1976), 47ff, also Chapter VI of this volume. Also Baird, "Uniform Civil Code and the Secularization of Law," *Religion in Modern India*, ed. Robert D. Baird (Delhi: Manohar, 1981, first edition), 417ff, and Chapter IX of this volume.

2. cf. Baird, "Human Rights Priorities and Indian Religious Thought," A Journal of Church and State, Vol. XI, No. 2, 1969, and Chapter XII of this volume.

3. cf. "Uniform Civil Code and the Secularization of Law." Also, Baird, "Religion and Legitimation of Nehru's Concept of the Secular State," *Religion and the Legitimation of Power in South Asia* (Leiden: E. J. Brill, 1978), 83ff, and Chapter VII of this volume.

4. *Commissioner, H. R. E., Madras* v. *Sirur Mutt* (1954 SCJ 348).

5. *Digyadarshan R. R. Vayu* v. *State of A. P.* (AIR 1970 SC 181).

6. *Sardar Sarup Singh* v. *State of Punjab* (1959 SCJ 1123).

7. *Commissioner H. R. E., Madras* v. *Sirur Mutt.*

8. *Seshammal and Others* v. *State of Tamil Nadu* (1972 SCC 11).

9. For an analysis of all cases relating to Article 25 on freedom of religion see the author's "Religion and the Secular: Categories for Religious Conflict and Religious Change in Independent India," Chapter VI.

10. Donald Eugene Smith, *India As a Secular State* (Princeton: Princeton University Press, 1963), 484.

11. *Constituent Assembly Debates* (CAD), Vol. VII, 570.

12. *Ibid.*, 571.

13. *Ibid.*, 572.

14. *Ibid.*, 574.

15. *Ibid.*

16. *Ibid.*, 575.

17. *Ibid.*, 576.

18. *Ibid.*, 577.

19. *Ibid.*, 578.

20. Smith, *India As a Secular State*, 485-486. Also P. C. Chatterji, *Secular Values for Secular India* (New Delhi: Pauls Press, 1984), 64.

21. 1958 SCJ 975.

22. *Ibid.*, 984.

23. *Ibid.*, 986.

24. *Ibid.*

25. *Ibid.*, 990.

26. *Ibid.*, 992.

27. *Ibid.*, 993.

28. *Ibid.*

29. *Ibid.*, 996.

30. *Ibid.*

31. *Ibid.*, 998.

32. *Ibid.*, 1004.

33. *Ibid.*, 1006.

34. *Ibid.*, 1007.

35. AIR 1961 SC 448.

36. AIR 1970 SC 96-97.

37. AIR 1986 SC 1205.

38. AIR 1986 SC 1213.

39. AIR 1952 Allahabad 753.

40 *Ibid.*, 758.

41. AIR 1953 Calcutta 333.

42. AIR 1958 Allahabad 198.

43. *Ibid.*

44. *Ibid.*, 204.

45. *Ibid.*

46. *Ibid.*

47. AIR 1962 Allahabad 22.

48. AIR 1963 Calcutta 565.

49. AIR 1964 Allahabad 106.

50. AIR 1965 Mysore 281.

51. AIR 1965 Tripura 22.

52. For an understanding of the role of the category of "superstition" in a court judgment written by the then Chief Justice Gajendragadkar see *Durgah Committee* v. *Hussain Ali* (SCJ, Vol. XXI, 1958, 975). For a more complete treatment of Gajendragadkar see Baird, "Mr. Justice Gajendragadkar and the Religion of the Indian Secular State," *Journal of Constitutional and Parliamentary Studies*, New Delhi, October-December, 1972, 47-64, and Chapter XI.

53. AIR 1965 Tripura 24.

54. *Ibid.*

55. *Ibid.*, 26.

56. AIR 1976 Allahabad 326.

11

Mr. Justice Gajendragadkar and the Religion of the Indian Secular State

Although she does not already embody the ideal, India intends to be and has a good chance of becoming a secular state. Donald E. Smith so interprets post–independent India while defining a secular state as

> ...a state which guarantees individual and corporate freedom of religion, deals with the individual as a citizen irrespective of his religion, is not constitutionally connected to a particular religion nor does it seek either to promote or interfere with religion.[1]

For Smith the secular state embodies three sets of relationships:

(1) religion and the individual (freedom of religion)
(2) the state and the individual (citizenship)
(3) the state and religion (separation of church and state)

V. P. Luthera, while operating with a definition of the secular state which is similar to that of Smith concludes that India neither intends to be nor is it desirable that she should be secular in terms of strict separation of state and religion.[2]

The term "secular state," however, has had and continues to have a variety of meanings both in the consciousness of the general citizen and on the more academic level. Mr. Justice Gajendragadkar presents a significant view of the secular state because his long career in the Indian judiciary makes his position of more than mere academic interest. A judge of the Bombay High Court from 1945 to 1957, P. B. Gajendragadkar was appointed to the Supreme Court of India where he served as a judge from 1957 to 1964 and as Chief Justice from 1964 to 1966. During his tenure the Supreme Court returned several decisions regarding "matters of religion" and he himself delivered the judgment for the

Court in *Durgah Committee* v. *Hussain Ali*,[3] and *Shri Govindlalji* v. *State of Rajasthan*.[4]

While Luthera places considerable weight on the fact that the Indian Constitution does not explicitly declare the Indian state a secular one Gajendragadkar does not.

> My thesis is that the Indian Constitution unequivocally provides for a secular state and has enjoined upon Indian democracy the task of creating a new social order where social equality will prevail, political and economic justice will be the order of the day, and secularism will govern the relations of all the citizens *inter se* and those of the citizens with the state.[5]

But if he differs from Luthera in this regard, Gajendragadkar differs from Smith in giving a content to the secular state which involves it in the transformation of the existing religions and in effect substituting one faith for another.

In this essay I intend to show that according to Gajendragadkar (1) the "religion" whose freedom is guaranteed by the Indian Constitution is not any historically existing religion (religion$_1$), but an ideal notion of religion (religion$_2$);[6] (2) that the religion (religion$_2$) which is guaranteed freedom in the secular democratic state of India is a religion relegated to personal experience and metaphysical speculation severed from political and economic expressions; (3) that Gajendragadkar's religion in terms of religio–historical analysis is a religion of nationalism where the goals of the state are ultimate and what he chooses to call religion (religion$_2$) is penultimate; (4) that this involves a reconception of religion (ultimate concern) which cannot be effected by law alone, but must be preached and taught to masses.

For Gajendragadkar the Constitution does not guarantee freedom to Indians to define their religious beliefs and duties for themselves, but the possibility of elevating the demands of a liberal, secular democratic state to the level of ultimacy and reconceiving a previous pattern of ultimacy in such a way that it becomes penultimate. Though this is an analysis of the thought of P. B. Gajendragadkar it is important for understanding Supreme Court decisions dealing with "matters of religion" made under Gajendragadkar's leadership.[7]

Religion$_1$ and the Secular State

For Gajendragadkar the Indian secular state involves the rejection of the

Pakistan theocratic state as well as the "wall of separation" doctrine which in effect makes religion almost irrelevant.[8] Equally contrary to the spirit of Indian secularism is the position of the social thinker M. N. Roy.

> According to Roy, true spiritual freedom means not freedom to choose from among various religious doctrines, but freedom of the human spirit from the tyranny of all of them.[9]

Indian secularism is not anti–God nor anti–religion for there exist conditions under which taxes could be used for the support of religion.[10]

When Gajendragadkar stresses that "religion" is relevant to Indian secularism, what is the meaning of "religion?" In this context it is not religion$_1$ but religion$_2$. There are many things about religion$_1$ (the existing religions) which are in conflict with Indian secularism. It is quite possible for religion$_1$ to come in conflict with the goals of the secular state even though in a fully enlightened society there need be no conflict between religion$_2$ and society.

Religion$_1$ tends to lack tolerance which is a necessary ingredient of secularism. It tends to hold that it has a monopoly on truth. Religion$_1$ sometimes manifests itself in the form of extra–territorial loyalties which are inconsistent with the secular state.[11] It is often fanatic and obscurantist, relying on tradition and texts and being unwilling to test its tenets with reason and common sense. Religion$_1$ is frequently opposed to change even though such opposition is based on ignorance.

> Opposition to social change from the traditional section of any community is based on ignorance and is born of obscurantism. Obscurantism represents an attitude of mind which accepts tradition and traditional beliefs and usages blindly and is not prepared, and is even averse, to test the said beliefs and usages by the touchstone of reason and experience. Sometimes, these traditional beliefs and usages are inconsistent even with the true spirit of the religion by which the traditional sections swear.[12]

Hence the Hindu community resisted the Hindu Code Bill and the Muslim community resisted and continues to resist a uniform civil code which would involve modifications in Muslim personal law. It is religion$_1$ which has made a religious doctrine out of untouchability — a practice which has been outlawed by the Constitution. Whatever is meant when Gajendragadkar says that "religion" is relevant to Indian secularism, he clearly does not intend to refer to religion$_1$.

> I have attempted to show that when I am referring to the relevance of religion in the context of the evolution of a modern secular state, I am not referring to religion as it is organised in the traditional way or as it is preached from the pulpit or platform by ignorant traditionalists, priests, pundits, or kazis.[13]

So, while "religion" and Indian secularism are not incompatible, the "religion" which is relevant is not religion$_1$.

> Are religion and modernism incompatible? When I refer to religion in this context, I am not referring to religion as it practised by ignorant men following different religions, or as it is preached by ignorant and bigoted priestly caste belonging to different religions. Religion as practised by superstitious people and as preached by unenlightened priests seeking to interpret the letter rather than the spirit of their respective religious texts, tends to become narrow and exclusive. It is pedantic, backward–looking and static. It creates walls of exclusiveness. It leans on scripture rather than on reason.[14]

Leaving India's youth under the influence of such obscurantist religious leaders jeopardizes the secular state.[15]

The historically existing religions must realize, however, that they cannot stand in the way of the creation of a secular state. For, if a conflict does arise on the historical–empirical plane between religion$_1$ and socio–economic goals, religion$_1$ must always yield the right of way. It is religion$_1$ to which Gajendragadkar refers when he says:

> ...If there is any conflict between religion and public order or morality or health or any other provision of Part III, *religion has to yield*; and that establishes the basic proposition of Indian secularism that consideration of public order, morality and health, and considerations relating to fundamental rights enshrined in Part III play a paramount role, and religion will not be allowed to conflict with them.[16]

Religion$_2$ and the Secular State

If religion$_1$ is frequently in conflict with secularism but religion$_2$ is relevant to Indian secularism, what is the content of religion$_2$, and how does it relate to the secular state? Gajendragadkar is speaking of religion$_2$ when he says:

> ...The task of secularism is to separate the secular from the essentially religious, and to allow the secular to be governed by the state, leaving the essentially religious to be dealt with by religion.[17]

The above statement also clarifies a basic point in the religion of the secular state. Religion$_2$ only exists freely in the secular state after it has been disentangled from the secular. Before the disengagement it is religion$_1$. After the separation what remains and is guaranteed freedom under the Constitution is religion$_2$. Religion$_1$ tends to take everything within reach and label it "religious." But, within the modern secular democratic state this is no longer possible. Freedom of religion is guaranteed in the Constitution, but it is only "religion" which has been disentangled from the secular, i.e., religion$_2$. Gajendragadkar is fully aware that his distinction between religion (religion$_2$) and the secular is not traditional but modern.

> I recognise that all religions, like laws, in all primitive and medieval societies, tend to cover the totality of the life of the individual and the community. Similarly, religious scriptures deal not only with purely religious and ethical matters, but also cover social and secular aspects of human life. In fact, in the earlier stages of human society, a clear or sharp distinction was not made between law and religion. *Dharma*, for instance, as contemplated by the Hindu Smiritis dealt with religion and religious practices as well as personal law and several other secular topics pertaining to human life from the cradle to the grave.[18]

What, then, is the realm of the secular? What are those problems or issues the solutions to which religion has no relevance? To begin with, citizenship is determined without any reference to religion (religion$_1$ or religion$_2$). Furthermore, socio–economic justice must also be handled without recourse to religion. It may be that untouchability and caste distinctions have had religious sanction in terms of religion$_1$, but in the secular state they are secular matters of a social nature and fall under the authority of the state.

> ...untouchability has to be abolished, *whether or not* it formed part of Hindu religion,. Untouchability inevitably affects the social status of the citizen and his right to be treated on a footing of equality along with other citizens of the country. The problem, therefore, becomes a social problem and cannot be considered in the light of any religious texts.[19]

Matters of economics and the management of property are also purely secular regardless of their relationship to temples or maths. The appointment of members of temple boards or trustees is a secular matter and when the state enters this realm it is not interfering with religion.

> ...While religion is guaranteed full freedom within its legitimate domain, secular matters such as the administration of property are within the purview of the legislature and can be regulated reasonably without offending the fundamental rights of any citizen or without invading the guarantee for freedom of religion.[20]

Also important as a new realm for activity by the secular state is the realm of personal law. Personal law, that is, law regarding marriage, divorce, owning property, inheritance rights, etc., "is a secular matter, social in character."[21] Law and religion must be separated. When law is secularized, then the state can regulate matters of personal law.

> ...The Constitution–makers were keen that, whereas religion may play its legitimate role in the lives of citizens who owe allegiance to any religion, the state has to discharge its functions in its own sphere, uninfluenced and hampered by any considerations of religion. Secular law, the Constitution says, is a social matter with which religion has no concern.[22]

The so–called Hindu Code Bill which, after considerable opposition, was finally passed in the form of several independent bills, illustrates both the religious sanction given to Hindu law in the minds of Hindus and also the inevitable and (as Gajendragadkar sees it) justifiable separation of Hindu law from Hindu religion (religion$_2$). The struggle against it illustrates resistance to "social change" and not "religious change."[23] This is a necessary inference after having secularized law. One should not seek to justify the provisions of Hindu law by quoting the sacred scriptures, for it is a secular matter to be justified on "grounds of justice, equity and good conscious..."[24]

> Obsolete considerations based on the performance of rituals such as the offering of oblations had, in the context of modernism, no relevance in determining the priority of heirship and the shares awardable to different heirs, and it was no longer possible to treat marriage as a sacrament and not a matter of secular civil contract. Therefore, it would be not exaggeration to say that the adoption of the Hindu Code by the Indian Parliament constitutes an important step taken by Indian democracy in secularising the outlook of the Hindu community and assisting the creation of a new social order within the community itself.[25]

In the history of Hindu law, commentators on the ancient texts were the vehicles of social and legal change. But now legislators have replaced the commentators. "With the arrival of democracy, the age of commentators has come to an end and the age of legislators has begun."[26] The logical implication is that whatever Hindus might think about it, within the context of the Indian secular state, there can be permitted no connection between Hindu religion and Hindu law. Hindu religion (in the form of religion$_2$ and not religion$_1$) is within the domain of religion, but Hindu law is clearly within the province of the state. When the state legislates in the area of Hindu law, it is not in any way interfering with religious freedom inasmuch as Hindu law and Hindu religion$_2$ are not connected.

What is true for the Hindus and the Hindu Code is equally true for Muslims and their opposition to a uniform civil code. Many Muslims honestly feel as did many Hindus that invasion into the domain of personal law is an invasion into religion. They must be educated to see that this is not so. They must be taught the legitimate realms of religion$_2$ and the secular state.

> While educating Muslim public opinion in regard to the necessity and significance of secularising the personal law, it would be idle to ignore the fact that in the traditional minds of the common Muslim men and

> women we notice resistance to any social change and this resistance proceeds from the honest, though mistaken, belief that a change in personal law necessarily invades the realm of Muslim religion. Traditional Muslims oppose any effort to secularise the Muslim law just as the traditional Hindu did, and we must satisfy the generality of Muslim men and women that no invasion of *Muslim religion properly so called* is intended when the adoption of a common civil code is advocated by the secular intellectuals of this country.[27]

What then is the realm of religion$_2$? Gajendragadkar recognizes that the "religion" whose freedom is protected by the Constitution is not defined in the Constitution. It is the disengagement of religion from the realm of the secular which leaves us with the realm of religion$_2$. It is necessary to distinguish between the essential part of religion$_1$ and its non–essential historical accretions. The latter are "secular in character, may be social, economic or political, and as such they may be disengaged from the sphere of religion."[28] Gajendragadkar gives us no more help in effecting the separation than does Toynbee whom he follows.[29]

Since "religion" is not defined in the Constitution, Gajendragadkar wants to rely on the judgments of the Supreme Court. It is particularly in *Commissioner, H.R.E.* v. *Lakshmindra* that religion is defined.[30] In that judgment the definition of religion used in the American case *Vide Davis* v. *Benson*[31] that religion"has reference to one's views of his relation to his Creator and to the obligation they impose of reverence for His Being and character and of obedience to His will." The theistic dimension of the "American" definition is rejected because it does not include "Buddhists" and "Jains." However, religion is seen as "a matter of faith with individuals or communities."[32] But religion ought not to be limited to mere belief.

> A religion may not only lay down a code of ethical rules for its followers to accept, it might prescribe rituals and observances, ceremonies and modes of worship which are regarded as integral parts of religion, and these forms and observances might extend even to matters of food and dress.[33]

P. B. Gajendragadkar further expands the "matter of faith." The realm of religion$_2$ is to inquire into the mystery of the universe, to deal with the problem of the future life if there is such, to engage in metaphysical speculations. Religion$_2$ deals with "eternal verities" if there be such.

> It is this quest for the mystery of the unknown depths of the universe on which religion is engaged. It involves an inquiry into the origin of the universe, into the future of man after life becomes extinct, into the question as to whether there are any eternal verities and in all problems which are supernatural. These may not be solved merely by human logic and reason, and intuition may play a part in such investigation. It is these metaphysical speculations with which religion and ethics are primarily concerned. It is religion and ethics in this sense to which Nehru refered and it is such religion that is relevant under Indian secularism.[34]

Intuition is part of religious investigation. But after one finds what one considers an answer to these religious questions regarding the unseen, one is not able to allow one's understanding to interfere with the ordering of the social, political and economic realms. In these secular areas reason and common sense reign supreme and intuition has no place.

Once religion$_1$ is stripped of its non–essential historical accretions and results in religion$_2$, it can be seen that all religions have an element of truth and none of them has a monopoly on the truth. This is understandable since each religion$_1$ contains religion$_2$. But Gajendragadkar goes still further in stating that each religion is entitled to equal respect since no religion is superior or inferior to another. This sounds as though he is referring to the historically existing religions (religion$_1$), but it must be remembered that religion$_1$ is not even guaranteed freedom under the Constitution as Gajendragadkar interprets it in the light of his concept of the secular state. This must then mean that all religions are entitled to equal respect to the extent to which they approximate or embody religion$_2$.[35]

For Gajendragadkar the doctrine of equal validity is basic to his understanding of tolerance. Tolerance is not the ability to permit religions to exist which one is convinced are wrong, but the recognition that equal respect is due to all religions since none is to be considered inferior or superior to another.

> The importance of tolerance in the creation of a secular order cannot be overemphasised. Whereas in India,

> many religions are practised, the followers of every religion must, *without any mental reservation*, recognise the fact that their individual religion is not the monopolist of spiritual wisdom; that all religions are entitled to equal respect under the Indian Constitution, which means, no religion is superior and no religion is inferior. The Hindus must give up unhesitatingly the concept of *Mlechcha*, which in old traditional days was associated with non–Hindus; and the Muslims must equally unhesitatingly and without mental reservation give up the concept of *Kafir*.[36]

If one comes to understand one's religion (religion$_1$) in terms of religion$_2$, one's tolerance or recognition of the truth of all religions will prevent one from propagation of religion$_1$ with the view to converting another to it. For such propagation implies the superiority of one's religion (religion$_1$) over that of another. If tolerance, or the recognition of the truth of all religions, is an important implication of Indian secularism, so is the avoidance of propagation.

> If the true spirit of tolerance receives acceptance from all religions, on principle there would really be no scope for concerted or organised efforts at propagation of religion or for making efforts at proselytising...Propagation of one's faith with the idea of converting a person belonging to another faith to one's own necessarily assumes the belief that the religion propagated is superior to the religion of the person sought to be converted; and such an assumption is inconsistent with the spirit of tolerance and is opposed to the philosophy on which modern Indian secularism is based.[37]

Article 25 of the Constitution does recognize the individual's right to propagate his religion. But for Gajendragadkar that simply means the right of discussion in an academic manner. If as a result of such discussion one desires a religious change that is permissible. But article 25 ought not to be taken as encouragement for persistent or enthusiastic propagation.[38]

In what context are we to understand the truth of all religions? All religions are true not in their concreteness, but to the extent to which they correspond to Gajendragadkar's model and have been severed from their non–essential accretions. But to get the public to accept that will take "concerted and consistent propagation" and should enlist all educators and educational institutions in behalf of such propagation.[39] But what does this do to Gajendragadkar's notion of tolerance? All religions are true if they conform to his model. Those who hold to a superiority doctrine cannot be tolerated within the secular state. Monopolist religion must be converted to Gajendragadkar's ideal model of the content and function of religion devoid of superstitions and cut off from the secular in which case they will be tolerated because they are the same (hence they will also tolerate each other), or they cannot be tolerated at all.

What is the source of Gajendragadkar's view of religion$_2$ in the secular state? While Donald E. Smith is partially correct in stating that the Hindu past is not a strong basis for secularism, Gajendragadkar argues that the spirit of tolerance of which he speaks and which is a prerequisite for secularism, is a legacy of the Hindu tradition.

> But the point which I wish to emphasise is that the spirit of tolerance, born out of a firm conviction that all religions are entitled to freedom and each one of them has an element of truth, while none has the monopoly of truth — this is a legacy of Hindu philosophy, and that is the cornerstone of secularism of which I am speaking. This is a special feature of Hindu philosophy, religion and culture and as such it is on this foundation that the whole edifice of secularism rests. This aspect of Hindu tradition is, and, I venture to suggest, does form the theoretical basis of our secularism.[40]

One must remember that it is not all existent religions which are entitled to freedom, but religion$_1$ transformed according to religion$_2$. It is on that model that the whole edifice of secularism is asked to rest.

How does Gajendragadkar operate when he has to apply his ideal model of religion (religion$_2$) to a real historical situation (religion$_1$) ? In *Durgah Committee* v. *Hussain Ali*,[41] he introduces two means for handling the problem. The first is that for a practice to be treated as religion$_2$ it "must be regarded by the said religion as its essential and integral part....[42] For a practice to be treated as religion$_2$ it must be considered by religion$_1$ as essential to its existence. Non–essential practices are considered secular even though they are often unnecessarily clothed in religious form. This first criterion could, if strictly applied, reduce a historical religion to skin and bones. Not infrequently the essential beliefs and practices of a religion have implications which while not themselves the essence, give form to the essence and without them the religion would be rendered enemic. Historical religious communities are a complex of beliefs and practices, many of which may not be "essential" but are part of a pattern, and their removal would significantly change the previous pattern of ultimacy.

His second criterion is more difficult to apply. If a practice springs from superstition, even though it is now considered essential and hence would otherwise qualify as $religion_2$, it may be treated as an accretion to $religion_2$ itself. That is, superstitions which attach themselves to the ideal model need not be guaranteed freedom. How does one identify superstition? Gajendragadkar does not say. Ultimately it is probably any deviation from his ideal model of religion. In the *Durgah* case, the petitioners argued that what is religion to one is superstition to another.

> The Court rejected this as being of no relevance. If an obviously secular matter is claimed to be a matter of religion, or if an obviously secular practice is alleged to be a religious practice, the Court would be justified in rejecting the claim because the protection guaranteed by Art. 25(1) and Art. 26(b) cannot be extended to secular practices and affairs in regard to denominational matters which are not matters of religion.[43]

But now the criterion for determining a "matter of religion" is gone. If a believer contends a given practice is essential and thereby qualifies as $religion_2$ and the Court rejects this because it is "obviously a secular practice," then the determination of a legitimate "matter of religion" (i.e. $religion_2$) becomes arbitrary. If, on the other hand, the criterion of "essentiality" is maintained, then nothing is "obviously secular." Its secularity can only be determined by a careful examination of the value system of the adherent or his community.

There are then two realms: $religion_2$ and the secular. The latter must be disengaged from $religion_1$ if the secular state is to become a reality. While intuition may play a role in $religion_2$, reason, justice and common sense rule the realm of the secular. The two realms would seem to be clearly distinguished and separate with no relationship between them. But, once the secular is disengaged from $religion_1$, leaving $religion_2$, and once $religion_2$ sees that it cannot assume a position of ultimacy and accepts its penultimacy, Gajendragadkar believes it will not only not interfere with the goals of secularism but will provide a driving force for these goals.

> Therefore, unlike the extreme advocates of secularism in the western sense who believe in the elimination of religion from life altogether, Indian secularism tolerates and even recognises the relevance of religion in the lives of citizens individually and collectively, but imposes an inexorable limitation on such relevance and validity of religion by declaring that secular matters are out of bounds for religions of all kinds. On this basis it is not unreasonable to suggest that in the effort to build a secular social order, faith and morality and ethics may furnish a driving force.[44]

Religion of Nationalism

Having examined Mr. Justice Gajendragadkar's view of religion$_1$, religion$_2$, and the secular state, it now remains for us to inquire as to what we have found means within the categories of religio–historical analysis. In other words, what qualifies for religion in terms of ultimate concern in the thought of Gajendragadkar? What does he say is of highest importance? We have already noticed that religion$_1$ had to give way to the secular state by giving up the realm of the "secular" and limiting itself to religion$_2$. Now we must address ourselves to this phenomenon more explicitly.

As Gajendragadkar sees it, historical events have changed our theories about human beings and the goals of life itself. The historical events to which he refers are two world wars and the emergence of communist power in Russia. The significance of the First World War is seldom appreciated.

> When the first shot was fired across the Austrian border and it led to the First World War (1914-1918), it was not realized that the shot would bring to an end the epoch of liberal philosophy which glorified individual freedom and fondly anticipated an inevitable and uninterrupted progress of the human race towards happiness and perfection.[45]

By the end of the First World War communist power became a reality in Russia and this posed a threat to democracies. Nazi Germany and fascist Italy were totalitarian responses to the threat of communism. Of importance for the development of democracy, however, was the Beveridge Report which gave birth to the idea of the welfare state.[46] The result was that the democratic state assumed certain responsibilities which it had not thus far assumed. The modern democratic state acts as protector, dispenser of social services, industrial manager, economic controller, and arbitrator. Once the democratic state dedicates itself to the cause of the common citizen and the establishment of socio–economic justice, if it also values individual freedom, the latter must be preserved but adjusted to the demands of the former.

> We reach a stage in the progress of the democratic way of life where law ceases to be passive just as democracy ceases to be passive and the purpose of law like that of democracy becomes dynamic; and that naturally raises the eternal question about the adjustment of the claims of individual liberty and freedom on the one hand, and the claims of social good on the other.[47]

With the emphasis of the welfare state on social justice, freedom and liberty must give some ground. "The catchwords became *welfare* and *quality* rather than freedom."[48]

> As soon as the ideal of a welfare state is accepted by democracy it leads to one important consequence, and that is that the claims of social justice must be treated as *paramount* and *primary* and if the freedom of the individual and his individual rights need to be regulated in order to achieve social justice, the regulation is a part of the price which democratic citizens must cheerfully pay in order to sustain the democratic way of life.[49]

Without the provisions of the welfare state, democracy is likely to fall to communism. But the welfare state provides certain freedoms by the curtailment of others. Freedom of the press, for example, can be restricted reasonably "in the interests of the security of the state, friendly relations with foreign states, public order, decency or morality, and in relation to contempt of court, or defamation, or incitement to an offense."[50] It was in response to communism that the welfare state was born, and its success will falsify the prediction of communism as the inevitability of a violent class–war.[51]

However, the birth of the democratic welfare state requires that problems be faced on a rational and scientific basis. This is indeed the "first basic postulate" of the democratic way of life.

> In a secular democracy, pseudo–metaphysical considerations or considerations based on technical,

> traditional, and religious hypothesis are irrelevant. All socio–economic problems have to be attacked in a rational and intellectual way and their solution sought by the adoption of a rational and scientific approach. In dealing with such socio–economic problems there is no scope for invoking any dogma or creed, for the very essence of a rational and scientific approach is that there are no absolutes in socio–economic matters.[52]

All spiritual techniques are inappropriate in the democratic view of life. Fasting as a method of putting pressure on the government is therefore undemocratic and irrational.

By relegating $religion_2$ to penultimacy and arguing that $religion_1$ must not regulate affairs, Gajendragadkar has in effect offered another pattern of ultimacy as a world view. It is a pattern of ultimacy and hence a religious system because it is more important than anything else. It is explicitly said to be *paramount.*

> It has been said earlier and I wish to emphasise it again, that Article 25 guarantees the right of freedom of religion subject to the distinct proviso that matters of social reform and matters covered by public order, morality and health and other fundamental rights are *paramount.* In other words, the non–essential part of religion must be disengaged from the essential and in regard to the former, which is secular in character, the state has complete authority of regulation.[53]

Indian secularism is "not merely a political doctrine. It is not a passive or negative doctrine. It is a comprehensive, forward–looking, dynamic doctrine."[54] Secularism is a new faith which is paramount and which demands the re–adjustment of historical religious expressions if they choose to continue their existence in a secular context. Secularism stands with the Constitution and the Courts, and hence it is $religion_1$ which must re–adjust its scope in the face of this ultimacy.

> Secularism says to the Hindus that in regard to the demand for a total ban on cowslaughter, let us discuss the problem as a social and economic problem and let us not introduce religious scriptures into the debate. Secularism says to the Muslim citizens that in regard to the problem of enacting a common civil code, let us

> discuss the reasonableness of the proposal in the light of principles of justice, equity and good conscience, but let us not introduce Muslim scriptures in the debate. To the Roman Catholic citizens, secularism says that the programme of family planning must be examined as a social problem, in the discussion and decision of which the Papal Encyclical has no relevance. Thus the sweep of secularism is *comprehensive* and its objective is to rationalise and modernise the social structure of the Indian community. It is to this objective that secularists belonging to all the communities in this country must dedicate themselves.[55]

Although the secular faith is transnational in that it invokes values which "transcend racial and national limits,"[56] nevertheless, the realization of the objectives of the secular democratic welfare state requires unquestioned national loyalty. Extra–territorial loyalty is a threat to this new faith of the secular state. After the burning of Jerusalem's Al Aqsa Mosque in August 1969, by an Australian later judged insane by an Israeli state psychiatric board, Indian Muslims took to the streets in protest, calling for Jihād. For Gajendragadkar the manner of conducting the protest illustrated the extra–territorial loyalties which were part of the faith of some Muslims and which threatened the goals of the secular state. Citizens must realize that the goals of the secular state are paramount and that reaching those goals requires unquestioned loyalty to India.

> It seems to me, it would be legitimate to suggest that if processions are taken out to protest against the damage done to a mosque situated in a foreign place like Jerusalem and cries of Jehad are raised, they are likely to awaken in the minds of Muslim masses a sense of extra–territorial loyalty born of a feeling of Muslim brotherhood which transcends national bounds. It is precisely this extra–territorial loyalty based on religious affinity which is not consistent with secularism and the obligations of citizenship. That is why, even on occasions when anger is roused and resentment is inevitable, it is the duty of the leaders to channelise the anger and resentment into forms of protest which will try to avoid the injection of Chauvinistic sentiments in the minds of those who join in such protests. Therefore, it is of the utmost importance that progressive Muslim intellectuals

> should inculcate in the minds of their fellow religionists the *paramount necessity of unquestioned loyalty to India and complete dedication to and identification with the cause of secularism enshrined in the provisions of the Indian Constitution.*[57]

The last statement communicates ultimacy. In terms of religio–historical analysis, the nation is elevated to the religious position and hence it cannot accept extra–territorial loyalties which might make it penultimate rather than ultimate.

After the communal incidents at Ahmedabad in 1969, an All–Party Conference convened by the Prime Minister unanimously adopted a statement offered by the National Integration Council which included the following statement endorsed by Gajendragadkar. "While religion plays an important role in life, it should not stand in the way of building a modern society and a secular state as envisaged in our Constitution."[58] One of the reasons why the state cannot be denied the right to legislate within its rightful domain, is that communities which retain their own distinct laws tend to become a nation to themselves and hence threaten the nation from within.[59]

Gajendragadkar is concerned to show the neutrality of the state in religious matters when he says, "Indeed, the state as such has no religion."[60] He seems to mean that the state is not in support of any form of religion$_1$. But the thrust of his position requires the reformulation of religion$_1$ in terms of religion$_2$. And this reorientation points to a new religion in terms of religio–historical analysis. The secularism of modern India in the thought of Gajendragadkar is not the separation of religion and the state as Donald E. Smith proposes, but the inculcation of a new faith. In the Indian context the separation of "religion" from the "secular" or better the separation of the secular from religion$_1$ amounts to the formulation of a new faith. But even the *content* of the secular has become a faith, a secular*ism* for Gajendragadkar. It is a faith in the ability of reason to solve socio–economic problems and even its relevance to the re–ordered sphere of religion$_2$ as a safeguard against "obscurantism" and "fanaticism." Furthermore, it is a faith of universal validity.

> This secular faith is universal in character because its values are inherited from the best elements of religions which transcend racial and national limits.[61]

This new faith or religion requires a conversion on the part of the masses if it is to be fulfilled. The traditional practice of granting religious sanction (as in $religion_1$) to "secular" matters has to be given up. "How," asks Gajendragadkar, "are you going to bring about a revolution in the outlook of the traditional community?"[62] One of the agents is the Indian intellectual who should take a lead in inculcating such secular ideals in the lives of the masses. The educator is particularly responsible for achieving the new goals of the secular state.

> When I refer to education as an instrument of social change, what do I mean? I mean that education must inculcate in the minds of students faith in a proper sense of values. This task cannot be achieved merely by prescribing textbooks. The philosophy on which a democratic and secular sense of values is founded has to be imparted by teachers to their students unceasingly, both in the curricular and in the co-curricular activities of university life...[63].

It should be noted that what Gajendragadkar calls social change or the secular, has been shown in terms of religio–historical analysis to be religious change and religion. *Nirvāṇa* was a term traditionally used to refer to liberation from the endless cycles of birth and death. As such, it was ultimate, final, the supreme goal. But for Gajendragadkar there is a new ultimacy, a new *Nirvāṇa*. Social reformers and liberals and humanists must continue to direct us to "...the road to the modern *Nirvana* of secularism free from obscurantism, free from fanaticism and from communalism."[64]

Notes

1. Donald E. Smith, *India as a Secular State* (Princeton: Princeton University Press), 1963, 4.

2. Ved Prakash Luthera, *The Concept of the Secular State and India* (Calcutta, Oxford University Press), 1964.

3. A. I. R. 1961 SC 1402.

4. A. I. R. 1963 SC 1638.

5. P. B. Gajendragadkar, *Secularism and the Constitution of India* (Bombay, Bombay University Press), 1971, 51.

6. The word "religion" is ambiguous and is used in several senses in the thought of P. B. Gajendragadkar and in religio–historical analysis. For the sake of clarity we will use the following symbols to distinguish three distinct meanings:
religion = ultimate concern, a functional definition useful in religio–historical analysis. The ultimate concern of a given person or community is that which is to him, her, or it, more important than anything else in the universe. For an extended discussion of this definition and the method of religio–historical analysis see Robert D. Baird, *Category Formation and the History of Religions* (The Hague, Mouton & Co.), 1971.
$religion_1$ = the historically existent religions. Not necessarily the "ism" traditions such as "Hinduism," "Buddhism," "Christianity," etc., but religions as found in their actual historical settings.
$religion_2$ = true religion which is relevant and permissible within Gajendragadkar's view of the secular state. Gajendragadkar's ideal model of religion.
Hence, whenever the term religion or its cognate form is used alone, we are referring to a category of religio–historical analysis. $Religion_1$ and $religion_2$ refer to two distinct uses of the term in Gajendragadkar's thought.

7. For a discussion of "matters of religion" in Indian Supreme Court decisions see B. Parameswara Rao, "Matters of Religion," *Journal of the Indian Law Institute*, October–December, 1963, Vol. 5 No. 4, 509-513.

8. *Secularism and the Constitution of India*, 52.

9. *Ibid.*, 11.

10. *Ibid.*, 58.

11. *Ibid.*, 149.

12. *Ibid.*, 118.

13. *Ibid.*, 98.

14. *Ibid.*, 42.

15. *Ibid.*, 86.

16. *Ibid.*, 69-70 (*emphasis added.* Article 25 of the Indian Constitution reads as follows:

"25 (1) Subject to public order, morality and health and to the other provisions of this Part, all persons are equally entitled to freedom of conscience and the right freely to profess, practise and propagate religion.

(2) Nothing in this article shall effect the operation of any existing law or prevent the State from making any law–

(a) regulating or restricting any economic, financial, political or other secular activity which may be associated with religious practice;

(b) providing for social welfare and reform or the throwing open of Hindu religious institutions of a public character to all classes and sections of Hindus.

Explanation I — The wearing and carrying of *kirpans* shall be deemed to be included in the profession of the Sikh religion.

Explanation II — In sub–clause (b) of clause (2), the reference to Hindus shall be construed as including a reference to persons professing the Sikh, Jain or Buddhist religion, and the reference to Hindu religious institutions shall be construed accordingly."

17. *Ibid.*, 120.

18. *Ibid.*, 90.

19. *Ibid.*, 82 (emphasis added).

20. *Ibid.*, 112-113.

21. *Ibid.*, 57.

22. *Ibid.*, 57-58.

23. *Ibid.*, 118.

24. *Ibid.*, 155.

25. *Ibid.*, 121.

26. *Ibid.*, 120.

27. *Ibid.*, 151 (emphasis added).

28. *Ibid.*, 95. The reference here is to $religion_2$.

29. For a critical discussion of Toynbee's attempt at separating the essence from the non–essential historical accretions see my *Category Formation and the History of Religions.*

30. A. I. R. 1954 SC 290. Judgment delivered by B. K. Mukherjea, J. (as he then was).

31. (1888) 133 U. S. 333 at 342.

32. A. I. R. 1954 SC 290.

33. *Ibid.*

34. *Secularism and the Constitution of India,* 90.

35. It is appropriate at this juncture to point out that the Constitution does not imply equal religious validity (in terms of $religion_1$), but protects the freedom of one to hold to the superiority of his religion

(religion 1) and propagate it. An examination of the *Constituent Assembly Debates* shows that the inclusion of "propagate" was at the insistence of the Christian community whose propagation had conversions in view.

36. *Secularism and the Constitution of India*, 96.

37. *Ibid.*, 97.

38. *Ibid.*

39. *Ibid.*, 85-86. Apparently here "concerted and consistent propagation" is not only permissable but essential.

40. *Ibid.*, 101.

41. A. I. R. 1961 SC 1402.

42. A. I. R. 1961 SC 1415.

43. *Secularism and the Constitution of India*, 81 cf. also A. I. R. 1961 SC 1415.

44. *Secularism and the Constitution of India*, 89.

45. P. B. Gajendragadkar, *Law, Liberty and Social Justice* (Bombay, Asia Publishing House, 1965), 58.

46. *Ibid.*, 62.

47. *Ibid.*, 64.

48. *Ibid.*, 75.

49. *Ibid.*, 80 (emphasis added).

50. *Ibid.*, 100.

51. *Ibid.*, 128.

52. *Ibid.*

53. *Secularism and the Constitution of India*, 152 (emphasis added). Cf. also *Law, Liberty and Social Justice*, 80.

54. *Ibid.*, 173.

55. *Ibid.*, 173-174 (emphasis added).

56. *Ibid.*, 50.

57. *Ibid.*, 149 (emphasis added).

58. *Ibid.*, 168.

59. *Ibid.*, 152-153.

60. *Ibid.*, 55.

61. *Ibid.*, 50.

62. *Ibid.*, 158.

63. *Ibid.*, 85.

64. *Ibid.*, 158.

12

Human Rights Priorities and Indian Religious Thought

Most discussions of human rights in the United States assume that the articles of the Universal Declaration of Human Rights proclaimed by the General Assembly of the United Nations in 1948 are indeed universal. The inference from such an assumption is that the only problem is the implementation of such rights where they have not been realized by reason of injustice and prejudice. Hence, even where the task is seen as educative, the passage of legislation is interpreted as part of the educative process. That such human rights are based on the religious views of the Enlightenment which are not themselves universally affirmed is seldom appreciated. It is the intention of this essay to show that the Universal Declaration is indeed a religious point of view, that it is in conflict with other widely held religious points of view, and that if implementation does not proceed with care, one endangers a basic human right guaranteed by the same document — religious freedom.

The Nature of Religion

One commonly praises religion because it has served as a cohesive force in either human personality or in society, or one condemns it because it has not functioned as one may have wished in alleviating poverty, discrimination, or mental illness. These are the kinds of judgments and questions that are raised by persons whose main concern is this world, the human personality, and human society. While it is true that some religious positions are this–worldly, not all have been, and not all are. The view of the Enlightenment that the value of religion is that it functions as the moral guardian of the community is simply not acceptable to all religious people.

The ultimacy of religion which is such a commonplace among scholars is consistently ignored in human rights discussions. "Religion, in the largest and most basic sense of the word," wrote Paul Tillich, "is ultimate concern."[1] That is, religion has to do with what really matters and is not merely a means to an end that matters more. To be sure, religion contains within its own system both means and ends, but the ends are not always socially oriented. Although a devout Muslim may well have a social conscience, to suggest that his submission to Allāh — which is what it means to be a Muslim, which is final and an end in itself, and which is symbolized by a prostrate position in prayer — is good not because it is ordered by Allāh, but because it is useful in putting into practice what someone else considers to be a good society, may be objectionable to the believer. To suggest that the loving devotion that is expressed when an Indian places flowers reverently on an image of Vishnu may be useful in motivating him to practice family planning may occur to a public administrator but may be objectionable to the devotee. For him, the deity which is the object of such devotion is the end and not merely the means to some other end which is more socially oriented in the mind of a Western–educated administrator. If the difference between such points of view is not seen and to some extent appreciated, it shows how far one is from simply understanding other people.

Let it be assumed that articles on religious freedom are included in human rights statements in order to make it possible for religious people to be religious,[2] rather than to make it possible for less religiously inclined power structures to dissolve religion or to transform it into a form more acceptable to its own goals. At this point an acute logical problem arises, for there is a sense in which the Universal Declaration is itself a religious statement. For some people it is a statement of their ultimate concerns. While it may be affirmed by others on less ultimate grounds, it is difficult to see how it may make room for a religious statement which rejects it.

The Universal Declaration is a religious point of view. Furthermore, regardless of how many official representatives of respective countries endorsed it, it is not in fact universal in any descriptive or phenomenal sense. It is universal in a normative sense, namely, that those who believe it also believe that it should be believed and practiced by all humankind — even those whose religious points of view are presently opposed to it. In order to clarify this point, certain aspects of religion in India which seem uncomfortable in the company of the Universal Declaration will be discussed. Such a discussion is valuable lest it be assumed that the human rights articulated in the United Nations statements are not universal either because all have not heard what their rights are, or because those whose value system rejects them are insincere. The concern here is not with human prejudice, but with articulated points of view which have had and continue to have religious sanction in the minds of religiously articulate people.

Aspects of Indian Religious Thought

There are certain religious ideas traditionally and contemporaneously held in India which in their traditional garb are unsupportive of the Universal Declaration. There is an initial reason why Indian religion has placed less emphasis than the West on one assumed article of faith found in the Universal Declaration: "the dignity and worth of the human person." While the Indian religious tradition is varied in its evaluation of the person, there are important and influential strains in that tradition which, while not necessarily denying this statement, certainly place the emphasis elsewhere. One view of human nature that has been influential in the Indian philosophical tradition and has had considerable influence on other levels of Indian religion as well is the view of Śankara (788-820). The Absolute in Śankara's system is called nirguṇa brahman or brahman without attributes. Nirguṇa brahman is indivisible and indescribable. Ultimately, one can only speak of nirguṇa brahman in terms of what "it" is not. The person's essence for Śankara is *ātman*. "Ātman, for Advaita Vedanta, is pure, undifferentiated self–shining consciousness, timeless, spaceless, unthinkable, which is not–different from Brahman and which underlies and supports the individual human person."[3] Ātman is not part of *brahman* but *is brahman* when spoken of with reference to the individual. Hence the *ātman* can only be accurately presented in the negative as well. In the *Bṛhadāraṇyaka Upaniṣad*, Yajnavalkya says of the *ātman*: "That self is (to be described as) not this, not this."[4]

For Śankara, ātman–brahman is not individualized in any ultimate sense. The individual person which most use as a focus for self–identification and which the Universal Declaration seems to have in mind is of a lower order of being than *ātman*.[5] While the phenomenal personality is not entirely unreal (*asat*), it is not ultimately Real (*Sat Paramārthika*), and over–concern for the phenomenal self and its welfare can hinder or at least postpone full self–realization — the union of *ātman* and *brahman*.

> The individual human person, the *jiva*, is a combination of "reality" and "appearance." It is "reality" insofar as atman is its ground; it is "appearance" insofar as it is identified as finite, conditioned, relative. The individual self is then empirically real, for it is a datum of objective and subjective experience; but it is transcendentally unreal, for the self in essence, is identical with the Absolute.[6]

In terms of human rights, the self which is of less concern to Śankara, i.e., the *jīva*, is the very self which is the primary concern of the Universal Declaration. One cannot deny freedom of expression or due process to the *ātman*, but only to the *jīva*. For Śankara and many Hindus today,[7] the dominant motif of life is religious, and their chief concern is salvation. The social problems of adequate food supply or overpopulation may sidetrack some of them, but many continue to pursue a religious end — the union of *ātman* and *brahman* or devotion to their god in terms of *bhakti*. The phenomenal world of which the *jīva* is a part is *māyā* or illusion, which simply means that it is not what it appears to be. The phenomenal self (*jīva*) appears to be more real than it is.

There is another area in which the Indian tradition and the Universal Declaration appear together with a certain amount of discomfort. Articles one and two say that "all human beings are born free and equal in dignity and rights" and that the rights and freedoms enumerated in the Universal Declaration are for all "without distinction of birth or other status." The Indian sacred texts traditionally define four castes. There are Brāhmans who are the intellectuals and spiritual seers, the Kṣatriyas who are the warriors and political leaders, the Vaiśyas who are the craftsmen, and the Śudras who do menial tasks. There developed another group called outcastes, since they were excluded from all castes; and their social ostracization was emphasized by their untouchability. In an attempt to elevate them, Gandhi referred to them as *harijans* (children of God). Their present official designation in India is "scheduled castes." Social reformers have sometimes tried to maintain that this is not actually a part of religion in India, but only part of the social context in which religion is found. They argue that caste can be separated from religion without inflicting any injury on the latter. Hence, since a separation between religion and caste is possible, one could retain the one while eliminating the other (Gandhi). Others have attempted to justify the caste system while recognizing that it has come in need of some reform (Radhakrishnan).

To suggest that religion and society are separable is already evidence of secularizing influence, for such a distinction was not made in ancient India; nor is it made by many village Indians today. On one level of investigation the caste system is a subject for the sociologist. Nevertheless, it has for the majority of Indians been under a religious sanction. How the caste system arose, and the social conditions of the time are interesting and increase one's understanding of the practice, but they do not alter the fact that the so-called social practice is given religious sanction. The earliest mention of the four castes is in the *Ṛgveda* (X, 90, 11-12). In a cosmogonic hymn the primeval *puruṣa* is divided in a sacrificial act (X, 90, 6-9), and his portions account for the created world. This creation includes the four castes which, it seems, are as basic to the nature of things as man himself. Man does not develop the castes but comes into existence in terms of the castes (X, 90, 11-12).[8] Also implied in the Vedic text is the descending order of the castes.

Caste is assumed in the *Bhāgavadgītā*. *Kṛṣṇa*, who in the *Gītā* is identified with *brahman* (X, 12ff), is made the originator of the castes with their appropriate *guṇas* and *dharmas*.[9] Basic to the *Gītā* is the situation in which Arjuna, a Kṣatriya, does not want to involve himself in killing persons in battle whom he recognizes as his relatives. One of the answers given to him is that he must fight since it is his caste duty. The basic caste structure is assumed throughout the *Gītā*, which even devotes several stanzas to a definite statement of it.

> Of Brahmans, warriors and artisans,
> And of serfs, scorcher of the foe,
> The actions are distinguished
> According to the strands that spring from the innate nature.
>
> Calm, (self–) control, austerities, purity,
> Patience, and uprightness,
> Theoretical and practical knowledge, and religious faith,
> Are the natural–born actions of Brahmans.
>
> Heroism, majesty, firmness, skill
> And not fleeing in battle also,
> Generosity, and lordly nature,
> Are the natural–born actions of warriors.
>
> Agriculture, cattle–tending, and commerce
> Are the natural–born actions of artisans;
> Action that consists of service
> Is likewise natural–born to a serf.
>
> Taking a delight in his own special king of action,
> A man attains perfection....10

The *Laws of Manu*, which is the first comprehensive statement of Indian law, was looked on as authoritative from the second century A.D. The first chapter of the book indicates the book's divine origin by describing how the great sages approached Manu, the descendant of Brahman, and requested an explanation of the sacred law. Basic to many of the laws is the four–fold caste distinction. The Brahmin is clearly favored, is "a very great deity," and is to be served by the Śudra. Regardless of a Brahmin's crime, a king may not kill him — the most severe punishment is banishment. To kill a Brahmin is the worst of all possible crimes and punishable by death. On the other hand "his (a Shudra's) killing by a Brahmin is equivalent merely to the killing of a cat, a mongoose, a blue jay, a frog, a dog, a lizard, an owl, or a crow."[11]

> Tonsure (of the head) is ordained for a Brahmana (instead of) capital punishment; but (men of) other castes shall suffer capital punishment.
>
> Let him never slay a Brahmana, though he have committed all (possible) crimes; let him banish such an (offender), leaving all his property (to him) and (his body) unhurt.
>
> No greater crime is known on earth than slaying a Brahmana; a king, therefore, must not even conceive in his mind the thought of killing a Brahmana.[12]

That the Brahmin's hand is clear in all of this does not alter the fact that it was received with a religious sanction.

Further support of the religious sanction is the manner in which the doctrine of *karma* is utilized to make caste more bearable.

> Again, the caste system does provide for the various functions necessary to social life, functions ranging from education to scavenging, from government to domestic service of the most menial kind; and it makes this provision under the sanction of a religious dogma, the belief in *karma*, which renders the superficially inequitable distribution of functions acceptable as being part of the divine order of the universe and a transient episode in the prolonged existence of the individual soul, which by acquiring merit in one existence may rise in the scale in the next, or which may be suffering from a degradation in caste merely by reason of its transgressions in a previous life.[13]

Manu has a lengthy section describing the qualities which issue in various types of rebirths. Certain types of life lead one to the heavens or hells or to subhuman existences such as fishes, snakes, tortoises, or worse. "Elephants, horses, Sudras and despicable barbarians, lions, tigers and boars (are) the middling states, caused by (the quality of) darkness."[14] In verse 38 of Book XII, the mark of darkness is given as "craving after sensual pleasures." Hence if one is born as a member of the lowest of the four castes, it is one's own doing.

Karma has been popularly defined as "the moral law of cause and effect."[15] What is meant is that the effects of a deed always follow a deed. In the moral realm this posed a problem since the righteous did not always prosper, and sometimes those who effected evil did not appear to be recompensed for it. But for many Indians, time is much less compact than for others. Time continued unceasingly throughout endless cycles. For the individual this meant that what was not reaped in one life would be effected in a subsequent life. This relationship between karma and rebirth is still close for many Indians. The person who affirmed such a view of human destiny knew that his actions in his present life would affect his future births and that the state of his present existence was the result of past actions. One could, of course, be born into a subhuman state, but even if one were born into a human state there were distinctions. The potentialities for spiritual realization were greater for the Brahmin than for other castes. Others could, by proper action, hope for rebirth as a Brahmin. Although some persons were born into an existence that would have to be considered a far cry from the conditions indicated in the Universal Declaration, they were not there by reason of some accident of birth or blind fate. Persons alone are responsible for their birth. If they are born as Śudras or outcastes, or even crippled or maimed, it is certainly because of actions committed by them in a previous existence. The answer to such a situation was not for low–caste persons to agitate for the privileges of the Brahmins but to fulfill the responsibilities of their situation in life with the hope that such a fulfillment would issue in a better birth next time.

Limitation of Religion

The implementation of human rights presents problems not always because the notion of human rights is rejected entirely, but because of disagreement regarding priorities. When conflict is genuine, which human right should be given priority? By reason of the very nature of religion (ultimate concern), it seems that every effort should be made to guarantee the largest scope of religious freedom possible in terms of highest priority. If statements on human rights do not grant priority to what is in fact of ultimate concern, one cannot expect religious people to be jubilant when they are offered a bill of human rights that provides for their penultimate concerns, withholds their ultimate concerns, and then by implication substitutes the former for the latter.

The conflict of the human right of religious freedom is resolved in three possible ways.[16] The first two solutions tend to dissolve religious freedom in favor of other human rights, while the third permits the retention of both while granting priority to religious freedom.

The first alternative is to guarantee religious freedom and then proceed to define what one will include in religion, leaving outside the definition such practices which conflict with other rights. In this case the non–believer is put in the position of telling the believer what religion is. Such an alternative has become part of the process of secularization. An illustration of this tendency in India is the movement toward the secularization of law.

Since religion involves ultimate concern it is not surprising that traditionally it has not made the kinds of distinctions now commonly made between religion and law or between religion and society. Such a distinction was not made in the Old Testament, and traditional Indian thought ignored such a distinction as well. So–called "Hindu Law" is based on the *Vedas*, the *Dharmaśāstras*, and custom. Indian religion is *dharma*, which is an extension of the *Vedic Ṛta*. The difficulty of rendering the Sanskrit with one English term is due to its varied usage and meaning.

> The law of the Dharmashastras is a mixture of morality, religion and law. The distinction drawn by modern jurists between positive law and moral law is not observed in Hindu jurisprudence. According to Hindu conception, law in the modern sense was only a branch of *dharma*, a term of the widest significance. The term *dharma* includes religious, moral, social and legal duties and can only be defined as the whole duty of man....[17]

The secularization of law is becoming an increasingly important problem in working out the implications of a secular state in India. Presently the legal structure is not unified, and areas of marriage, divorce, and inheritance, to name a few, are different for "Hindus," "Christians," and "Muslims." The Indian government has committed itself to the establishment of a uniform civil code.[18]

The opposition that the government faces in bringing this goal to fruition is due to the fact that many Indian people are seriously religious, and such a modification or secularization of law in which previously religious matters are brought under the authority of the secular state is looked upon as an infringement on religious freedom. Due to religious differences even among those termed "Hindus," it has not yet been possible to formulate a unified Hindu Code. When it became impossible to pass a Hindu Code Bill, separate measures were passed including the Hindu Marriage Bill which passed in 1955. The attempt to legalize divorce brought the following response from N.C. Chatterjee, former head of the Hindu Mahasabha: "In all humility...I appeal to all sections of the House, don't tamper with the Hindu sacramental marriage and introduce divorce into it."[19] Such laws are frequently looked upon as an encroachment on Hinduism and a clear infringement on religious freedom. Chatterjee's interpretation of the movement toward the secularization of law is to the point. "Imbued with western ideas some people in power are seeking to change the basic concepts of Hindu *dharma* by making laws which are repugnant to the basic principles of Hinduism."[20] In this case religious freedom is being limited not through explicitly imposed limitations as much as through an implicit definition of religion which, through the secularization of law, is progressively eliminating from the area of religion something that was previously indistinguishable from it and remains indistinguishable in the minds of many Indians.

Limitation of Religious Freedom

The second logical alternative is that, instead of guaranteeing religious freedom and limiting what one intends by religion, one can frankly recognize that certain restrictions must be placed upon religious freedom. The United Nations' "International Covenant on Economic, Social and Cultural Rights" guarantees religious freedom "subject only to such limitations as are prescribed by law and are necessary to protect safety, order, health, or morals or the fundamental rights and freedoms of others." Article 25 of the Indian Constitution reads: "Subject to public order, morality and health and to the other provisions of this part, all persons are equally entitled to freedom of conscience and the right freely to profess, practise and propagate religion."[21]

The ability of the state to legislate matters which are clearly within the domain of religion is seen in legislation which touches on animal sacrifices and temple prostitution. In 1950, legislation was passed in the state of Madras which prohibited the sacrifice of animals or birds within the precincts of temples in Madras state.[22] Particularly in the case of the worship of Kali such sacrifices are enjoined and still take place in the Kali temples in Bengal. Some argued that it was against the doctrine of *ahiṁsā* and ignored the fact that sacrifices were enjoined in Vedic times. Smith describes the hopeless attempt to justify such legislation:

> Among those who participated in the debate, there was complete unanimity as to the desirability of the measure but disagreement regarding the basis for its justification. One member attempted to interpret the legislation as a law–and–order measure, claiming that "hundreds and thousands" of riots and murders would be prevented, as disputes frequently arose among the villagers over whose animal was to be sacrificed first! This farfetched argument apparently impressed no one in the assembly. Some attempt was made by the law minister to describe the object of the bill as the prevention of a public nuisance, but it was pointed out that ample legislation already existed to deal with any act which could be so described. A number of members stated that they supported the bill because they wished to end the revolting and gruesome scenes of animal sacrifice. But it was obvious that no one was compelled to witness such scenes.[23]

There were those who were interested in the legislation because it would eliminate a form of worship which tended to put Hinduism in a bad light. This was hardly a justifiable reason for legislation in a secular state and illustrates the ever–present threat to religious freedom which hovers over this second logical alternative.

Another case, less arbitrary legally, was the Devadasis Bill of 1947 passed in Madras. Devadasis ("servants of God") were young girls dedicated to the deities in the Temples. They danced and sang before the images in the temples, and some engaged in prostitution. The Madras bill not only prohibits such dedication, but eliminates the possibility of certain acts associated with the devadasis such as women dancing in the temples.

The historian of religions is well aware that prostitution has frequently been a part of religious expression. This was true of Canaanite religion, certain Hindu practices, and Tantric Buddhism. That there is involved in such practices a religious expression is difficult to deny in the light of certain studies in the history of religions.

> For but one example, we need only think of the prestige that sexual union as ritual acquired in Indian tantrism. India strikingly illustrates how a physiological act can be transformed into ritual and how, when the ritualistic period is ended, the same act can be valorized as mystical technique. The husband's explanation in the *Brihadaranyaka Upanisad*, "I am heaven, thou art earth," follows the transfiguration of the wife into the Vedic sacrificial altar (VI, 4,3). But in tantrism woman ends by incarnating Prakriti (=nature) and the cosmic goddess, Shakti, while the male is identified with Shiva, the pure, motionless, serene spirit. Sexual union (maithuna) is above all an integration of these two principles, cosmic nature–energy and spirit. As a tantric text expresses it: "The true sexual union is the union of the supreme Shakti with the Spirit (atman); other unions represent only carnal relations with woman" (Kularnava Tantra, V, 111-112). There is no longer any question of a physiological act, there is a mystical rite; the partners are no longer human beings, they are detached and free, like the gods. The tantric texts never tire of emphasizing that a transformation of carnal experience occurs.[24]

The reason given for the Devadasis Bill was not health or the prevention of disease. Were this the case, other precautions would have been taken. The threat of epidemic and cholera at large religious festivals has always been an ominous threat. Governmental precautions did not, however, eliminate the possibility of religious festivals but provided health stations and immunization shots. In the Devadasis Bill the issue was clearly moral. The incorporation of prostitution was deemed immoral, and hence the legislative restriction was constitutional. The question as to whether the argument of immorality could be used to justify the elimination of temple dancing as well as prostitution may well require another answer. In any case, the concern here is not so much with a limitation of the meaning of religion. The discussions prior to passage indicate that the religious domain of animal sacrifices was not questioned, nor was the religious dimension of the devadasis denied. Even if the secularization of common law were to become a reality, it is not likely that such religious matters would fall within the secular realm. Rather, these are cases in which that which is recognized as religious is limited for reasons of public order, health, or morality deemed detrimental to society.

Religious Re–emphasis and Reinterpretation

A third logical possibility depends on the natural diversity of religious traditions. Rather than involving legislation, this possibility takes place within the traditions themselves. Since religious traditions are diverse, re–emphasis or reinterpretation commonly occurs. An example of this is the "Neo–Hinduism" of Sarvepalli Radhakrishnan, past President of India. Among other things, he has articulated his views on caste, karma, and the relation of man to the world.

Radhakrishnan deals with caste in at least three of his books: *The Hindu View of Life* (1926), *Eastern Religions and Western Thought* (1939), and *Religion and Society* (1947). In the first book he sees the castes as a significant Hindu insight and contribution. Pointing out that the word *varṇa* refers to color, Radhakrishnan argues that caste was the Hindu way of accommodating incoming races without inflicting hindrances on either the existing or the incoming group. Racial fusion is not possible in a short period of time. Hence while occasions of intermarriage are noted, the practice is not encouraged. Since each racial group is allowed to develop without impeding the progress of others, the caste system is lauded as "democratic."

> Caste was the answer of Hinduism to the force pressing on it from outside. It was the instrument by which Hinduism civilized the different tribes it took in. Any group of people appearing exclusive in any sense is a caste. Whenever a group represents a type a caste arises. If a heresy is born in the bosom of the mother faith and if it spreads and produces a new type, a new caste arises. The Hindu Society has differentiated as many types as can be reasonably differentiated, and is prepared to accept new ones as they arise. It stands for the ordered complexity, the harmonized multiplicity, the many in one which is the clue to the structure of the universe.25

For Radhakrishnan the four basic castes are part of the very nature of things, representing the four basic types of men: men of thought, men of action, men of feeling, and men in whom none of these characteristics is highly developed. The caste system is a democracy since it allows for all the possibility of developing their nature. But it is a special kind of democracy — a spiritual democracy.

> While the system of caste is not democracy in the pursuit of wealth or happiness, it is a democracy so far as the spiritual values are concerned, for it recognizes that every soul has in it something transcendent and incapable of gradations, and it places all beings on a common level regardless of distinctions of rank and status, and insists that every individual must be afforded the opportunity to manifest the unique in him.[26]

While in *The Hindu View of Life* some dissatisfaction is shown with the perversions of caste and while mention is made of occasions in Hindu texts where people changed castes and where "conduct counts and not birth," it is also pointed out that the general rule was to rest caste determination with birth.[27] In this discussion Radhakrishnan states: "While caste has resulted in much evil, there are some sound principles underlying it."[28] In *The Hindu View of Life* the emphasis is on the "sound principles" rather than on the "evil."

In his later discussion in *Religion and Society* he dwells more on the evils which exist in the phenomenon. There he describes untouchability and other discriminations against the harijans. "Places of worship, public wells, and public utilities such as cremation grounds and bathing ghats, hotels, and educational institutions should be open to all."[29] Anything that is presently being done in this regard is not justice or charity but atonement. One senses a certain awareness of guilt in the pages of this volume. The spirit that has been so divisive must go.

> Caste divisions have prevented the development of homogeneity among the Hindus. To develop a degree of organic wholeness and a sense of common obligation, the caste spirit must go. We have to get rid of the innumerable castes and outcastes, with their spirit of exlusiveness, jealousy, greed and fear.[30]

A. R. Wadia observes, "In his treatment of castes Radhakrishnan does not present a consistent position."[31] While the consistency or validity of Radhakrishnan's interpretation is not the present concern, at least a clear change in emphasis is detected between his earlier and later thought.

The book that was written between the two already mentioned clarifies some of the divergency. In *Eastern Religions and Western Thought*, a distinction is made between class and caste. In this book, as before, he argues that "hierarchy is not coercion but a law of nature."[32] Man by nature falls into four classes and each class has duties and contributions to make to society. In keeping with his tradition he emphasizes duties more than rights. The four classes are not only for Hindus but pertain to humanity at large. This division of mankind into four classes goes back to the *Ṛgveda*, and even there it may have been in some sense related to birth. Each society, for example, needs a class of Brahmins who are leisure class people devoted to the pursuit of truth and who are unconcerned with the problems of ruling society which falls to the *Kṣatriyas*. But the life of a Brahmin requires special training and "the special training cannot be postponed until the age of examinations. If the training is to start early enough we must choose the members soon after birth. Is it to be by lot? The Hindu assumed that birth in a family which had the traditions of the leisured class might offer the best solution."[33] Nevertheless, there existed the exception to the rule, and there are illustrations of those who changed their class.

Siding with this view of class distinctions, Radhakrishnan opposed the caste system. When the elements of birth became foremost, the classes degenerated into caste. The three chief characteristics of caste are heredity (one cannot change his caste), endogamy (one cannot marry outside his caste), and commensal restrictions (one does not eat or drink outside one's caste). By arguing that the Vedic reference is to class but not to caste, Radhakrishnan is trying to say that a rejection of the present evils of caste is not a rejection of Hinduism. When he says, "Caste in its rigour became established by the time of Manu and the Puranas, which belong to the period of the Gupta kings (A.D. 330 to 450),"[34] he is in effect conceding that the caste system has become a part of Hinduism for the majority of Hindus and that it has had a considerable history. But by distinguishing between class and caste and by relating Hinduism to the former and decrying its connection with the latter, Radhakrishnan is attempting to interpret the Hindu tradition in such a way as to make more room for human rights. But human rights are not to be equated with human equality and equal responsibility.

> The truth underlying the system is the conception of right action as a rightly ordered expression of the nature of the individual being. Nature assigns to each of us our line and scope in life according to inborn quality and self–expressive function. Nowhere is it suggested that one should follow one's hereditary

> occupation without regard to one's personal bent and capacities.[35]

The accuracy of the last statement quite apart, the change in tone is clear. Instead of finding a lesser penalty for irresponsible Brahmins, Radhakrishnan would remind them of their greater responsibilities. He interprets the classes not so much in terms of their respective rights which differ by class, but in terms of their respective responsibilities which differ in terms of their natural capacities.

Another shift in emphasis is seen in Radhakrishnan's interpretation of karma. Radhakrishnan is aware of the criticism that karma implies a denial of freedom, and he responds to it. He argues that it does not actually come in conflict with freedom. Karma may be inflexible, but it is not deterministic. According to karma, one's past is settled, and one is what one is because of that past. But the future lies ahead with considerable possibility for choice. Radhakrishnan admits that karma was sometimes confused with fatality in India, which led people not to do their best.

> The principle of karma reckons with the material or the context in which each individual is born. While it regards the past as determined, it allows that the future is only conditioned. The spiritual element in man allows him freedom within the limits of his nature. Man is not a mere mechanism of instincts. The spirit in him can triumph over the automatic forces that try to enslave him. The *Bhagavadgita* asks us to raise the self by the self. We can use the material with which we are endowed to promote our ideals. The cards in the game of life are given to us. We do not select them. They are traced to our past Karma, but we can call as we please, lead what suit we will, and as we play, we gain or lose. And there is freedom.[36]

Radhakrishnan also recognizes the role that karma plays in explaining the station of one's birth, but his discussion emphasizes instead its potentialities for freedom in determining the future. Whether or not he has presented a consistent case is one thing. But he has taken a traditional doctrine and has stressed its other side — the side that magnifies human potentialities.

When Radhakrishnan turns to man and his nature in relation to the world, he again stresses points within the Hindu tradition which put a new emphasis on human possibilities. It is true that for Radhakrishnan man is essentially spiritual in his goals and that undifferentiated Atman is Ultimate Reality. He emphasizes, however, that the doctrine of maya is not illusionism, but refers to the mystery involved in the relationship between God and the world. As he sees it,"Śankara believes that it is not possible to determine logically the relation between God and the world. He asks us to hold fast both ends. It does not matter if we are not able to find out where they meet."[37] Furthermore, there are other aspects of Hindu thought that relate human beings to the world in a direct way. Hindus traditionally have held to four stages of life (*aśrama dharma*). The duty of the *gṛhastha* (householder or second stage) is to maintain and ensure as a social responsibility the continuity of the family. This stage is hardly world–renouncing. In addition to this, with the exception of the Brahmin caste, the other castes have as their primary responsibility and dharma the concerns of the world. While their ultimate goal is spiritual, it is reached by fulfilling the *varṇa dharma* which might be fighting a war, ruling society in righteousness, or doing manual labor. It would hardly do to suggest that the phenomenal personality which concerns modern society is only relatively real. The answer given is that far from denying the significance of the individual, Hinduism affirms his divinity. While one may point out that the divinity does not apply to the individual (*jīva*) except in a relative way, the shift in emphasis is unmistakable.

Radhakrishnan has done a great deal in permitting a certain type of Indian to retain his or her heritage and also to enter into the modern world which among other things, is concerned with rights on a human basis. His voice has been most persuasive.

Historically all three logical solutions have been utilized, consciously and unconsciously, side by side. But if such types of reinterpretation and re–emphasis represented in Radhakrishnan become more common, the gap between some religious expressions and some human rights will narrow. This is not a speedy process, but it has the advantage of appealing to religious people on religious grounds. In such a manner religious freedom is not lost.

Notes

1. Paul Tillich, *Theology of Culture* (New York: Oxford Press, 1959), 7-8.

2. Article 18 of the *Universal Declaration of Human Rights* reads: "Everyone has the right to freedom of thought, conscience and religion; this right includes freedom to change his religion or belief, and freedom, either alone or in community with others and in public or in private, to manifest his religion or belief in teaching, practice, worship and observance."

3. Eliot Deutsch, "The Self in Advaita Vedanta," *International Philosophical Quarterly*, VI (March 1966), 6.

4. S. Radhakrishnan, *The Principal Upanisads* (London: Unwin & Allen Ltd., 1953), 286.

5. In the Indian religious traditions one does not ordinarily distinguish entities as simply real or unreal. The frame of reference is one of "degrees of reality." The higher degrees of reality are more reliable and lasting, and for Śankara only Brahman is ultimately real and indestructible.

6. Eliot Deutsch, *op. cit.*, 10.

7. Cf. E. Luther Copeland, "Neo–Hinduism and Secularism," *A Journal of Church and State*, IX (Spring 1967), 200.

8. Ralph T. H. Griffith, *The Hymns of the Ṛgveda*, 4th ed. (Varanasi: Chowkhamba Sanskrit Series Office, 1963), II, 519.

9. *The Bhagavad Gītā*, trans. Franklin Edgerton, Harper Torchbook Series (New York: Harper, 1964), 24, IV, 13.

10. *Ibid.*, 87-88. XVIII 41-45a.

11. J. H. Hutton, *Caste in India*, 4th ed. (Bombay: Oxford University Press, 1963), 92.

12. *The Laws of Manu*, trans. G. Buhler, S.B.E. (Delhi: Motilal Banarsidass, 1964), 320.

13. Hutton, *op. cit.*, 121-122.

14. Buhler, *op. cit.*, 493. XII, 43.

15. Huston Smith, *The Religions of Man* (New York: Harper and Row, 1965), 76.

16. I am speaking here in terms of logical categories and not in terms of practical implementation. As for the actualities of history, the three logical possibilities usually exist side by side.

17. S. V. Gupte, *Hindu Law in British India* (Bombay: N. M. Tripathi Ltd., 1947), 3.

18. Directive Principles of State Policy, Article 44: "The state shall endeavor to secure for the citizens a uniform civil code throughout the territory of India."

19. For a discussion of this and other bills involved, see Donald Eugene Smith, *India as a Secular State* (Princeton: Princeton University Press, 1963), 281 ff.

20. Speech in New Delhi under the auspices of the All India Convention on the Hindu Code, April 15, 1955. Quoted in Donald Eugene Smith, *ibid.*, 287.

21. *Ibid.*, 184.

22. *Ibid.*, 235 ff.

23. *Ibid.*, 236.

24. Mircea Eliade, *The Sacred and the Profane* (New York: Harper Torchbook, 1961), 170-171.

25. S. Radhakrishnan, *The Hindu View of Life* (New York: The Macmillan Company, 1962), 75. Original lectures delivered in 1926.

26. *Ibid.*, 83.

27. *Ibid.*, 79.

28. *Ibid.*, 90.

29. *Religion and Society* (London: Allen and Unwin Ltd., 1947), 134.

30. *Ibid.*, 133.

31. A. R. Wadia, "The Social Philosophy of Radhakrishnan," in *The Philosophy of Sarvepalli Radhakrishnan*, ed. by Paul Arthur Schlipp (New York: Tudor Publishing Company, 1952), 766.

32. *Eastern Religion and Western Thought* (New York: Oxford University Press, 1959), 366.

33. *Ibid.*, 359.

34. *Ibid.*, 372.

35. *Ibid.*, 378.

36. Radhakrishnan, *The Hindu View of Life*, 54.

37. *Ibid.*, 49.

PART THREE

INDIAN RELIGION

IN THE UNITED STATES

13

Swami Bhaktivedanta: Karma, Rebirth and the Personal God

Swami Bhaktivedanta, founder of the International Society for Kṛṣṇa Consciousness, does not present his views on karma and rebirth in either a systematic or an academic fashion. He sees himself as in the Vaiṣṇava tradition, resting firmly on the *Bhagavadgītā*, *Śrīmad Bhāgavatam*, and the teachings of Sri Caitanya. He also presents himself as a bona fide spiritual master in disciplic succession from Sri Caitanya.

As such, although he has written several topical books, his views on karma and rebirth are largely to be found by examining his commentaries on the above-mentioned texts. There is no work or chapter in which he systematically develops these themes. Moreover, he disdains the work of academics who are labelled "mental speculators." He does not concern himself with comparing and contrasting his position with the position of other modern thinkers. Occasionally there is a stray reference, but only to indicate the errors that are engendered by not relying on a bona fide teacher. His purpose is not academic, nor does he follow academic procedures. Above all he seeks to lead all persons to spiritual realization.

When he speaks on karma and rebirth he does not present his teaching as containing novelty, only fidelity to the Vaiṣṇava tradition. His is, therefore, a decidedly theistic approach to the world, and this approach dominates the way he sees karma and rebirth. He has a strong view of the laws of nature and their inexorability. But, above and within those laws and the operation of karma is the guidance and control of God.

Karma

The Realm of Karma

Swami Bhaktivedanta writes of the material world and the spiritual world. The human being is an eternal soul or living entity (*jīva*) within a material body which has a gross and subtle aspect. As long as the living entity is associated with a material body, that body is governed by the laws of material nature and karma.

From the smallest germ up to Indra, King of Heaven, all living beings are subject to the law of karma and suffer the results of attachment to their work.[1] Technically speaking, the soul is neither born nor does it die. It is the material body associated with it which is subject to birth and death. It is the body that is the locus of karma and reaps its harvest.[2]

There are 8,400,000 species of life into which the living entity can be born and a body is assigned according to one's karma.[3] These bodies may range from a demigod in one of the heavenly planets, to a human, animal, or vegetable form on this planet, to some form in a lower planet or hell. In each case a body is forced upon the living being by the laws of material nature and one's karma.[4] The living entity has no power to change the laws of material nature relating to the body which is acquired. If one is born as a dog or cat or hog, one must live like those animals.[5]

Karma, the results of fruitive activities, follows the living entity even when there is a dissolutionment of the world and a new creation. The same karma simply moves from actuality to potentiality to actuality again.[6]

Specific Karma

While Swami Bhaktivedanta does not attempt to give a complete account of specific acts which produced identifiable results, there are some specifics given and hints of a more general nature exist. To begin with, one's situation in the three *guṇas* has some generally predictable effects. Material bodies are dominated by one of the three *guṇas* of *prakṛti*. The mode of goodness (*sattva*) makes one wiser than others in the conditioned state.[7] Ideally, the *brāhmaṇa* is supposed to be situated in the mode of *sattva* and is more or less free from sinful reactions. By pious activities in the mode of goodness one is purified. One who dies in the mode of *sattva* is reborn in one of the higher planetary systems, enjoying godly happiness in Brahmaloka or Janaloka. While there are impurities in the material world regardless of which mode one is in, the mode of *sattva* is the purest form of existence and those who die there are "elevated to the planets where great sages and great devotees live."[8]

> There is an upper planetary system, consisting of the heavenly planets, where everyone is highly elevated. According to the degree of development of the mode of goodness, the living entity can be transferred to

> various planets in this system. The highest planet is Satyaloka, or Brahmaloka, where the prime person of this universe, Lord Brahmā, resides. We have already seen that we can hardly calculate the wondrous condition of life in Brahmaloka, but the highest condition of life, the mode of goodness, can bring us to this.[9]

Unfortunately, the mode of *sattva* is part of *prakṛti* and a person so situated may think of himself or herself as advanced in knowledge and therefore superior to others. Even here, then, there is little likelihood of liberation or being transferred to the spiritual world.

> Repeatedly, one may become a philosopher, a scientist, or a poet, and, repeatedly, become entangled in the same disadvantages of birth and death. But, due to the illusion of the material energy, one thinks that that sort of life is pleasant.[10]

The mode of passion (*rajas*) is characterized by the attraction between man and woman. Modern society is dominated by the mode of *rajas*. Those predominantly in this mode want honor in society with a happy family and a nice house. Hence, in order to please wife, society, and keep up one's prestige, one has to work hard. But, "if there is no liberation for those in the mode of goodness, what of those who are entangled in the mode of passion?"[11]

> The mode of passion is mixed. It is in the middle, between the modes of goodness and ignorance. A person is not always pure, but even if he should be purely in the mode of passion, he will simply remain on this earth as a king or a rich man. But because there are mixtures, one can also go down. people on this earth, in the modes of passion or ignorance, cannot forcibly approach the higher planets by machine. In the mode of passion there is also the chance of becoming mad in the next life.[12]

A person who is predominantly in the mode of *tamas* or ignorance possesses little understanding. It should be obvious that all people will die, but one in the mode of *tamas* continues to seek the accumulation of money and is not much interested in spiritual advancement. Such people are lazy in spiritual things, and are inclined to sleep more than is required (six hours of sleep a night is sufficient). Such persons also appear to be dejected and are addicted to intoxicants. To fall into this mode is very risky since all that remain are subhuman forms.

> Beneath the human level there are eight million species of life: birds, beasts, reptiles, trees, etc., and, according to the development of the mode of ignorance, people are brought down to these abominable conditions. The word *tāmasāḥ* is very significant here. *Tāmasāḥ* indicates those who stay continually in the mode of ignorance without rising to a higher mode. Their future is very dark.[13]

Those in the lower modes of passion and ignorance can be elevated to the mode of goodness if they practice Kṛṣṇa consciousness. But, the ultimate goal is to achieve liberation through elevation above all the modes.[14]

There are some activities for which Bhaktivedanta is more specific. Killing animals for the eating of meat will result in the guilty person becoming an animal in a future life and in the animal having a body suitable to kill him.[15] Also, those who eat meat would seem to deserve birth in a body of those creatures who do such things.

> They are such fools that they do not know what will happen to them in their next life. Although they see varieties of living creatures eating abominable things — pigs eating stools, crocodiles eating all kinds of flesh, and so on — they do not realize that they themselves, because of their practice of eating all kinds of nonsense in this life, will be destined to eat the most abominable things in their next life.[16]

Killing on the battlefield or killing animals sacrificially, however, has a different effect since it is ordained.

> The animal sacrificed gets a human life immediately without undergoing the gradual evolutionary process from one form to another, and the *kṣatriyas* killed in the battlefield also attain the heavenly planets as do the *brāhmaṇas* who attain them by offering sacrifice.[17]

A woman is someone who was previously a man who was overly attached to his wife. If one is too attached to his wife, he thinks of her at the time of death and in his next life takes the body of a woman. But, if a woman thinks of her husband at the time of death, she becomes a man in the next life. While the bodies of men or women are merely one's bodily dress, it is easier to get out of the clutches of material nature from the body of a man. A woman is generally fond of household furnishings, ornaments and dresses, and children. Her attachment to the man is the result of his providing her with these things. Ideally, neither the man nor the woman should be attached to each other, but to the Lord.[18] The ideal is for the husband and wife to help each other advance in spiritual life. Sex and eating are both essential, but should be governed by this principle. Sex should be engaged in only in order to propagate Kṛṣṇa conscious children. Unfortunately, in this age, men and women unite for "unrestricted sexual enjoyment. Thus they are victimized, being obliged to take rebirth in the form of animals to fulfill their animalistic propensities."[19]

People who mock and jeer at Kṛṣṇa are born into lower and lower situations.

> Their destiny is certainly to take birth after birth in the species of atheistic and demoniac life. Perpetually, their real knowledge will remain under delusion, and gradually they will regress to the darkest region of creation.[20]

Inexorable Karma and Divine Control

There is a sense in which the results of fruitive actions are automatic and inevitable.

> Even in the present life, the body changes from childhood to boyhood, from boyhood to youth, and from youth to old age; similarly, when the body is too old to continue, the living being gives up his body and, by the laws of nature, *automatically* gets another body according to his fruitive activities, desires and ambitions. The laws of nature control this sequence, and therefore as long as the living entity is under the control of the external, material energy, the process of bodily change takes place *automatically*, according to one's fruitive activities.[21]

The laws of material nature are not to be contravened. Karma is fruitive action for which there is always a reaction, either good or bad.

Every fruitive activity must have its effect and cannot be nullified by some other activity. There would seem to be no place for counteractive karma. "A sinful activity cannot be counteracted by a pious activity."[22] So relentless is karma that attempts by philanthropists and social reformers to make significant changes in material conditions are doomed to failure. "Material conditions are already established by the superior administration according to one's *karma*."[23] One should not concern oneself with material conditions, but seek instead to raise people to Kṛṣṇa consciousness which results in transcending that material nature.

Swami Bhaktivedanta is interested in raising the living entity to Kṛṣṇa consciousness and bringing all beings "back to Godhead." He repeatedly castigates those who think they are the controllers or who think that somehow nature works without God. Although in one sense karma is inexorable, even to the extent of excluding counteractive karma, these laws do not operate independently. The material nature is the Lord's external energy and both the laws of nature as well as the effects of karma are controlled and administered by the Lord. "Therefore victory and defeat come according to the result of one's *karma*, and the judgment is given by the Supreme Lord."[24] On several occasions Swami Bhaktivedanta counters what he takes to be the materialistic position of the *karma mīmāṃsā* in which karma is the cause of everything, even to binding the Supreme Controller to act in a given way.[25] Karma is not the original cause of one's position. Behind it all is the hand of God, who administers his justice with the help of his agents, the demigods.

Is determinism, then, merely raised from the level of material nature to the level of divine control? There are statements that would seem to suggest that.

> Since we act under the control of the Supreme according to our *karma*, no one is independent, from Brahmā down to the insignificant ant. Whether we are defeated or victorious, the Supreme Lord is always victorious because everyone acts under his directions.[26]

> Victory is always with the Supreme Personality of Godhead. As for the subordinant living entities, they fight under that arrangement of the Supreme Personality of Godhead. Victory or defeat is not actually theirs; it is an arrangement by the Lord through the agency of material nature.[27]

Swami Bhaktivedanta cannot countenance a view of the world that omits reference to the Supreme Controller. To grant that there is anything that is not in the control of Kṛṣṇa would be to admit that some things happen on their own. But neither is he interested in affirming a determinism that diminishes human responsibility. So, although Kṛṣṇa is the "ultimate doer" of everything, He is not thereby responsible for the plight of the living souls.

> Although the Supreme Personality of Godhead is the ultimate doer of everything, in His original transcendental existence He is not responsible for the happiness and distress, or bondage and liberation, of the conditioned souls. These are due to the results of the fruitive activities of the living entities within this material world.[28]

There is a hierarchy of causes for every act. Although nothing is without its cause, human beings are responsible for their actions within the context of those causes. The supreme cause of all is the Lord. But, the Lord works through material nature and the karma of the living entity.

> In the material creations, the Lord is the only supreme cause. The immediate cause is material nature by which the cosmic manifestation is visible. The created beings are of many varieties, such as the demigods, human beings and lower animals, and all of them are subject to the reactions of their own past good or bad activities. The Lord only gives them the proper facilities for such activities and the regulations of the modes of nature, but He is never responsible for their past and present activities.[29]

The Lord does not create the particular situations into which living entities are placed. Rather, they desire to be placed into these situations, and impartial as He is, the Lord grants all such desires. But, He does not interfere with the desires of independent living beings.[30]

It has been observed that the Lord controls the working of karma which is not set loose to operate on its own.[31] It has also been seen that the Lord is impartial to all. Yet there are instances where the Lord is free to change the results of actions.[32] Swami Bhaktivedanta explicitly denies that the Lord, as Lord of karma, is bound to its results.

> We must always remember that the Lord is the supreme will, and He is not bound by any law. Generally the law of *karma* is that one is awarded the results of one's own

> actions, but in special cases, by the will of the Lord, such resultant actions are changed also. But this change can be effected by the will of the Lord only, and no other...the Supreme Will is absolutely free to do whatever He likes; and because He is all–perfect, there is no mistake in any of His actions or reactions. These changes of resultant actions are especially rendered by the Lord when a pure devotee is involved.[33]

Since the Lord is impartial and not arbitrary, and since the laws of material nature and of karma itself are due to Him, before one concludes that the Lord sometimes acts in such a way as to set aside such laws one should remember that the intellectual capabilities of the living entity are not sufficient to understand the workings of the infinite.

> The activities of the Lord are always inconceivable to the tiny brain of the living entities. Nothing is impossible for the Supreme Lord, but all His actions are wonderful for us, and thus He is always beyond the range of our conceivable limits.[34]

Therefore, what might appear to be contrary to karma or the laws of material nature might be quite reasonable within the divine intelligence.

Karma and the Devotee

A devotee of the Lord is not under the laws of karma and cannot be punished for past karma. We will see later that this involves transcending the sphere of karma rather than interfering with it from within. For example, only the foolish would think that one's life could be extended beyond one's karmically determined time.[35] But the Lord can extend the duration of the devotees' time and in effect nullify the results of his karma.

> When one becomes a devotee, however, he is not destined to die according to a limited duration of life. Everyone has a limited duration of life, but a devotee's lifetime can be extended by the mercy of the Supreme Lord, who is able to nullify the results of one's karma....A devotee is not under the laws of karma.[36]

A devotee who is less than a pure devote is still capable of misusing his position and thereby having to be born in a lower form. But, the punishment is different than it is for ordinary materialistic persons. By the grace of the Lord the devotee is punished in such a way that his desire to achieve Kṛṣṇa consciousness is increased which enables him to achieve liberation during his next lifetime.[37] Swami Bhaktivedanta comments on the case of Bharata Mahārāja, who due to his compassion for a young deer was compelled to take the body of a deer for a short time to rectify that mistake.

> He was very anxious to get out of his deer body, and this indicates that his affection for devotional services was intensified, so much so that he was quickly to attain perfection in a *brāhmaṇa* body in the next life.[38]

But, "such punishment is only for a short period, and it is not due to past *karma*. It may appear to be due to past *karma*, but it is offered to rectify the devotee and bring him to pure devotional service."[39] The devotee is also aware that whatever punishment is given him is to bring him to the right path.[40]

In the theism of Bhaktivedanta, then, the Lord is in complete control as the ultimate cause of all the laws of material nature and of karma. Nothing takes place outside of His will or knowledge. But the living entity is still free and thereby responsible for his destiny. And, one should not lightly think that the Lord sets aside His karmic laws.

Transmigration

Transmigration, like karma, applies only to the world of material nature. The original nature of the living entity is spiritual and that is the destiny to which it should return. Hence, although the various bodies with which the living entity is associated differ widely, one's ultimate goal is to transcend them all and return to a spiritual existence. Being caught in the cycles of birth and death is the result of desire. How this gets started is described by Swami Bhaktivedanta as follows.

> Originally the living entity is a spiritual being, but when he actually desires to enjoy this material world, he comes down....The living entity first accepts a body that is human in form, but gradually, due to his degraded activities, he falls into lower forms of life — into the animal, plant and aquatic forms. By the

> gradual process of evolution, the living entity again attains the body of a human being and is given another chance to get out of the process of transmigration. If he again misses his chance in the human form to understand his position, he is again placed in the cycle of birth and death in various types of bodies.[41]

Bodies are arranged according to a gradual evolution from the lower species of life to the higher or human forms. Humans are distinguished from the lower vegetable forms in that they have consciousness, and from animal forms in that the animal cannot control itself and has no sense of decency.[42] The living being passes through a natural evolutionary process until it reaches a human body at which time the will becomes significant for future progress. Only in human life is liberation possible.[43]

If one wastes one's human years in sense gratification, one will transmigrate in the next life to the body of an animal such as a dog, cat, or hog.[44] One may even take the form of a tree.[45] Swami Bhaktivedanta parts with theosophical thought in believing that one can be born in a subhuman form after having attained the human level. He also sees Darwin's theory as incomplete because although it describes evolution from ape to man, it does not take into account the reverse condition as a possibility.[46] If one misuses the opportunity provided by the human body one will slip to subhuman forms, but if one utilizes the human opportunity one will be elevated to higher planetary systems in the next life.

Not only, then, does the living entity transmigrate from one life to another on earth, but rebirth takes place on planets above and below our present planetary system.[47] Life on the higher planets is more pleasurable and of longer duration. Each of the higher planets is ruled over by a demigod whose life span is immense. Lord Brahmā, who rules over Brahmaloka, the highest planet in the system, lives for a very long time. But, unlike Kṛṇṣa, even Brahmā is subject to death. Living entities who are born in one of the upper planetary systems are usually reborn later as humans. It is even possible to be born as a demigod and thereby become a further purified devotee and return to Godhead.[48] By worshipping the demigod who presides over it, one goes to that planet at death.[49] But all of these planets are part of the material universe and unless one transcends them to the spiritual universe of Vaikuṇṭha one will never escape the rounds of birth and death.[50]

> In the higher planets of the material world, the *yogīs* can enjoy more comfortable and more pleasant lives for

> hundreds and thousands of years, but life in those higher planets is not eternal. Those who desire eternal life enter into the anti–material universe through mystic powers at certain opportune moments that are created by the demigod administrators.[51]

One of these heavenly planets is the moon. One who goes there still possesses some material desire.[52] When that is entirely gone one travels to Kṛṣṇa's abode which is the spiritual world of Vaikuṇṭha.

The Material Body

The living entity transmigrates through a variety of bodies until it is finally liberated and returns in its spiritual body to Godhead. During that time, the bodies that it inhabits are composed of a variety of elements. There is the gross body that is visible to the eye and which is composed of the five elements of material nature: earth, water, fire, air and sky. There is also the subtle body, unperceived by the material senses, which is composed of the three subtle elements: mind, intelligence, and ego.[53]

At the time of death it is the gross body that is burned in cremation.[54] However, unless the living entity is liberated, the subtle body remains and carries the soul to its next gross body.[55] Throughout life and even at the moment of death the gross body acts to form the disposition of the subtle body. After death, the subtle body continues and is responsible for the determination of the next gross body.[56]

If, at the time of sex, the secretions of the mother are more profuse, the child will receive a female body, while if the secretions of the father are more profuse, the body will be male. These are the laws of nature, but they act according to desire. Hence the gross body is determined by the subtle body. The way to change this situation is to change the subtle body.

> If a human being is taught to change his subtle body by developing a consciousness of Kṛṣṇa, at the time of death the subtle body will create a gross body in which he will be a devotee of Kṛṣṇa, or if he is still more perfect, he will not take another material body but will immediately get a spiritual body and thus return home, back to Godhead.[57]

The subtle body continues in the womb even though the gross body is not fully developed.[58] Even after birth it takes some time for the effects of one's karma to manifest themselves in the gross body. Hence, although small children may appear to be innocent, this should not be confused with the state of liberation. The effects of one's fruitive activities are simply held in reservation in the subtle body to appear at a later stage in development.[59]

In dreams, the living entity, encased in the subtle body, is able to leave the gross body for a time.[60] When we sleep we forget the identity of the gross body, and when we awaken we forget the identity of the subtle body.[61] It is possible to experience things in a dream which have never been seen or heard of in this life because they have been experienced in previous lives. And novelty may result from combining experiences.[62] The stage of development of the senses may also influence the subtle body and one's dreams.

> In a dream a young man may experience the presence of a young woman because at that time the senses are active. Because of undeveloped senses, a child or boy will not see a young woman in his dreams. The senses are active in youth even when one dreams, and although there may be no young woman present, the senses may act and there may be a seminal discharge (nocturnal emission). The activities of the subtle and gross bodies depend on how developed conditions are.[63]

Usually one does not remember previous lives nor know the type of body one will have next. However, there are exceptions. If one has come to the end of the usefulness of his present gross body and knows that the next one will be a step down, one may want to retain the one that he has. While the forces of nature are too strong to counteract, this desire for retention may cause one to lie in a coma for an extended period before death occurs.[64]

If one is overly attracted to one's life situation, one is not given another gross body and is forced to remain as a ghost in a subtle body without a gross body. Such a one is a disturbance to others in a society since ghosts seek a body to inhabit.[66]

It is said repeatedly that the living entity who is not liberated is forced to take another material body according to the laws of material nature and one's karma. But as before, we see that the Supreme personality of Godhead has a hand in the formation of the material body. Not only are the laws of material nature and karma determined by Him, but material nature is His external energy. In addition, one has not only a subtle and gross body and a living soul (*jīva*), but is endowed with a Supersoul. This Supersoul is a form of the Supreme which resides within the individual. It transmigrates from body to body along with the original soul and reflects the divine guidance of the whole procedure. The Lord remains the ultimate cause in control of the universe and uses mediate causes to accomplish His purpose.

> The Supersoul is said to be friendly because the Supreme Personality of Godhead is so kind to the original soul that when the original soul transmigrates from one body to another, the Lord goes with him. Furthermore, according to the desire and *karma* of the individual soul, the Lord, through the agency of *māyā*, creates another body for him.[67]

At the appropriate time, then, the next body is prepared and the individual soul and the Supersoul transfer to the "particular bodily machine."[68] There is a close connection between saying that material nature forces one to take a particular body and saying that the Lord prepares a particular body.[69] Actually the Lord works in a orderly fashion according to the laws of material nature which He guides.

> At the time of death, according to his mental condition, the living being is carried by the subtle body, consisting of mind, intelligence and ego, to another gross body. When higher authorities have decided what kind of gross body the living entity will have, he is forced to enter such a body, and thus he automatically gives up his previous body.[70]

But the moment of death is more specifically sketched out.

Death

Death always comes at the right time.[71] There is even a gracious and timely element to capital punishment. If a murderer were permitted to live he might commit future murders and have to suffer the inevitable karmic results of such activities.[72]

At death the gross body divides and the gross elements go back to their source. After the destruction of the gross body, the soul and Supersoul remain.[73] In cremation it is the gross body that is destroyed and if there is no more desire for material enjoyment the subtle body is also ended.[74] If, however, further transmigration is required, attachment to the old body makes cremation desirable.[75]

At death one might transmigrate to higher planets or to Vaikuṇṭha. Or, one may go to Yamarāja, the controller of sinful activities.[76] In the latter case, the messengers of Yamarāja, the Yamadūtas, punish the living entity. To an extent that the living entity is able to tolerate, he must suffer the consequences of sense gratification. While passing from this planet to the planet of Yamarāja, the culprit meets many dogs who bark and bite to remind him of his criminal activities of sense gratification.[77] He passes a vast distance in a few moments. In this passage,

> The subtle body is covered by the constables so that the living entity can pass such a long distance quickly and at the same time tolerate the suffering. This covering, although material, is of such fine elements that material scientists cannot discover what the coverings are made of. To pass 792,000 miles within a few minutes seems wonderful to the modern space travellers. They have so far travelled at the speed of 18,000 miles per hour, but here we see that a criminal passes 792,000 miles within a few seconds only, although the process is not spiritual but material.[78]

It should be understood that Yamarāja is not a fictitious character. he is truly the king of his abode, Pitṛloka. He is appointed by the Supreme Personality of Godhead to see that human beings do not violate His regulations.[79] The punishment inflicted on the planet of Pitṛloka is intended as remedial, but those so punished often continue to follow their sensual ways.

> The conditioned souls, who have come to this material world for sense gratification, are allowed to enjoy their senses under certain regulative principles. If they violate these regulations, they are judged and punished by Yamarāja. He brings them to the hellish planets and properly chastises them to bring them back to Kṛṣṇa consciousness. By the influence of māyā, however, the conditioned souls remain infatuated with the mode of ignorance. Thus in spite of repeated punishment by Yamarāja, they do not come to their senses, but continue to live within the material condition, committing sinful activities again and again.[80]

The concentration of the mind at the moment of death determines one's next destination. "Whatever state of being one remembers when he quits his body, that state he will attain without fail."[81] It is not a magical moment, however, since one is bound to act characteristically. The point is that "whatever we do in life will be tested at the time of death."[82] Mahārāja Bharata thought of a deer and became one in his next life. If one has had no thoughts other than how to maintain his family throughout life, he will think of them at the moment of death. He may even in his last words ask that someone look after his family. Such a one will surely be reborn.[83]

The ultimate goal of one's life will be reached if one is able to remember the Lord at the moment of death. One way to do this is to chant the *mahāmantra*. But even this is not possible for the person who has not practised Kṛṣṇa consciousness throughout life.

> Anyone who quits his body in Kṛṣṇa consciousness is at once transferred to the transcendental abode of the Supreme Lord. The word smaran (remembering) is important. Remembering of Kṛṣṇa is not possible for the impure soul who has not practised Kṛṣṇa consciousness in devotional service. To remember Kṛṣṇa one should chant the mahāmantra....[84]

The significance of this has to do with the importance of the subtle body in forming the next gross body and the formative influence of the mind in the process. At the time of death the mind and intelligence create the subtle form of the body for the next life. If the thought is not congenial, the next life will be unfavorable. But if one thinks of Kṛṣṇa one is translated to His abode. If one is worshipping one of the demigods one will be transferred to their planet. But that will entail future rebirths.[85]

In death as in life, one should understand that the process is not purely naturalistic. There are laws which determine death and the transfer to another body. But these are governed by the Lord. For "Lord Viṣṇu is even the Supreme Lord of death...."[86] The living entity generally does not remember his previous life and hence forgets where he was in the process of God realization. However, the Lord in the form of Paramātman is present in the transmigration and supplies the remembrance which enables the living entity to renew his work where the last life ended.[87] The whole process of death is neither accidental nor wholly explained through natural law. For that law is under the control of the Supreme Personality of Godhead.

Birth and Life in the Womb

The birth of the human being's body takes place as the result of a mixture of semen and ovum, but that mixture does not always produce pregnancy.[88] Unless the soul enters the mixture there is no pregnancy. Therefore, it is important to note that the father and mother, while agents in the production of the material body, do not create the living entity which is put into the semen according to its karma.[89] One should not even say that the semen creates the living entity, for the soul merely, "takes shelter in a particle of semina and is then pushed into the womb of a woman."[90] The soul is transferred to the semen of a man who is karmically suitable to become the material father.[91]

Death usually involves being in a trance for seven months. When at the end of seven months the being awakens from the trance and finds himself in the womb he feels confined. In this condition he often prays to the Lord to liberate him from his condition.[92] The miserable condition of material existence, then, is felt not only when one emerges from the womb, but when one is confined within. But once one is born, *māyā* conceals from the living entity the miserable condition of material existence. It is possible within the womb to understand one's relationship to Vasudeva, and such a one has his liberation assured.[93] The existence of the child in the womb is a precarious one. "On one side of where the child is floating there is the heat of gastric fire, and on the other side there is urine, stool, blood and discharges."[94] Not only does the child pray to the Lord for deliverance from the womb, but, knowing that one forgets his relationship to the Lord after birth, sometimes prays to remain in the womb.

> It is said that Sukadeva Gosvāmî, on this consideration, remained for sixteen years within the womb of his mother; he did not want to be entangled in false bodily identification. After cultivating such knowledge within the womb of his mother, he came out at the end of sixteen years and immediately left home so that he might not be captured by the influence of *māyā*.[95]

It is possible, within the womb, to be conscious of one's situation, to pray, and to be constantly absorbed in Kṛṣṇa consciousness.[96]

As we have seen before, this process operates according to the laws of material nature and one's karma. But that is not the final explanation. In the ultimate sense, the body is created by the Lord who is the original.[97]

> Whether the body is of *sattva-guṇa, rajo-guṇa* or *tamoguṇa*, everything is done by the direction of the Supreme Lord through the agency of the external energy (*pṛthak sva-māyayā*). In this way, in different types of bodies, the Lord (*Īśvara*) gives directions as Paramātma, and again, to destroy the body, He employs the *tamo-guṇa*. This is the way the living entities receive different types of bodies.[98]

Liberation

One usually achieves liberation only after many births.[99] However, if one surrenders to the Lord, it can happen earlier.[100]

> After many, many births, and after attaining the platform of transcendental knowledge, one becomes perfect when he surrenders unto the Lord. This is the general procedure. But one who surrenders at the very beginning...at once surpasses all stages simply by adopting the devotional attitude.[101]

If "unalloyed devotion is the ultimate goal of life,"[102] it is because it issues in liberation or ultimate freedom in a transcendental or spiritual world. The material spheres have three divisions of planets. But no matter how high one is elevated in the material planets, one is always subject to birth and death. Liberation involves transcending the material universe and entering one of the spiritual planets.[103] There is nothing superior to Goloka Vṛndāvan, Kṛṣṇa's spiritual abode, which is one's ultimate destination.[104] True liberation is above the three *guṇas* of *prakṛti* and is called Kṛṣna consciousness.[105] This ultimate abode is uncompromisingly spiritual.[106] When in liberation one transcends the material worlds one also receives a spiritual body.[107] This spiritual body is one's original state before contamination by the material world.

> The result of perfection in Kṛṣna consciousness is that after giving up one's material body, one is immediately transferred to the spiritual world in one's original spiritual body to become an associate of the Supreme Personality of Godhead. Some devotees go to Vaikuṇṭhaloka, and others go to Goloka Vṛndāvana to become associates of Kṛṣṇa.[108]

This ultimate freedom does not mean the loss of the individual identity of the soul. Just as there is variegatedness in the material world, so is this true of the spiritual world in which there are eternal distinctions. To be born in this spiritual world also means that one is no longer affected by the creation and destruction of the material world in the day and night of Brahmā.[109] Liberation means that one learns that all living beings are merely part and parcel of the Lord and that their bodily existence that induces them to think of themselves as independent is *māyā*.[110] "Liberation means to be situated in one's constitutional position as the eternal servitor of Kṛṣṇa (Kṛṣṇa consciousness)."[111] And, since all of the material world is nothing more than the Lord's external energy, the one who is Kṛṣṇa conscious understands the situation of the living entity and the process of karma and rebirth as well.

In the final analysis full illumination and death are simultaneous.

> And in due course of time, when a pure devotee is completely prepared, all of a sudden the change of body occurs which is commonly called death. And for the pure devotee such a change takes place exactly like lightning, and illumination follows simultaneously. That is to say that a devotee simultaneously changes his material body and developes a spiritual body by the will of the Supreme.[112]

However, "even before death, a pure devotee has no material affection due to his body being spiritualized like a red–hot iron in contact with fire."[113] Although one can be involved in the practice of Kṛṣṇa consciousness and fall into material desire, the pure devotee is already spiritualized during his life.

> One who is always busy serving Kṛṣṇa, in whatever condition he may live, is understood to be liberated even in this life. Such a person, who is a pure devotee, does not need to change his body; indeed, he does not possess a material body, for his body has already been spiritualized. An iron rod kept constantly within a fire will ultimately become fire, and whatever it touches will burn. Similarly, the pure devotee is in the fire of spiritual existence, and therefore his body is *cin–maya*; that is, it is spiritual, not material, because the pure devotee has no desire but the transcendental desire to serve the Lord.[114]

It is for this reason that the pure devotee is said to be unaffected by karma. He is living above it. The devotee lives transcendentally and not on the material level as it might appear.[115]

The impersonal experience of *advaita* is only preliminary to the final liberation which has three stages.

> Brahman is the beginning of transcendental realization. Paramātmā, the Supersoul, is the middle, the second stage in transcendental realization, and the Supreme Personality of Godhead is the ultimate realization of the Absolute Truth. Therefore, both Paramātmā and the impersonal Brahman are within the Supreme Person.[116]

The person who is fully engaged in Kṛṣṇa consciousness is no longer engaged in sense gratification,[117] for he knows that he is not the body, but a "fragmental portion of the Supreme Personality of Godhead."[118]

To be liberated, then, is to live above the realm of material nature and the karma that operates there. It is also to cease to be reborn since one is elevated to a spiritual planet from which one does not return.[119]

Means to Liberation

One must begin by pointing out that one cannot reach liberation by worshipping the demigods.[120] Nor is *jñāna* sufficient for liberation.[121] *Jñāna* and karma yoga both ultimately lead to bhakti which is the supreme yoga.[122] One is not able to engage in counteractive karma to cancel out past karma and achieve liberation. Instead it is necessary to be raised above the level of karma to a transcendental level.

> One has to *act* in the status of spirit soul, otherwise there is no escape from material bondage. Action in Kṛṣṇa consciousness is not, however, action on the fruitive platform. Activities performed in full knowledge strengthen one's advancement in real knowledge. Without Kṛṣṇa consciousness, mere renunciation of fruitive activities does not actually purify the heart of a conditioned soul. As long as the heart is not purified, one has to work on the fruitive platform. But action in Kṛṣṇa consciousness automatically helps one escape the result of fruitive action so that one need not descend to the material platform.[123]

Swami Bhaktivedanta sometimes talks of cleansing all sinful reaction, or of burning up reactions.[124] But in addition to having reactions to one's work burned up through Kṛṣṇa consciousness, one's existence is raised to the transcendental level. The means that are used, then, should not be seen as "good" karma as over against "bad" karma. They are actions which, rather than counteracting karma, raise one above its sphere until one's very material body is "spiritualized."

It should not be surprising, then, to learn that no matter what one does, it is not sufficient apart from the grace of the Lord. For, whatever one does is done on the level of material nature. Only the Lord who lives above this plane and is untouched by it can raise one above it.[125] "Therefore He is the Supreme, and only He can deliver the conditioned soul from the onslaught of material nature...."[126]

The Lord rescues living entities by His causeless or uncompelled nature.[127] But, the Lord is not arbitrary. Although His mercy is causeless and cannot be forced, He does respond to surrender and devotional service. Personal striving is on the level of desire. But the pure devotee does not even desire promotion to the spiritual world.[128] This is why the pure devotee receives liberation and elevation to the spiritual planet at death. He is surrendered entirely to the Lord which is the only way to be liberated. "That supreme abode can be achieved only by surrender and by no other means."[129]

This position that liberation is the result of the causeless mercy of the Lord does not mean that there is nothing that the individual can do. Indeed, the causeless mercy of the Lord is commonly given to those who surrender to Him and who engage in devotional service,

> ...which consists of nine different activities: hearing, chanting, remembering, serving, worshipping, praying, obeying, maintaining friendship and surrendering everything. By the practice of these nine elements of devotional service one is elevated to spiritual consciousness, Kṛṣṇa consciousness.[130]

Devotional service is so pure that once one has started it, one is dragged eventually to ultimate success.[131] For devotional service is above mundane causes and cannot be affected by them.[132] Devotional service, "being transcendental in nature, it frees one from reaction."[133] Rather than being merely a form of counteractive karma, devotional service seems to raise one above both good and bad reactions to a transcendental level.[134] The more one is engaged in devotional service, the more is one fixed on that transcendental plane.[135] The soul is cleansed from material contamination and one rises to the level of *sattva* and then finally to Kṛṣṇa's abode.

The gracious ingredient of liberation is further seen in the fact that when the devotee surrenders to Kṛṣṇa, Kṛṣṇa takes away all sinful reactions of the devotee. Likewise the spiritual master, as the eternal manifestation of Kṛṣṇa, takes on the sinful reactions of the disciples that he initiates.

> As Kṛṣṇa takes away all the sinful reactions of a person immediately upon his surrender unto him, similarly the external manifestation of Kṛṣṇa, the representative of Kṛṣṇa who acts as the mercy of the Supreme Personality of Godhead, takes all the resultant actions of the sinful life of the disciple immediately after the disciple's initiation.[136]

When a spiritual master gets sick, or has bad dreams, it is not the result of his karma, but of that of his disciples.[137] It is for this reason that Śri Caitanya urged not to make many disciples. But, in the process of preaching, for Bhaktivedanta, that became a necessary risk. But even here, grace is operative. Only the Supreme Personality of Godhead Himself is powerful enough to neutralize fully the reactions of sinful deeds. But if the spiritual master becomes overloaded with his disciples' sinful reactions, Kṛṣṇa neutralizes those for his servant as well.

> No one but the Supreme Personality of Godhead is able to neutralize the reactions of sinful deeds, whether one's own or those of others. Sometimes the spiritual master, after accepting a disciple, must take charge of that disciple's sinful past activities and, being overloaded, must sometimes suffer — if not fully, then partially — for the sinful acts of the disciple....The poor spiritual master is kind and merciful enough to accept a disciple and partially suffer for that disciple's sinful activities, but Kṛṣṇa, being merciful to His servant, neutralizes the reactions of sinful deeds for the servant who engages in preaching His glories.[138]

Even karma is a form of grace when one realizes that the laws of material nature and karma are the external energy of the Lord. It is through this, and his residence within as Supersoul, and His role as spiritual master that the Lord seeks to reclaim conditioned souls.

> This means that the conditioned souls are being reclaimed by the Lord both ways, namely by the process of punishment by the external energy of the Lord, and by Himself as the spiritual master within and without. Within the heart of every living being the Lord Himself as the Supersoul Paramātmā becomes the spiritual master in the shape of scriptures, saints and initiator spiritual master.[139]

Swami Bhaktivedanta does not present a full range of logical arguments for karma and rebirth. He speaks with confidence while denouncing the views of materialists, mental speculators, advaitins, academics and others who are caught in the web of ignorance. Nor does he claim to be innovative or to modify a teaching in the light of modern academic knowledge. For, a bona fide teacher in disciplic succession merely passes on an authentic and ancient truth. A proper response is not to challenge but to submit.

But, while Swami Bhaktivedanta's understanding is not novel in terms of his tradition, in the light of other contemporary approaches to karma and rebirth it stands out decisively as a view that consistently interprets these doctrines within the control of a personalized God. Material laws and karma can not be circumvented. But this is not because material nature runs on its own or is out of God's control, but because both immanently (in His external energy and as Supersoul) and transcendentally (as the Supreme Personality of Godhead), Kṛṣṇa guides every aspect of the universe. And, if one finally transcends these material rounds of birth and death in a spiritual planet and existence, that too is the result of the Supreme Lord.

NOTES

1. A. C. Bhaktivedanta Swami Prabhupāda, *Śrīmad–Bhāgavatam* (Los Angeles: The Bhaktivedanta Book Trust, 1972), I, 1, 305. (Bhaktivedanta's 29 volumes of this set were published from 1972 to 1980. The roman numeral refers to the *Canto*, the first number thereafter refers to the *Part*, and the last number to the *page*. Hereafter, references to this set will simply read *Ś. B.*)

2. A. C. Bhaktivedanta Swami Prabhupāda, *Bhagavad–gītā As It Is* (New York: Collier Books, 1972), 99. (Hereafter referred to simply as *Bhagavad–gītā*).

3. *Bhagavad–gītā*, 412.

4. *Ś. B.*, IV, 1, 371.

5. *Bhagavad–gītā*, 646.

6. *Ś. B.*, IV, 1, 311.

7. *Bhagavad–gītā*, 699ff.

8. *Ibid.*, 677.

9. *Ibid.*, 682.

10. *Ibid.*, 670.

11. *Ibid.*, 671.

12. *Ibid.*, 682.

13. *Ibid.*

14. *Ibid.*, 682-683.

15. *Ibid.*, 679.

16. *Ś. B.*, VII, 2, 254.

17. *Bhagavad–gītā*, 114.

18. *Ś. B.*, III, 4, 1358.

19. *Ś. B.*, VII, 3, 112.

20. *Bhagavad–gītā*, 463.

21. *Ś. B.*, X,1, 64-65; (*emphasis mine*).

22. A. C. Bhaktivedanta Swami Prabhupāda, *The Nectar of Instruction* (Los Angeles: The Bhaktivedanta Book Trust, 1975), 3.

23. *Ś. B.*, V, 1, 279.

24. *Ś. B.*, VI, 2, 223.

25. *Ś. B.*, VI, 3, 44.

26. *Ś. B.*, VI, 2, 223.

27. *Ś. B.*, VI, 2, 222.

28. *Ś. B.*, VI, 3, 189.

29. *Bhagavad–gītā*, 237.

30. *Ibid.*, 288.

31. *Ś. B.*, IV, 1, 371 and VI, 2, 223.

32. *Ś. B.*, I, 3, 712-713.

33. *Ibid.*

34. *Ś. B.*, I, 2, 389.

35. *Bhagavad–gītā*, 737.

36. *Ś. B.*, VII, 2,313.

37. *Ś. B.*, V, 1, 300.

38. *Ś. B.*, V, 1, 295.

39. *Ś. B.*, V, 1, 295-296.

40. *Ś. B.*, VIII, 3, 160.

41. *Ś. B.*, IV, 4, 1376.

42. *Ś. B.*, III, 4, 1334.

43. A. C. Bhaktivedanta Swami Prabhupāda, *Śrī Īśopaniṣad* (Los Angeles: The Bhaktivedanta Book Trust, 1969), 108-109.

44. *Ś. B.*, VII, 2, 3-12.

45. *Ś. B.*, VIII, 2, 225-226.

46. *Ś. B.*, VII, 3, 109.

47. *Ś. B.*, III, 3, 1360.

48. *Ś. B.*, X, 2, 197.

49. *Śrī Īśopaniṣad*, 65, 70.

50. *Ibid.*, 83.

51. A. C. Bhaktivedanta Swami Prabhupāda, *Easy Journey to Other Planets* (Los Angeles: The Bhaktivedanta Book Trust, 1970), 31.

52. *Bhagavad–gītā*, 127-128.

53. *Ś. B.*, VI, 3, 83.

54. *Ś. B.*, IX, 1, 214.

55. *Ś. B.*, X, 1, 6.

56. *Ś. B.*, VI, 1, 76.

57. *Ibid.*

58. *Ś. B.*, IV, 4, 1462.

59. *Ś. B.*, IV, 4, 1463.

60. *Ś. B.*, IV, 4, 1446.

61. *Ś. B.*, IV, 4, 1461.

62. *Ś. B.*, IV, 4, 1456.

63. *Ś. B.*, IV, 4, 1462.

64. *Ś. B.*, IV, 4, 1468.

65. *Ś. B.*, IV, 4, 1468-1469.

66. *Ś. B.*, X, 2, 51.

67. *Ś. B.*, Vi, 1, 46-47.

68. *Ś. B.*, VI, 1, 47.

69. *Bhagavad–gītā*, 656.

70. *Ś. B.*, X, 1, 66.

71. *Ś. B.*, V, 1, 314.

72. *Ś. B.*, IV, 1, 189.

73. *Bhagavad–gītā*, 654.

74. *Ś. B.*, IX, 1, 124.

75. *Ś. B.*, VII, 1, 96.

76. *Ś. B.*, III, 4, 1298.

77. *Ś. B.*, III, 4, 1300.

78. *Ś. B.*, III, 4, 1302.

79. *Ś. B.*, V, 2, 439.]

80. *Ibid.*

81. *Bhagavad–gītā*, 8.6.

82. *Ibid.*, 411.

83. *Ś. B.*, III, 4, 1297.

84. *Bhagavad–gītā*, 415.

85. *The Nectar of Devotion*, 74.

86. *Ś. B.*, V, 2, 279.

87. *Bhagavad–gītā*, 713.

88. *Ś. B.*, VII, 2, 59.

89. *Ś. B.*, VI, 2, 228.

90. *Ś. B.*, III, 4, 1314.

91. *Ibid.*

92. *Ś. B.*, I, 2, 616.

93. *Ś. B.*, III, 4, 1325.

94. *Ś. B.*, III, 4, 1331.

95. *Ś. B.*, III, 4, 1336.

96. *Ś. B.*, III, 4, 1338.

97. *Ś. B.*, VI, 2, 228.

98. *Ś. B.*, VII, 1, 17.

99. *Bhagavad-gītā*, 349, 390; *Srī Iśopaniṣad*, 36.

100. *Bhagavad-gītā*, 158.

101. *Śrī Iśopaniṣad*, 109.

102. *Ś. B.*, I, 2, 426.

103. *Śrī Iśopaniṣad*, 83.

104. *Bhagavad-gītā*, 431.

105. *Ibid.*, 379.

106. *Ibid.*, 432.

107. *Ibid.*, 703-704.

108. *Ś. B.*, VI, 1, 133.

109. *Bhagavad-gītā*, 665.

110. *Ibid.*, 261.

111. *Ibid.*, 262.

112. *Ś. B.*, I, 1, 304.

113. *Ibid.*

114. *Ś. B*., X, 1, 103.

115. *Ś. B*., VIII, 3, 151.

116. *Bhagavad–gītā*, 690. See also p. 139.

117. *Ibid*., 312.

118. *Ibid*., 294.

119. *Ś. B*., VI, 1, 272.

120. *Śrī Iśopaniṣad*, 65 & 70.

121. *Bhagavad–gītā*, 274.

122. *Ibid*., 359.

123. *Ibid*., 274.

124. *Ibid*., 242-243; 263.

125. *Ibid*., 253.

126. *Ś. B*., VII, 2, 217.

127. *Ś. B*., I, 1, 295-296.

128. *Bhagavad–gītā*, 424.

129. *Ibid*., 702.

130. *Ibid*., 443.

131. *The Nectar of Instruction*, 36.

132. *Ibid*., 37.

133. *Bhagavad–gītā*, 272.

134. *Ibid.*, 135.

135. *Ś. B.*, I, 1, 110.

136. *Ś. B.*, IV, 3, 851.

137. *Perfect Questions Perfect Answers* (Los Angeles: The Bhaktivedanta Book Trust, 1977), 59-60.

138. *Ś. B.*, IX, 2, 6.

139. *Ś. B.*, I, 1, 323.

14

Swami Bhaktivedanta and the *Bhagavadgītā* "As it Is"

The encounter between the scholar and the believer is always an interesting one. Frequently in historical studies, however, the believers whom one studies are gone and therefore unable to respond to scholarly analyses of their work and thought. Sometimes the tradition itself is dead and there are not even any followers with whom one must reckon. This is not true for the subject at hand, for the movement founded by Swami Bhaktivedanta is a thriving and self–conscious movement today. It will become clear that Swami Bhaktivedanta has some exceedingly uncomplimentary things to say about the world of scholarship and the academic interest in the *Bhagavadgītā* in particular. The gulf between Swami Bhaktivedanta's presentation and that of the scholarly exegete is unbridgeable, for their purposes operate on different levels.

One way to deal with the gulf is to seek to circumvent it by crossing at another point, as does Edward Dimock in the "Foreword" to Bhaktivedanta's commentary. Dimock sees Bhaktivedanta's interpretation as an authentic interpretation within the Gauḍīya Vaiṣṇava tradition. My task, however, in this context, is not merely to see Swami Bhaktivedanta as an authentic proponent of Vaiṣṇavism, but to inquire how he interprets the *Gītā*. And it must be assumed that this examination is to be done within the context of academic scholarship and not as part of a devotional commitment. This also assumes that there are two objects to be considered. The first is the *Gītā* itself, and the second is Swami Bhaktivedanta's interpretation of it. While the devotee may be expected to merge the two, particularly when it is believed that the interpreter is in disciplic succession (*paramparā*), such an assumption is not permitted for the historian of religions. Hence, although from the standpoint of the devotee, the scholar's approach may lack integrity, the academic is bound by a scholarly integrity of his own.

The historian is interested in learning precisely what the text has to say. He or she wants to understand everything that might be implied in the words of the text without importing anything that is not actually there. Furthermore, he or she is interested in understanding the *ślokas* in their historical setting. Exoteric meaning is the only realm, for the esoteric tradition is closed to academic study. With this in mind we will turn to an examination of several passages and Swami Bhaktivedanta's interpretation of them. The passages are chosen to illustrate points or trends that are common in Swami Bhaktivedanta's handling of the *Gītā*. Since Swami Bhaktivedanta's purports go well beyond the exoteric meaning of the texts to which they are attached, they indicate some of the themes that are emphasized in his thought.

Treatment of the Text

Promulgation of Kṛṣṇa Consciousness

Many scholars see some degree of progression within the *Bhagavadgītā*. It is recognized that chapters one through six deal with unattached action and place little emphasis on the place of Kṛṣṇa as supreme Lord of the universe. Chapters seven through twelve expound the supreme nature of Kṛṣṇa, while chapters thirteen through eighteen return again to an emphasis on unattached action. While these are not mutually exclusive, they are clear emphases. Whether this difference in tone is to be explained as progressive teaching on the part of the author or as the result of the use of different source materials is a matter for discussion.[1] However, one of the striking features of Swami Bhaktivedanta's approach to the *Gītā* is that he reads the complete teaching of the book, indeed of vedic literature generally, into any passage. There is no recognition given to the possibility of progressive teaching in the text. This is particularly striking in some of the early passages of the book.

In chapter two the *Gītā* seems to be teaching that Arjuna will finally be unable to avoid action. Since action is inevitable, the key to liberation is action without attachment to the fruits. In 2.48 this is how *yoga* is defined. It is actions performed without attachment, indifferent to success or failure (*samatvaṃ yoga ucyate*). *Yoga*, then, is defined as indifference or evenness of mind. This would seem to be confirmed in 3.3 where *jñānayoga* is identified with *saṅkhya* (not necessarily the classical system by that name — *jñāna yogena sāṅkhyānāṃ*), while the term *yoga* is identified with *karmayoga* (*karma yogena yoginām*). Already, Swami Bhaktivedanta takes *karmayoga* not merely as unattached action, but in the light of later passages in the *Gītā*, as "devotional work."

This whole chapter which emphasized unattached work as the means to liberation is infused with Kṛṣṇa consciousness. The reference to Kṛṣṇa as the object of meditation is taken as a reference to Kṛṣṇa consciousness. R. C. Zaehner points out that in 2.61 we have the first instance in the *Gītā* in which Kṛṣṇa mentions himself. And, he points out that it is in connection with exercises that are essentially "Buddhistic and Sāṁkhya–Yoga" in nature. He continues:

> He is not at all offering Himself as a object of living devotion and veneration, but merely as a definite object on which to direct what is elsewhere called 'one–pointed' (*ekāgra*, cf. *Yoga–sūtras* 3.11,12) concentration.[2]

Zaehner goes so far as to say that "Hence, at the end of this chapter which from now on describes the ascent of the self to full liberation, there is no further mention of Kṛṣṇa as God: the goal is not God, but Nirvāna, the Buddha's goal."[3] Whether one wants to follow Zaehner in saying that the goal specified is the Buddha's goal, it certainly does not articulate a liberation in terms of Kṛṣṇa consciousness. Yet in 2.61 where Kṛṣṇa is the object of meditation, Swami Bhaktivedanta comments: "that the highest conception of *yoga* perfection is Kṛṣṇa consciousness is *clearly* (emphasis mine) explained in this verse."[4]

In 2.67 where the text merely states that the senses are roving and are capable of carrying away a person's mentality, Swami Bhaktivedanta comments that to avoid this, all the senses are to be "engaged in the service of the Lord" and that "all the senses must be engaged in Kṛṣṇa consciousness, for that is the correct technique for controlling the mind."[5] In 2.68 which says only that withdrawing the senses from the objects of sense stabilizes the mentality (*prajñā*), Swami Bhaktivedanta introduces not only Kṛṣṇa consciousness, but also the need for a bona fide spiritual master. "...Only by Kṛṣṇa consciousness is one really established in intelligence and...one should practice this art under the guidance of a bona fide spiritual master...."[6] In 2.70 the text (even by Swami Bhaktivedanta's translation) likens the person who is able to achieve peace to the ocean which has rivers emptying into it while remaining still. Swami Bhaktivedanta comments that this is true of the person

> ...fixed in Kṛṣṇa consciousness. As long as one has the material body, the demands of the body for sense gratification will continue. The devotee, however, is not disturbed by such desires because of his fullness.

> A Kṛṣṇa conscious man is not in need of anything because the Lord fulfills all his material necessities.[7]

When 2.71 says that the man goes to peace who is free from self interest and egoism (*nirmamo nirahaṅkāraḥ sa śāntim adhigaccati*), Swami Bhaktivedanta comments: "To become desireless means not to desire anything for sense gratification. In other words, desire for becoming Kṛṣṇa conscious is actually desirelessness."[8] He then goes on to describe the Kṛṣṇa conscious person as the eternal servitor of Kṛṣṇa. There is certainly no explicit reference to Kṛṣṇa in verses 62 through 71. Yet, when liberation is described as *brahma nirvāṇam* it is understood by Swami Bhaktivedanta as equivalent to Kṛṣṇa consciousness and being elevated to the spiritual plane in devotional service to the Lord.[9]

It would appear, then, that Swami Bhaktivedanta reads the notion of Kṛṣṇa consciousness into the second chapter where the text itself says much less. This tendency is found repeatedly in his interpretation of the *Gītā*. It suggests that he considers it legitimate to interpret any verse in the light of the whole system found in the *Gītā* whether it is explicitly mentioned in that verse of the *Gītā* or not.

Inculcation of a Vaiṣṇava Life Style

Not only does Swami Bhaktivedanta seem to disavow any principle of progression in the *Gītā*, but he also goes beyond specific texts and the *Gītā* itself when he makes it the occasion for the inculcation of a Vaiṣṇava life style. In several places Swami Bhaktivedanta credits Caitanya (1486-1534) with instituting the chanting of the *mahāmantra*. Yet in numerous places in his purports on specific verses, which never mention this practice of chanting, Swami Bhaktivedanta recommends it as the best way of achieving the goal of the text in the present age, *kali yuga*. In 4.39 the text says that one who has knowledge and has controlled the senses soon goes to the highest peace. Swami Bhaktivedanta says that such knowledge can be achieved by one who believes firmly in Kṛṣṇa and that this faith is achieved by acting in Kṛṣṇa consciousness and by chanting the *mahāmantra*.[10]

In 6.34 Arjuna calls attention to the fickle nature of the mind which is as difficult to restrain as the wind. In his purport, Swami Bhaktivedanta recommends chanting as the best method for restraining the mind. "The easiest way to control the mind, as suggested by Lord Caitanya, is chanting 'Hare Kṛṣṇa,' the great *mantra* for deliverance, in all humanity."[11] In 6.35 it is admitted by Kṛṣṇa that it is very difficult to control the mind, but it is said that it is possible through practice (*abhyāsena*) and detachment (*vairāgyeṇa*). The text does not specify precisely what practice is, but Swami Bhaktivedanta does in some detail. It is the practice of Kṛṣṇa consciousness and engaging in "nine types of devotional service to the Lord. The first and foremost of such devotional engagements is hearing about Kṛṣṇa."[12] This can purge the mind of all misgivings.

In 8.5 the text indicates that liberation to Kṛṣṇa's estate is guaranteed for one who remembers Kṛṣṇa alone at the time of death. However, Swami Bhaktivedanta reminds his readers that this is not possible for the "impure person" who has not practiced Kṛṣṇa consciousness and devotional service. The way to be certain is to chant the *mahāmantra*.

> To remember Kṛṣṇa one should chant the *mahāmantra*, Hare Kṛṣṇa, Hare Kṛṣṇa, Kṛṣṇa Kṛṣṇa, Hare Hare/ Hare Rāma, Hare Rāma, Rāma Rāma, Hare Hare, incessantly, following in the footsteps of Lord Caitanya, being more tolerant than the tree, humbler than the grass and offering all respect to others without requiring respect in return. In such a way one will be able to depart from the body successfully remembering Kṛṣṇa and so attain the supreme goal.[13]

This same advice about the *mahāmantra* is repeated in the purports for verses 7 and 8 as a means of remembering Kṛṣṇa even though the text itself says nothing about chanting. In 12.6-7, the text also indicates that one should work with the mind fixed on Kṛṣṇa, the means to which Bhaktivedanta again sees as chanting the *mahāmantra*. He recommends that one engage in one's vocation and at the same time chant the *mahāmantra*.

In 16.1-3 he indicates, as does the text, that sacrifice is useful. He says that one should preform vedic sacrifices, but because of the tremendous expense it is not really possible. The best sacrifice that one can offer in this age is the *mahāmantra*. Nowhere is this stated or implied in the text. A similar imposition is clear in 6.11-12 since the text recommends one thing and Swami Bhaktivedanta cancels that and offers the *mahāmantra*. This text tells how one should select the best place for meditation and go to a sacred place. Swami Bhaktivedanta indicates that this is fine in India, but that in Western societies it is not possible. Therefore, the *Brihan–Naradiya Purana* says that in the *kali yuga* when people in general are short–lived, slow in spiritual realization and always disturbed by anxieties, the best means of spiritual realization is chanting the name of the Lord. "In this age of quarrel and hypocrisy the only means of deliverance is chanting the holy name of the Lord. There is no other way. There is no other way. There is no other way."14 So, although nowhere in the text of the *Bhagavadgītā* is there any explicit mention of chanting the *mahāmantra*, it is recommended repeatedly as the best method in this age, and indeed as the *only* means of adequately concentrating the mind on the Lord.

Swami Bhaktivedanta also takes a number of occasions to proclaim the teaching of ISKCON (International Society for Kṛṣṇa Consciousness) of vegetarianism, of offering all food to Kṛṣṇa, and of eating *prasādam.* In 6.16 the text warns of eating too much or too little or sleeping too much. It is a good text to show how Swami Bhaktivedanta is more interested in expounding the principles of Kṛṣṇa consciousness than in merely explicating the text at hand. For, although the text also warns against those who do not eat at all, Bhaktivedanta does not comment on that. He does, however, expound on the Kṛṣṇa consciousness principles of not eating too much and eating only foods offered to Kṛṣṇa (not mentioned at all in the text), and not sleeping over six hours. He even indicates that eating animals is unnecessary and the result of one's being in the mode of ignorance. He uses 9.26 to enumerate some of the foods that are acceptable and unacceptable to Kṛṣṇa. Since ISKCON members eat only food offered to Kṛṣṇa (*prasādam*) it is also a list of acceptable food for them as well. Actually, 9.26 lists some of the physical things that are commonly offered to the image in *bhakti* worship. Swami Bhaktivedanta's translation is: "If one offers Me with love and devotion a leaf, a flower, fruit or water, I will accept it." The Kṛṣṇa conscious person will avoid anything that the Lord does not ask for and will limit his offering to the things specified. Thus, Swami Bhaktivedanta concludes that "meat, fish and eggs should not be offered to Kṛṣṇa. If He desired such things as offerings, He would have said so."[15] He continues: "Vegetables, grains, fruits, milk and water are the proper foods for human beings and are prescribed by Lord Kṛṣṇa Himself. Whatever else we eat cannot be offered to Him, since He will not accept it."[16] It is clear, however, that the text mentions flowers which are generally not eaten and makes no mention of vegetables, grains or milk. Nevertheless, Swami Bhaktivedanta uses the text to teach the dietary principles of ISKCON. Leaves, flowers, fruit and water hardly exhaust even the ISKCON diet.

In 17.8-10 various foods are classified according to the three *guṇas*. The text speaks of sattvic foods as being fattening. Swami Bhaktivedanta takes this to mean not animal fat, and goes to great length to indicate that one can get all the animal fat that one needs through milk, which rules out the need for killing innocent animals. None of this is mentioned in the text. Moreover, the text indicates that food that is cooked more than three hours before it is eaten is tamasic food. Although this is all that the text says, Swami Bhaktivedanta notes parenthetically "except *prasādam*, food offered to the Lord."[17] He also notes that remnants of food can be eaten only if they were first offered to the Lord or eaten first by saintly persons. Food that is offered to the Lord is transcendental and therefore not obliged to be eaten within three hours. This is all in keeping with the principles of ISKCON, but is not part of the text. In the purport to 18.3 which reports a difference of opinion about the usefulness of sacrifices, Swami Bhaktivedanta concedes that animal sacrifice is recommended in vedic literature, but that the animal is not actually killed! "The sacrifice is to give a new life to the animal. Sometimes the animal is given a new animal life after being killed in the sacrifice, and sometimes the animal is promoted immediately to the human form of life."[18]

Another important principle for ISKCON is the strict regulation of sexuality. Since 4.26 talks about offering up the senses in the fire of restraint, Swami Bhaktivedanta takes the opportunity to talk about how the *brahmacārī* does this through Kṛṣṇa consciousness, and how the householder does this through regulation of the senses dealing with intoxication, meat eating, and sexuality according to Kṛṣṇa consciousness principles. In the midst of a long list in which Kṛṣṇa is seen as the best of all categories, he is in 7.11 the might of the mighty (free from desire and passion), and he is also desire in creatures (so far as it is not inconsistent with right). Swami Bhaktivedanta's purport on this verse is short, but it is the occasion for teaching the regulation of sex. "Similarly, sex life, according to religious principles (*dharma*), should be for the propagation of children, not otherwise. The responsibility of parents is then to make their offspring Kṛṣṇa conscious."[19] Since both *Kāma* and *dharma* are in the text, he fills them with his content.

Articulation of a Theology of Kṛṣṇa

Swami Bhaktivedanta does not develop his theological themes in a systematic manner, but one can see in his purports the use of the text to present aspects of his theology of Kṛṣṇa. An interesting passage is 4.6-8, since it shows how Swami Bhaktivedanta's theology is brought to bear on a text on which scholars have generally agreed. Here in verse 6 the text is translated by

Edgerton, Deutsch, and Zaehner to indicate that though Kṛṣṇa's *ātman* is eternal and unborn, by his own mysterious power (*māyā*), he does take on *prakṛti*.[20] The next verse indicates that this happens when *dharma* languishes and *adharma* thrives. Swami Bhaktivedanta takes this to mean that although unborn, Kṛṣṇa's transcendental body never deteriorates. *Prakṛti* is taken as transcendental form. This means that although Kṛṣṇa appears he does not assume a new body as living entities do. When the Lord appears, he does so in the same original body, by his internal potency (*ātma–māyayā*).

> In other words, Kṛṣṇa appears in this material world in His original external form, with two hands, holding a flute. He appears exactly in His eternal body, uncontaminated by this material world. Although He appears in the same transcendental body and is Lord of the universe, it still appears that he takes His birth like an ordinary living entity.[21]

However, Swami Bhaktivedanta comments, although the Lord grows from childhood to boyhood, he never goes beyond youth.

> At the time of the Battle of Kurukṣetra, He had many grandchildren at home; or, in other words, He had sufficiently aged by material calculations. Still He looked just like a young man twenty or twenty–five years old. We never see a picture of Kṛṣṇa in old age because He never grows old like us, although He is the oldest person in the whole creation — past, present, and future.[22]

In 4.7 it is stated that Kṛṣṇa incarnates when *dharma* declines and *adharma* ascends. According to Bhaktivedanta, the principles of religion are laid down in the *Vedas* and any discrepancy in executing the rules of the *Vedas* makes one irreligious, i.e. adharmic. These principles are clearly indicated throughout the *Gītā* and the highest principle at the end of the *Gītā* is to surrender to Kṛṣṇa only, nothing more. Swami Bhaktivedanta relies on the *Bhāgavatam* and holds that Buddha was an incarnation of Kṛṣṇa. In Buddha's time, materialists were claiming the authority of the *Vedas* while participating in animal sacrifices contrary to vedic principles. So Buddha appeared to establish the vedic principle of nonviolence. Each *avatāra* has its own purpose, but no *avatāra* should be accepted as such unless it is specifically referred to in scriptures.

In 3.11 it would seem that the text is sketching the vedic view of sacrifice. The sacrifices are offered to the *devas*. For Swami Bhaktivedanta the *devas* are the demigods who are the administrators of material affairs under the supreme Lordship of Kṛṣṇa. He goes into some detail to indicate how the demigods each have their realm of responsibility, but that they serve under Kṛṣṇa and that even though some *yajñas* are for their benefit, it is ultimately Lord Kṛṣṇa who is the beneficiary of the *yajñas*. Now the text explicitly says none of this. "Some of the *yajñas* are meant to satisfy particular demigods; but even in so doing, Lord Viṣṇu is worshipped in all *yajñas* as the chief beneficiary."[23]

Kṛṣṇa Consciousness as the Fulfillment of Religion

In addition to using texts of the *Gītā* to teach Vaiṣṇava life style and thought, Bhaktivedanta often seeks to show the superiority of the Vaiṣṇava position and the error of other positions. Sometimes, he asserts, the positions are wrong, occasionally he holds those who hold them are ignorant or lacking intelligence, and if they do not recognize the ultimate reality of Kṛṣṇa as the personal god, they are preliminary positions that are fulfilled in Kṛṣṇa consciousness. The position that is attacked with the most regularity and vigor is that of Advaita Vedānta. Its advocates are called māyāvādīns, impersonalists, or monists.

In the path to spiritual realization there are three stages which are outlined. The first is an experience of the impersonal Brahman, the second is the experience of God as localized Supersoul, while the third is the experience of the Supreme Personality of Godhead. Apparently, the text does not need to refer to impersonalism or the preliminary nature of its experience. In 7.19 the text indicates that after many rebirths the man of knowledge finally comes to Kṛṣṇa. Swami Bhaktivedanta takes the occasion to point out that early in one's attempt to give up attachment to materialism there is an experience of impersonalism, but as one becomes more advanced spiritually one surrenders to Kṛṣṇa.[24] In 18.53-54 one is described as *brahma-bhūtaḥ*, which Edgerton translates as "becoming Brahman." Swami Bhaktivedanta takes this as an impersonal experience that is merely the first stage.

> To the impersonalist, achieving the *brahma-bhūta* stage, becoming one with the Absolute, is the last word. But for the personalist, or pure devotee, one has to go still further to become engaged in pure devotional

> service. This means that one who is engaged in pure devotional service to the Supreme Lord is already in a state of liberation, called *brahma-bhūta*, oneness with the Absolute.25

There are passages which seem to support Swami Bhaktivedanta's interpretation but which make no mention of other views as being inferior. One of them would seem to be 13.23. Here Swami Bhaktivedanta takes the occasion to show that this text supports his view more than that of the monists, who take the knower of the body to be one and hence fail to distinguish between the individual soul and the Supersoul.

> The individual soul enjoys the activities of a particular field, but the Supersoul is present not as finite enjoyer nor as one taking part in bodily activities, but as the witness, overseer, permitter and supreme enjoyer. His name is *paramātmā*, not *ātmā*, and He is transcendental. It is distinctly clear that the *ātmā* and *Paramātmā* are different.26

In the purport to 7.24, Swami Bhaktivedanta makes it clear that the impersonalists who think that they have experienced the final truth do not yet know the ultimate feature of the Absolute (which is personal). He is even harder on modern impersonalists who, unlike Śankara, do not recognize Kṛṣṇa as the Supreme Personality of Godhead.

> Persons who are under the impression that the Absolute Truth is impersonal are described as *asuras*, which means one who does not know the ultimate feature of the Absolute Truth. In the *Śrīmad-Bhāgavatam* it is stated that supreme realization begins from the impersonal Brahman and then rises to the localized Supersoul — but the ultimate word in the Absolute Truth is the Personality of Godhead. Modern impersonalists are still less intelligent, for they do not even follow their great predecessor, Śaṅkarācārya, who has specifically stated that Kṛṣṇa is the Supreme Personality of Godhead.27

Swami Bhaktivedanta goes on to indicate that the truth cannot be realized through mental speculation, but that one can only come to know Kṛṣṇa through devotion and that one should begin to practice it by chanting the *mahāmantra*. He continues; "Nondevotee impersonalists think that Kṛṣṇa has a body made of the material nature and that all His activities, His form and everything, are *māyā*. These impersonalists are known as Māyāvādī. They do know the ultimate truth."[28] Devotional service is not a temporary activity that is only preliminary to liberation. Actual devotional service continues after liberation, indeed, one can even say that in the best sense it does not begin until liberation.[29]

That it is difficult to achieve liberation through renunciation without yoga is indicated in 5.6. Swami Bhaktivedanta takes this occasion to show the inferiority of the māyāvādīn view. Studying *sāṅkhya* and *vedānta* and engaging in speculation, they do not place much stock in devotional service. But since their speculation becomes tedious, they sometimes revert to the *Bhāgavatam*, although they do not properly understand it. They also have the tendency to fall from the path of realization and enter materialistic activities of a philanthropic and altruistic nature which are merely material entanglements.[30] "Therefore, the conclusion is that those who are engaged in Kṛṣṇa consciousness are better situated than the *sannyāsīs* engaged in simple Brahman speculation, although they to come to Kṛṣṇa consciousness, after many births."[31]

Swami Bhaktivedanta, then, does not deny that the māyāvādīns have a valid experience. The impersonal Brahman is real, but it is merely the "personal effulgence of Kṛṣṇa."[32] It is the personal god who is the cause of everything. All the incarnations are only expansions of the Lord as are the living entities which are part and parcel of the Supreme Lord. The māyāvādīns do not properly understand this truth. "The Māyāvādī philosophers wrongly think that Kṛṣṇa loses His own separate existence in His many expansions. This thought is material in nature."[33] *Māyā* does not teach that the distinctions that are made are unreal, but that living entities think that they are separate from Kṛṣṇa.

> For want of sufficient knowledge in the absolute science, we are now covered with illusion, and therefore we think that we are separate from Kṛṣṇa. Although we are separated parts of Kṛṣṇa, we are nevertheless not different from him....The whole teaching of the *Gītā* is targeted toward this end: that a living being, as His eternal servitor, cannot be separated from Kṛṣṇa, and his sense of being an identity apart from Kṛṣṇa is called *māyā*.[34]

Since the liberation of the impersonalists is only partial, they stand the risk of returning again to this material world.[35] A text such as 4.11 does not have to mention the impersonalists to provide Swami Bhaktivedanta with an opportunity to criticize them. Kṛṣṇa helps even them by absorbing them into his effulgence, but they "return to this material field to exhibit their dormant desires for activities."[36]

Not only is Advaita only fulfilled in the personal god, but in 6.46-47 Swami Bhaktivedanta sees *bhaktiyoga* as the fulfillment of all other yogas. Although the text indicates that of all yogis, the ones who revere Kṛṣṇa with faith are the best, Bhaktivedanta makes use of this to teach that *bhaktiyoga* is best. "The culmination of all kinds of *yoga* practices lies in *bhakti–yoga*. All other *yogas* are but means to come to the point of *bhakti* in *bhakti–yoga*. *Yoga* actually means *bhakti–yoga*; all other *yogas* are progressions toward the destination of *bhakti–yoga*."[37]

In 4.29 Swami Bhaktivedanta explains the purposes of *prāṇāyāma*, of inhalation and exhalation, and how its practice can prolong life by many years. However, the person who is Kṛṣṇa conscious is seen as accomplishing all that this is intended to accomplish and more. Even the practice of reducing the intake of food is done automatically when the devotee limits his intake of food to *prasādam*. In the purport to 6.3, Swami points out that the practice of the eight–fold yoga is particularly difficult in the *kali yuga*. Also, early attempts at such practice are only fruitive activities and only near the end of such practice do disturbing mental activities cease. A Kṛṣṇa conscious person is superior since from the very beginning he thinks only of Kṛṣṇa. The purpose of yoga, then, is fulfilled in Kṛṣṇa consciousness.

> Kṛṣṇa is realized in different degrees as Brahman, Paramātmā and the Supreme Personality of Godhead. Kṛṣṇa consciousness means, concisely, to be always engaged in the transcendental loving service of the Lord. But those who are attached to the impersonal Brahman or the localized Supersoul are also partially Kṛṣṇa conscious, because impersonal Brahman is the spiritual ray of Kṛṣṇa and Supersoul is the all–pervading partial expansion of Kṛṣṇa. Thus the impersonalist and the meditator are also indirectly Kṛṣṇa conscious. A directly Kṛṣṇa conscious person is the topmost transcendentalist because such a devotee knows what is meant by Brahman or Paramātmā. His knowledge of the Absolute Truth is perfect, whereas the impersonalist and the meditative *yogī* are imperfectly Kṛṣṇa conscious.[38]

Theoretical Background for Swami Bhaktivedanta's Approach

If Swami Bhaktivedanta does not interpret the text of the *Gītā* in the manner of modern scholars, and if we find in his purports discussions that go beyond the context of the text itself, we must ask if there are any principles at work which will explain why he takes this approach without any evidence of discomfort. There are a number of such principles which provide such an explanation, and to those we now turn.

The Nature and Extent of Vedic Literature

The *Vedas* are eternal, are given by Kṛṣṇa, and have the knowledge of Kṛṣṇa as their end.[39] However, when Swami Bhaktivedanta speaks of the *Vedas* he means more than the four *Vedas*; vedic literature extends to include all of what is commonly taken as *śruti* as well as much of *smṛti*. For example, the vedic literature is seen as including the four *Vedas*, *Vedānta-sūtras*, the *Upaniṣads* and *Purāṇas*. "In all Vedic literature, beginning from the four *Vedas*, *Vedānta-sūtras*, and the *Upaniṣads* and *Purāṇas*, the glories of the Supreme Lord are celebrated."[40] "*Veda* refers to all kinds of Vedic literature, namely the four *Vedas* (*Ṛg*, *Yajur*, *Sāma*, and *Atharva*) and the eighteen *Purāṇas* and *Upaniṣads*, and *Vedānta-sūtra*."[41] Also included in vedic literature are the *Mahābhārata* and certain other authorized texts in the Vaiṣṇava tradition (e.g. *Caitanya-Caritāmṛta*). Kṛṣṇa is the source of the whole corpus of vedic literature and is the final author of it all. Swami Bhaktivedanta indicates the relative purposes of the texts as follows:

> First, He divided the *Vedas* into four, then He explained them in the *Purāṇas*, and for less capable people He wrote the *Mahābhārata*. In the *Mahābhārata* there is given the *Bhagavad-gītā*. Then all Vedic literature is summarized in the *Vedānta-sūtra*, and for future guidance He gave a natural commentation on the *Vedānta-sūtra*, called *Śrīmad-Bhāgavatam*.[42]

Of all the revealed scriptures, however, the *Bhagavad-gītā* is best.[43] The reason for this is that "it is the essence of all Vedic literature and...is spoken by the Supreme Personality of Godhead."[44] Furthermore, the only aim of the *Vedas* is to enable devotees to gain Kṛṣṇa consciousness, to realize that they are part and parcel of the Lord, to go back to Godhead. That is not only true of the *Bhagavad–gītā* and *Bhagavata Purāṇa* which are explicit in this regard. It is also true of the four *Vedas*, the *Upaniṣads*, and the *Vedānta–sūtras*. "All the *Vedas*, therefore, aim only toward Kṛṣṇa. Whatever we want to know through the *Vedas* is but a progressive step to understand Kṛṣṇa."[45] Since the Lord in his incarnation as Vyāsadeva is the author of the texts, it stands to reason that even the earliest ones will have the same message as the later ones. "The *Vedas* offer knowledge of the Supreme Personality of Godhead, Kṛṣṇa, and Kṛṣṇa in His incarnation as Vyāsadeva is the compiler of the *Vedānta–sūtra*. The commentation on the *Vedānta–sūtra* by Vyāsadeva in the *Śrīmad–Bhāgavatam* gives the real understanding of *Vedānta–sūtra*."[46] Not only is the *Gītā* the best for the reasons indicated above, but one can come to the goal of vedic literature by reading it alone. Furthermore, if one comes to Kṛṣṇa consciousness and acts in Kṛṣṇa consciousness, one also automatically fulfills all other vedic injunctions and sacrifices.

Use of Other Texts to Explain the Gītā

If the extent of vedic literature is as we have indicated, and if the end of it all is Kṛṣṇa, then it could be expected that Swami Bhaktivedanta would quote from these other texts to indicate what the intention of the *Gītā* is. This is in fact the case and some of the texts that Swami Bhaktivedanta quotes come before and some after the composition of the *Gītā*. But these texts are used in such a way that they are not referred to merely to illuminate the text, but are quoted as though they have the same authority as the *Gītā* itself. They are used in much the same way that later passages of the *Gītā* are used to explain the meaning of earlier passages. The time line is erased in their use.

In 3.9 the Sanskrit is as follows:

yajñārthāt karmaṇo'nyatra
loko'yaṁ karma–bandhanaḥ

This is rendered by Edgerton as: "Except action for the purpose of worship, this world is bound by actions." The point seems to be that karma or work is binding except when it is done as a sacrifice. Swami Bhaktivedanta, however, sees *yajña* as referring to Viṣṇu, and interprets the passage as follows: "*Yajña* means Lord Viṣṇu, or sacrificial performances. All sacrificial performances also are meant for the satisfaction of Lord Viṣṇu. The *Vedas* enjoin: *yajño vai viṣṇuḥ*. In other words, the same purpose is served whether one performs prescribed *yajñas* or directly serves Lord Viṣṇu."[47] Swami

Bhaktivedanta then continues by saying that the *varnāśrama* institution was created for the purpose of serving Lord Viṣṇu. This is supported by a text in the *Viṣṇu Purāṇa* (3.8.8). The conclusion is that "one has to work in Kṛṣṇa consciousness to satisfy Kṛṣṇa (or Viṣṇu); and while performing such activities one is in a liberated stage."[48]

In the following verse (3.10), *Prajāpati*, the Lord of creatures, is taken as an equivalent of Viṣṇu by Swami Bhaktivedanta. The *yajñas* which he created are seen as sacrifices to Viṣṇu. The principle of the vedic hymns is to understand Kṛṣṇa, and when it is found in *Bhagavatam* 2.4.20 that Lord Viṣṇu is described as *pati* in many ways, it becomes clear that *Prajāpati* is Viṣṇu. There are many yajñas which are prescribed for worship of Kṛṣṇa in the vedic literature, but perhaps the best for the *kali yuga* is the *saṅkīrtana-yajña*. This is mentioned in the *Bhāgavatam* and was introduced by Caitanya who was an incarnation of Lord Kṛṣṇa.

> In this age of Kali, the *saṅkīrtana-yajña(the chanting of the names of God) is recommended by the Vedic scriptures, and this transcendental system was introduced by Lord Caitanya for the deliverance of all men in this age. Saṅkīrtana-yajña* and Kṛṣṇa consciousness go well together. Lord Kṛṣṇa in his devotional form (as Lord Caitanya) is mentioned in the *Śrīmad-Bhāgavatam*....[49]

In 3.22, Kṛṣṇa tells Arjuna that although he is not bound to do anything in the three worlds, he acts anyway. Swami Bhaktivedanta quotes a lengthy passage from the *Śvetāśvatara Upaniṣad* (6.7-8) to illuminate the nature of the one who so acts.

> The Supreme Lord is the controller of all other controllers, and He is the greatest of all the diverse planetary leaders. Everyone is under His control. All entities are delegated with particular power only by the Supreme Lord; they are not supreme themselves. He is also worshipable by all demigods and is the supreme director of all directors. Therefore, He is transcendental to all kinds of material leaders and controllers and is worshipable by all. There is no one greater than Him, and He is the supreme cause of all causes.

> He does not possess bodily form like that of an ordinary living entity. There is no difference between His body and His soul. He is absolute. All His senses are transcendental. Any one of His senses can perform the action of any other sense. Therefore, no one is greater than Him or equal to Him. His potencies are multifarious, and thus His deeds are automatically performed as a natural sequence.

In 4.8 the text indicates that Kṛṣṇa incarnates himself to annihilate the evil doers and to protect the good (*sādhūnām*). According to Swami Bhaktivedanta a *sādhu* or holy man is a man in Kṛṣṇa consciousness. An evil doer (*duṣkṛtam*) refers to one who does not care for Kṛṣṇa consciousness. He then quotes from the *Caitanya–Caritāmṛta* of Kṛṣṇadasa Kaviraja for amplification. He delineates the various kinds of *avatāras* according to Vaiṣṇava theology, while emphasizing that Lord Kṛṣṇa is the fountainhead of all *avatāras*. He then appeals to the *Śrīmad–Bhāgavatam* for support for the view that the incarnation of the Lord in the *kali yuga* is Lord Caitanya. That Caitanya is an incarnation of Kṛṣṇa is in earlier vedic texts even though it is not stated openly, but secretly.

> Lord Caitanya as the incarnation of Kṛṣṇa, the Personality of Godhead, is described secretly but not directly in the confidential parts of the revealed scriptures, such as the *Upaniṣads, Mahābhārata, Bhāgavatam,* etc. The devotees of Lord Kṛṣṇa are much attracted by the *saṅkīrtana* movement of Lord Caitanya. This *avatāra* of the Lord does not kill the miscreants but delivers them by the causeless mercy of the Lord.[50]

Sometimes the puranic stories are used to illustrate the point of the text as in 6.43. But for Swami Bhaktivedanta this is not mythology at all but literal history.

In 2.17 the text states that the soul is indestructible, and that it pervades the body. Swami Bhaktivedanta uses both the *Śvetāśvatara Upaniṣad* (5.9) and the *Bhāgavatam* (no reference given) to confirm that the soul is the size of one ten thousandth of the upper portion of the hair point. This is further confirmed by a quotation from the *Muṇḍaka Upaniṣad* (3.1.9). The *Kaṭha Upaniṣad* (1.2.20) is quoted to support the distinction between the soul and the Supersoul. The *Vedānta–sūtras* are also referred to without any specific reference given. In all, a wide range of texts are used to serve as authorities for understanding the *Gītā*. Swami Bhaktivedanta not only treats specific texts in a way that would be unusual among Western scholars, but he sees specific texts in the light of the *Vedas* in general.

The History of the Gītā

That Kṛṣṇa first instructed Vivasvān who instructed Manu who in turn taught his teaching to Ikśvāku is found in 4.1. Swami Bhaktivedanta expands on this and thereby indicates his understanding of the history of the *Gītā* itself. In this millennium the sun god is known as Vivasvān who is the origin of the planets within the solar system. The *Gītā*, therefore, is not a speculative treatise but knowledge direct from the Supreme Personality of Godhead from remote time. How remote is indicated in Swami's interpretation of the following passage from the *Mahābhārata* (*Santiparva* 348.51-52):

> In the beginning of the Tretā–yuga [millennium] this science of the relationship with the Supreme was delivered by Vivasvān to Manu. Manu, being the father of mankind, gave it to his son Mahārāja Ikṣvāku, the King of this earth planet and forefather of the Raghu dynasty in which Lord Rāmacandra appeared. Therefore, *Bhagavad–gītā* existed in the human society from the time of Mahārāja Ikṣvāku.

Swami Bhaktivedanta comments:

> At the present moment we have just passed through five thousand years of the Kali–yuga, which lasted 432,000 years. Before this there was Dvāpara–yuga (800,000 years), and before that there was Tretā–yuga (1,200,000 years). Thus, some 2,005,000 years ago, Manu spoke the *Bhagavad–gītā* to his disciple and son Mahārāja Ikṣvāku, the King of this planet earth. The age of the current Manu is calculated to last some 305,300,000 years, of which 120,400,000 have passed. Accepting that before the birth of Manu, the *Gītā* was spoken by the Lord to His disciple, the sun–god Vivasvān, a rough estimate is that the *Gītā* was spoken at least 120,400,000 years ago; and in human society it has been extant for two million years.[52]

Five thousand years ago it was observed by Kṛṣṇa that the disciplic succession was broken and that the purpose of the *Gītā* was lost. So, he spoke it again to Arjuna to reestablish the disciplic succession. It is the *Gītā* as understood in the disciplic succession that accounts for the title of Swami Bhaktivedanta's commentary. It is the *Gītā* as it is from the hands of disciplic succession (*paramparā*) and not as the result of mental speculation of unaided academic interpretation.[53]

It should be noted that Arjuna is a devotee of the Lord, one of those devotees who is a constant companion of the Lord and was therefore incarnated whenever the Lord incarnated. This means that he was present when Kṛṣṇa spoke the message of the *Gītā* to the sun god Vivasvān. When Arjuna questions Kṛṣṇa, then, it is not so much for himself as for those who do not believe in the Supreme Personality of Godhead.

> Arjuna is an accepted devotee of the Lord, so how could he not believe in Kṛṣṇa's words? The fact is that Arjuna is not inquiring for himself but for those who do not believe in the Supreme Personality of Godhead or for the demons who do not like the idea that Kṛṣṇa should be accepted as the Supreme Personality of Godhead; for them only Arjuna inquires on this point, as if he were himself not aware of the Personality of Godhead, or Kṛṣṇa.[54]

The Structure of the Gītā

It should not come as a surprise to learn that Swami Bhaktivedanta does not seem to be interested in giving a great deal of attention to the establishment of the overall structure of the text. It is true that often either at the beginning or end of a chapter he indicates what he considers the essential purport of the chapter, and sometimes refers to previous chapters as a point of reference. Nevertheless, at no point in the commentary, not even in the introduction, does he offer an outline of the book. This is understandable if one recognizes that for Swami Bhaktivedanta, "In every chapter of *Bhagavad-gītā*, Lord Kṛṣṇa stresses that devotional service unto the Supreme Personality of Godhead is the ultimate goal of life."[55] Structure shows a sense of progression, and while there is some development as Swami Bhaktivedanta sees it, the purpose of *Gītā* study is not to offer textual analysis but spiritual development.

Swami Bhaktivedanta, however, does see the *Gītā* as broadly falling into three sections of six chapters each. But, while some commentators see devotion to Kṛṣṇa as not prevalent in the first six chapters, Swami Bhaktivedanta sees it everywhere. He characterizes the first six chapters of the *Gītā*, then, as dealing with "the knower of the body, the living entity, *and*[emphasis mine] the position by which he can understand the Supreme Lord..."[56] In the middle six chapters (which Bhaktivedanta considers of prime importance), "the Supreme Personality of Godhead and the relationship between the individual soul and the Supersoul in regard to devotional service are described."[57] In the final six chapters, "how the living entity comes into contact with material nature, how he is delivered by the Supreme Lord through the different methods of fruitive activities, cultivation of knowledge, and the discharge of devotional service are explained."[58] It is clear from this that there are different emphases in the content of the *Gītā* in each of the units, but that each unit in one way or another aims at Kṛṣṇa consciousness.

There are places where Swami Bhaktivedanta singles out a certain section or a certain chapter as a high point. But given the frequency with which several texts are seen as the "essence" of the *Gītā*, we quickly realize that it is not structure that is the object of concern. In the purport to 4.35, he comments: "The whole teaching of the *Gītā* is targeted toward this end: that a living being, as His eternal servitor, cannot be separated from Kṛṣṇa, and his sense of being an identity apart from Kṛṣṇa is called *māyā*."[59]

Swami Bhaktivedanta starts his purport on 7.1 by saying that "In this Seventh Chapter of *Bhagavad-gītā* , the nature of Kṛṣṇa consciousness is fully described."[60] And, at the end of chapter eight he indicates that the middle chapters of the *Gītā* are "the essence of the *Gītā*."[61] But chapter nine begins with the comment that "This chapter of *Bhagavad-gītā* is called the king of education because it is the essence of all doctrines and philosophies explained before."[62] Yet in his purport to 14.1, Swami Bhaktivedanta sees Kṛṣṇa further enlightening Arjuna, and says, "The knowledge explained in this chapter is proclaimed by the Supreme Lord to be superior to the knowledge given so far in other chapters."[63] And further, "Thus it is expected that one who understands this Fourteenth Chapter will attain perfection."[64]

Chapter 11, which contains the 'vision' of Kṛṣṇa in his universal form, is sometimes seen as the high point of the *Gītā*. But it is not so singled out by Swami Bhaktivedanta. Indeed, there is a sense in which it is less significant than many other chapters. The text indicates that Arjuna has heard of the nature of Kṛṣṇa, but that now he desires "to see thy form as god" (Edgerton). Arjuna's request comes through even in Swami Bhaktivedanta's rendering: "I yet wish to see how you have entered into this cosmic manifestation."[65] Swami Bhaktivedanta, however, explains in his purport that Arjuna is not asking for himself, but to convince others in the future who might have some doubt.[66] Of course, Kṛṣṇa knows this too. The explanation is as follows:

> Arjuna's asking the Lord's permission is also significant. Since the Lord is the Supreme Personality of Godhead, He is present within Arjuna himself; therefore He knows the desire of Arjuna, and He can understand that Arjuna had no special desire to see Him in His universal form, for he is completely satisfied to see Him in His personal form of Kṛṣṇa. But He can understand also that Arjuna wants to see the universal form to convince others.[67]

Since this is the beginning of a new *paramparā* it is particularly important that this confirmation be made so that it will be less easy for imposters to pose as incarnations of the Lord. Furthermore, the true devotee is not concerned to see this universal form.[68] The purports on this chapter are frequently short, something that comes as an initial surprise until one understands the relative unimportance of the chapter. The form that is revealed in chapter eleven is on the material level; hence it is only temporary and not the highest knowledge. "This universal form is material and temporary, as the material world is temporary. But in the Vaikuṇṭha planets He has His transcendental form with four hands as Nārāyana."[69] This also explains why the universal form "is not attractive for pure devotees, who are in love with the Lord in different transcendental relationships."[70] Actually those who think this form is wonderful are those who are "involved in elevating themselves by fruitive activities."[71]

It comes as a bit of a surprise, then, to find that 11.55 is "the essence of *Bhagavad–gītā*."[72] Again, this is not a comment on the structure of the *Gītā*. Rather, it is its essence, just as are chapters six through eleven, and several other passages, indeed, wherever Kṛṣṇa consciousness is clearly taught. Here at the end of chapter eleven, since the text teaches that if one is engaged in devotional service to Kṛṣṇa and without attachment and "mental speculation," one will come to Kṛṣṇa, it teaches the essence of the *Gītā*.

Qualifications for Understanding the Gītā

As we have seen, for Bhaktivedanta the ultimate goal of vedic literature and of the *Gītā* which is its essence, is to bring people back to the Supreme Personality of Godhead, to get them to surrender to the Lord, and thereby live in Kṛṣṇa consciousness as part and parcel of the Lord. However, not everyone is equally qualified to interpret, to understand, or to teach the *Bhagavad-gītā*. Scholars in particular come under Swami Bhaktivedanta's condemnation because they are merely "mental speculators." They are also called "mundane wranglers" (4.1), "insignificant" (4.1), "demonic persons" (4.2), "foolish and ignorant" (9.11), and persons who are engaged in "foolish speculation" (10.2), and "speculative reasoning" (13.26). Since these scholars are not surrendered to Kṛṣṇa, they are not Kṛṣṇa conscious; they are merely offering their own ideas rather than the truth within the *paramparā* system.

> The next class of *duṣkṛtina* is called *māyayapāhṛta-jñāna*, or those persons whose erudite knowledge has been nullified by the influence of material illusory energy. They are mostly very learned fellows — great philosophers, poets, literati, scientists, etc. — but the illusory energy misguides them, and therefore they disobey the Supreme Lord.
>
> There are a great number of *māyayapāhṛta-jñāna* at the present moment, even amongst the scholar of the *Gītā*.[73]

There are numerous statements in the *Gītā* which indicate that Kṛṣṇa is the Supreme Personality of Godhead, but these scholars deride the Supreme Lord by considering him as simply another human being. The result is that their work on the *Gītā* is not only not illuminating, but a distinct barrier in the path of spiritual understanding.

> All the unauthorized interpretations of the *Gītā* by the class of *māyayapāhṛta-jñāna*, outside the purview of the *paramparā* system, are so many stumbling blocks in the path of spiritual understanding. The deluded interpreters do not surrender unto the lotus feet of Śrī Kṛṣṇa, nor do they teach others to follow this principle.[74]

Ordinary knowledge like that offered in the university is on the level of matter and is not that to which the *Gītā* aspires.[75] Hence it is unlikely that one will find a true understanding of the *Gītā* there. Such are not simply passing remarks, but are repeated with such frequency that one must see them as a major concern on the part of Swami Bhaktivedanta. Even in texts where one would be hard pressed to draw the inference (6.8), the purport rails against "mundane scholarship" and "mere academic knowledge."[76] The Kṛṣṇa conscious person is above all of this. "He is transcendental because he has nothing to do with mundane scholarship. For him mundane scholarship and mental speculation, which may be as good as gold to others, are of no greater value than pebbles or stones."[77]

There would seem to be two qualifications if one is to understand the *Bhagavadgītā* "as it is." The first qualification resides with the teacher while the second resides with the disciple. First, then, is to be taught the meaning of the *Gītā* by one who is in disciplic succession (*paramparā*). Any teaching other than this is mental speculation and not the *Bhagavadgītā* "as it is." This is very important, for Kṛṣṇa took the trouble to reestablish this succession some 5000 years ago when it was clear that it had been broken. "If we want to understand *Bhagavad-gītā*, we should accept the statements in these two verses (10.12-13). This is called the *paramparā* system, acceptance of the disciplic succession. Unless one is in the disciplic succession, he cannot understand *Bhagavad-gītā*."[78] On the part of the disciple, the essential requirement is submission to a bona fide spiritual master. The *Gītā*'s teachings should also be heard in the company of other devotees. A striking quality of Swami Bhaktivedanta's treatment of the *Gītā* is now understandable. He points out the errors of other positions, and makes it clear that those who do not hold to his position are in error. But he seldom engages in the kind of argumentation that scholars are accustomed to when deciding between alternative interpretations. Most commonly he merely announces what is correct. For if he were using "mundane scholarship" he would have to present arguments, but a spiritual master within disciplic succession merely declares. If the hearer surrenders and accepts, he will ultimately achieve liberation. If he does not, he will sink lower and lower into material bondage and degradation. Not only, then, can one in disciplic succession properly interpret the *Gītā*, but only a devotee can understand it.[79] Others are like bees licking on a bottle of honey!

NOTES

1. For a thorough discussion of introductory matters see Robert N. Minor, *Bhagavad-Gītā: An Exegetical Commentary* (South Asia Books, 1982), xv-lx.

2. R. C. Zaehner, *The Bhagavad-Gītā* (Oxford University Press, 1969), 153.

3. *Ibid.*, 153-54.

4. A. C. Bhaktivedanta Swami Prabhupada, *Bhagavad-gītā As It Is* (Collier Books, 1972) Complete Edition, 147.

5. *Ibid.*, 153-54.

6. *Ibid.*, 154.

7. *Ibid.*, 156.

8. *Ibid.*, 157.

9. *Ibid.*, 158-59.

10. *Ibid.*, 265.

11. *Ibid.*, 344.

12. *Ibid.*, 345.

13. *Ibid.*, 415.

14. *Ibid.*, 320.

15. *Ibid.*, 478.

16. *Ibid.*

17. *Ibid.*, 761.

18. *Ibid.*, 782.

19. *Ibid.*, 377.

20. Franklin Edgerton, *The Bhagavad Gītā* (Harper & Row, 1964, first pub. in 1944); Eliot Deutsch, *The Bhagavad Gītā* (Holt, Rineart and Winston, 1968); also cf. Zaehner and Minor.

21. Bhaktivedanta, *Bhagavad–gītā*, 222-23.

22. *Ibid.*, 223.

23. *Ibid.*, 173.

24. *Ibid.*, 390-91.

25. *Ibid.*, 822.

26. *Ibid.*, 648.

27. *Ibid.*, 398.

28. *Ibid.*

29. *Ibid.*, 447-48.

30. *Ibid.*,278-79.

31. *Ibid.*,279.

32. *Ibid.*, 261.

33. *Ibid.*

34. *Ibid.*

35. *Ibid.*, 228.

36. *Ibid.*, 232.

37. *Ibid.*, 359.

38. *Ibid.*, 318.

39. *Ibid.*, 713.

40. *Ibid.*

41. *Ibid.*, 581.

42. *Ibid.*, 24.

43. *Ibid.*, 266.

44. *Ibid.*, 28.

45. *Ibid.*, 469.

46. *Ibid.*, 713.

47. *Ibid.*, 170. *Taittirīya Saṃhitā* 1.7.4 says, "the sacrifice is Viṣṇu" and Śankara quotes this at this point in his commentary.

48. *Ibid.*, 171.

49. *Ibid.*, 172.

50. *Ibid.*, 227.

51. *Ibid.*, 215.

52. *Ibid.*

53. *Ibid.*

54. *Ibid.*, 218.

55. *Ibid.*, 780.

56. *Ibid.*, 621.

57. *Ibid.*

58. *Ibid.*

59. *Ibid.*, 261.

60. *Ibid.*, 362.

61. *Ibid.*, 439.

62. *Ibid.*, 444.

63. *Ibid.*, 664.

64. *Ibid.*

65. *Ibid.*, 541.

66. *Ibid.*, 541-42.

67. *Ibid.*, 542.

68. *Ibid.*, 546-47.

69. *Ibid.*, 577.

70. *Ibid.*, 590.

71. *Ibid.*

72. *Ibid.*, 591.

73. *Ibid.*, 385.

74. *Ibid.*

75. *Ibid.*, 497.

76. *Ibid.*, 316.

77. *Ibid.*

78. *Ibid.*, 511-12.

79. *Ibid.*, 88.

15

The Response of Swami Bhaktivedanta to Religious Pluralism

By the time Swami Bhaktivedanta arrived in New York to engage in what would lead to the founding of the International Society for Kṛṣṇa Consciousness, he was sixty–nine years of age.[1] Although he would encounter new ideas and practices in his remaining years, his Vaiṣṇava theology and the attitudes which provided the setting for his response to other religions had long since been fixed on Indian soil. He is particularly interesting since the general perception of his movement is that it engages in vigorous conversionism in a manner that contradicts the usual generalities about Hindu tolerance. Some of Bhaktivedanta's statements about adherents of other religions are indeed harsh, but his strongest condemnations are reserved for Advaita Vedānta, the system of thought that is commonly used to provide the structure for Western understandings of "Hinduism."

Ultimate Concern and Ultimate Reality

Swami Bhaktivedanta does not leave the content of his ultimate concern to chance. The "real purpose of life is to revive our dormant love for God."[2] This is not the only way it can be stated. "One's real desire should only be to achieve the state of living transcendental service to the Lord."[3]

What is the system and the analysis of the human condition that provides the basis for this statement of ultimacy? Vaiṣṇavism, *sanātana dharma, varnāśrama dharma* are ways that his system is designated. It is presented as a system that is as old as Kṛṣṇa himself, but has been passed on in disciplic succession (*paramparā*) down to and including Swami Bhaktivedanta. This system describes the highest principle as the Supreme Personality of Godhead. Unlike Advaita, which sees the personal god on the level of *vivarta* and only *nirguṇa brahman* as ultimate *sat*, Bhaktivedanta sees the truth in reverse order. There are three phrases to the realization of Absolute Truth: the impersonal Brahman, Paramātman, and Bhagavān.[4] Bhaktivedanta's view is a form of panentheism. Everything is contained in the Supreme Lord, but the Supreme Lord is not exhausted by everything that is in the world. All of these phases are really one and the same truth, but they constitute different features of it.[5]

> Brahman is the beginning of transcendental realization. Paramatma, the Supersoul, is the middle, the second stage in transcendental realization, and the Supreme Personality of Godhead is the ultimate realization of the Absolute Truth. Therefore, both Paramatman and the impersonal Brahman are within the Supreme Person.[6]

The Advaitin realization of the impersonal, therefore, is only a partial realization of the ultimate. It is the realization of the *sat* feature of the Supreme Personality of Godhead. The complete whole, however, is not formless. So Advaitin experience is true but incomplete.[7]

The human condition is that people are unaware of their position as part and parcel of God. This ignorance of one's position in Bhagavān is the cause not only of personal, but also of societal suffering and discontent. "Because of this lack of Kṛṣṇa consciousness in human society, people are suffering terribly, being merged in an ocean of nescience and sense gratification."[8]

The world is ultimately real. To designate it as *māyā* means that it is not the complete reality. *Māyā* points to "forgetfulness of one's relationship with Kṛṣṇa."[9] It is failure to realize that one is part and parcel of the Supreme Lord.

> Thus it is false to think that the living entity has no connection with the Supreme Lord. He may not believe in the existence of God, or he may think that he has no relationship with God, but these are all "illusions," of *māyā*. Due to absorption in this false conception of life, man is always fearful and full of anxieties. In other words, a godless concept of life is *māyā*.[10]

One's goal, then, is to return to Godhead, or as the ISKCON magazine is titled, come *Back to Godhead*.

True religion can only be given by the Supreme Personality of Godhead.[11] People have sought numerous human methods to search for God. Such methods will not work and will ultimately side–track the individual so that the route to Kṛṣṇa consciousness is longer and more arduous than necessary. "If one actually wants to become religious, he must take up the chanting of the Hare Kṛṣṇa *mahāmantra*....[13]

Historians and philosophers operate on the level on which no "truth" can be more than highly probable. But religious believers exude with a confidence and certainty that seems to leave no room for the possibility of error. This is true of Swami Bhaktivedanta. Anyone outside of the *paramparā* system is merely a "mental speculator," and it is that which leaves room for doubt. Bhaktivedanta never concedes, explicitly or implicitly, that there is any possibility that he might be wrong in his Vaiṣṇava theology, his assessment of the human condition, his proposed means to correct it and bring people "back to Godhead."

> Whatever one's position, *everyone* in this age of Kali needs to be enlightened in Kṛṣṇa consciousness. That is the greatest need of the day. *Everyone* is acutely feeling the pangs of material existence. Even in the ranks and files of the American Senate, the pinpricks of material existence are felt, so much so that April 30, 1974, was actually set aside as Prayer Day. Thus *everyone* is feeling the resultant pinpricks of Kali–yuga brought about by human society's indulging in illicit sex, meat–eating, gambling and intoxication...Kṛṣṇa consciousness should be distributed to *everyone* indiscriminately. In this way the *entire world* will be peaceful and happy, and *everyone* will glorify Śri Caitanya Mahāprabhu, as He desires.[14]

Pungent Judgment on Other Religions

In the light of the principles of *paramparā*, absolute certainty, and universal validity, it should not be a surprise to find that Bhaktivedanta has some harsh things to say about the numerous erroneous positions that stand outside his *paramparā* system. Some approaches to life are condemned by the Lord..."[15] Misguided descendents of Advaita and others who have no use for Kṛṣṇa worship are "like the dead branch of a tree."[16] Those who show Kṛṣṇa no respect and even despise him are asuras, demoniacs, and products of the Kali yuga.[17] According to Bhaktivedanta Māyāvādins hold that it is proper to worship any of the Indian deities, and that this is as good as worshipping Kṛṣṇa. Such "rascals" are actually leading people to atheism since they do not recognize the Supreme Personality of Godhead. "This philosophical hodge–podge exists under the name of the Hindu religion, but the Kṛṣṇa consciousness movement does not approve of it. Indeed, we strongly condemn it."[18] Advaitins who encourage this are "foolish."[19]

The Cārvākas are, expectedly, atheists and ignorant.[20] But, the "...desire to merge in the impersonal Brahman is the subtlest type of atheism. As soon as such atheism, disguised in the dress of liberation, is encouraged, one becomes completely unable to traverse the path of devotional service to the Supreme Personality of Godhead."[21] Even the young hippies in New York were not "offenders" as the Advaitins since they were attracted to Kṛṣṇa and joined the movement. Caitanya found that even "Mohammedans" were easier to convert than Advaitins. "We therefore conclude that the so–called *mleccas* and *yavanas* of the Western countries are more purified than offensive Mayavadis of atheistic impersonalists."[22]

Since there is a gulf between approved practice within *paramparā* and human creativity, it is not surprising that the goal of Bhaktivedanta is most appropriately reached through conversion. Since there is only one approved system and it is for all human beings, Bhaktivedanta comfortably quotes from the *Bhagavadgītā* 18.66. "Abandon all varieties of religion and just surrender unto Me. I shall deliver you from all sinful reaction. Do not fear."[23]

The importance of Caitanya's example can hardly be over–emphasized in this regard. "During his journey he had discussions with the Buddhists, the Jains and the Mayavadis in several places and converted his opponents to Vaiṣṇavism."[24] It is clear that Caitanya's preference was for conversion. Whether this is part of a hagiographical account is not important. For, as it stands, it is a biographical model for Bhaktivedanta and those who would follow him.[25]

At certain points Bhaktivedanta appears to suggest a less vigorous opposition to other religions, but such statements are not permitted to stand without qualification. On the one hand, "In every system of religion, it is accepted that God is the supreme father of all living entities."[26] On the other hand, this statement is qualified by saying that "any religion that does not accept the Supreme Lord as the absolute father is called *kaitava–dharma*, or a cheating religion."[27] Again, "it does not matter whether one is a Christian, Mohammedan or whatever. He must simply accept the sublime position of the Supreme Personality of Godhead and render service to Him. It is not a question of being Christian, Mohammedan or Hindu. One should be purely religious and freed from all these material designations."[28] On the other hand it is because of this that "the Kṛṣṇa consciousness movement is gaining ground throughout the world."[29] To be part of the Bhāgavatam movement is to be beyond the *guṇas* of *prakṛti*, while to be a member of another religion is to be bound by matter. In the end it is clear that there is no final acceptance of pluralism as a status quo.

> In this present day, man is very eager to have one scripture, one God, one religion, and one occupation. So let there be one common scripture for the whole world — *Bhagavad-gītā*. And let there be one God only for the whole world — Śri Kṛṣṇa Kṛṣṇa, Hare Hare/Hare Rama, Hare Rama, Rama Rama, Hare Hare. And let there be one work only — the service of the Supreme Personality of Godhead.[30]

The Principle of Isolation

Another principle that helps to explain Bhaktivedanta's treatment of other religions is the principle of isolation. To begin with, a primary characteristic of a devotee's behavior is to avoid unholy association.

> Here the main point is that one should always stay aloof from unholy association. That is the sum and substance of a devotee's behaviour. And what is unholy association? It is association with one who is too much attached to women and with one who is not a devotee of Lord Kṛṣṇa. These are unholy persons. One is advised to associate with the holy devotees of the Lord and carefully avoid the association of unholy nondevotees.[31]

Moreover, the devotee is to be devoted totally in transcendental service to the Lord, thereby avoiding all speculative activities. One should listen to the recitation of the *Bhāgavatam* and other Vaiṣṇava texts, but not from persons who are not in disciplic succession.[32] "No one should hear or take lessons from a person who is not a Vaiṣṇava. Even if he speaks about Kṛṣṇa, such a lesson should not be accepted, for it is like milk touched by the lips of a serpent."[33] If one is to read commentaries on accepted texts, they should be written by Vaiṣṇavas such as Rāmānuja, Madhva, Viṣṇusvāmi or Nimbārka.[34] Māyāvādī commentaries should be avoided. When one indulges in Māyāvādī philosophy one will gradually fall from devotional service. Since it is devotional service that is the means to the goal, such texts should be shunned.[35] Not only will unauthorized commentaries cause one to commit a great blunder, but as long as one persists, progress back to Godhead will be impossible.[36]

Moreover, Bhaktivedanta's translation of a verse in *Śrī Caitanya-caritāmṛta* has profound implications for his approach to other religions. "The devotee should not worship demigods not should he disrespect them. Similarly, the devotee should not study or criticize other scriptures."[37] A careful reading of the many works and commentaries of Bhaktivedanta supports the view that he followed this advice himself. There is little to suggest that he read Māyāvādī commentaries (much less that he studied them), that he read the "Koran," the Christian scriptures or any philosophers or theologians in those traditions. While specific references are cited when he refers to the *Bhagavadgītā, Śrīad Bhāgavatam* or *Śrī Caitanya–caritāmṛta*, no such specificity is given in alien scriptures. What he knows about other religions comes largely from references to them in his own texts, from occasional personal contact and interviews with persons of other faiths, from information given by devotees converted from other faiths, and from hearsay. The point is that one cannot acquire real knowledge or make progress back to Godhead by reading the works of mental speculators. And, if one is not in disciplic succession, if one is not a devotee of the Lord, one is indeed a mental spectator. "One who disbelieves in this *śāstras* is an atheist, and we should not consult an atheist, however great he may be. A staunch believer in the *śāstras*, with all their diversities, is the right person from whom to gather real knowledge."[38] This principle will appear repeatedly in our discussion of specific religions.

Treatment of Other Religions

As we move to consider Bhaktivedanta's view of specific other religions, we will first pause to consider his assessment of religions in general and his view of how they arose.

Other Religions in General

One's original nature is to be transcendental to material nature. But when one forgets one's relationship to the Supreme Personality of Godhead, one comes into contact with material nature and generates faiths that are on the material platform. These faiths can be good, passionate or ignorant according to the *guṇa* that is dominant.[39] Bhaktivedanta believes that the entire world was originally under one culture that was Vedic.[40] Presently the earth is divided into many countries, religions and political parties. But these are all external divisions on the platform of matter. Some of them may have limited validity, but they can never provide the unity and Truth that is found on the transcendental level. Religions on the material level are able partially to satisfy the different bodies and minds that people have.[41] But the ultimate goal of human beings is reached only on the transcendental level.

We noted that one of the terms used to describe service to the Lord is *sanātana–dharma*. According to Bhaktivedanta, *sanātana–dharma* is, like the living entity itself, without beginning or end. In terms of reality, the rendering of service is the eternal religion of the living entity.[42] Hence, *sanātana–dharma* is, like the living entity itself, without beginning or end. In terms of reality, the rendering of service is the eternal religion of the living entity.[42] Hence, *sanātana–dharma* is not a sectarian religion on the platform of matter, and "when we mention the name Kṛṣṇa we do not refer to any sectarian name."[44] Ultimate unity is found only by transcending the plane on which religions exist. It is by becoming a vaiṣṇava, that is, engaging in devotional service to Kṛṣṇa and in effect by becoming part of the Kṛṣṇa consciousness movement that one reaches the transcendental level.[45] On the material level there are many religions, but they are *dharma kaitavah*, cheating religions. "None of these religions are actually genuine."[46]

Worship of Other Indian Deities

Swami Bhaktivedanta thinks that Christians and Muslims have a misconception about the "Hindu religion." They think that in Hinduism there are many gods. But there is only one god. There are many powerful entities called demigods who are delegated areas of responsibility and carry out the orders of the Supreme Lord.[47] But it is out of ignorance that people worship the demigods as though they are God. Bhaktivedanta does not deny that certain results come from such worship. Not only are there definite material benefits which accrue from worshipping the demigods, but such worship also determines the place of rebirth for the worshipper.[48] But while the worship of Kṛṣṇa is not sectarian, the worship of the demigods is. It is motivated by lust,[49] and is condemned by Kṛṣṇa and Caitanya.[50]

Demigods are merely "different energies of the Supreme Viṣṇu."[51] This means that "...directly or indirectly, all types of worship are more or less directed to the Supreme Personality of Godhead, Kṛṣṇa. In *Bhagavad-gītā* it is confirmed that one who worships the demigods is in fact only worshipping Kṛṣṇa because the demigods are but different parts of the body of Viṣṇu, or Kṛṣṇa."[52] The mistake made by such worshippers is that they mistakenly think they are worshipping God when they are merely worshipping one of his energies. Hence such worship is said to be *avidhi-purvakam*, improper. "One who worships demigods worships the Supreme Lord indirectly. One can worship Him directly."[53]

For this reason Bhaktivedanta makes even stronger statements about demigod worship. Since such worship is done in ignorance and improperly, it should not be done. Bhaktivedanta offers several texts to show that such worship should be avoided.[54] After all, all of the planets of the demigods such as Candraloka, Suryaloka, Indraloka, etc., are merely creations of Kṛṣṇa. As manifestations of Kṛṣṇa's energy they are on the level of matter, and can only be transcended through worship of Kṛṣṇa. "One should directly approach Kṛṣṇa, for that will save time and energy. For example, if there is a possibility of going to the top of a building by help of an elevator, why should one go by the staircase, step by step."[55]

Indian Philosophies

We have already noticed that Kṛṣṇa can be realized as Brahman, Paramātman, and as the Supreme Personality of Godhead. And these are realized through speculation (*jñāna*), through the yoga system (*aāja*) and through devotional service (*bhakti*).[56] This would suggest that the philosophies which emphasize one of the preliminary types of knowledge of Kṛṣṇa are correct and valid as far as they go. "But those who are attached to the impersonal Brahman or the localized Supersoul are also partially Kṛṣṇa conscious, because impersonal Brahman is the spiritual ray of Kṛṣṇa and Supersoul is the all-pervading partial expansion of Kṛṇṣa."[57] However, such systems are, like the worship of the demigods, only indirectly and hence imperfectly Kṛṣṇa conscious.[58] Since the so-called "orthodox" schools of Indian philosophy do not affirm the supremacy of the Supreme Personality of Godhead, they are all the result of mundane philosophy.59 Hence they will never take one beyond the *guṇas* to the transcendental realm.

> Impersonal speculation, monism (merging into the existence of the Supreme), speculative knowledge, mystical yoga and meditation are all compared to

> grains of sand. They simply cause irritation to the heart. No one can satisfy the Supreme Personality of Godhead by such activities, nor do we give the Lord the chance to sit in our hearts peacefully. Rather, the Lord is distributed by them.[60]

Bhaktivedanta seems to accept the Sāṇkhya philosophy's analysis of the twenty-four elements of the material universe.[61] But what the Sāṇkhya philosophers do not realize is that these elements are "originally offshoots from Kṛṣṇa's energies and are separated from Him."[62] The Sāṇkhya philosophers are atheistic since they "do not know Kṛṣṇa as the cause of all causes."[63] It is not possible to attain Absolute Truth by following Sāṇkhya or by practicing Patañjali's yoga. Since they do not follow Kṛṣṇa as the Supreme Personality of Godhead, their ambition will never be fulfilled. If this is true of philosophies that have a spiritual goal, how much more would it be true for the Lokāyata's who are classed with modern "materialistic scientists and anthropologists."[64] Those who do not believe in the existence of the soul are even further from the truth than those who do without recognizing the Lord there.

While there may be some truth in other Indian philosophies and some of them at least may be an indirect worship of Kṛṣṇa, in the end all kinds of yogis (*karma, jñāna, haṭha*, etc.), have to move on to *bhakti* and Kṛṣṇa consciousness to reach devotional perfection. None of them are therefore approved means of reaching back to Godhead.

Advaita Vedānta

Advaita receives more attention from Bhaktivedanta than any other Indian philosophical system. It is also inescapable that the harshest statements made with incredible frequency are reserved for the "impersonalists," "Māyāvādīs," "followers of Śaṅkara's Advaita," and "monists." While it might seem strange that Advaitins would be more harshly censured than Muslims or Christians, several things must be kept in mind. The attitude of Swami Bhaktivedanta is molded by what he finds in his accepted scriptures, and it is clear that some of Caitanya's most serious disagreements came with Advaitins. He had more difficulty in converting them than in converting Muslims, and they sometimes vigorously attacked his position. It is a general principle that those who attack the Vaiṣṇava position are worse off than those who are merely ignorant of it. Furthermore, of primary importance to Bhaktivedanta is the Supreme

Personality of Godhead, Kṛṣṇa. Hence those positions which deny the ultimate supremacy and reality of the personal God are more harshly condemned than those who affirm the ultimate reality of the personal deity as do Muslims and Christians.

Māyāvādīs consider themselves Vedantists. But according to Bhaktivedanta, the Vedānta philosophy is found in the *Bhagavadgītā* and its compiler is Kṛṣṇa, not Śaṅkara. There is also the tendency to be less harsh with the founder of a movement than with the tradition itself. In the present case, "Śaṅkarācārya preached Māyāvādī philosophy in order to bewilder a certain type of atheist. Actually he never considered the Supreme Lord, the Personality of Godhead, to be impersonal or to have no body or form."[65] But this concession to Śaṅkara is not consistently followed, and usually he is associated with the impersonalists who followed him.

Those who direct the masses of people to the impersonal rather than to the Personality of Godhead are "scholarly demons."[66] After a tirade against the *prakṛta–sahajiyās*, because they do not consult the Vedic scriptures and because they are "debauchees, woman hunters and smokers of Ganja,"[67] Bhaktivedanta goes on to say that they are, nevertheless, "more favorable than the impersonalists, who are hopelessly atheistic. The impersonalists have no idea of the Supreme Personality of Godhead."[68] To support their atheistic theory, "the Māyāvādīs cite false scriptures, which make people bereft of transcendental knowledge and addicted to fruitive activities and mental speculation."[69] Because they do not accept the Supreme Person they are "atheistic rascals."[70] Bhaktivedanta's quarrel with the impersonalists is particularly striking since he alludes to them even when the text on which he is commenting seems not to be addressing the issue. He deals with them whenever his flow of thought brings them to mind.[71]

Nevertheless, Advaitins are not without truth and what they experience is real. But they do not go far enough, often denying there is something beyond their experience of the impersonal absolute. The impersonalist has only achieved the first stage in the realization of the Lord. But as we have seen, there is the experience of Brahman, Paramātman and Bhagavān.

> These three aspects can be explained by the example of the sun, which also has three different aspects, namely the sunshine, the sun's surface and the sun planet itself. One who studies the sunshine is only the preliminary student. One who understands the sun's surface is further advanced. And one who can enter into the sun

> planet is the highest. Ordinary students who are satisfied by simply understanding the sunshine — its universal pervasiveness and the glaring effulgence of its impersonal nature — may be compared to those who can realize only the Brahman feature of the Absolute Truth.[72]

At what points, then, does Bhaktivedanta differ from the impersonalists? If the Māyāvādīs take the designation of Brahman as *nirguṇa* to mean that the ultimate is without qualities, Bhaktivedanta holds this to mean that the Absolute Truth is without material qualities, certainly not without spiritual ones.[73] Their respective views of the world also affect the way they perceive temple worship. The Māyāvādī sees the image of the deity as an imaginary form since the ultimate is without form. But the Vaiṣṇava sees the image as being both one and different simultaneously according to Caitanya's *acintya bhedābheda* philosophy. "Yogurt is nothing but milk, but at the same time it is not milk."[74] The Māyāvādīs even deride temple worship, saying "that since God is everywhere, why should one restrict himself to temple worship."[75] Bhaktivedanta retorts that if God is everywhere that includes the temple deity!

There is also a difference over the use of the *mantra*. Śaṅkara sees *tat tvam asi* rather than the Hare Kṛṣṇa mantra as the primary vibration. Actually, *tat tvam asi* is a warning to people not to mistake the body for the self. Therefore, it is meant for the conditioned soul, while the Hare Kṛṣṇa *mantra* is meant for the liberated soul.[76] The Māyāvādīs see devotional service as suitable only prior to liberation. But for Bhaktivedanta, devotional service continues even after liberation. Since liberation does not do away with distinctions one is continually engaged in serving the Lord. It is the liberated one who can truly chant the *mahāmantra*.[77] In the end it is unfortunate that they do not know that "there is no conflict between personalism and impersonalism" which is reconciled in Caitanya's doctrine of *acintya bhedābheda*.[78]

Buddhism

I have noticed the tendency to be more charitable toward the founder of a religious tradition than toward the subsequent tradition itself. The Buddha is a case in point. He was an incarnation of Kṛṣṇa whose intention was to stop the atheists from killing animals. The Buddha did not speak of God because the people were unable to understand that and so he limited himself to speaking against killing.[79] On the other hand, Buddhists are teachers of "voidism" which is hardly distinguishable from Advaita.[80]

In the *Śri Caitanya-caritāmṛta*, it is stated that Caitanya had an encounter with the leader of a Buddhist cult who attempted to establish his "nine philosophical conclusions" by logic.[81] Bhaktivedanta lists them along with his refutation. This is instructive for several reasons. In the first place it indicates the validity of the principle that he acquires knowledge of other religions either through personal encounter (as did Caitanya here) or through material internal to his own tradition. It also reveals that although the Buddha is purportedly an *avatār* of Kṛṣṇa, some of the doctrines attributed to him by followers are deficient and erroneous. Finally, it is the philosophy of an unnamed cult leader whose views are unacceptable.

Briefly, then, the nine principles are as follows. First, "the creation is eternal; therefore there is no need to accept a creator." But if annihilation or dissolution is the highest truth, as the Buddhists say, then one cannot say that the creation exists eternally. For his part, Bhaktivedanta accepts the beginning of creation and a creator who existed before creation. Second, "the Buddhists argue that the world is false..." This is wrong since the world is temporary, but not false. The suffering and pleasures of sentient existence are factual. Third, "the Buddhists maintain that the principle 'I am' is the Ultimate Truth, but this excludes the individuality of 'I' and 'you.'" He seems to mean that the Buddhist excludes the Supreme Personality of Godhead from reality. But if there is no duality, the individual soul and Supersoul, there can be no argument since argument rests on duality. This constitutes a refutation of Buddhism since it tries to rest its case on logic but undercuts what is necessary to make a logical argument. Fourth, "there is repetition of birth and death." Fortunately, the Buddhists accept transmigration, but they do not properly explain the next birth. According to Bhaktivedanta there are 8,400,000 species of life and the next life may not be human.[82] Fifth, "Lord Buddha is the only source for the attainment of knowledge." This is necessary since the Buddha did not accept the authority of the Vedas. But, "if everyone is an authority, or if everyone accepts his own intelligence as the ultimate criterion — as is presently fashionable — the scriptures will be interpreted in many different ways, and everyone will claim his own philosophy supreme." The only adequate solution is disciplic succession. Six, "the Buddhists theorize that annihilation, or *nirvaṇa*, is the ultimate goal." According to Bhaktivedanta, it is true that annihilation applies to the body, but not to the soul. If all physical bodies were to be annihilated, then the soul would have to obtain a nonmaterial or spiritual body if there is to be another birth. And this is the case. If the soul is to return to Godhead, it does not become void or zero, but accepts a spiritual body. Seven, Bhaktivedanta cannot accept the view "that the Buddhist philosophy is the only way" for it contains too many defects. Only Vedānta philosophy, that is, the Vaiṣṇava system taught by Kṛṣṇa is without defect. Eight, "according to the Buddhist cult, the *Vedas* are compiled by ordinary human beings." This does not square with Bhaktivedanta's understanding of the matter. In the creation, Brahma did not create the *Vedas*, but after the creation, "the Supreme Person imparted Vedic knowledge within the heart of Brahma." The only conclusion, then, is the *Vedas* are not the work of a human being. Even Śaṅkara accepts this fact. Finally, "it is stated that mercy is one of the qualities of the Buddha, but mercy is a relative thing." Mercy can only be shown from a superior to an inferior. Hence without the Supreme Being, Buddhist mercy is ultimately defective. Also, one must know what true mercy is. It is to preach Kṛṣṇa consciousness so as to revive "the lost consciousness of human beings."

It is not clear what sect the "Buddhist leader" might have represented. Bhaktivedanta is aware of the "Hinayana" and "Mahayana" philosophies. But some of the above principles do not fall clearly within either camp, while others would appear to be inferences made by the Vaiṣṇava school from other assertions that can be located more clearly. That the creation is eternal is the type of speculation avoided by the Pali canon. That *nirvaṇa* is annihilation is also going further than that body of texts would permit. The third principle of "I am" is probably an inference made by Vaiṣṇavas from the "Buddhists'" denial of the reality of the Supreme Person.

Islam and Christianity

Bhaktivedanta's references to Islam are few. Muslims are not criticized for their doctrines since they hold that the Supreme Lord is personal. However, Muslims (Bhaktivedanta refers to them as Mohammedans) are the objects of conversion by Caitanya. They are persons of low cultural practices since they are meat–eaters.[83] Bhaktivedanta advised avoiding contact with such abominable persons who eat meat. Thus, although he had ample opportunity to understand them as the largest religious minority in India, he learned about them from his own texts and presumably avoided contact with them himself. There is virtually no discussion of their theology or law.

Bhaktivedanta's knowledge of and contact with Christians seems to have been nonexistent until he arrived in New York in 1965 at age 69. As before, the principle of isolation comes to play. It is pointless to read Christian books or to study Christian scriptures. Referring to "some Bishop in Boston" who wants to change "Thou shalt not kill" into "Thou shalt not murder" in order to preserve animal slaughter, he writes, "We have all respect for these great preachers, but we do not require to study books save and accept for some reference."[84] In the same letter he advises, "So these Christian and Buddhist scriptures were delivered for a different class of men, and we needn't spend our time in studying their doctrines. You should read our own books over and over again and as far as possible do not try to enter into controversy. We do not concern ourselves with any other religion. Our religion is to become the servant of the servant of the servant of Kṛṣṇa." Again, it would seem that he followed his own advice. In a letter to a disciple Tosan Kṛṣṇa, he says, "Regarding New Testament, we can simply agree that the New Testament accepts God is great and the creation came into existence by His Word. I do not know the details of New Testament, but I do so fat (*sic*) that it is stated there that all creation is made by God."[85]

In a letter to disciple Dasarha, he encourages the disciple to avoid arguments with Christians since they are predominantly sentimentalists and have no philosophy. But he advises,

> Regarding your other question, you should not read such nonsense books, nor allow your mind to dwell on such subject matter. Instead utilize your time for advancing Krishna consciousness by reading our books. We have got sufficient stock, and if you simply go on reading them, chanting regularly 16 rounds, engaging yourself 24 hours in Krishna's business, then all your questions will be answered automatically, because Krishna promises to his sincere devotee that He will give him the intelligence to understand Him.[86]

Bhaktivedanta's repeated criticism of Christianity has to do with meat–eating. He holds that the command "thou shalt not kill" has to do not only with murder but with killing animal life for consumption. He holds that those who read it as a prescription against murder have changed the text. Bhaktivedanta is convinced that the *Bible* teaches "thou shalt not kill" but is not sure where to locate the statement. He repeatedly attributes it to Jesus. It is difficult to trace the development of Bhaktivedanta's thought on this issue. This is partly a difficulty in dating. Some of his interviews in *Back to Godhead* can be dated, while others can only be assigned a publication date rather than an interview date. Likewise the distinction between the interview date and publication date creates another problem. In a selection from *Science of Self–Realization* in the December 1977 issue of *Back to Godhead* (12.12), Jesus is designated as the source of this teaching when he says, "A preacher of God consciousness is a friend to all living beings. Lord Jesus Christ exemplified this teaching, 'Thou shalt not kill.'"[87] In an undated interview published in November of 1977, he says, "Jesus Christ said, 'Thou shalt not kill.' So why is it that the Christian people are engaged in animal killing?"[88] In a conversation with some disciples in Hyderabad in April of 1974, but published in January of 1982, he still attributes the statement to Jesus Christ when he says, "Jesus Christ says, 'Thou shalt not kill.'"[89] In a conversation with some disciples in Dallas in March 1975, and published in 1983, he identifies the source correctly as the Ten Commandments when he says, "In the Ten Commandments the Bible clearly says, 'Thou shalt not kill.' But they'll not obey. That is sinful."[90] One might think that the clarification was made sometime between April of 1974 and March of 1975. However, in a letter dated March 2, 1969 to a disciple Shivananda, it is clear that Bhaktivedanta thinks that it is Jesus Christ who gave the Ten Commandments. "If we wish to criticize Christian faith we can do so, and we can prove that hardly there are any sincere Christians. In the Ten Commandments we see Lord Jesus Christ advised 'Thou shalt not kill.'"[91] This would pose no problem for development since it is an early letter. However, in an interview with a journalist published in *Back to Godhead* in 1979 but given in late 1968 (hence prior to the 1969 letter) Bhaktivedanta is quoted as locating the statement with some precision. "For instance, in the Old Testament there are the Ten Commandments, and one commandment is 'Thou shalt not kill.'"[92] It is possible that the 1968 interview was edited in line with his later understanding.

However one settles the issue, it would seem clear that Bhaktivedanta has no acquaintance with the texts of which he speaks. This should not make us lose sight of his argument, however, which remains constant throughout. It is that Christians have changed the words and intent of Jesus so as to enable them to eat meat. Hence they are to be faulted not because of error in the teaching but because of their unwillingness to obey it.

Not only did he believe that Jesus was teaching the truth in this regard, but that he also taught *saṅkīrtana*. He must have been told that Jesus Christ approved of his activities. He responds, "Perhaps you have marked it in my preaching work that I love Lord Jesus Christ as good as Krishna; because he rendered the greatest service to Krishna according to time, circumstances and society in which he appeared."[93] In the same letter he continues with advise that Kirtananda should prepare a small book on *saṅkīrtana* in the Bible. "And because it is approved by Lord Christ (*sic*) at least the Christian world will accept our Kirtan procedure. I have seen in the Bible that Lord Jesus Christ (*sic*) recommended this Kirtan performances in the Bible. You know better than me and I would request you to write a small book on SANKIRTAN MOVEMENT IN THE BIBLE."

He also discovered a book titled *Aquarian Gospel* which led him to believe that Jesus lived for some time in the Jagannath temple in Puri. Since non–devotees would not have been allowed to live there, Jesus must have been a devotee of Kṛṣṇa.

> There is a book called *Aquarian Gospel* in which it is stated that Lord Jesus Christ lived in the temple of Jagannath. Without being His devotee, how could he live there and how the authorities could allow a non–devotee to live there? From that book it appears that Lord Jesus Christ lived in intimate relations with the priest order. So far as possible, you should prepare yourself for future writings that our movement is not against the philosophy of Jesus Christ, but it is in complete collaboration with his line of religiosity.[94]

By November of 1969 he wrote disciple Hansadutta that he would not accept a book like *Aquarian Gospel* as authoritative since sometimes it contains words not actually spoken by Christ.

While Bhaktivedanta's knowledge of Christianity is limited and his judgments on Christians are sometimes harsh, there are also ameliorating dimensions. For example, he says on a number of occasions that he is not seeking to convert Christians to Hinduism. "Yes, I don't say that Christians should become Hindu. I simple say, 'Please obey your commandments.' I'll make you a better Christian. That is my mission. I don't say, 'God is not in your tradition — God is only here in ours.' I simply say, 'Obey God.' I don't say, 'You have to accept that God's name is Kṛṣṇa and no other.' No. I say, 'Please obey God. Please try to love God.'"[95] In that same interview he states that comparing his approach with that of Christianity, the end and the methods are the same. The difference is that he is teaching people practically how to follow it. Any religious scripture one follows might give you enlightenment. However, the inference drawn from this is not that

Bhaktivedanta will cooperate to enhance the institutional forms of these other religions or encourage people to stay therein. Rather, he says, "Similarly, any religious scripture you may follow will give you enlightenment. But if you find more in this Kṛṣṇa consciousness movement, then why should you not accept it?"[96]

Likewise, Bhaktivedanta argues that Christ is merely a form of Kṛṣṇa. The name is the same.

> *Christ* comes from the Greek word *Christos*, and *Christos* is the Greek version of the word Kṛṣṭa. When an Indian person calls on Kṛṣṇa, he often says Kṛṣṭa. Kṛṣṭa is a Sanskrit word meaning 'the object of attraction.' So when we address God as 'Christ,' 'Kṛṣṭa,' or 'Kṛṣṇa,' we indicate the same all–attractive Supreme Personality of Godhead.[97]

But again, the inference of this identity is not only to eliminate unnecessary conflict but also to enlist support for his movement. "Therefore, the Christian clergymen should cooperate with the Kṛṣṇa consciousness movement. They should change the name Christ or Christos and should stop condoning the slaughter of animals. This is not some philosophy I have fabricated; it is taught in the Bible."[98] Since the names are the same, he can counsel his disciple Jadunandan that he can chant any name of God, but Kṛṣṇa is to be prefered.[99]

Finally, although Bhaktivedanta says that it is not his intention to make Christians into Hindus, that does not mean that he does not expect them to associate with the Kṛṣṇa consciousness movement. For,

> The religion of the *Bhagavad–gītā* is not Hindu religion or Christian religion or Mohammedan religion. It is the essence of religion — the reciprocation, the exchange of dealings, between God and the Soul, the Supreme and the subordinate living entity. To accept Kṛṣṇa as our Lord, to surrender to the lotus feet of Kṛṣṇa — this is bhakti, or real religion.[100]

If one accepts the *sanātana dharma*, the essence of all religion, one accepts devotion to Kṛṣṇa. The completion of this would be to associate with devotees, and lend support to the Kṛṣṇa consciousness movement by becoming part of it. In a letter to his disciple Jadunandan, Bhaktivedanta indicates that "So we are teaching love of Godhead, not any particular type of religion. Our

Kṛṣṇa conscious movement is not a religious movement; it is a movement for purifying the heart."[101] It is not a religion, it is not Hinduism, but it is a movement with which one should align oneself. For above the quotation just made, Bhaktivedanta discusses a strategy for converting Christians. "...When you want to convert Christians into Krishna Consciousness, you should understand first of all the philosophy of Krishna Consciousness. Without understanding the philosophy of Krishna Consciousness, if we try to convert Christians into Krishna Consciousness, it will be utter failure."

Conclusion

There is no place in the corpus of Bhaktivedanta's writings where one can go for a systematic treatment of his approach to other religions. However, scattered through his writings one can find principles stated and judgments made which enable one to weave together a coherent account. There is truth in all religions. But they are inevitably incomplete, and if one is to return to Godhead, one must finally resort to *bhakti*, which alone raises one above the mundane plane to the transcendental level. While one's goal is not to convert people to "Hinduism," Kṛṣṇa consciousness is not "Hinduism" but *sanātana dharma* or the eternal religion. On balance there is more criticism of religions than praise. His principle of isolation makes it unlikely that one will acquire accurate factual knowledge of traditions other than one's own. But Bhaktivedanta has passed on. As the movement moves from sect to denomination, there is evidence to suggest the Bhaktivedanta's more ameliorating statements will be held up and his more characteristic harshness will be tempered.

Notes

1. The author wishes to express his appreciation to Śubhananda dāsa, Senior Editor of Bhaktivedanta Book Trust, who made available unpublished letters of Swami Bhaktivedanta dealing with other religions.

2. A. C. Bhaktivedanta Swami Prabhupada, *Teachings of Lord Caitanya* (Bhaktivedanta Book Trust, 1974), 242.

3. *Ibid.*, 61.

4. A. C. Bhaktivedanta Swami Prabhupada, *Śrī Caitanya-caritāmṛta* — hereafter referred to as *CC* (Bhaktivedanta Book Trust, 1975) *Madhya-līlā*, VI, 144.

5. *Ibid.*

6. A. C. Bhaktivedanta Swami Prabhupada, *Bhagavad-gītā As It Is* (Collier Books, 1972), 690.

7. A. C. Bhaktivedanta Swami Prabhupada, *Śrī Iśopaniṣad* (Bhaktivedanta Book Trust, 1972), 1-2.

8. *CC, Ādi-līlā*, III, 89.

9. *Teachings of Lord Caitanya*, 60.

10. *Ibid.*

11. *CC, Madhya-līlā*, VIII, 199.

12. *CC, Madhya-līlā*, VI, 262.

13. *Ibid.*

14. *CC, Madhya-līlā*, IV, 20 (*emphasis mine*).

15. *Bhagavad-gītā As It Is*, 181.

16. *CC, Ādi-līlā*, III, 41.

17. *CC, Ādi-līlā*, 165.

18. *Ibid.*, 257.

19. *Ibid.*, 256.

20. *Ibid.*, 111.

21. *CC, Ādi–līlā*, I, 79.

22. *CC, Madhya–līlā*, VII, 80.

23. *CC, Madhya–līlā*, IX, 223.

24. *The Teachings of Lord Caitanya*, xx.

25. *Ibid.*

26. *CC, Madhya–līlā*, VIII, 155.

27. *Ibid.*

28. *CC, Madhya–līlā*, IX, 306.

29. *Ibid.*

30. *Bhagavad–gītā As It Is*, 28.

31. *The Teachings of Lord Caitanya*, 122.

32. *CC, Madhya–līlā*, VIII, 404-405.

33. *CC, Antya–līlā*, IV, 171.

34. *CC, Antya–līlā*, I, 169.

35. *CC, Madhya–līlā*, IV, 163.

36. *Bhagavad–gītā As It Is*, xii.

37. *CC, Madhya–līlā*, VIII, 397-398.

38. *CC, Ādi–līlā*, I, 380.

39. *Bhagavad–gītā As It Is*, 754.

40. *CC, Madhya–līlā*, IX, 403-404.

41. *CC, Madhya–līlā*, VII, 100.

42. *Bhagavad–gītā As It Is*, 16.

43. *Ibid.*, 18.

44. *Ibid.*, 17-18.

45. *CC, Madhya–līlā*, IX, 363.

46. *CC, Madhya–līlā*, VII, 99.

47. *CC, Ādi–līlā*, III, 157.

48. *CC, Ādi–līlā*, II, 241.

49. *Bhagavad–gītā As It Is*, 18.

50 *CC, Ādi–līlā*, III, 158.

51. *Teachings of Lord Caitanya*, 66.

52. *Ibid.*

53. *CC, Madhya–līlā*, VII, 98.

54. *CC, Madhya–līlā*, IX, 272.

55. *Bhagavad–gītā As It Is*, 470.

56. *Teachings of Lord Caitanya*, 69.

57. *Bhagavad–gītā As It Is*, 318.

58. *Ibid.*

59. *CC, Madhya–līlā*, IX, 326-328.

60. *CC, Madhya–līlā*, V, 66.

61. *Bhagavad–gītā As It Is*, 13.

62. *Ibid.*, 368.

63. *Ibid.*

64. *Ibid.*, 107.

65. *Teachings of Lord Caitanya*, 214.

66. *Ibid.*, viii-ix.

67. *CC, Madhya–līlā*, I, 18-19.

68. *Ibid.*

69. *CC, Madhya–līlā*, II, 304.

70. *CC, Madhya–līlā*, IX, 52-53.

71. See the author's "Swami Bhaktivedanta and the *Bhagavad–gītā* 'As It Is'" in *Modern Indian Interpreters of the Gita*, edited by Robert N. Minor (State University of New York Press, 1986), also Chapter XIV of this volume.

72. *Bhagavad–gītā As It Is*, 73-74.

73. *Teachings of Lord Caitanya*, 34.

74. *CC, Madhya–līlā*, IV, 103.

75. *Bhagavad–gītā As It Is*, 461.

76. *CC, Madhya–līlā*, II, 269.

77. *Bhagavad–gītā As It Is*, 447.

78. *Ibid.*, 374.

79. *CC, Madhya–līlā*, IX, 320.

80. *Teachings of Lord Caitanya*, 22.

81. *CC, Madhya–līlā*, III, 314.

82. For a complete discussion of Bhaktivedanta's views of karma and rebirth see the author's "Swami Bhaktivedanta: Karma, Rebirth and the Personal God," in *Post–Classical Indian Views of Karma and Rebirth*, edited by Ronald Neufeldt (State University of New York Press, 1985), also Chapter XIII of this volume.

83. *CC, Madhya–līlā*, VIII, 33.

84. Letter to Hansadutta, November, 1969, copy on file.

85. Letter to Tosan Kṛṣṇa, June 23, 1970, copy on file.

86. Letter to Dasarha, March 4, 1972, copy on file.

87. *Back to Godhead*, 12/12 (December 1977), 16.

88. *Back to Godhead*, 12/11 (November 1977), 12.

89. *Back to Godhead*, 17/1 (January 1982), 14.

90. *Back to Godhead*, 18/6, (June 1983), 14.

91. Letter to Shivananda, March 2, 1969, copy on file.

92. *Back to Godhead*, 14/2-3 (February/March 1979).

93. Letter to Kirtananda, April 7, 1967, copy on file.

94. Letter to Hayagriva, July 31, 1969, copy on file.

95. *Back to Godhead*, 14/2-3 (February/March 1979), 5.

96. *Ibid.*

97. *Back to Godhead*, 12/12 (December 1977), 16.

98. *Ibid.*

99. Letter to Jadunandan, April 13, 1968, copy on file.

100. *Back to Godhead*, 19/4 (April 1984), 22.

101. Letter to Jadunandan, April 13, 1968, copy on file.

16

ISKCON and the Struggle for Legitimation

Although the roots of the International Society for Kṛṣṇa Consciousness (ISKCON) go back to Caitanya in fifteenth–century India (and even before), it is considered a new religious movement because it was first introduced in western countries in the 1960s. In its early years in the United States ISKCON was perceived as a movement engaged in kidnapping, brain–washing, deceptive fund–raising, and aggressive proselytizing. My concern is not with the legitimacy or illegitimacy of these perceptions, but rather with the undisputed fact that such charges reflect a commonly accepted image of this religion which engendered hostile reaction on the part of numerous segments of American society.

In this context it is striking that during the lifetime of Swami Bhaktivedanta and increasingly since his demise (1977), ISKCON has sought legitimation through the courts, through courtship of the approval of scholars, and through an increasingly open or positive approach to other religious traditions. These attempts are not mutually exclusive. The attempt at legitimation in U.S. courts was buttressed by an appeal to scholars and religious leaders who were sympathetic to the cause. Just as I am not attempting to assess the legitimacy of the general image of ISKCON, neither am I attempting to assess the relative success of their attempt at legitimation. It is the phenomenon of religious change within the movement that is under consideration.

Legitimation in U.S. Courts

In 1965 the founder of ISKCON, A. C. Bhaktivedanta Swami Prabhupada, brought his message to New York City. He was then seventy years old. One year after his arrival in the United States, he founded the New York Temple. Committed to the thought and practices of Caitanya, he and his disciples engaged in preaching and chanting in parks and streets, and later engaged in solicitation of funds and the distribution of literature at airports, fairs and wherever they could engage people in religious discussion. Their simple life–styles were a confrontation to middle–class values, and their manner of dress, coupled with their rules against eating meat, gambling, use of drugs or stimulants, and illicit sex were in sharp contrast to the life–styles followed by many who were part of the counter–culture of the 1960s. Their frequently aggressive manner and their early tendency to renounce family ties and values provoked a vigorous reaction on the part of family members and people in general. So strong was this reaction that some parents had their children (often of legal age) kidnapped with the purpose of having them deprogrammed. The charge was that ISKCON brainwashed their converts, who had to be deprogrammed in order to return to a more normal and acceptable life–style. When professional deprogrammers encountered legal difficulties they turned to the thirty–day conservatorship. During that time the deprogramming and neutralizing of the presumed mind–control took place. Converts were usually subjected to mental and physical violence with the intention of getting them to renounce their new–found faith. One of the arguments used against ISKCON members was that they were not entitled to the protection of the First Amendment of the U. S. Constitution since they were not part of a *bona fide* religion, only a "cult."

A celebrated case which has a bearing on the struggle to be considered a *bona fide* religion began with a Queens County (NY) Grand Jury hearing requested by the New York Temple of ISKCON because of the kidnapping of Merylee Kreshower (aged 24) and Ed Shapiro (aged 22). Both had been living in the Temple. Miss Kreshower's mother had arranged a kidnapping for the purpose of deprogramming. Ed Shapiro had requested $20,000 from a fund of stocks and bonds set up for him by his father. Shapiro intended to turn the money over to ISKCON. His father committed him for psychiatric examination, but he was found to have no mental disorder.

Upon release, Kreshower pressed charges against her mother and the detective who had organized the kidnapping. The case went before a Queens Grand jury which, instead of pursuing the circumstances of the kidnapping, inquired into the teachings and practices of ISKCON. This led to the arrest on 12 October 1976 of Adi Kesava (Angus Murphy) and Trai Das (Harold Connolly) who were charged with unlawful detainment by use of mind–control techniques. They were also charged with extortion, alleging a threat that Shapiro Senior would never see his son again unless he released the $20,000. The direction of the grand jury investigation and the subsequent arrests indicate the high level of public hostility towards, and suspicion of, ISKCON. On 17 March 1977, however, the New York Supreme Court dismissed the charges and affirmed the "The Hari Kṛṣṇa movement is a *bona fide* religion with roots in India, that go back thousands of years."[1] The court also stated that "the entire and basic issue before this court is whether or not the two alleged victims in this case and the defendants, will be allowed to practice the religion of their choice...and this must be answered with a resounding affirmation."[2]

In an attempt to strengthen their case as a *bona fide* religion, the movement sent representatives to the 1976 joint meeting of the American Academy of Religion, Society for Biblical Literature and American School of Oriental Research in St. Louis. There they acquired the signatures of almost 200 scholars on a petition that affirmed that the movement was a *bona fide* religion and should be afforded freedom under the First Amendment.

A symposium was held at the Center for the Study of World Religions at Harvard University on 22 November 1976 at which issues relating to ISKCON and "mind–control" were discussed by Harvey Cox (Professor of Theology, Harvard Divinity School), Jeremiah Gutman (Civil Liberties Attorney), Stephen Chorover (Professor of Psychology, MIT), Diana Eck (Lecturer in Sanskrit, Harvard) and two representatives of ISKCON. The tone of the symposium was supportive of the movement.

Statements were also issued in support of the movement by the World Fellowship of Religions, by James Redington, SJ (doctoral student in Indian religions), by Robert A. McDermott (Baruch College), by Joseph T. O'Connell (University of Toronto) and by a number of Indian professors. In a series of newsletters sent to academics following the 1976 meeting in St. Louis, representatives of ISKCON thanked those scholars who had had an influence on the outcome of the Kreshower/Shapiro case.

A series of bills were to come before the state legislatures of Vermont, Massachusetts, Texas, Pennsylvania and Florida which would enable any citizen to gain custody of a person in a "cult," and hold that person for thirty days while he/she was being deprogrammed. A strong appeal by scholars was influential in seeing that none of those bills were voted into law. But it was the New York Supreme Court that settled the issue of whether ISKCON was a religion and entitled to protection under the First Amendment.

In certain other areas the movement took a more aggressive stance in the courts, arguing that under the First Amendment they had the right to proselytize and solicit funds in airports, state fairgrounds, on city streets and on federal park land. On 21 March 1975, the U.S. District Court in Dallas ruled on a request for an injunction against an ordinance enforced by the Dallas–Fort Worth Regional Airport Board that would prohibit solicitation of funds and distribution of literature in terminal buildings. The court did not say that the ordinance was free of constitutional defects, but considered the injunction improper at the time.[3] On 30 January 1979, an opinion was filed in which a permanent injunction restrained the defendants from enforcing the ordinance in question. The District Court judge felt it necessary to comment on the possible reception of his judgment. He commented on the view of many that the Krishnas were harassing airline travellers and that their views were not currently shared by many Americans. Nevertheless, he continued, it is the purpose of the Bill of Rights to protect holders of unpopular ideas.[4]

Between the time of the original request for an injunction (1975) and the final adjudication (1979), there were no less than eight other cases involving airport solicitation. Most of them were settled in favour of ISKCON. A civil rights suit and permanent injunction was filed to enable devotees to perform *saṅkīrtan* at the Kennedy, LaGuardia and Newark airports. The suit was dismissed because there were no prosecutions pending against the plaintiffs.[5] On 17 January 1977, an injunction was granted against an ordinance prohibiting solicitation and distribution of literature without written permission of the Kansas City airport director. The fact that money was solicited in connection with the preaching of religion did not make it a commercial undertaking, and it was protected under the First Amendment.[6]

In a case involving the rights of devotees to solicit at O'Hare Airport in Chicago, it was ruled that a regulation that does not state standards to guide officials in granting permits suppresses First Amendment rights and is a means of censorship.[7] A similar injunction was granted for the Houston Airport.[8] Granting the same rights at the Greater Pittsburgh International Airport, it was held that a ten dollar permit fee was unconstitutional, but that solicitation could be limited in cases of fraudulent solicitation and that devotees were not to engage in physical contact with a prospective donor unless the individual had already agreed to make a contribution.[9] Requirement to acquire a permit to distribute literature and solicit donations at the Los Angeles International Airport was judged unconstitutional.[10] A similar judgment was rendered for the Milwaukee Airport.[11] Regulations imposing a fee for a permit issuance based on the applicant's character coupled with prohibition of any solicitation within the New Orleans airport terminal was ruled unconstitutional on 1 August 1978.[12]

In keeping with its policy to go where one can encounter large numbers of people, another set of cases involved the rights of devotees to have access to state and county fairs. A series of injunctions was handed down voiding regulations that would have restricted devotees from entering the pedestrian thoroughfares of the fair, talking to persons about their religion, distributing literature and soliciting donations. This was the situation for the Ionia Free Fair,[13] the Wisconsin State Fair (August 1979) , the State Fair of West Virginia (August 1978), and Erie County Fair (August 1978). In the latter case, certain restrictions limited the number of devotees soliciting at any time to ten, required them to conduct religious discussions on an individual basis with no more than one member confronting a member of the public at one time, and forbade them to leave literature unattended which would be conducive to litter. In some of the judgments it is stated that to confine devotees to a booth would be to inhibit their rights to practice their religion freely. But in a case regarding the Ohio State Fair it was ruled that to confine devotees to specific booths was not such an infringement on First Amendment rights. Here the ruling was that the state had the right to regulate such activities even though it could not prohibit them.[14] On 1 September 1978, however, an injunction granted the right of unrestricted movement at the Nebraska State Fair, and a similar injunction was granted for free solicitation at the Indiana State Fair.[15]

On 9 September 1978, a restraining order was handed down to enable solicitation at the Kansas State Fair although in this case a number of conditions were attached. Members were to wear cards identifying themselves as solicitors for ISKCON. The number of members soliciting at one time was to be limited to twenty, and they were not to use the word 'fair' in such a way as to suggest sponsorship. They were not to touch unconsenting persons even for the purpose of pinning flowers on them. No more than two members were to engage a person in discussion at one time. There were seventeen rules to be followed. On 12 September, a temporary restraining order was granted for the performance of *sańkīrtan* at the Eastern States Exposition in Massachusetts. A judgment relating to the State Fair of Texas ruled that devotees had the right to solicit donations and distribute literature outside the confines of a booth unless they concealed their identity. "...But if members of a sect (*sic*) went in disguise and gave away flowers with no distribution of literature or disclosure of their religious purpose, they would be required to obtain a booth."[16] It seems that members were wearing wigs and street clothing in place of their traditional identifying garb and were not explicit about the purpose for the donations.

A number of judgments overturned restrictions on proselytizing and soliciting donations on the public streets of major U. S. cities. A New Orleans ordinance that made solicitations illegal in the French Quarter of the city was judged unconstitutional.[17] An ordinance in Sacramento, California that required a prior permit to engage in charitable solicitation was deemed unconstitutional.[18] A Chicago ordinance which made it unlawful "for any person to engage in the business of a peddler without a license" was inapplicable since the solicitation of religious donations was not a commercial enterprise but a religious act and protected under the First Amendment.[19]

A state licensing law, applied to the devotees, that prohibited them from soliciting donations at rest–stops on state highways in Florida was judged unconstitutional.[20] But the regulation of certain areas as off limits to such solicitation in national park areas was indeed constitutional.[21] Finally, ISKCON sought an injunction to enjoin arrest and prosecution of members who solicited on certain segments of the pavement leading to the entrance of Knott's Berry Farm (a popular amusement park in California). This was denied on the ground that the portion of the street, though resembling a public thoroughfare, was the private property of Knott's Berry Farm.[22]

Overall, these cases from 1975 to 1979 were exceedingly successful in granting members of ISKCON protection under the First Amendment as a legitimate religion. The result was an extension of freedom to engage in distribution of literature and in solicitation of donations in a variety of forums where they might encounter a large number of people. Although the extent to which these cases changed public opinion is uncertain, ISKCON's legal place alongside other legitimate denominations was assured.

Legitimation Through Appeal To Scholars

In tracing the attempt to achieve legal room for ISKCON, we have already noticed the role played by scholars as expert witnesses. But the use of scholars and scholarship to enhance legitimacy has extended beyond this legal purpose.

In a series of newsletters from ISKCON to scholars following the St. Louis petition of 1976, several scholars offered their services as sources of information about the movement for concerned parents of converts. They also urged other scholars in metropolitan areas around the country to do the same.

In 1980-83, the six–volume *Śrīla Prabhupāda–līlāmṛta* was published by the Bhaktivedanta Book Trust. Each volume of this authorized biography of Swami Bhaktivedanta contains a preface by a scholar whose name would be immediately recognizable in academic circles. This is regularly mentioned in advertising. In a footnote to a later article, Śubhānanda dās notes, "Each volume of *Līlāmṛta* is introduced by a noted scholar of religion."[23]

In the editor's preface to *Hare Krishna, Hare Krishna: Five Distinguished Scholars on the Krishna Movement in the West*,[24] Steven J. Gelberg, (Śubhānanda dās) deals with caricatures of ISKCON and its devotees. He asserts that devotees can be rational, are not zealots or cultic zombies and should not be considered merely a part of pop culture. ISKCON is a legitimate religious tradition. But he recognizes that this assertion would be less convincing were it to come from a devotee than if it were to come from the mouth of a respected academic.

> At one point, I realized that a collection of systematic dialogues with some of ISKCON's academic observers might serve as a useful introduction to the movement — an introduction that might be *more credible* than one attempted by a committed member with an apologetic motive. This book is the product of that realization.[25]

Included are scholars who can be trusted not to wage an attack. Not every statement if laudatory. If Professor Shinn (then of Oberlin College) confesses his difficulty in relating to the role of the guru in the Vaiṣṇava tradition, and if Professor Basham says "Although I could never belong to it myself," (190) in reference to the movement, it makes many of their other statements even more forceful in the legitimation process.

Several themes are stated repeatedly by all of the scholars here interviewed. ISKCON is not a cult, not even a "new" religious movement. Not only is it said by Harvey Cox (24), but also by Larry Shinn (63), by Thomas Hopkins (120ff), by A. L. Basham (180ff), and at length by Shrivatsa Goswami, an Indian Vaiṣṇava with an MA in Indian Philosophy from Banaras Hindu University (105ff). For Professor Basham to say that "the Hare Krishna movement is very definitely a religion" (163) and to have that repeated by other scholars can do nothing but assist in the legitimation of ISKCON as a *bona fide* religion. And when Harvey Cox says that deprogramming is "reprehensible, destructive to human personality, and in every way evil" (55), this is certain to be more effective than if it were to come from a devotee. This and also the accusation of brainwashing is also countered by Professor Shinn when he says, "...'brainwashing' — if we mean by that 'mind–control,' 'coercive persuasion,' or 'thought reform'...is clearly not, in any sense, an explanation of how people get into the Hare Krishna movement." (64)

This volume leaves the distinct impression that there are reputable scholars who hold that ISKCON is a *bona fide* religion, a movement that is rapidly becoming more of a denomination than a sect, which has a strong mystical dimension coupled with a strong intellectual base and a long and illustrious history in India. The scholars are afforded considerable freedom to express their views, but they are led by carefully crafted questions that direct their attention to topics that are of concern to the intellectual side of the movement today. On a few occasions when the view expressed is considered at least partially wrong, the editor takes the opportunity to clarify the issue, for example, on the guru–disciple relationship (79).

For a number of years the Bhaktivedanta Book Trust has made its presence known at the annual meetings of the American Academy of Religion through its book display. At the 1982 annual meeting of the AAR, an entire session was devoted to a discussion of ISKCON. There were four presentations, two by "outsider" scholars and two by "insiders." The presentations were followed by a response, replies to the response, and a general discussion. By participating in this forum, the "insiders" took the same rostrum as other scholars and hence participated in a form of legitimation.

A final use of scholars and scholarship for legitimation is the inauguration, in Spring 1985, of *Iskcon Review: Academic Perspectives on the Hare Krishna Movement*. The first issue was devoted to the above–mentioned session on ISKCON at the 1982 AAR meeting. The *Review* is an attempt to present the intellectual side of ISKCON, and it invites contributions from those within the movement, as well as academics. In describing the primary audience of this new journal, its editor, Śubhānanda dās, writes,

> It is directed towards a wide, particularly academic and professional audience including Hindu studies scholars, sociologists and psychologists of religion, students of American religious history, theologians, mental health professionals, and clergy...as well as interested members of ISKCON.26

Other "new religions" have also made an appeal to scholars, most notably the Unification Church. They have held numerous conferences. The proceedings have often been published and the editing handed over to "outsider" scholars. ISKCON has not gone quite so far and has maintained editorial control of such publications. But the growing relationship with scholars is another dimension of the legitimation of ISKCON.

Legitimation Through Irenic Approach To Other Religions

In a previous article, I examined Swami Bhaktivedanta's statements about other religions and sought to explain their predominantly critical nature in the light of his theology.[27] As the movement has matured, devotees have not only sought to engage scholars in discussion, but have developed a more ameliorating approach to other religions. This attempt at a more positive statement is another dimension of the struggle for legitimation.

In July 1985, ISKCON held a conference at New Vrindavan in West Virginia on the theme "Krishna Consciousness in the West: A Multidisciplinary Critique." Twenty–five scholars from colleges and universities in North America were invited, along with a number of devotees. Among the devotees was a Harvard graduate student in religion, Graham M. Schweig, who presented a paper on "Bhakti, 'The Living Religion of the Day': A Study of the ISKCON Vaiṣṇava View of Other Religions." In his paper, Schweig makes an effort to construct a "total" ISKCON view of how devotees view other religions. Basing his thought on the words of Bhaktivedanta, Schweig attempts to use the three levels of spiritual advancement in God–realization to present a "total" ISKCON view. Although these three levels are discussed by Bhaktivedanta, he offers no systematic attempt to relate this to one's attitude to other religions. This, then, is a new theological development.

The lowest level (*kanistha*) is a devotee who has deep faith in God, but "his vision is narrower and parochial, and he maintains an exclusivistic stance in relation to any other tradition because he cannot discern the religiousness of others."[28] The intermediate level devotee (*madhyama*) combines an exclusive and inclusive stance. He has developed God–consciousness to the degree that he is able "to distinguish between a God conscious person, a novice, an innocent person, and an irreligious person whether such a person is a Vaiṣṇava or not."[29] The advanced devotee (*uttama*) has an inclusivist vision of other traditions. "He, like the beginner devotee, is indiscriminate, but with his highly developed vision sees everyone as a devotee of God."[30] All of these attitudes are seen as a total ISKCON view. This construction has the potential of enabling one to account for both positive and negative attitudes on the part of devotees by assessing their level of spiritual advancement. But this scheme is not systematically carried through in Schweig's paper.

Instead, what seems to take Schweig's attention is an examination of Bhaktivedanta's view in terms of inclusive and exclusive. "We shall see how

Prabhupada's every statement signifies or implies a very specific and particular balance between inclusivistic and exclusivistic stances."[31] Since it can hardly be assumed that Bhaktivedanta is an intermediate devotee, one can only assume that his statements which operate on the lower or middle levels operate there for the sake of lower of middle devotees. Then the positive ones would be his higher view. But this is not worked out either. What is striking about this attempt, however, is that a devotee is seeking to emphasize a more positive approach without ignoring the exclusive dimensions. He sees that Bhaktivedanta distinguishes between true and false religion. But it is emphasized that true religion means devotion to God, and that can take place in any tradition. Of course, the Pali Canon and advaita are less instructive in this regard because of their denigration of the personal God.

Repeatedly in the works of Bhaktivedanta, advaitins are called "the dead branch of a tree," asuras, demoniacs and products of the Kali yuga, rascals and offenders. The model of Caitanya was conversion, not dialogue. Any religion that does not accept the Supreme Lord is a cheating religion (*kaitava–dharma*). Devotees are discouraged from worshipping other deities (demigods) or from reading scriptures other than Vaiṣṇava ones. There is a tendency to be more charitable to the founder of a religion than to his followers. This is true of Śankara, the Buddha, Christ, and Mohammed. Muslims and Christians violate the prohibition against killing (i.e. they eat meat).[32]

What is striking about Schweig's construction is that none of this strong language is present. Moreover, there is a tendency to deal with the positive or inclusive statements first and at some length before moving to a less extensive treatment of the exclusive statements. Nowhere do terms like "rascals," "offenders," "demoniacs," or other such pungent words that abound in Bhaktivedanta's writings appear in Schweig's paper. Schweig's is a serious attempt at a balance between inclusive and exclusive attitudes. But, within the context of Bhaktivedanta's work, it is its emphatically affirmative tone that stands out.

Also in 1985, the first American disciple of Swami Bhaktivedanta and the founder of the New Vrindavan community in West Virginia, Kirtananda Swami Bhaktipada, published a book, *Christ and Krishna: The Path of Pure Devotion*.[33] In a question and answer format, Bhaktipada explores the essential unity of the message of Christ and Kṛṣṇa. The book also contains six short chapters of his conversations with a variety of Christians. Early in the book he states,

> I am not condemning any *bona fide* religion because the principles of *bona fide* religion are the same everywhere. Religion means the laws of God. One who abides by these laws is truly religious. The laws of God, as stated in all scriptures, demand surrender to God.[34]

As the son of a Baptist minister, Bhaktipada believed that to accept Christ meant to condemn other religions. Now he sees that Christ, the perfect son of God, is not the only avatāra. Kṛṣṇa corresponds to God and tells people to "love me." Christ told them to "love God." There is no contradiction between the two. As for the Christian teaching that one can only come to God through Christ, Bhaktipada likens that to the need for a *jagad–guru*. Bhaktipada's openness does not extend to all views. Those who reject God or who are impersonalists are in error. But the emphasis in his book is clearly positive.

Bhaktipada is concerned primarily with the relationship between Kṛṣṇa consciousness and Christianity. He sees no problem in affirming the virgin birth of Christ or the doctrine of the trinity. "A follower of the Vedas can understand this mystery of 'three in One' because we also speak of three aspects of God: the impersonal Brahman, the localized Paramatma, and Bhagavan, the Supreme Personality of Godhead. Still, there is unity."[35] Since reincarnation is taught by Christ and is found in the Bible, it is a short step to see the Christian doctrine of the resurrection of the body as a reference to reincarnation.[36]

Bhaktipada is willing to engage in philosophical discussion, finding the arguments for God convincing. Particularly affirmed are the arguments from design and first cause. In the end, however, we learn the truth of God from the scripture. But God has given scriptures to many peoples at various times and places. This includes not only the Vedic corpus, but also the Bible, Qu'ran, and Buddhist sutras (54). The main difference between the Bible and the Vedic literature is not the difference between error and truth but the difference between a small and large dictionary. The Vedic literature is simply more complete. One can achieve consciousness of God even while remaining a Christian. ISKCON members chant the *mahāmantra*. But if chanting the name of Kṛṣṇa is uncomfortable, one can chant the name of Christ, since they are the same anyway. Chanting any of the *bona fide* names of God will be effective (43ff).

An important chapter for our purposes in entitled "The Universal Church." Bhaktipada states that the real church is not an organization, but a "spiritual unity composed of those who believe in God and love Him" (111). This church cannot be sectarian. While one can change one's faith, religion cannot be changed since it is one. It is "*sanatan dharma*, the eternal nature of things, which specifically indicates the inherent, changeless nature of the living entity: to render loving service to God" (112). The only limits placed on this universal church is a denial of God or unwillingness to serve him in loving devotion. Hence communists would be excluded. The subsequent chapters entitled "conversations with Christians" are illuminating, but are less conversations than a continuation of the question and answer format.

Bhaktipada's wide range of knowledge of biblical texts and of western traditions is in striking contrast to the dearth of such knowledge in Bhaktivedanta.[37] Biblical texts and Vaiṣṇava texts are woven together to present a complete picture of *sanātan dharma* which is quite harmonious. The use of biblical texts by modern Indian religious thinkers to show the universal quality of their thought is often strained. But Bhaktipada frequently chooses just the right text to make his point. This book grew out of his encounter with Christians who visited New Vrindavan, and is another dimension of the struggle for legitimation.

Dialogue is something that Bhaktipada has not found instructive and is where he would draw the line. "Such dialogues generally end up as so much impersonal hogwash. I don't know anything other than what I have learned from Srila Prabhupada" (146). It is thus a further step when Śubhānanda dās, formerly Directory for Interreligious Affairs, ISKCON, writes a lengthy article entitled "The Catholic Church and the Hare Krishna Movement: An Invitation to Dialogue."[38] Śubhānanda reacts to the statement of the "Vatican Report on Sects, Cults and New Religious Movements" (1986) that "there is generally little or no possibility of dialogue with the sects" by pointing out that Swami Bhaktivedanta "met and spoke at length with Sergio Cardinal Pignedoli, the second president of the Secretariat for Non–Christians, and with Jean Cardinal Daniélou of France (both now deceased) as well as with many Catholic clergy, religious and seminarians throughout the world."[39] He continues by pointing out that members of ISKCON have repeatedly accepted invitations to speak at Catholic schools, colleges and seminaries, and that he himself has engaged in extensive dialogue with "Benedictine, Cistercian, and Camaldolese monks at monasteries in the United States, Canada, Australia, and Ireland." He concludes that ISKCON is quite open to dialogue.

The article seems to imply that the ball is in the court of the Catholic Church. Most of the remainder of the article deals with Catholic attitudes toward cults and with which attitudes are inappropriate. It also analyzes a series of generic criticisms of cults along with answers which are intended as a corrective. Each criticism is seen as somewhat stereotypical. But, to the extent that it is true, it is a belief of practice held in common with the Catholic Church. Even the anti–cult rhetoric is similar to that anti–Catholic rhetoric in the nineteenth–century United States which is not entirely dead today. Bigotry is attacked, and Catholic writers who are sympathetic to such dialogue are quoted extensively.

The first step to dialogue is the overcoming of ignorance and prejudice (36). Such is extensive among Christians, and how better to minimize it than to hear from authentic devotees. Since the essay is addressed to the Church, it concentrates on Catholic attitudes, theology and their ignorance of ISKCON. There is little discussion of what type of groundwork might be required of ISKCON for such dialogue. They are ready! One of the advantages to the Church will be "increased awareness of an appreciation for God's universal saving grace; and a deepening of one's own spirituality" (39). That is, one will see ISKCON as a means of God's grace.

If entering into dialogue presupposes that each party treats the other as an equal, then ISKCON will be treated as a legitimate religious movement and not a mere cult. Śubhānanda contends that ISKCON will continue to exist with or without dialogue with the Catholic Church. It seems that Catholics have the most to lose by ignoring this sincere invitation. But he also recognizes that such dialogue would lend credibility to the dialogue partner,[40] and it is therefore a part of the struggle for legitimation.

ISKCON, then, has through the courts, through the influence of scholars and scholarship, and through an increasingly open approach to other religions, sought to enhance its image as a legitimate religion alongside others in a pluralistic society.

Notes

1. *New York Law Journal*, 21 March 1977, 12, col. 4.

2. *Ibid.*, 13, col. 4.

3. *ISKCON* v. *Dallas–Ft. Worth Regional Airport Board*, 391 F. Supp. 606 (1975).

4. *Susan Fernandes* v. *Leonard Limmer* et. al., US District Court for Northern District of Texas, Dallas Division.

5. *ISKCON* v. *NY Port Authority* 425 F. Supp. 681 (1977).

6 *ISKCON* v. *Englehardt* 425 Suppl 176 (1977).

7. *ISKCON* v. *Rochford* 425 F. Supp. 734 (1977).

8. *ISKCON* v. *Collins* 452 F. Supp. 1007 (1977).

9. *ISKCON of Western PA, Inc.* v. *Griffin* 437 F. Supp. 666 (1977).

10. *People, Plaintiff and Respondent* v. *Fogelson* Sup., 145 Cal. Rptr. 542.

11. *ISKCON* v. *Wolke* 453 F. Supp. 869 (1978).

12. *ISKCON* v. *Lentini* 461 F. Supp. 49 (1978).

13. *Anderson et. al.* v. *Ionia Free Fair Association*, US District Court, Western District of Michigan, 7 August 1978.

14. *ISKCON* v. *Evans* 440 F. Supp. 414 (1977).

15. *ISKCON* v. *Bowen* 456 F. Supp. 437 (1978).

16. *ISKCON* v. *State Fair of Texas* 461 F. Supp. 719 (1978).

17. *ISKCON* v. *City of New Orleans* 347 F. Supp. 945 (1972).

18. *ISKCON of Berkeley* v. *Kearnes* 454 F. Supp. 116 (1978).

19. *ISKCON* v. *Conlisk* 374 F. Supp. 1010 (1972).

20. *ISKCON* v. *Hays* 438 F. Supp. 1077 (1977).

21. *Liberman* v. *Schesventer* 447 F. Supp. 1355 (1978).

22. *ISKCON* v. *Reber* 454 F. Supp. 1385 (1978).

23. *Iskcon Review*, 2 (1986), 50, note 3.

24. *Hare Krishna, Hare Krishna: FIve Distinguished Scholars on the Krishna Movement in the West* (New York: Grove Press, 1983).

25. *Ibid.*, 18-29, emphasis mine.

26. *Iskcon Review*, 1, (1985), no. 1, inside cover.

27. "Swami Bhaktivedanta and the Encounter with Religions," *Modern Indian Responses to Religious Pluralism*, ed. Harold Coward (Albany: State University of New York Press, 1987), also Chapter XV of this volume.

28. Manuscript copy, 3.

29. *Ibid.*

30. *Ibid.*

31. *Ibid.*, 4.

32. All of these views are developed in "Swami Bhaktivedanta and the Encounter with Religions."

33 *Christ and Krishna: The Path of Pure Devotion* (Bhaktipada Books, 1985).

34. *Ibid.*, 2.

35. *Ibid.*, 17.

36. For a complete discussion of Bhaktivedanta's view on karma and rebirth, see Robert D. Baird, "Swami Bhaktivedanta: Karma, Rebirth and the Personal God," *Karma and Rebirth: Post Classical Developments*, ed.

Ronald W. Neufeldt (Albany: State University of New York Press, 1986), and Chapter XIII of this volume.

37. "Swami Bhaktivedanta and the Encounter with Religions."

38. *Iskcon Review*, 2 (1986).

39. *Iskcon Review*, 2 (1986), 2.

40. *Iskcon Review*, 2 (1986), 49.

17

Religious or Non–Religious: TM in American Courts

The Transcendental Meditation movement is one among numerous movements in the U. S. today that is firmly rooted in Indian religio–philosophical traditions. However, TM consistently seeks to be understood simply as a technique and its spokespersons strongly deny that it is a religion. It is the credibility of this disavowal that has enabled TM to get support for its programs from correctional institutions run by the state, state legislatures, departments of the federal government and local school officials.

It is the purpose of this paper to show that in the mind of Maharishi the proper understanding of TM is uniformly linked with a theoretical or metaphysical explanation which has been variously called "The Science of Being" or the "Science of Creative Intelligence," and that this linkage is found in Maharishi's writings and has been recently uncovered in the courts.

There are two contentions which stand out in introductory lectures on TM and in the promotional literature which is offered to potential meditators: (1) TM is not a religion; and (2) TM has many benefits which are scientifically verifiable.

As for the benefits, TM is supposed to improve one's reaction time, make one more stable, make one a better athlete, a better student, more productive in one's work, improve one's relationships with co–workers and supervisors, decrease anxiety, improve one's mental health, decrease blood preassure, reduce dependence on alcohol, cigarettes or drugs, improve one's resistance to disease, help cure insomnia, and assist in the normalization of weight. All these effects are scientifically verifiable, according to TM, and can be verified in one's own experience. One is counselled that he or she does not have to believe anything in particular in order to practise TM. Having been given a *mantra* specifically chosen for the individual, its repetition will refine the nervous system and one can easily experience the effects to which I have just referred. One does not have to understand the workings of this any more than one has to understand the workings of electricity in order to turn on the light.

Understanding TM: Necessity of a Theoretical Explanation

Although one does not have to understand metaphysics in order to *practice* TM, Maharishi makes it clear that one cannot *understand* the workings of TM without understanding its underlying philosophy. In his *The Science of Being and the Art of Living*, later available in paperback as *Transcendental Meditation: Serenity Without Drugs*, Maharishi begins with metaphysics and a discussion of the nature of the reality on which TM is based.

> To those who have never had an interest in metaphysical study, the section on "Science of Being" may first appear to be highly abstract, but once they have stepped into "Life" and "Art of Living" and have completed the section on "Fulfillment," they will find that without dwelling on the abstract features of the science of Being, the whole wisdom of the book would have no practical basis.[1]

In TM, as one progresses beyond the introductory and promotional level, it becomes more important to learn something about the philosophy on which the practice is based. Maharishi sees the two as inseparable. He is willing to divorce the two temporarily in order that persons will begin the practice of TM believing that later they will learn about its philosophy when they have found its practice beneficial. This temporary divorce is based on a principle which is commonly found in Indian religious traditions, a principle that Buddhists called *upāya* or skill in means. It means that the *guru* or spiritual leader knows the truth and is able to approach any person on his or her respective level of ignorance or insight. If people were generally receptive to religion, TM could be presented as religion, but because the mass consciousness is not favorable to religion, TM will not be so designated.

> Whenever and wherever religion dominates the mass consciousness, transcendental deep meditation should be taught in terms of religion. Whenever and wherever metaphysical thinking dominates the consciousness of society, transcendental deep meditation should be taught in metaphysical terms, openly aiming at the fulfilment of the current metaphysical thought...[2]

In the present time politics and economics dominate the consciousness and so TM should be approached from this perspective.[3] Hence the emphasis on happiness as the end of life, improved physical and psychological benefits, and improved job performance. One finds what people see as their most profound and pressing needs, and then TM is presented as meeting that need.

> The techniques of imparting transcendental deep meditation to the people is to find out what they are aspiring for in life, find out what they want to accomplish, what their desires are, and then tell them of the gains of transcendental deep meditation in terms of their desires and needs and aspirations in life.[4]

Metaphysical ideas are pushed aside until a later stage when practitioners will be more open to them.

The theoretical basis for TM is termed the Science of Creative Intelligence (SCI). The same theory was earlier expounded as "The Science of Being." "Science," there, was defined as "systematized knowledge." The "Science of Being" meant "systematized knowledge of the Being — systematized knowledge of existence or the actuality of life."[5] In 1963 the "Science of Being" functioned as the theoretical explanation for TM much as its terminological equivalent SCI does today. Within the earlier terminology, the theoretical explanation might be condensed as follows.

The ultimate and essential aspect of all is Being. Being permeates everything. Sometimes this is called "God," but ultimately it is not personal. Being exists in its absolute state as unchanging, and in its relative state as changing.[6] All of reality is Being either in its absolute or its relative state. Being is like a vast ocean, silent and ever the same, while the waves which are part of the ocean, though different, represent the phenomenal phases of daily life. The imperishable Being lies beyond all the relative existence of mental and material life.

Human beings are essentially one with the Being.[7] That is, the ultimate reality which is at the base of nature is also at the base of human nature. On the surface there is change and suffering and hypertension. But at the base of human nature is "the Being" — the infinite reality which is none other than man himself. That which is ultimately real is not to be found by looking without, but within.

All suffering is due to not knowing the way to unfold the divine glory within oneself. If one only had the knowledge to "dive" within oneself, the root of all ills and sufferings would be eliminated. Our inner being is the unmanifested absolute Being which manifests itself in the ego, intellect, senses and mind.[8] But we have lost contact with Being and hence identify ourselves with the surface manifestations. We mistake the waves, as it were, for the total ocean.

The solution is to contact the eternal Being lying deep within.[9] One then becomes one with the absolute eternal Being. For Maharishi, one can bring this experience into the plane of the relative through the technique of transcendental deep meditation.

> The practice of transcendental deep meditation results in such a great impact of the nature of the Being on the nature of the mind that the mind begins to live the nature of the eternal Being and yet continues to behave and experience in the field of relative existence.[10]

In meditation the mind comes in contact with eternal Being, that state which lies beyond all seeing and hearing and touching, smelling and tasting.[11] One becomes able to live the Being through the practice of transcendental deep meditation and through engaging in activity after meditation. When in contact with Being, there is identity.

> The mind loses its individuality and becomes cosmic mind, it becomes omnipresent and gains pure eternal existence. In the transcendent it has no capacity for experience. Here the mind does not exist, it becomes existence.[12]

Meditation increases clarity of mind and all the other promised benefits because the mind has come in contact with Being and one is now living the Being.

SCI/TM in District Court

In the fall of the 1969 Jerry Jarvis, director of SIMS and IMS (branches of the TM movement), taught a course at Stanford University entitled "The Science of Creative Intelligence." The enrollment of over three hundred students generated interest on the part of the academic community and enthusiasm within the TM movement for presenting SCI/TM in educational institutions. Jerry Jarvis commented:

> Since then there have been more SCI courses established and Maharishi has been working to prepare comprehensive courses for teaching SCI at all levels of education.[13]

This endeavour resulted in an attractively produced text–book, *Science of Creative Intelligence for Secondary Education.* During the 1975-76 academic year it was the basis for an elective course taught in five New Jersey public high schools, entitled "Science of Creative Intelligence–Transcendental Meditation." The course was taught four or five days a week by teachers trained by the World Plan Executive Council–United States, an organization whose objective it is to disseminate the teachings of SCI/TM throughout the U. S. Each student that elected the course, was required to attend a *Puja* ceremony as part of the course, at which time he or she received a *Mantra* and was trained in its use.

A suit was filed in the United States District Court, District of New Jersey, involving twelve plaintiffs and twenty defendants. Among the defendants was the United States Departments of Health, Education and Welfare through which WPEC–US had received a $40,000 grant. Plaintiffs moved for a partial summary judgment to enjoin the teaching of the course on the ground that it violated the establishment clause of the first amendment. Their argument was based on the text book, *puja*, deposition testimony of the president of WPEC–US, Jerry Jarvis, and the deposition of two people who taught the SCI/TM course. It is pointed out that the facts of the case were agreed upon by both sides, the only issue being their interpretation.

Defendants argued that TM is a technique of meditation in which the meditator contemplates a meaningless sound (*mantra*). This results in the many benefits which we have already enumerated. The "Science of Creative Intelligence" is a theory promulgated by Maharishi which purports to explain what occurs within a meditator's mind during meditation and intends to describe an entity or concept called creative intelligence. During TM, a meditator reverses the process through which thought develops until the meditator's mind reaches the field of pure creative intelligence which is at the source of thought.[14] District Court Judge Meanor's Opinion is seventy–eight pages in length and centers around the text book and the *puja*.

The Text Book

The science of creative intelligence holds that during meditation the meditator's mind moves from conscious thought to the source of thought, where the mind comes in contact with the unmanifest and unbounded field of pure creative intelligence (T at 29) which is present everywhere in the universe and within every individual.[15] Attainment of contact with pure creative intelligence places the meditator in a "fourth state of consciousness" known as "restful alertness" or "transcendental consciousness" (T at 30). During TM the meditator experiences the field of pure creative intelligence directly (T at 29). This infuses the meditators' mind with creativity (T at 26), clarifies and strengthens the meditators' thoughts (T at 32), expands perceptions (T at 30), and refines the meditator's nervous system (Jarvis deposition at 866a). Regular practice of TM will further refine the nervous system so that the expanded perceptions experienced during TM will carry over into the meditator's conscious thought and activities. (T at 38, 86). Continued practice of TM may lead one's mind to be infused with "expanded awareness" with perceptions experienced during meditation carrying over to the waking, sleeping and dreaming states. This is called "cosmic consciousness" or "the fifth state of consciousness" (T at 86). Continued practice may lead to further refinement of the nervous system and increased faculties of perception until a state called "unity consciousness" is reached. This highest level of refinement of the nervous system is called "God consciousness" or "Brahman consciousness."[16] The teachers did not mention either "unity consciousness" or "Brahman consciousness" to their classes.

The field of pure creative intelligence is unmanifest and the home of all the qualities which constitute the universe. Creative intelligence is a force which springs from the field of pure creative intelligence which is the source of everything in the universe (T at 26, 40, 260). Creative intelligence, unlike pure creative intelligence, possesses all the qualities that can be conceived of. "Every quality that is ever expressed in creation is the expression of creative intelligence" (T at 40). The text book takes 255 pages to discuss fifty specific qualities of creative intelligence.

One should not seek to imitate the qualities of creative intelligence, but should allow them to be displayed spontaneously as a result of TM. TM is not only the automatic means of attaining all the qualities of creative intelligence, but also the exclusive manner of obtaining these qualities (T at 94, 132, 217, 262).

While the field of pure creative intelligence, is described as silent, non–changing, and immovable, the text book describes creative intelligence as perpetually active in all aspects of the universe.

> The entire field of life, from the individual to the cosmos, is nothing but the expression of never-changing pure creative intelligence in the relative ever–changing expressions of life. (T at 92). So, nothing occurs in random fashion.

In addition to activity, creative intelligence possesses the anthropomorphic qualities of being thoughtful, loving and just, decisive and sweet, precise and truthful. Furthermore, creative intelligence is omnipotent since its power is unlimited (T at 108), and it is the basis of all knowledge (T at 189). It is also omnipresent (T at 23) and eternal. It "has existed for all times. It is, always has been, and always will be the non–changing basis of life, the fountainhead of all currents of creativity" (T at 242). The field of pure creative intelligence is the "field of unlimited happiness" (T at 32, 56), "the unbounded ocean of bliss" (T at 152), and "universal existence" (T at 292) or "perfection of existence" (T at 118).

The defendants argued that no matter what statements are to be found in the text book, those statements are "not intended or understood as an (*sic*) religion, religious study of God" (Jarvis affidavit). The defendants sought to present the view that creative intelligence is merely a philosophic idea or a "philosophic concept" but the court responded that the text–book contradicted such claims: "Creative intelligence is not just an abstract concept or idea it is a concrete reality that can be practically applied to bring success and fulfilment to every phase of living" (T at 250).

The defendants also selected certain statements from the text–book in an attempt to show that they were only apparently religious. The court saw this as an attempt to "refute their obvious meanings" through "unpersuasive analogies" and "bald assertions of belief." Although Judge Meanor's Opinion offers numerous examples, the following will indicate the nature of the argument and the court's response.

(1) The analogy of gravity. The text–book states the creative intelligence "guides and sustains every aspect of the universe" (T at 174). But in his affidavit, Jarvis explains,

> Creative intelligence is not understood or taught as sustainer of the universe in a religious sense. It "guides and sustains" in a scientific–philosophic sense, much in the same manner that gravity guides and sustains the path of the planets.

The court responded by pointing out that creative intelligence, unlike gravity, is the source of life–energy, the home of all knowledge and wisdom, and the origin of all power in the universe. Unlike creative intelligence, gravity is not kind, or an ocean of love.

(2) The analogy from the principles of freedom, truth and justice.

Defendants admit that creative intelligence is eternal and state that "purely secular ideas and principles, such as freedom and the concepts of truth and justice, are eternal and 'go on and on' devoid of religious connotations" (Jarvis, 42). But the court pointed out that the analogy was weak since freedom, truth and justice do not have the other characteristics attributed to creative intelligence. Neither is a "concrete reality" (T at 250) that "can be contacted" (T at 13), and which "accomplishes all things with no effort" (T at 108). Furthermore, the text–book states that freedom, truth and justice are only three of a multitude of qualities contained within the field of creative intelligence.

(3) The analogy of matter and energy. The court rejected the analogy of matter and energy since neither possess the tiniest fraction of the characteristics of creative intelligence. Neither matter nor energy is bliss–consciousness, nor unbounded awareness, nor a field of "unlimited power, energy, existence, peace and happiness," as is creative intelligence (T at 121, 262, 102).

The defendants also sought to have creative intelligence understood not as an objective metaphysical principle but as subjective qualities which develop in the practitioner as a result of meditation (Jarvis Affidavit, 41).

> While the text–book attempts to describe certain qualities of creative intelligence, it contains nothing intended or understood as inherently religious. Thus, attributes such as loving, just, gentle, strong, efficient, kind, clean, purifying, "a person of full heart," self–sustaining and self–sufficient, are simply human qualities that develop as a result of personal growth.

The court replied that while it may be true that these qualities do develop in an individual as a result of personal growth, the text–book attributes these "simply human qualities" with the exception of "a person of full heart," to a non–human, unmanifest, uncreated "concrete reality" (T at 250, 214-221, 100-107).

Depositions from three clergymen: a Catholic priest, a United Presbyterian minister, and a rabbi, were also presented. All of them testified that they did not consider SCI/TM a religion, nor did they consider their *pujas* a religious activity. None of the clergymen, however, had actually read the entire text–book and two of them saw it first on the day of their depositions. The third said that he had the text for several weeks and had "looked over it kind of carefully." The latter indicated that he had studied portions of the text–book, but could not remember any reference to the term "bliss–consciousness" which occurs frequently throughout the book. In a footnote to the opinion, Judge Meanor states:

> The same clergyman testified that there was no connection between the teachings embodied in the Science of Creative Intelligence and the technique of Transcendental Meditation. The clergyman was apparently oblivious to the fact that defendants teach that the Science of Creative Intelligence explains the mechanics of the practice of Transcendental Meditation, including the teaching that the alleged benefits of the practice of Transcendental Meditation, derive not from the contemplation of a meaningless sound but from contact with the unmanifest field of life known as the field of pure creative intelligence (e.g. T at 23, 24, 26, 38).[18]

The defendants also submitted Affidavits from two SCI/TM teachers and eleven students in the courses who said they did not see the course as a study of religion. The judge indicated, however, that the issue was the content of the course and not how some people subjectively characterized it.

> The subjective characterizations by individuals of teachings as religious or not religious in their systems of characterization cannot be determinative of whether or not the teachings are religious within the meaning of the first amendment.[19]

The Puja

The second item around which discussion centred was the *puja*. Each student was required to attend a *puja* which was performed in a closed room by the teacher in the presence of the student. *Pujas* were conducted off the school premises and on Sundays. Each student was asked to bring a clean white handkerchief, a few flowers and some fruit. Each student removed his or her shoes before entering the room. Inside the room was a table covered with a white sheet on which were placed containers for candle and incense, camphor, and three dishes for water, rice and sandal–paste. At the back of the table was an eight by eleven inch color picture of Guru Dev.[20] The handkerchief, fruit and flowers brought by the student were also placed on the table. The student stood or sat in front of the table while the teacher sang a chant in Sanskrit lasting three or four minutes.[21] At the conclusion of the chant the teacher gave the student a *mantra* and then instructed the student in the technique for using it. The student then meditated with the use of the *mantra* for some twenty minutes after which the teacher and student discussed the student's experience. The whole procedure took 1 1/2 to 2 hours. A week or two prior to the *puja*, the student was required to sign a document in which the student promised never to reveal his or her *mantra*. The teachers told the students that the *puja* was not a religious exercise or prayer.

The court points out that the *puja* chant takes the form of expressions of reverence for "the Lord," other named entities or individuals, "the tradition of our Master," and Guru Dev, who is portrayed as a personification of a divine being or essence.

> To the glory of the Lord I bow down again and again, at whose door the whole galaxy of gods pray (*sic*) for perfection day and night.

Commenting on this passage from the *puja*, the court indicates in a footnote:

> The court is aware that defendant Jarvis, although not an expert in the culture, history or religions of India, (see Jarvis Deposition at 908, 1020), testified that it is his personal understanding that the use of the word "Lord" in the term "Lord Narayana" denotes "merely the highest possible human appreciation and esteem (for human beings), like we would say Lord Mountbatten or something like that." (Jarvis Deposition at 966). Ignoring for the moment the inaccuracies in this weak analogy and accepting the statement *arguendo*, Mr. Jarvis' understanding of the word "Lord" when the word is attached to a proper noun can have no application to the term "the Lord" standing alone. In addition, it is impossible to imagine that "the whole galaxy of gods pray for perfection" at the door of "Lord Mountbatten" or at the door of any other titled person.

Guru Dev is seen as the personification of "the essence of creation" and is referred to as "Him." The only other referent to "Him" with a capital "H" is "the Lord." The court points out that many of the epithets applied to Guru Dev are similar to those applied to the field of creative intelligence in the text book: Guru Dev is called "the unbounded," "the omnipresent in all creation," "bliss of the Absolute," "transcendental joy," "the self-sufficient," "the embodiment of pure knowledge which is beyond and above the universe like the sky," "the One," "the Eternal," "the Pure," "the Immovable," and "the true preceptor." The chant ends with another offering and two more obeisances to "Him," to Guru Dev.

> Guru in the glory of Brahma, Guru in the glory of Vishnu, Guru in the glory of the great Lord Shiva, Guru in the glory of the personified transcendental fullness (*sic*) of Brahman, to Him, to Shri Guru Dev adorned with glory, I bow down.

The court concluded: "Manifestly, no one would apply all these epithets to a human being."[23] The court noted an inconsistency as to whether the *puja* is performed for the student or for the teacher, but agreed to accept the position that it is performed for the initiator with the student's participation limited to attendance and the contribution of certain offerings.

The defendants argued that the *puja* was not religious, but merely a ceremony of gratitude. This is supported with depositions by Jarvis, three clergymen, two professors of religion and two teachers who performed the ceremony. The court was not impressed with an argument which avoided an analysis of the text in favour of subjective interpretations. It pointed out that it is difficult to see the ceremony as one of gratitude since the chant did not reveal one word of gratefulness of thankfulness. The chant actually takes the form of a double invocation of Guru Dev. Jarvis stated that it was his personal understanding that the *puja* was merely a ceremony of gratitude to the tradition of past teachers and that similar ceremonies were performed in secular contexts in India. The court pointed out that Jarvis was not an expert in Indian things and that when asked what the word *puja* meant, he was unable to say. When asked if he were familiar with any *puja* "other than the one that is performed by the teacher at the time a *mantra* is assigned," he answered "No." The court pointed out that none of the depositions analysed the text of the chant, but merely indicated that they did not see it as religious.

When asked to what the gratitude of the ceremony was expressed, the reply was to the tradition of teachers who have preserved the teaching, or "to the knowledge" which each teacher in the chant is purported to have had. The court argued that the problem with this was that none of the described recipients was capable of receiving the gratitude. In common English usage, when one performs a ceremony of gratitude, there must be a recipient. One may be grateful *for* a body of knowledge or *for* a tradition, while gratitude extends *to* the preservers of a tradition.

> One would no more perform a ceremony of gratitude to a tradition or to a body of knowledge than one would perform a ceremony of gratitude to a chair or to a useful contrivance or to a machine or to any other inanimate object which would be entirely incapable of perceiving human communication.[24]

Most of the teachers addressed in the *puja* have been dead for thousands of years, and the most recent for nearly a quarter of a century.

Furthermore, the court pointed out that the *puja* was seen as indispensable to Maharishi.

> Maharishi Mahesh Yogi places such emphasis on the singing of this chant prior to the imparting of a mantra to each individual student that no *mantras* are given except at *pujas* and no one is allowed to teach the Science of Creative Intelligence/Transcendental Meditation unless he or she performed the *puja* to the personal satisfaction of Maharishi Mahesh Yogi or one of his aids.[25]

SCI/TM and the First Amendment

Having analysed the text book and the *puja*, the court set out to determine whether SCI/TM was religious under the meaning of the first amendment, and concluded that it was. It rejected the subjective criterion and indicated that it was particularly suspect in a case where the proponents "have enlisted the aid of governmental entities in the propagation of their beliefs, teachings, theories and activities."[26] To use subjective characterization by defendants to determine the religious extent of activities or beliefs "would be to inject a variable into the first amendment test which would preclude a fair and uniform standard."[27] Then the only inquiry left to the courts would be to determine the sincerity of the defendants.

> "Religion" under the first amendment would take on a different meaning in each case, and similar or virtually identical practices would be religious or not religious under the first amendment depending on the classification system of a particular proponent.[28]

The defendants request that the court define religion was seen as unnecessary. Courts had not defined "press" either. It was important that such terms should not be rigidly defined so that as comparable items unforeseen by the founding fathers arose they could be included.

> Owing to the variety of form and substance which religions may take, the courts have avoided the establishment of explicit criteria, the possession of which indelibly identifies an activity as religious for purposes of the first amendment. This court, therefore, must be guided by the type of activity that has been held to be religious under the first amendment by the courts.[29]

The only issue, then, was what judicial precedent included in the designation "religion," and how that applied to the case at hand.

By ruling as unconstitutional the recitation of a non–denominational prayer (*Engel* v. *Vitale*, 370 U. S. 421-1962), the Supreme Court made it clear that an activity may be religious even if it is not derived from a "societally recognized religious sect."[30] When in *Torcasco* v. *Watkins* (367 U. S. 488-1961), the Supreme Court ruled as unconstitutional the Maryland requirement that appointees to state offices affirm their belief in the existence of God, it made it clear that "religion" under the first amendment was broader than theism. Indeed, it could include Buddhism, Taoism, Ethical Culture and Secular Humanism.

Furthermore, the court found that Scientology was "religious" even though it "postulated the existence of no supreme essence or being and disavowed mysticism and supernaturalism."[31] Another important feature of the Scientology case was the fact that whether it was a religion under the first amendment was not dependent upon the representations of its proponents, but was a proper issue for the courts to determine.

Turning to TM, the court pointed out that the first organization in this country to offer instruction in TM (in 1959) was called the "Spiritual Regeneration Movement Foundation." One of the articles of the certificate of incorporation stated: "This corporation is a religious one." The court also found a remarkable similarity between the "Hindu" concept of the Supreme Being as Truth, Knowledge and Bliss and the qualities attributed to the field of pure creative intelligence. Regarding the contention that this has to do with philosophic concepts and not religion, the court explained:

> A philosophy well may posit the existence of a supreme being without functioning as a religion in the sense of having clergy and houses of worship. For purposes of the first amendment, these philosophies are the functional equivalent of religions. Surely the prohibition of the establishment clause could not be avoided by governmental aid to the inculcation of a belief in a supreme being through philosophical instruction instead of through conventionally recognized religious instruction.32

The court found that the characteristics of creative intelligence in the text book were equivalents to the term "God" in common usage.

Having determined that the SCI/TM course was religious, it remained for the court to decide if it was in violation of the first amendment. Under *Committee for Public Education* v. *Nyquist* (413 U. S. 756-1973), three tests were used to determine whether a religious activity constituted a violation of constitutional provision.

> The activity first, must reflect a clearly secular legislative purpose, second, must have a primary effect that neither advances not inhibits religion, and third, must avoid excessive government entanglement with religion.33

The court found that the SCI/TM course violated the constitutional provisions on all three counts. In the first place, the secular purpose of government in the SCI/TM course was to make available to students the alleged benefits of TM. But the simple technique was not all that was taught. Seventy percent of the time was devoted to teaching the theory of the Science of Creative Intelligence. Defendants did not teach merely that the use of a *mantra* will bring about certain beneficial physiological changes, but that a *mantra* is a vehicle which will bring a practitioner of TM into direct contact with an unmanifest, pure perfect, eternal and infinite field of life — the field of pure creative intelligence. Hence the government agencies have sought to effect a secular goal by the propagation of a religious concept, and this is prohibited by the establishment clause. In the case of the second test, the promulgation of a belief in the existence of a pure, perfect, infinite and unmanifest field of life clearly has primary effect of advancing religion and religious concepts. Under the third test, the aid given to the course in SCI/TM by the Federal Government and the State of New Jersey clearly constituted an "excessive government entanglement in religion." The court concluded: "The teaching of the SCI/TM course in New Jersey public high schools violates the establishment clause of the first amendment, and its teaching must be enjoined."[34]

The Appeal Decision

The immediate reaction of TM spokesmen was to downplay the importance of the decision. Admittedly it was a judgement about a specific course taught in New Jersey. However, it had definite implications for other situations as well. What implications might it have for public support in teaching TM in penal institutions? The case was appealed before the U. S. Court of Appeals, Third Circuit, and was argued on December 11, 1978. The opinion of the appeal was filed on February 2, 1979. The Appeal Court agreed that the SCI/TM course was religious in nature and agreed with the application of the Nyquist test. It was no more impressed with the appelant's arguments that the text book and *puja* were not religious than was the District Court. All of the parties among the original plaintiffs were represented in the appeal. However, defendants before the lower court included the U. S. Department of Health, Education and Welfare, the New Jersey Department of Education, and the several local school boards. None of these governmental defendants joined the World Plan Executive Council–U. S. in its appeal.

While this case only deals with a specific course, its implications are broad. To the extent to which this opinion is followed, whenever SCI is a part of TM the endeavour is religious under the first amendment because SCI, is at least an equivalent of religious teaching. Even if TM were to be taught without the accompaniment of SCI, the necessity of the *puja* makes it religious as well. Moreover, this case raises serious questions about any use of public funds as a subsidy for TM.

Notes

1. Maharishi Mahesh Yogi, *Transcendental Meditation* (New York: New American Library, 1968), xvi.

2. *Ibid.*, 299.

3. *Ibid.*, 299-300.

4. *Ibid.*, 296.

5. *Ibid.*, xvi.

6. *Ibid.*, 31.

7. *Ibid.*, 33.

8. *Ibid.*, 36.

9. *Ibid.*, 44ff.

10. *Ibid.*, 42.

11. *Ibid.*, 46.

12. *Ibid.*, 54.

13. Quoted in Jack Forem, *Transcendental Meditation* (New York: E. P. Dutton, 1974), 217.

14. "Pure creative intelligence" corresponds to the "Being" in its absolute state as expounded in *The Science of Being and the Art of Living*.

15. The description is that of the court while the references given by the court are to the text book. Hence "T at 29" refers to page 29 of the text book.

16. These levels of consciousness are also enumerated in Maharishi Mahesh Yogi, *On the Bhagavad–Gita: A New Translation and Commentary with Sanskrit Text* (Penguin Books, 1969), 20.

17. *Malnak* v. *Maharishi*, Opinion, 23.

18. *Ibid.*, 35.

19. *Ibid.*, 36.

20. Maharishi's teacher was Swami Brahmananda Saraswati, often referred to as Guru Dev.

21. An English translation of the *puja* was provided by the defendants.

22. *Ibid.*, 43.

23. *Ibid.*, 43.

24. *Ibid.*, 45.

25. *Ibid.*, 50.

26. *Ibid.*, 64.

27. *Ibid.*, 61.

28. *Ibid.*, 61.

29. *Ibid.*, 52.

30. *Ibid.*, 52.

31. See *Founding Church of Scientology v. United States*, 499 F. 2nd 1146 (D. C. Cir. 1969).

32. *Malnak* v. *Maharishi*, Opinion, 69.

33. *Ibid.*, 71.

34. *Ibid.*, 78.

Index

A

Abdul Ameed v. *Chitradurga Municipality*, 218
Abdul Hakim v. *State of Bihar*, 212
Abishiktananda, Swami, 49
adoption, 180, 195
Advaita Vedanta, 47, 68, 251, 289, 309, 312, 329-332, 337-339
Agamas, 105, 112, 113
Agrawal, Kasturchand, 182
ahimsā, 205, 258
Allāh, 61-62, 190, 250
All India Santan Dharma Mahasabha, 181
American Academy of Religion, 355, 360
archaic man, 31, 34, 35
Archaka, 105, 106, 202
archetype, 32
atman, 251, 264, 308, 310
avatar, 20, 67, 308, 316, 340, 363
Ayyangar, M. A., 149

B

Bahadur, B. Pocker Sahib, 175
Bakr Id Day, 109, 206, 208, 218
Baig Sahib Bahadur, Mahoob Ali, 154, 175
Beard, Charles, 86, 91
Becker, Carl, 73-75, 79-87, 91
Berger, Peter, 120, 122
Bhagavadgītā, viii, 4, 20, 150, 214, 253, 263, 271, Chapter 14
bhakti, 19, 20, 252, 306, 336, 337, 346
Bhaktipada, Swami Kirtananda, 262-264
Bhargava, Thakur Dass, 203, 207, 210
Bible, 150, 342, 343, 344, 345, 348, 363, 364
Bira, Kishore Deb v. *State of Orissa*, 104
Bleeker, C. J., 9, 15, 16, 21, 34,40
Bombay Hindu Places of Public Worship Act, 111
Bombay Prevention of Excommunication Act, 106-107
Bramaloka, 272, 273, 280
Brahman, 20, 61, 66, 251-254, 265, 276, 279, 339, 363
Brahmans, 96, 97, 112, 171, 216, 254, 255
Bṛhadāranyaka Upaniṣad, 259
Brinton, Crane, 81
Buddha, 46, 51, 61, 303, 308, 339, 340, 341, 362
Buddhism, 10, 13, 14, 22, 24, 39, 46, 109, 120, 121, 137
Buddhists, 100, 115, 232, 244, 332, 340, 341, 342, 362, 370
Buddhu v. *Allahabad Municipality*, 215

C

Caitanya, Sri, 271, 291, 304, 305 313, 315, 331, 332, 334, 337, 339, 340, 353, 362
Callois, Roger, 28
Carman, John, 45, 46, 48
caste, 112, 130, 131, 132, 158, 160, 171, 174, 187, 188, 201, 228, 252, 253, 260, 261, 262
Caste Disabilities Removal Act of 1850, 107
Chisti Order of Sufis, 110

K

L

M

N

O

P

Q

R

S

T

TORONTO STUDIES IN RELIGION

This series of monographs and books is designed as a contribution to the scholarly and academic understanding of religion. Such understanding is taken to involve both a descriptive and an explanatory task. The first task is conceived as one of 'surface description' involving the gathering of information about religions, and 'depth description' that provides, on the basis of the data gathered, a more finely nuanced description of a tradition's self-understanding. The second task concerns the search for explanation and the development of theory to account for religion and for particular historical traditions. The series will, furthermore, cover the phenomenon of religion in all its constituent dimensions and geographic diversity. Both established and younger scholars in the field will be included and will represent a wide range of viewpoints and positions, producing original work of a high order at the monograph and major study level.

Although predominantly empirically oriented the series will also encourage theoretical studies and even leave room for creative and empirically controlled philosophical and speculative approaches in the interpretation of religions and religion.

Toronto Studies in Religion will be of particular interest to those who study the subject at universities or colleges but will also be of value to the general educated reader.